"The Imperial Navy's submarine force in World War II is still barely understood in the West. Geoghegan has given us one of the first detailed glimpses into the workings of Japan's undersea fleet. His detailed coverage of the Imperial Navy's *I-400* program is uniquely interesting."

—JONATHAN PARSHALL, author of *Shattered Sword*

"Anyone who believes there are no more hidden secrets to World War II will feel differently on seeing this book. I've been reading about the war all my life, but knew nothing of the extraordinary weapon whose story John Geoghegan tells here. And tells, I might add, in a riveting, vivid, suspenseful way that makes it hard to stop reading once you've begun. It's a remarkable tale."

—ADAM HOCHSCHILD, bestselling historian and author of *To End All Wars* and *King Leopold's Ghost*

"Just when we were beginning to think that every conceivable World War II topic worthy of study has already had a shelf's worth of books devoted to it, John Geoghegan's *Operation Storm* combines painstaking research and crisp writing to bring to life, for the first time in English, the fascinating story of Japan's late war *I-400* experimental submarine program."

—M. G. SHEFTALL, author of *Blossoms in the Wind: Human Legacies of the Kamikaze*

"*Operation Storm* does for Japanese submarines what *Das Boot* did for U-boats, showing the human side of a remarkable story no less extraordinary for being true. Geoghegan's splendid research combined with his writing skill makes *Storm* a genuine page-turner."

—COL. (RET.) WALTER J. BOYNE, former head of the Smithsonian National Air and Space Museum

"Impressively documented and lucidly written, here is a lively, well-balanced account of the Japanese Imperial Navy's huge *I-400* class submarines and their eleventh-hour 'game-changer' mission."

—CARL BOYD, coauthor of *The Japanese Submarine Force and World War II*; professor emeritus, Old Dominion University; and U.S. Navy submariner 1954–1958

OPERATION STORM

JAPAN'S TOP SECRET SUBMARINES AND
ITS PLAN TO CHANGE THE COURSE OF
WORLD WAR II

JOHN J. GEOGHEGAN

B\D\W\Y
BROADWAY BOOKS
NEW YORK

Book design by Lauren Dong
Illustrations by Emil Petrinic
Cover design by Chris Brand

First Paperback Edition

146122990

For Emma and Nina,
because it's always better to know
both sides

Contents

AUTHOR'S NOTE

Under the supervision of the Demobilization Bureau, the basic material contained in this monograph was compiled and written in Japanese by former officers ... The paucity of original orders, plans and unit journals, which are normally essential in the preparation of this type of record, most of which were lost or destroyed during field operations or bombing raids rendered the task of compilation most difficult ... However, while many of the important orders, plans and estimates have been reconstructed from memory and therefore are not textually identical with the original, they are believed to be generally accurate and reliable.

—*Japanese Operational Monograph*, Japanese Research Division, Military History Section, Headquarters, Army Forces Far East, 1946, preface, p. v.

Rashomon is a Japanese term that describes how different witnesses to the same event can shape its story differently, based on individual perception. *Rashomon* also applies to the history of the *I-400* submarines because the memories of their officers and crew sometimes differ. As the preface to the Allied monograph on Japanese military history indicates above, many Japanese records were destroyed during or immediately after the war. As a result, I have relied primarily on first-person accounts either oral or written. When accounts differ, I have indicated the differences in a footnote.

Additionally, Japanese records show an event happening a day later than U.S. records. This is because Japanese time is 13 to 16 hours ahead of U.S. time, depending on the U.S. time zone and daylight savings. For example, the attack on Pearl Harbor happened on Monday, December 8, in Japan, but the date is emblazoned in American memory as Sunday, December 7. The fact that many Japanese records were lost, or intentionally destroyed, at the end of the war means dates can be difficult to establish. When dates are in conflict or doubt, a footnote explains the difference. Any errors are my own.

Finally, Japanese names appear in Western style, with the family name coming last. In the interest of simplicity, I have also omitted any macrons. Ages are also stated in Western terms. (Prior to World War II, Japanese children were considered one year old when they were born.) And though the Japanese do not refer to ships as male or female, I have done so throughout the text to maintain consistency with Western convention.

Principal Actors

IMPERIAL JAPANESE NAVY
(IJN, OR *DAI-NIPPON TEIKOKU KAIGUN*)

Naval General Staff (*GUNREIBU*)

- *Cdr. Yasuo Fujimori,* staff officer submarines. He was dedicated to steering the *I-400* program through a hostile bureaucracy.
- *Cdr. Shojiro Iura,* staff officer submarines. He opposed the *I-400* program, even though he wanted to bomb Oregon.

Combined Fleet (*RENGO KANTAI*)

- *Adm. Isoroku Yamamoto,* commander in chief of the Combined Fleet. He dreamed up the *I-400* submarines as a follow-up punch to Pearl Harbor.
- *Capt. Kamato Kurojima,* Yamamoto's chief staff officer. He helped make sure a resistant naval bureaucracy built Yamamoto's underwater aircraft carriers.

Sixth Fleet (IJN Submarine Force, or *Dai-roku Kantai*)

Submarine Squadron 1 (SubRon 1, or *Daiichi Sensuitai*), sometimes called *Sensuikan tokugata* (Special submarine), or *Sen-toku* for short. In some instances the *I-400* submarines were also referred to as *tokugata*, or "special model" subs.[1]

- *Cdr. Tatsunosuke Ariizumi,* squadron commander. The British may have called him "the Butcher," but his reputation inside the Imperial Japanese Navy was just as tough.

I-401 (Squadron Flagship) Key Officers and Crew

- **Lt. Cdr. Nobukiyo Nambu,** commanding officer. The emotional instability of his superior officer forced him to make the toughest decision of his life.
- **Lt. Muneo Bando,** chief navigator. He knew how to ingratiate himself with the enemy as much as with his boss.
- **Lt. Tsugio Yata,** chief gunnery officer. He helped repel the enemy's first attack.

I-400

- **Cdr. Toshio Kusaka,** commanding officer. His crew respected him, even though he'd massacred prisoners.

I-14

- **Cdr. Tsuruzo Shimizu,** commanding officer. He was as lucky as he was skilled.

I-13

- **Cdr. Katsuo Ohashi,** commanding officer. Last to be ready, his crew would pay the price.

631st Air Group (Assigned to SubRon 1)

- **Lt. Cdr. Tadashi Funada.** One of Japan's foremost test pilots, he came up with the *Seiran*'s poetic nickname.
- **Lt. Cdr. Masayoshi Fukunaga,** executive officer. Loved by some, he was viewed as incompetent by others.
- **Lt. Atsushi Asamura,** *Seiran* squadron leader, *I-401*. He would gladly give his life in support of the mission.
- **Ens. Kazuo Takahashi,** *Seiran* pilot, *I-400*. He questioned whether they really had what it took to succeed.
- **WO (warrant flying officer) Nobuo Fujita,** seaplane pilot, *I-25*. He was the first enemy pilot to bomb the U.S. mainland.

U.S. NAVY

ComSubPac
(Commander Submarine Force, U.S. Pacific Fleet)

- *Vice Adm. Charles A. Lockwood,* commander, submarine force, U.S. Pacific Fleet. His subs helped bring an end to the war with Japan.

USS *Segundo* (SS 398)

- *Cdr. James D. Fulp, Jr.,* commanding officer (May 1944–June 1945). His crew trusted him like no other skipper.
- *Lt. Cdr. Stephen Lobdell Johnson,* commanding officer (June 1945–February 1946). His seeming inexperience rattled his crew.
- *Lt. John E. "Silent Joe" Balson,* executive officer. Steady under the worst of circumstances, he would lead the *I-401*'s boarding party.
- *Lt. (jg) L. Rodney Johnson.* When he first saw the *I-401,* he thought it was a ship.
- *Lt. (jg) Victor S. Horgan.* He was ready to sink the *I-401* the moment it was required.
- *QM3c (quartermaster third class) Carlo M. "Charlie" Carlucci.* He wasn't sure whom to fear more, the *I-401* or his trigger-happy crewmates.

WEST COAST CITIES TARGETED
BY OPERATION PX

EAST COAST CITIES TARGETED
BY I-400 SUBMARINES

SAN FRANCISCO
LOS ANGELES
SAN DIEGO

NEW YORK
WASHINGTON

PANAMA CANAL

OPERATION STORM

Ominato Naval Base (Honshu, Japan)

Yokosuka, Japan

Saipan, Mariana Islands

Ponape (now Pohnpei)
Micronesia

Ulithi Atoll

Truk (now Chuuk)
Micronesia

OPERATION STORM LEGEND

1 — Planned rendezvous point
for I-400 and I-401

2 — Planned launch point for *Seiran* aircraft

3 — US Naval Anchorage at Ulithi Atoll

·········· Route taken by submarine I-14

– – – Route taken by submarine I-400

——— Route taken by submarine I-401

Ominato Naval Base
(Honshu, Japan)

Sasebo Naval Base
(Nagasaki, Japan)

Singapore Naval Base

C

B

D

COLOMBIA

E

ECUADOR

PANAMA CANAL ATTACK LEGEND

A — Aircraft launch point 100 sea miles
west of Ecuador

B — Fly to Colombia's north coast,
then turn west

C — Approach Colón, Panama, from north

D — Attack target, Gatun lock gates

E — Ditch aircraft near launch point,
swim to submarines

A

PANAMA CANAL ATTACK

Illustration by Emil Petrinic

Part I

PROLOGUE

CHAPTER I

FACE-OFF

THE USS *SEGUNDO* (SS 398) WAS FIVE DAYS OUT OF MIDWAY heading toward Japan when her crew received news that the Japanese government had accepted peace terms. As the submarine's executive officer, Lt. John E. Balson, noted in the boat's Fifth War Patrol Report:

HEARD THE GOOD WORD OF THE SURRENDER—AND IN
ELEVEN LANGUAGES, TOO![1]

Balson was second in command of the Balao-class sub, one of the newest U.S. fleet boats. Nicknamed "Silent Joe" for his reticent manner, Balson was responsible for ensuring that the captain's orders were carried out in a correct and timely manner. He'd been with the *Segundo* since before her commissioning and had served on all five of her war patrols. Twenty-eight years old and already balding, Balson was a man of sly wit if few words. His all-cap entry was an uncharacteristic display of emotion for the normally phlegmatic officer. Then again, the war with Japan was finally over.

The *Segundo* had been patrolling the Kuril Islands when the cease-fire was announced. She hadn't seen much activity except for a few Russian vessels.[2] Nevertheless, the Sea of Okhotsk could be dangerous. Sometimes when fog blanketed the ocean's surface, the *Segundo*'s sail protruded as much as 10 or 15 feet above the cloud bank, making the sub perilously visible. Other times the water was so calm, you could hear a bird take off, which meant the *Segundo*'s engines could be heard as well. And it was cold even in August—so cold, in fact, that you had to recycle the boat's vents, or the valves froze, preventing the sub from diving.[3]

These weren't the only ways the Kurils could kill you. The Russians had been threatening to invade Hokkaido, and Japan was close enough that a stray mine or determined patriot could still sink the sub. But now that the war was over, there was no point remaining in the area.

On August 24, 1945, the *Segundo* was ordered to Tokyo Bay to represent the U.S. submarine force at the upcoming surrender ceremony. The invitation was an honor for the *Segundo*'s crew, but they weren't ready to relax just yet. They were still in enemy territory, and though the cease-fire agreement specified that the Japanese military were to lay down arms, some units hadn't got the message.

It was two weeks since the Japanese emperor had asked his subjects to "endure the unendurable," and the *Segundo* was heading to Tokyo with orders to mop up remnants of the once-formidable Japanese fleet.[4] Not much was left of the Imperial Japanese Navy (IJN), and what was, wasn't expected this far north. There was isolated resistance though so the *Segundo* continued on a wartime footing.

So far the patrol had proven uneventful.[5] There'd been one encounter with a Japanese fishing boat, but as Balson noted: "there wasn't much fight coming from him and none from us . . . [so we] called it a draw and retired from the scene."[6]

The *Segundo* had been an aggressive boat despite the diminishing number of enemy targets. Her first skipper, Cdr. James Douglas Fulp, Jr., had been assigned to the sub while she was still under construction at the Portsmouth Navy Yard in New Hampshire. Fulp had put an indelible stamp on the boat's crew while commanding her first four war patrols. During that time, he'd sunk two Japanese warships, eight merchants, and seven sampans and earned the *Segundo* a total of four battle stars. These results weren't surprising given the fact that Fulp was an experienced sub captain. Tall, athletic, and matinee-idol handsome, he radiated the kind of confidence his men had come to respect. He was 34 (old for a sub captain) and quiet by nature. But that only contributed to his command presence.

Fulp prosecuted the war with just the right balance of aggressiveness and caution. His crew knew he was somebody they could count on to sink a combatant ship and bring them home safely. They also appreciated his fairness. Some commanding officers (CO) were despots, but Fulp was even-handed when dealing with his men. He never dressed them down in front of one another, and he listened more than he spoke. Though he could be remote, that wasn't unusual for a CO. It was better for Fulp to be distant than overly familiar, since the crew's lives depended on his objectivity. In other words, the *Segundo*'s first skipper had everything a crew liked in a sub captain: he was mature, steady, and reliable. They happily served under him.

All this had changed, however, before the *Segundo* departed on her fifth and final war patrol. The sub was still in Midway undergoing refit when Fulp received orders transferring him to Pearl Harbor. He had eight war patrols under his belt and was due for rotation. But Fulp had built the *Segundo* into a formidable fighting machine. And if it's true that a combat submarine operates like a family, then Fulp's departure was like depriving the crew of their father. The men were sorry to see him go.

Unfortunately, the boat's new skipper, Lt. Cdr. Stephen Lobdell Johnson, was a different breed of captain. He was younger than Fulp with a cockiness that put his crew on edge. The first time S1c (seaman first class) Richard "Fox" Binkley saw Captain Johnson at Midway, his new skipper was shooting dice with the men. To Binkley, Johnson didn't make a good impression. He acted more like a crew member than an officer, not the kind of captain he was used to serving under.[7]

Lt. (jg) Victor Horgan also had concerns about his new CO. Horgan had overheard the tall, lanky Johnson tell his officers, "When we get off this patrol, they'll be throwing medals down our hatch." Was this the kind of guy you could respect? Horgan wasn't sure.[8] He too had seen Johnson play dice with the men. It wasn't how the CO of a combat submarine, not to mention an Annapolis graduate, was supposed to act.[9]

In fact, the more the crew saw of Johnson, the more they worried he was a "Hollywood skipper." He may have had other capabilities, but he was noticeably lacking in Fulp's gravitas. It almost seemed as if the *Segundo* was the 29-year-old Johnson's first command. It wasn't, it was his third. If his officers had known this, it would have worried them all the more.[10]

Horgan wasn't the only one who sensed a problem. One night before the *Segundo* left on her fifth war patrol, he went drinking with his fellow officers at a Midway bar. While his friends drank beer and gossiped about their new CO, Horgan played a slot machine. Frustration had been building ever since Johnson's arrival, and the beer loosened their tongues. As the night wore on, a consensus grew that it might be time to ask off the boat.

While Horgan played the slots, Lt. (jg) Lewis Rodney Johnson (no relation to Captain Johnson) called over:

"You going to stay with the boat, Vic?"[11]

Horgan was tired of losing to the aptly named one-armed bandit and moved to a new machine. Pulling the lever, he stood motionless as a jackpot fell into place. Not believing his luck, he switched to another machine, and the same thing happened. Trying a third machine, he again hit the jackpot. Horgan was feeling lucky.

"Yeah, I'll stay," he said.

"We will too, then."

And that was the end of that.[12]

Lieutenant Balson remained as the *Segundo*'s executive officer (XO) after Fulp left. He recognized that their new captain was different. Johnson was a smooth talker, highly polished and well dressed. Even his nickname was "Slick," which wasn't always a compliment.

Balson knew a change in command was nothing to worry about. He'd seen his share of sub captains, and no two were alike. Given time, most crews adjusted to a new skipper's foibles.[13] If not, the U.S. sub force was 100 percent volunteer—you could always ask off the boat.

The biggest issue Captain Johnson faced was the *Segundo*'s tight-knit crew. Most of the men had been aboard since the boat's commissioning 15 months earlier, and they'd been shaped by

Fulp's command style. Importantly, Fulp had gotten them out of some pretty tight spots. Would their new skipper be as talented? A change in command was not to be taken lightly, but Balson expected the crew would come around. Time had a habit of sorting out problems.

Of course, Captain Johnson's presumed impetuosity was less of an issue now that the war was over. The one thing the men didn't want though was for something stupid to happen. Sailors are a superstitious lot, and now that a cease-fire was in place, they didn't want any last-minute screwups sending them to the bottom. Home was the preferred direction.

There were still plenty of mines in Japanese waters, and tales of suicide attacks continued to circulate. The recent communiqué from Adm. Chester W. Nimitz, Commander in Chief of the Pacific Fleet, stressed the uncertainty of their situation:

MAINTAIN DEFENSIVE AND INTERNAL SECURITY MEASURES AT HIGHEST LEVEL AND BEWARE OF TREACHERY OR LAST MOMENT ATTACKS BY ENEMY FORCES OR INDIVIDUALS.[14]

It was another way of saying, anything could still happen.

IT WAS FIFTEEN minutes before midnight on August 28, 1945, when Lieutenant Johnson relieved Lt. "Mac" McLaughlin as officer of the deck. Watch officers customarily appeared early when relieving each other. Extra time was needed to conduct the handover since important information had to be exchanged. The two men huddled on the bridge as McLaughlin passed along the sub's course, her speed, and the captain's latest orders. When they finished, Lieutenant Johnson went to the sub's fantail to begin his watch.[15]

The *Segundo* was on the surface about 100 miles off Honshu, heading south toward Tokyo.[16] It was the fourteenth day of the cease-fire, and not one enemy warship had been sighted since her patrol had begun. It was a cold night and visibility was poor,[17] but the ocean was calm,[18] and Lieutenant Johnson decided to take advantage of what little moonlight there was to scan the horizon.

When he first spotted an object south of the sub, Johnson thought his eyes were playing tricks on him. But the more he looked the more certain he became that something was out there. Meanwhile Alex "Snoopy" Leitch was sipping coffee in the conning tower when a blip appeared on his radar screen. Leitch was surprised at how large the object was. Something that size should have been picked up at 15,000 yards, yet it hadn't appeared until it was within a third of that distance.[19]

Leaping the few steps to get under the bridge hatch, Leitch shouted, "Radar contact; 5,500 yards!"*

At first nobody was sure what they were dealing with.[20] No U.S. ships were reported in the area, and it was unlikely to be an enemy vessel this far north.[21] There was no mistaking the blip, though, which was sizable and doing 15 knots.[22] If it was American, fine. But if it was Japanese, they had a problem.

Captain Johnson flew up into the conning tower demanding the target's range and bearing. Determined to take a closer look, he called for "Tracking Stations."[23] When the *Segundo* closed to within 3,000 yards,[24] the dark silhouette materialized into the shape of a gigantic submarine.[25] The sub was so big, it looked like a surface ship. It easily dwarfed the *Segundo*. Since the Allies had nothing remotely close in size, the sub had to be Japanese.

Before Johnson could declare battle stations sparks began flying out of the mysterious sub's diesel exhaust.[26] Clearly, they'd been spotted. As Johnson scrambled his men, the Japanese sub rabbited into the night at flank speed.[27]

---

* Alex Leitch, the *Segundo*'s radar operator on duty, recalled spotting the *I-401* at a distance of only 3,000 yards, while the Patrol Report says the sub was spotted at 5,500 yards. Since the Patrol Report indicates that the *Segundo* closed to within 3,000 yards of the target, it's more likely that the *I-401* was spotted 5,500 yards out; otherwise there would have been no distance to close. See *Segundo*, Fifth War Patrol Report, August 28, 1945, 2353; Alex Leitch, "The Chase, Capture, and Boarding of a Japanese Submarine," *Polaris*, December 1985, http://home.earthlink.net/~richandannie/id71.html.

Lieutenant Horgan was in the control room plotting the enemy's course as the chase ensued. Horgan knew fighting was still going on in the Pacific, but he couldn't understand why a Jap sub would run away. After all, the war had been over for 14 days. Nevertheless, the situation seemed dangerous as hell.[28] Here they were chasing an enemy sub without knowing what they were dealing with. Any way you looked at it, they had a tiger by the tail.[29]

As the chase extended into the early morning hours, Johnson pushed the *Segundo* to 20 knots.[30] Every time he tried drawing near, the Japanese sub pulled away. Johnson didn't trust the enemy not to fire on them, so he settled off their stern quarter at a distance of 4,000 yards.[31] He also made sure his torpedo tubes were loaded and ready. If the Jap sub tried anything funny, he'd sink her first.

The *Segundo*'s new captain found himself in an uncomfortable position. Had it not been for the cease-fire, he'd have let go with a spread and sent her to the bottom. But Johnson's orders prevented him from sinking the sub unless fired upon even though fleeing could be considered a hostile action.[32] Not surprisingly, he didn't want to give the enemy that chance.[33]

To complicate matters, he was having trouble reaching his superiors at ComSubPac (Commander, Submarine Force, U.S. Pacific Fleet).[34] At the very least, he wanted to inform them of the situation and request permission to torpedo the sub. The *Segundo*'s captain wasn't going to play cat and mouse forever, but he was unsuccessful in reaching his command.[35] For the time being, he was on his own.[36]

First one hour passed, then another. As the pursuit dragged on, the crew began speculating. No one had expected an unescorted Japanese sub this close to Tokyo, least of all one heading in the opposite direction of the main sub base at Yokosuka. The fact she'd turned tail and run only added to their curiosity.

But as dawn approached, something unusual happened. The enemy sub began slowing. Johnson wasn't sure what she was up to. Maybe she was ready to surrender, or maybe she was getting into firing position. Fortunately, he'd reached ComSubPac, which advised him to capture the enemy if possible. If they resisted, he was free to sink them.[37]

Shortly after four o'clock the morning of August 29, Johnson called QM3c Carlo Carlucci to the bridge. It was Carlucci's first war patrol. A tough kid from the Bronx whose accent was like a punch in the face, he'd been sleeping when the *Segundo* first spotted the Japanese sub. He was wide awake now though, as he "horsed" the cast iron signal lamp to the *Segundo*'s bridge.[38] Rapidly flicking its shutters, Carlucci pounded out the international code for "stop."

The enemy sub failed to acknowledge the message even though it was impossible to misunderstand its meaning. The sub may have slowed, but she showed no signs of stopping. Finally, after a few minutes, Carlucci received an affirmative reply.[39] Two minutes later the enemy sub lay dead in the water.[40]

As dawn slowly illuminated the Japanese sub, Johnson and his men were in for a big surprise. They weren't facing a typical submarine. It was, in fact, the largest submarine the *Segundo*'s crew had ever seen. Horgan thought she was huge, at least twice as big as the *Segundo*. Carlucci was convinced she was three times as large, and MM (machinist's mate) Wallace C. Karnes, Jr., could have sworn she was four times bigger. Whatever her actual size, the Japanese sub loomed over the Balao-class boat.

Johnson knew they'd stumbled across something unusual. The enemy sub was big all right, but what he didn't realize was that he faced the largest submarine in the world, a sub so huge she would remain the largest until the USS *Triton* (SSRN 586) was commissioned in 1959.

Johnson's men had every reason to feel small. At just over 400 feet in length, the "Jap sub" was longer than a football field. And at 5,223 tons,[41] her surface displacement was more than three times that of the *Segundo*'s. It wasn't just her size that made for such a menacing spectacle; the Jap sub also bristled with weaponry. With a 5.5-inch gun on her aft deck; three triple-barrel 25mm antiaircraft guns; and a single 25mm mount on the bridge, the Japanese sub was all business. There were also eight torpedo tubes in her bow, two more than the *Segundo* had, and it was reasonable to assume she carried the deadliest torpedoes of the war: the Type 95, based on the "Long Lance."* The Type 95 packed an 891-pound warhead with way more punch than the *Segundo*'s Mark 14s.[42] Johnson wanted to avoid the Japanese torpedoes like the horns of a bull. Not only did they have a third more explosive power than his own torpedoes; they had nearly three times the range and were faster to boot.[43] Whatever the boat's weaponry, the crew of the *Segundo* had no doubt that they were dealing with a monster sub; a sub that not only dwarfed her in size but was armed to the teeth and whose intentions were painfully unclear.

The boat's size and weaponry weren't the only things intimidating the *Segundo*'s crew; the ungainliness of her superstructure also looked nefarious. Her monolithic sail was as high as a three-story building. It should have painted an enormous radar signature, but it appeared to be sitting on an indented base designed to reflect radar waves back into the sea. The most noticeable aspect of the superstructure though was a huge compartment running the length of her deck. The housing was more than 100 feet long and so massive, her sail had to be offset nearly seven feet to starboard to keep the sub from tipping over.

It wasn't hard to guess what the cavernous structure held, because a catapult stretched from a gigantic, bulbous door toward the bow. This was a plane-carrying sub. But what kind of plane was carried inside such an enormous hangar? The Japanese sub fleet was known to carry scouting planes, biwinged "put-puts" strictly for reconnaissance. This sub was more like an underwater aircraft carrier.

If Captain Johnson felt alarm at the enemy sub's contradictory behavior, he didn't show it. But you could never underestimate the

---

* Rear Adm. Samuel Eliot Morison was the naval historian who came up with the nickname "Long Lance." Another term popularized by the West rather than the Japanese was *kamikaze*. According to M. G. Sheftall, *Blossoms in the Wind: Human Legacies of the Kamikaze* (New York: NAL Caliber, 2006), p. 60, the Japanese used the term *tokko* to describe their suicide tactics. The term *kamikaze*, for suicide attack, came into fashion only after the war and largely because American media and historians popularized it.

ferocity of the Japanese military even in defeat. If Johnson misjudged the situation even slightly, the *Segundo* was in for trouble. To ensure that didn't happen, he brought his bow torpedo tubes to bear on his adversary and ordered his helmsman to close the distance.[44]

As Johnson aimed his binoculars at the Japanese sub a short distance away he could detect nothing wrong with her. In fact, she looked to be in good condition.[45] He could make out five figures atop her sail, at least two of which were staring at him through their own binoculars. It appeared to be a Mexican standoff.

By all rights the Japanese sub should surrender. But her decision to flee and her reluctance to stop, especially after being chased, suggested they didn't intend to give up easily. Yes, they were flying the black surrender flag and her deck guns were pointed downward. Yet nothing else in the sub's behavior indicated that Johnson should take the flag seriously. After all, she still flew her naval ensign, the *Asahi,* with the red and white rays of the rising empire.

One thing was for sure—nobody in the United States Navy had ever seen a sub like this. For the submarine the *Segundo* now confronted was the *I-401,* the largest, most powerful class of sub built by Japan during World War II. She had been designed for a mission so secretive that the U.S. military didn't know anything about it, a mission that Admiral Yamamoto, the architect of the attack on Pearl Harbor, had planned himself, a mission so audacious that the Imperial Japanese Navy saw it as a way to change the course of the war in their favor.

As Captain Johnson watched the sub float menacingly in the distance, he carefully considered his options. Depending on what happened next, a resumption of hostilities was likely. If the Japanese refused to follow his orders, he'd have no choice but to blow them out of the water.

What Captain Johnson didn't appreciate was just how reluctant the *I-401* was to surrender. Not only was the sub part of a top secret squadron of underwater aircraft carriers, it was the flagship that carried the squadron commander, Tatsunosuke Ariizumi.

Commander Ariizumi had been involved with the development

of the *I-400* subs almost from their beginning. Some people considered him their father.[46] He certainly knew they'd been designed to attack the U.S. mainland. Why, only a month previously, the planes stored in the sub's enormous on-deck hangar had been painted to resemble American aircraft, to help slip past U.S. air defenses.

Given her pedigree, the *I-401* wasn't going to surrender without a fight. In fact, surrendering to the enemy would be more than unacceptable to Commander Ariizumi; it would be an embarrassment and a disgrace. It went against all his years of training as a loyal subject of the emperor and a commander in the Imperial Japanese Navy.

And so, much to their surprise, the men of the USS *Segundo* were about to learn that World War II wasn't over quite yet because, along with their unproven skipper, they found themselves in what promised to be the last great shooting match of the Pacific war.

CHAPTER 2

THE *I-401*

Lt. Cdr. Nobukiyo Nambu stood on the *I-401's* bridge, squinting through his binoculars at the American submarine 400 yards off their starboard side. He'd done nothing to antagonize the enemy. Nevertheless, the American sub seemed insistent on a showdown.

The *I-401* was one of the last survivors of the Sixth Fleet, the submarine arm of the *Teikoku Kaigun,* the Imperial Japanese Navy. It was a testament to Captain Nambu's skill, forbearance, and luck that he'd survived this long, especially since his combat career had begun at Pearl Harbor. But the *I-401* was an offensive weapon and Nambu a successful and aggressive skipper. He didn't like being challenged.

Nambu was fiercely proud of his command. Not only was the *I-401* the world's largest submarine; she could travel one and a half times around the globe without refueling. She had a top surface speed of 19 knots (six and a half submerged)[1] and could dive in 56 seconds,[2] no small feat for such a large sub. Finally, she could remain on patrol for 120 days,[3] twice as long as the *Segundo's* typical voyage.

But the *I-401's* most unusual feature was her three state-of-the-art special attack planes, carried in her watertight hangar. Purpose-built to bomb New York City and Washington, D.C., the Aichi M6A1 planes were so secret, the Allies didn't know about them until after the war. This means, the *I-401* wasn't just a major offensive weapon in a submarine fleet forced to play defense—she was an underwater aircraft carrier designed to hold three of Japan's most secret and technologically advanced torpedo bombers, built to attack the U.S. mainland.

As Nambu watched through his binoculars, the American sub acted as if she were in a western quick-draw contest. It didn't help that Commander Ariizumi stood beside him expressing unhappiness with the situation. Both men had been reluctant to accept the emperor's surrender announcement when it was broadcast on August 15.[4] They'd been overhearing Allied radio programs all week[5] indicating that Japan was about to give in. Nambu had dismissed them as propaganda and carried on as if nothing were wrong.[6] But it was hard to ignore the *Taikai Rei,* or Imperial Rescript, when it finally arrived. Even though its language was so archaic they had trouble understanding it,[7] Nambu threw his hands up in anger when he read "endure the unendurable." He knew it meant surrender.

"Could they really do something this stupid?" he cried.[8]

Everyone knew the war was going badly. Nobody expected to return home alive. But what were they supposed to do after five long years of fighting? Surrender to the enemy? What was command thinking?

Squadron Commander Ariizumi was so incensed by the news, he didn't even finish reading the decree.[9] Neither Ariizumi nor Nambu informed the crew that Japan had surrendered.[10] Instead, they submerged the sub and continued on their deadly mission.

When the *I-401* next surfaced, it was the evening of August 16, and a flood of communiqués deluged the radio room.[11] The orders were so contradictory, it was hard to understand their mission status. Order number 114 confirmed that peace had been declared and a cease-fire was about to be signed.[12] But the order also stated: "All submarines shall execute predetermined missions and attack enemy if discovered."[13] Clearly, the *I-401* was being told to complete her mission despite the cease-fire. Subsequent orders suggested otherwise.

Nambu recognized the confusion as the death throes of the empire.[14] What he didn't appreciate was just how chaotic things were.

At Kure, Japan's second-largest sub base, Sixth Fleet junior officers had broken into the armory, commandeered weapons, and requested permission to continue the war.[15] Meanwhile six Japanese subs intent on attacking the enemy had put out to sea of their own accord.[16]

Things were no better at the Sasebo sub base. One sub captain sent a defiant telegram to Admiral Tadashige Daigo, commander in chief of the Sixth Fleet, proclaiming: "Though defeated in war, Japan will never die. We will fight to defend our country until the last soldier. We depart . . . today to attack the enemy."[17]

The Imperial Japanese Navy had never planned on surrender, and since individual initiative wasn't highly prized, many commanders didn't know what to do. The situation was unprecedented.

Nambu had been taught that when torn between surrender and death, it's best to choose death,[18] yet deep in his heart he wished to return to his family. Though he'd never admit to such feelings, Nambu was as human as the next man. He was also reluctant to surrender. The reason was more than just pride—it was belief in the entire imperial system. To surrender would be shameful; to die for the emperor, glorious.

Such thinking wasn't unusual for a Sixth Fleet sub captain. But Nambu was different in other ways. Over six feet tall with an erect bearing and a handsome face, Nambu had a full head of hair that he brushed straight back from his forehead. Despite his modest upbringing, he'd demonstrated intellectual acumen at an early age.[19] His parents had high aspirations for their only son, hoping he'd go into medicine, politics, or the military; the only routes for advancement in a stratified society. But Nambu and his sister were orphaned at an early age, curtailing their options. Fortunately, when it came time to take the naval academy's famously difficult entrance exam, Nambu's precocity paid off. He was one of only two boys from his prefecture to be admitted.*

What really differentiated the 34-year-old sub captain was his

---

* Nambu graduated with Etajima's sixty-first class in November 1933.

command philosophy. Nambu took a different approach when it came to his crew, and the results showed. Thoughtful, deliberate, and always in control, he had his men's welfare at heart, and they trusted him because of it. He didn't have to command respect, he earned it.

Ariizumi, by contrast, couldn't have been more different.

Raised in a well-to-do family with a history of naval service, Arizumi had had a comfortable upbringing. Loyalty to the emperor and filial piety were so ingrained in him that he probably had taken it for granted that he'd attend the naval academy.

The commander's family traced their roots back to samurai, but the difference between Ariizumi and Nambu extended beyond upbringing. Ariizumi had at least ten more years of experience in the Imperial Japanese Navy. He'd not only captained submarines—he was the Naval General Staff's senior submarine officer when the war began. He'd also planned the midget sub attack against Pearl Harbor and had participated in the development of Yamamoto's *I-400* subs. In other words, Ariizumi knew his way around the halls of the Navy Ministry, while Nambu was still a line officer. Ariizumi set policy; Nambu carried it out. Though this understates Nambu's command ability, naval roles left little room for deviation. They may have had their share of disagreements, but Ariizumi was Nambu's superior officer, period.

Ariizumi's rank didn't make him good-looking though. Best described as roly-poly, he had a round, pudgy face, shiny skin, and limp black hair that he parted neatly on the left. When standing side by side, Ariizumi and Nambu looked more like a bowling ball and a tenpin than a superior officer and a subordinate.

The differences weren't just cosmetic though; they were stylistic as well. Ariizumi was a forbidding autocrat with a reputation for being meticulous and demanding. He also had a temper. Sometimes he even struck his men—not an uncommon practice in the Imperial Japanese Navy. Admirers described him as tough. Detractors called him ruthless. Unsurprisingly, the *I-401*'s crew were intimidated by Ariizumi. Some even feared him.

About the only thing Ariizumi and Nambu had in common, besides their loyalty to the emperor, was their mustaches. Ariizumi preferred his thin and clipped, while Nambu's was almost luxuriant. The crew so admired Nambu's mustache, they said it made him look like a movie star.[20] But Nambu wasn't vain; he was straightforward and predictable. Ariizumi, on the other hand, was volatility personified.

The surrender announcement had shaken both men to the core, especially since neither was the type to give up. And now that an American submarine menaced them, they were faced with an important decision. Nambu was responsible for a top secret, state-of-the-art sub, as well as the lives of its 204 crew. He also had a commanding officer with no intention of allowing a despised enemy to capture his flagship. But Nambu's thinking had evolved since his first pained acknowledgment of Japan's surrender. The more he thought about the emperor's edicts, the more he realized they were being called home to help rebuild the nation. That meant returning his men safely to Japan.

Ariizumi disagreed.

Nambu knew their fate depended on how he managed the commander, but he could not go against his superior officer. Ariizumi was responsible for all the aircraft and submarines in SubRon 1 (Submarine Squadron 1), not just the *I-401*. Since the war's end, however, SubRon 1 lay sunk or scattered. Additionally, Nambu had purposefully kept the *I-401*'s whereabouts secret, despite repeated calls from Sixth Fleet headquarters to disclose their location.[21] Both men were determined to operate on their own terms, and both were desperate to complete their self-appointed missions.

Still, the change in circumstances had muddled the *I-401*'s command structure. The crew only took orders from Nambu, but Ariizumi commanded the squadron. It was possible he might cross the line and begin issuing orders himself, especially if Nambu wouldn't. Ariizumi's unpredictability didn't help matters. If he began telling Nambu's crew what to do, would they obey him?

Ironically, they'd been only ten hours from their final destination when they crossed paths with the enemy. And they wouldn't have stopped if their port engine hadn't broken down.[22] But now that they faced an American submarine, all bets were off.

Ariizumi wasn't ready to surrender, especially outside Japanese waters. Unfortunately, the American sub wasn't giving him much alternative. As Nambu saw it, they only had three choices: to run, to attack, or to surrender. If they repaired their engine in time, they could try to run, but the American submarine was likely to sink them before they got very far. They could attack the U.S. sub, using the few resources they had left, but Nambu well knew they were at a disadvantage. Finally, they could surrender, but neither Nambu nor Ariizumi wanted the loss of face. It was the perfect doomsday scenario, each option leading to catastrophe.

There was one option, though, that Nambu hadn't considered—one he'd completely overlooked. Unfortunately, it was the one option that Commander Ariizumi presented to him, and he did so as a fait accompli. They would scuttle the *I-401* with all hands on board. Everyone would die for the emperor.

Ariizumi's decision made sense on one level. The *I-401* was his flagship, and he didn't want it captured by the enemy. It was also an honorable way to die. But Ariizumi's option made Nambu ache with regret. Here they were, the war finally over, practically in sight of their homeland, and the commander wanted to bury them at sea. Yes, it avoided the ignominy of capture while preserving the honor of the Imperial Japanese Navy, but it wasn't the fate Nambu wanted for his men.

Nambu knew the lives of his crew depended on what he did next. Unfortunately, in all his years as a naval officer, he'd never faced such a dilemma. Would he violate the command structure he'd sworn to uphold? Would Ariizumi even stand down if confronted?

Nambu had to do something, and he had to do it quickly—otherwise Ariizumi would act in his place. Time was running out. He had to act now.

That is, if the *Segundo* didn't sink them first.

PART II

PREPARATION

CHAPTER 3

BIRTH

ON CHRISTMAS EVE 1941, LESS THAN THREE WEEKS AFTER THE attack on Pearl Harbor, Adm. Isoroku Yamamoto, commander in chief of Japan's Combined Fleet, gathered his senior officers to discuss their next move.

Yamamoto's attack on Pearl Harbor had gone better than planned. Though he hadn't destroyed any aircraft carriers, he'd succeeded in knocking the United States out of the Pacific for six months, buying Japan the time she needed to continue her southern advance and consolidate territorial gains. Yamamoto was wise enough to know Japan stood little chance of defeating the United States in a protracted war, so the challenge remained: what to do next?

Yamamoto understood his enemy well. He'd first visited America in 1919 as a naval representative. During this time he read *Life* magazine,[1] attended Harvard University,[2] and visited the U.S. Naval War College.[3] When he returned again in 1923, he made it a point to tour Detroit's auto factories and Texan oil wells.[4] He'd even lived in Washington, D.C., the seat of American power, when he was later appointed naval attaché to the Japanese embassy. Yamamoto's time in America meant he understood that the country's natural resources and industrial capacity far outstripped Japan's. He knew what he was up against.

Japan needed a large geographic empire if she was going to take her place among the first-rank colonial powers; an empire with sufficient resources to support and strengthen the Japanese military machine. Her expansion into China, Burma, Indochina, and the Dutch East Indies had been made with this goal in mind. But Yamamoto needed time; time to establish a defense perimeter that would allow the Japanese Army to complete its southern advance and gain more than just a foothold in recently conquered territories. He also needed a way to make the war so painful for the United States that the American people would protest its continuation and demand that their leaders sue for an early peace. Japan's best chance for expanding her empire lay in forcing the United States to the negotiating table.

Many Japanese leaders were convinced that Americans were decadent and weak. They not only lacked the Japanese fighting spirit, they didn't have much tolerance for pain. Materialism had made them flabby.

Unfortunately, Japan didn't have the resources to fight a prolonged war. That wasn't the plan, however. The plan was to conquer those Pacific nations with the most vital commodities and to consolidate these gains behind a strong southern defense perimeter. Japan didn't need to defeat the United States outright; she just had to hold America off long enough to secure her footing in Asia.

And Yamamoto was off to a good start. After her defeat at Pearl Harbor, the United States faced a two-ocean war, with much of her Pacific fleet damaged or destroyed. Now the admiral needed to find a way to take the war directly to the American mainland. The question was how?

No one knows the exact date when Yamamoto first came up with the idea of an offensive squadron of underwater aircraft carriers, but from Japanese accounts,* he was toying with the thought in

---

* Both Fujimori, Naval General Staff's First Division chief, and Sato, Ariizumi's staff officer, credit Yamamoto as coming up with the idea for an underwater aircraft carrier. Though this is not conclusive proof, it is certainly substantive evidence, given both men were well positioned to know firsthand. It is important to note, however, that both Lt. Cmdr. Tatsunoke Ariizumi and Yamamoto's senior staff officer, Kamato Kurojima, have also been cited as potentially responsible for the idea. Clearly, both men played a crucial role in the development of the underwater aircraft carriers. Nevertheless, until definitive proof appears, it is the author's belief that Yamamoto was responsible for the idea behind the *Sen-toku* squadron. Less conclusive, though still appealing, is the sense that the innovative yet unorthodox nature of the underwater aircraft carriers has Yamamoto's personality stamped all over it.

December 1941.[5] After his carrier task force returned from Oahu, Yamamoto held a gathering of his senior commanders aboard his flagship, *Nagato.* His officers must have been impressed as they filed into the teak-paneled cabin, which looked more like the first-class saloon on a luxury ocean liner than a wardroom where officers met.[6] The battleship's 16-inch guns, thick armor plating, and acclaimed speed made her one of the most powerful warships of the day. In spite of the opulent setting, the Combined Fleet's commander in chief cared little for pomp and circumstance. He was famous within the IJN for being direct to the point of rudeness, an attribute appreciated by those Americans he'd met. As one colleague remarked, Yamamoto was a man who "succeeded in upsetting preconceived notions of the typical Japanese."[7] This trait was in contrast to the IJN, which preferred a more collaborative decision-making approach.

In spite of his diplomatic experience, Yamamoto disliked obfuscation, which was one reason Americans warmed to him. In addition to being a maverick, he also had a tough streak. (You didn't get to be CINC of the *Rengo Kantai* without one.) He also had a surprisingly mischievous side.[8] It wasn't unusual for the commander in chief to do a headstand at a party, as an ice-breaking trick.[9] Though he didn't drink (he'd learned as an ensign that he couldn't handle alcohol),[10] he had a sweet tooth[11] and a penchant for geisha houses. He also wrote mediocre poetry.[12] None of this was unusual for an Imperial Japanese naval officer, except perhaps his inability to drink. Etajima, Japan's naval academy, prided itself on turning out renaissance men, and Yamamoto was no exception.

Standing five feet three inches, Yamamoto was shorter than the average Japanese.[13] He had a prominent nose, a strong chin peppered with scars, and a shaved head. Besides his surprisingly thick lips, his only distinguishing feature was two missing fingers on his left hand. He'd lost them during the 1905 Russo-Japanese War, when the barrel of an overheated deck gun exploded. Yamamoto had been serving aboard the *Nisshin* when the accident happened, and his body bore its scars for the rest of his life. One story has it that geishas teasingly nicknamed him "eighty *sen*"—two fingers, or

20 *sen* less than the 100 *sen* cost of a manicure.[14] He accepted the name with characteristic good humor.

What Yamamoto enjoyed most of all was gambling. Whether it was *shogi*, go, mah-jongg, billiards, roulette, or bridge, Yamamoto lived for games of chance.[15] As an accomplished gambler, he was willing to take a risk so long as the odds were calculable. Pearl Harbor had been a risk, and he'd won. Now he was looking to make his next big bet—which was why he'd gathered his senior officers.

Though Yamamoto could be bold, he was also realistic. When invited to discuss the chance of victory in a war against the United States, he'd told Prime Minister Fumimaro Konoe, "If we are ordered to do it, I can guarantee a tough fight for the first six months, but I have no confidence as to what [will] happen if it went on for two or three years."[16]

The recent successes at Pearl Harbor, the Philippines, and Malaya had so exceeded expectations that the Japanese were feeling *sensho-byo,* or victory fever. Yamamoto remained calm despite the excitement over Japan's initial victories and counseled his officers to do the same.

"This is an all-night game of mah-jongg where you play until someone collapses," he warned. "Just because the wind was in our direction . . . doesn't mean we can relax."[17]

Clearly, Yamamoto's gambling instinct had resulted in victory at Pearl Harbor. By taking the battle to the enemy's doorstep, he'd achieved unprecedented success.* His strategy ran contrary to two of the IJN's strongest tenets: that a decisive naval battle should be conducted at sea, and that the bigger the battleship the better. Pearl Harbor had involved aircraft carriers, not battleships,

---

* Though at the time, the Japanese viewed the attack on Pearl Harbor as a success, certain miscalculations would later come back to haunt them. Chief among them was the fact that the attack united rather discouraged a U.S. population reluctant to go to war as well as its failure to destroy the sub pens, repair shops, and fuel storage tanks at Pearl Harbor. These oversights enabled the U.S. Pacific Fleet to bounce back faster than it might have, had essential resources such as oil and repair facilities been eliminated.

and the decisive battle had taken place in the sky over the enemy's home anchorage, not at sea. Now it was time to take his logic one step further.

The United States had already boasted that if it came to war, it would reduce Japan's wood and paper cities to ashes.[18] American cities might have been made out of concrete, but Yamamoto thought the strategy had merit.[19] As he told his commanders that day aboard the *Nagato*, "If we send a submarine aircraft carrier to the U.S. mainland and drop bombs like rain over their major cities, the American people will surely lose their will to fight."[20]

Naturally, the right target selection was key to achieving the desired effect. The cities had to have enough political, economic, and symbolic importance to persuade Americans that continuing the war would be too painful. Certainly bombing Washington, D.C., and New York City fulfilled these criteria. Yamamoto had visited both places and knew the important role they played in America's self image.

Yamamoto also knew that an air raid was unlikely to cause substantive damage—Japan couldn't muster enough resources for that. But the psychological effect would be devastating, especially since there'd be no trace of the attacker. Yamamoto would not only hit a proud country in her two most important power centers, he would demonstrate yet again what the Japanese people were capable of. American leaders had badly underestimated Japan once before. Would Americans tolerate a second such mistake?

Obviously, long-range bombers were required for an attack, but Japan was too far away to launch a successful air strike. Since they'd never slip another carrier task force past the United States without being discovered, Yamamoto's commanders discussed alternatives. The only IJN weapons platform that carried planes besides surface ships were submarines, but no submarine had ever been built with the capabilities Yamamoto required. Such a sub would need a long range to reach America's east coast and return without refueling, a journey of nearly 38,000 nautical miles. The sub would also have to be large enough to carry at least two bombers and serve as a stable platform for launching the planes.

Though IJN subs had been carrying aircraft for more than two decades, and nearly 20 percent of all Japanese subs were equipped to carry seaplanes, none of the Sixth Fleet's aircraft were suited for the task. The most common sub-borne plane, the Yokosuka E14Y1 floatplane, was used for reconnaissance. Its cruising speed was only 90 mph, making it easy pickings for enemy fighters. Besides, its bomb payload was tiny. Sending the Yokosuka to attack New York would be like sending a gnat to sting a bear. Importantly, IJN subs carried only a single plane, hardly enough to inflict psychological damage on a major U.S. city.

As they worked through the requirements, it soon became apparent that neither the right kind of plane, nor the right kind of submarine, existed in the Imperial Japanese Navy. That meant both weapons had to be designed from the ground up. This was asking a lot, given the competing demands the IJN faced for men and materials. Building these weapons would not be easy.

But Yamamoto was an innovative thinker. He appreciated novel ideas. He'd been one of the IJN's first officers to see the potential for naval aviation, at a time when most of his colleagues put their faith in big guns and super-size battleships.[21] Yamamoto was not a submariner though. He'd had little direct experience with the submarine force and virtually no exposure to the design and construction of submersibles. He had a limited understanding of what could be achieved.

Sometimes, a lack of preconceived notions can lead to an unexpected breakthrough. As commander in chief of the Combined Fleet, Yamamoto had every right to ask whether an underwater aircraft carrier could be built with enough range and cargo space to carry and launch attack planes against the east coast cities of the United States. When it came to the answer, Yamamoto turned to his senior staff officer and chief confidant, Kamato Kurojima.

The relationship between Yamamoto and Kurojima was an unusual one. Taciturn by nature, Yamamoto did not confide in many people. Kurojima was one of them. Yamamoto trusted his personal staff officer more than his own chief of staff. When the Navy Ministry's Personnel Affairs Bureau tried replacing Kurojima with a new officer, Yamamoto refused the change. This was highly unusual, given the rigid nature of IJN personnel decisions, yet Kurojima remained in place while Yamamoto's chief of staff turned over many times.[22]

Kurojima's special relationship with his boss caused jealousy among his peers. It didn't help that Kurojima's ideas could be as unconventional as Yamamoto's. Because of his unorthodox thinking, Kurojima was nicknamed the "Weirdo Officer,"[23] but there is little doubt he was a fierce advocate for Yamamoto. Together they presented a formidable front that IJN personnel both respected and resented.

One story avidly repeated in the Navy Ministry concerned how the Naval General Staff (NGS) had originally opposed Yamamoto's Pearl Harbor attack.[24] Yamamoto grew so frustrated with their conservative thinking, he sent Kurojima to tell the NGS officers he'd resign if they didn't support his plan. That got their attention, and NGS approval followed shortly thereafter. It's not surprising that when Yamamoto wondered whether an underwater aircraft carrier could be built, he sent Kurojima to find out.

Given Yamamoto's triumph at Pearl Harbor, NGS staff officers had to take Kurojima seriously. This time when he appeared, they paid attention. On January 13, 1942, less than a month after Yamamoto had raised the idea aboard the *Nagato,* the NGS had "studied the plan" and arranged for a meeting with the Bureau of Naval Construction to discuss specifics.[25]

The NGS staff officer in charge of submarines was Lt. Cdr. Tatsunosuke Ariizumi. Ariizumi would eventually command the *I-400* subs, but his job, for the time being, was to explore the idea with the IJN's foremost sub construction expert, Ariki Katayama.[26] Ariizumi and Katayama eventually agreed on specifications, yet what emerged was daunting. Yamamoto's sub would have to travel nearly 40,000 nautical miles without refueling. By comparison, the farthest cruising range for an existing IJN submarine was 20,000 nautical miles, with a more typical range of 15,000, or less than half. A U.S. Balao-class sub like the *Segundo* had an average range of 11,000 nautical miles, so Yamamoto's sub would have to have nearly four times the range of an American submarine. Clearly, Yamamoto was talking about a sub of an order of magnitude bigger than anything ever built.

A sub this size would require 1,750 tons of fuel to circumnavigate the globe as well as enough provisions for four months at sea.[27] (The average U.S. sub patrol was only 45 days.) Additionally, the sub would need room to carry two attack planes with a range of 600 miles, enough to reach the United States while carrying a single aerial torpedo, or the largest bomb in the naval aviation arsenal.[28] The plane also had to be fast enough to evade enemy aircraft and be capable of the steep dive necessary for attack.

Finally, the sub would need a watertight hangar on its deck big enough to house two aircraft. The hangar alone would have to be at least 100 feet long, have a big enough diameter to accommodate the diameter of an airplane's propeller, and be made of material thick enough to withstand not only the crushing pressure of the sea but machine-gun bullets from enemy planes.[29] As if this weren't enough, a powerful pneumatic catapult would have to be designed for the heaviest weight ever launched from the deck of an IJN sub.[30] And a collapsible deck crane capable of lifting a ten-ton airplane[31] was also needed to recover the attack planes and load them on board.

Despite its large size, the sub would have to be fast underwater. Seven knots* was almost as fast as a U.S. fleet sub,[32] while her safety depth of 330 feet was slightly better than the "official" safety depth of a Gato-class boat.[33] In addition to its plane-carrying responsibilities, the sub would have to carry offensive armament, including 27 Type 95 torpedoes and room to berth a crew of 147 to operate it.†[34] (This number would later be increased to 157.)[35] By comparison, U.S. fleet boats carried only 80 men.[36]

---

* Nambu says the *I-401* could do 7 knots underwater, while Western sources, such as Polmar and Carpenter, *Submarines of the Imperial Japanese Navy 1904–1945*, and Bagnasco, *Submarines of World War II*, cite 6.5 knots as the maximum underwater speed.

† According to Nambu, the interior configuration of the *I-401* was slightly different given her flagship status. Differences included living quarters for her squadron commander and a strategy room (among others).

Yamamoto's new submarine would ultimately top out at 400 feet, 3 inches long and displace 6,560 tons submerged.[37] This was three times the displacement of the largest boat in the American sub force at the time. Longer than a destroyer, Yamamoto's sub was essentially the size of a small cruiser. It wasn't an exaggeration, then, to say that Yamamoto was asking for something akin to a small underwater aircraft carrier.

Though Yamamoto was talking about building the largest submarine the world had ever seen, those involved realized that the conning tower, bridge, and deck hangar couldn't be so big that they'd hinder the sub's ability to dive or maneuver underwater. These goals were mutually exclusive, however. A submarine big enough to carry and launch two planes would have to be so big, its dive time would be compromised. And though size gave the sub an advantage when storing and launching its planes, it also made her a sitting duck.

The IJN had always built the largest possible weapons to offset treaty limits imposed by America, Great Britain, France, and Italy. For example, Japan built World War II's largest battleships (*Yamato* and *Musashi*), aircraft carrier (*Shinano*), and heavy cruisers. Constructing the largest sub was a natural step.

Clearly then, Yamamoto's submarine would have to break the conventional mold. And though some IJN officers saw it as an eccentric experiment, it wasn't a crazy idea, because the Sixth Fleet had more experience loading aircraft onto submarines than any navy in the world. In fact, repurposing inherently defensive sub-borne aircraft as offensive weapons was new strategic territory. It was the same kind of unconventional thinking that had enabled Yamamoto to conceive of carrier-borne aircraft taking the decisive naval battle to the home anchorage of the U.S. Pacific fleet.

Yamamoto wanted his follow-up punch to Pearl Harbor to be a knockout. The resulting plan called for building 18 monster subs carrying a total of 36 attack planes.[38] Original forecasts estimated it would take two years before the first sub was ready. This wasn't fast enough, and Kurojima lobbied to shorten the construction period. Though no one knew how the Pacific conflict would progress, it didn't matter. The sooner Yamamoto's *Sensuikan Toku* squadron ("Special Submarine," abbreviated as *Sen-toku*)[39] was ready, the sooner it could force America to the bargaining table.

Things moved quickly after Ariizumi's meeting with Katayama. Specifications for the sub's hull, engines, and armament were hammered out. Meanwhile the Air Technical Bureau began working on the plane design. The NGS insisted the program be treated with the highest possible security consideration,[40] the same classification given to the Imperial Navy's other superweapon, the battleship *Yamato*.[41] Nobody except a few NGS officers including Ariizumi knew anything about the project.

By March 1942, the preliminary design for Yamamoto's monster subs was complete.[42] After further refinement, the Naval General Staff reviewed the proposal on April 27,[43] a technology subcommittee meeting was held the next day, and the design was accepted on May 17.[44] It was an exceptionally fast turnaround,[45] especially in the consensus-building culture of the NGS. Yamamoto's sub was a top priority.

The IJN's Fifth Replenishment Plan–Revised, or *Kai Maru*–5, was issued in June 1942, with orders to build 18 of Yamamoto's gigantic subs. Officially referred to as the *I-400* class, the order shows the sub series numbered from *I-400* through *I-417*. Construction of the first five subs was to begin in January 1943. Not surprisingly, Katayama was assigned to supervise their construction since he'd been involved with their design from the beginning.

Admiral Yamamoto's follow-up to Pearl Harbor, a plan intended to change the course of the Pacific war, was now under way.

Chapter 4

NAMBU

The design for Yamamoto's underwater aircraft carriers was working its way through Tokyo's naval bureaucracy when Lt. Nobukiyo Nambu arrived in the glassy waters off San Diego. It was the morning of February 21, 1942, and Nambu was excited to find himself off the continental United States once again.

The man the IJN High Command would eventually select to captain the *I-401* was still an executive officer. It would be another three years before he captained the *Sen-toku* flagship. For the time being, he was second in command of the *I-17*, a frontline combat sub commissioned 11 months previously. The *I-17* was the newest generation of *Junsen*-class sub, a Type B with a floatplane in her watertight deck hangar and a range of 14,000 nautical miles—longer than that of a U.S. sub.[1] The added range was important. It allowed the *I-17* to reach the west coast without refueling, an essential feature for attacking the American mainland. Nambu's experience aboard a plane-carrying sub would prove useful when he took command of the *I-401*. In the meantime, he was still learning the ropes.

This was Nambu's second war patrol aboard the *I-17*. His first had been at Pearl Harbor. Nambu's sub had been stationed in the middle sentry arc north of Oahu when December 7 dawned. As the *I-17*'s executive officer, he was thrilled to find himself facing American territory for the first time. Though he was on the opposite side of the island from the air attack, he expected that many enemy ships would pass through his crosshairs as they fled the aerial bombardment. He was confident he'd sink at least one American battleship and maybe an aircraft carrier. But as the attack unfolded, not one ship had appeared.

The Imperial Japanese Navy deemed Pearl Harbor a success, even though the Sixth Fleet sub force contributed little to the effort. Not only had His Imperial Majesty's submarines failed to sink an aircraft carrier, they didn't sink a single capital ship. But Nambu didn't have to wait long for a chance to redeem himself. Shortly after the attack was over, the *I-17* was sent to the American west coast with orders to prevent naval reinforcements from reaching Hawaii.

It was December 16, 1941, when Nambu saw the U.S. mainland for the first time. Moved by the beauty of Oregon's snow-capped mountains, he couldn't believe he was so close to the enemy. It was surprising, though, how unprepared the Americans seemed. One of Nambu's colleagues in an I-boat off Long Beach saw "hundreds of people sunning themselves beneath colorful umbrellas."[2] Another said car lights on shore were so bright, he could have read a book at night.[3] The consensus among I-boat crews was clear.

"They certainly don't act like there's a war going on."[4]

Nambu sunk his first ship, the SS *Samoa*, 15 miles off Cape Mendocino early on the morning of December 18. The *I-17*'s second victim came two days later, when she torpedoed the SS *Emidio*, a 6,912-ton oil tanker bound for San Francisco. Three days later Nambu claimed his third merchant ship,[5] the 7,038-ton SS *Larry Doheny*.*

It's difficult for sub crews to know whether they've actually sunk a ship, since they can't usually linger to observe their handiwork. This means both sides often claimed more ships than were actually sunk.† Sixth Fleet subs attacked ten commercial ships off the U.S. west coast

---

* Interestingly, both the SS *Samoa* and the SS *Larry Doheny* escaped the *I-17*, though neither Captain Nishino nor Nambu realized it at the time. Nevertheless, fate caught up with the SS *Larry Doheny* on the evening of October 5, 1942, when the *I-25* sank her while she was en route from Long Beach, California, to Portland, Oregon. As a result, the total number of ships actually sunk by the *I-17* on her first war patrol was one.

† It was not unusual for both Japanese and U.S. sub commanders to mistakenly conclude that a torpedoed target had sunk. After the war, when shipping records were more closely scrutinized, sinkings by both sides were reduced to better reflect reality.

during a six-day period in December 1941, of which at least four were sunk.*

Though not every merchant ship claimed was a total loss, Yamamoto was doing his best to take the battle to the American mainland. The actual damage may have been limited, but the sub attacks had a profound psychological impact, leading many to fear a Japanese invasion was imminent. It wasn't the coup de grâce Yamamoto was looking for; the *I-400* subs would provide that. Nevertheless, the Sixth Fleet was on the offensive, and Nambu was off San Diego to keep up the pressure.

THE DAY THE *I-17* arrived off San Diego, the ocean was so calm, Nambu worried people on shore might hear his crew talking on the bridge.[6] The weather didn't last, unfortunately. By afternoon, the wind had picked up, rain started falling, and the sea grew so rough, the sub had difficulty maintaining periscope depth.[7] Despite the poor conditions, Nambu was eager to sink something big.[8]

San Diego was home to a major American naval base, so the pickings should have been excellent. But Nambu's sub searched the area without finding a single warship. The next day, the *I-17* received orders to shell the continental United States. Nambu was wary. He'd been through this drill once before and had been disappointed. The *I-17*, along with eight other I-boats,[9] had been ordered to shell west coast military installations on Christmas Eve 1941.[10] Shortly before shelling was to commence, Combined Fleet Headquarters inexplicably canceled the operation. It was a

---

* According to Zenji Orita, a Sixth Fleet conference in January 1942 summed up the results as "17 sinkings and 3 ships damaged." Specific breakdowns were as follows: "SubRon 1 was credited with 11 ships sunk and 2 damaged; SubRon 2 was credited with 4 sunk and 1 damaged; SubRon 3 was credited with 2 ships sunk." See Zenji Orita with Joseph D. Harrington, *I-Boat Captain: How Japan's Submarines Almost Defeated the U.S. Navy in the Pacific!* (Canoga Park, Calif.: Major Books, 1976), p. 45. However, once again these numbers proved to be inflated. The actual number of ships sunk was considerably less.

missed opportunity, given that every coastal city from Vancouver to San Diego was lit up like a carnival. Nambu suspected the mission had been called off out of respect for the Christian holiday.[11] If it had, it was a lousy reason. Maybe this time things would be different.

A list of targets was sent to the *I-17*, along with instructions to avoid San Diego.[12] Usually, sub captains had little discretion when it came to big decisions, so Nambu was thrilled when Captain Nishino called him to the wardroom to discuss target selection.[13] The *I-17*'s navigator and chief gunnery officers were also present and immediately began making suggestions.

"We should shell San Francisco!"

"No, we should shell Castroville!"

Captain Nishino was pleased. None of his officers lacked the proper fighting spirit. Still, he insisted they make their selection based on escape routes. After consideration, Nishino pointed to a spot on the map where an oil storage facility 12 miles north of Santa Barbara was located.

"This is our target!"[14]

The IJN knew how important oil was.*[15] It wasn't just the navy's life blood; the nation's entire industrial base couldn't function without it. The U.S. oil embargo against Japan had been a deciding factor in pushing them into war. Nambu understood that the *I-17*'s job was to send a message to America. It would let America know she wasn't safe with Japanese subs off her coast. And exploding oil tanks were a good way to make a dramatic statement.

Their target would be the Barnsdall–Rio Grande Oil Company, the forerunner of ARCO.[16] Considered one of the west coast's major oil facilities,[17] the target was a mile-long oceanfront oil field with producing wells, beachside docks, and a sizable tank farm. The area was remote, which meant the *I-17* could attack without

---

* Under interrogation, Japan's secretary of the Naval Ministry said: "You ask why we didn't shell some coastal U.S. city rather than . . . [the Santa Barbara] oil tanks. At Santa Barbara, it was our decision to shell oil tanks because we felt them important war assets. So it was with Fort Stevens. We didn't use these attacks to terrorize your people, but to strike war blows."

resistance. The target also offered an escape route, which was important to the practical-minded Nishino.

The Sixth Fleet was so bullish on the attack that it moved up the date.[18] When the captain broke the news to his crew, they were equally enthusiastic.

"We are now entering Santa Barbara Strait. We'll lie submerged and do recon with our periscope. Then tomorrow, we'll surface after dark and bombard the Ellwood oil field."[19]

A 1982 article in *Parade* magazine recalls a time before the war when Nishino was a tanker captain and visited the Ellwood facility. On his way to a welcoming ceremony, Nishino supposedly slipped and fell onto a cactus. While the proud captain plucked needles from his backside, refinery workers laughed at his predicament.[20] Or so the story goes. But it is fanciful. Nishino was never a tanker captain. Since admission to sub school in 1923, he'd served only aboard submarines,[21] leaving the reason for Ellwood's selection purely strategic.

Early in the morning of Monday, February 23, 1942, the *I-17* submerged and remained underwater all day. Captain Nishino occasionally raised the periscope to have a look around. Though the ocean remained clear of enemy patrols, the day still dragged for the crew. Lunch was canned *inari-zushi* (vinegar-flavored rice wrapped in fried tofu),[22] but it was hard to taste anything. Everybody was waiting for battle stations to be called. Even Nambu was nervous. At first he tried reading a book to calm his mind. When that failed, he got something to eat. It wasn't until later in the day that he finally relaxed enough to feel certain of success.[23]

It was 5:30 P.M., and the *I-17* was three miles offshore when Nishino raised the periscope.[24] The tank farm could be seen sitting above the beach. The hills behind were green from winter rain, and the surf was a steady thread of white. Nishino squinted through the periscope as sunlight glinted off the silver tanks. One tank marked RICHFIELD HI-OCTANE GASOLINE[25] held 80,000 gallons of aviation fuel. It would make a splendid target. And there was no indication of land or offshore patrols of any kind.[26] The area was deserted.

Nishino called Shimada, his gunnery officer, to the conning tower and instructed him to shell the storage tanks first, followed by the refinery. Then, at 6:30 P.M., Nambu heard the call they'd been waiting for.

"All hands to battle stations!"[27]

The men sprang into action, excited to make history. Shimada and his gun crew jammed into the tight confines of the conning tower, ready to jump on deck the moment the sub cleared the waves. All nine of Shimada's gun crew wore white headbands around their foreheads to signal their determination.[28] Shimada wore the same.

The *I-17* was about two miles off the coast, running parallel with the shore,[29] when the sub's starboard engine began malfunctioning.[30] The news might have deterred some sub captains,[31] but Nishino was determined to attack. Barking an order to fix the engine, he took one last look through the periscope, revealing both sea and sky to be clear. Then he turned to his hydrophone operator.

"Nothing detected, sir!"[32]

"Blow main ballast!"[33] Nishino commanded. "*Kyusoku fujyo!* [Rapid surface!] Prepare the deck gun!"[34]

The main ballast tanks were vented, and the bow and stern planesmen spun their wheels so quickly, the *I-17* leaped out of the water like a breaching whale. Once the bridge cleared the waves, the hatch was opened, and Shimada's gun crew dashed on deck. The sub was equipped with a 5.5-inch deck gun,[35] the same kind Japanese battleships used for their secondary battery.[36] Shells were kept on deck in a magazine, and though many were required to sink a ship, it would take only a few to set an oil field ablaze.

As the sun hung low in the sky, a crewman manhandled a shell into the gun breech. Then the pointer and trainer rotated the gun toward the shore. Once they were satisfied they'd lined up with the tank farm, the head gunner announced, "Mark, set!"

When the sub was almost abreast of the oil field, Nishino gave the order.

"Commence firing!"

It was 7:10 P.M.[37] when the first shot fired at the U.S. mainland since the War of 1812 was sent on its way. It was Washington's Birthday, and Roosevelt was giving a fireside chat at the time. The radio broadcast had begun promptly at seven o'clock, and though the purpose of the talk was to calm nervous Americans, local residents would find themselves in need of further reassurance once the *I-17* began her attack.

Shimada's first shot fell short, crashing into the sea. The trainer and azimuth-setter made adjustments, and the second shot landed on the beach, sending a dozen refinery workers scurrying for cover.[38] Further adjustments were made, but the trajectory was too high. One shell overshot the tank farm, burying itself in the hillside.[39] Another landed farther inland.[40]

The sub's rocking motion made a nearly flat trajectory difficult to achieve. But not all the shells missed their target. One ricocheted off a wooden pier and crashed into a pump house.[41] Another landed near the aviation fuel tank.[42]

Nambu was in the radio room when the shelling began, but it was impossible to stay once the deck gun sounded. Unable to stem his curiosity, he climbed into the conning tower and craned his neck out the bridge hatch.[43] The cannon fire was deafening.

The gun crews were doing a superb job as one volley after another arced toward the oil field. Nambu was sure at least one shell hit an oil tank.[44] Then again, it was hard to see everything.

Ten-year-old J. J. Hollister was at home with his family listening to Roosevelt's broadcast when he heard the first cannon report. Running outside, he saw a muzzle flash, followed by an eerie whistling noise as a shell landed near his house with a startling thump.[45]

Mrs. George Heaney was first to phone the police.[46] Bob Miller, an oil worker, also called to report that the refinery was being shelled.[47] Lawrence Wheeler, owner of Wheeler's Inn on nearby Highway 1, knew something was wrong when he felt his restaurant shake. Rushing outside to determine the cause, he was soon joined by his customers[48] and kitchen staff.[49] Wheeler's wife reported that the shell craters were so evenly spaced, it looked like a giant had walked up the beach.[50] Somewhere a siren began blaring.

Nishino kept the *I-17* running parallel to the coast as Shimada's men worked with precision.[51] Firing a shell every 30 to 60 seconds, the trainer and pointer continually adjusted their settings. The gun was targeting the refinery, but the hoped-for flames would have started more easily had they been using incendiaries. Surprisingly, they'd brought none.[52]

Backlit by the setting sun, the gun crew glowed a hellish red.[53] As the light faded, it soon became difficult to see. An evening mist settled on the mountains, and the coastal mustard fields were lost in darkness.[54] When Nishino gave the command to cease firing, the attack had lasted less than 30 minutes.

The gun crew quickly anchored their cannons, gathered their equipment, and disappeared down the bridge hatch. When two of the crew passed the radio room, they were buttonholed by the communications officer.

"What did we hit?"

"I don't know," one of them responded. "I had no time to confirm anything."

The radio officer celebrated anyway. "We're the first to bombard America!"[55]

Nambu knew the easy part was over. It was escaping that would be difficult.[56]

U.S. air patrols were already looking for them. The Santa Barbara Channel wasn't deep enough for the *I-17* to submerge, but coastal fog rolled in, providing much-needed cover. Fortunately, the *I-17*'s engine had been repaired, so Nishino called for 16 knots.

The *I-17*'s crew didn't relax until they'd submerged into the Pacific. Meanwhile Nambu thought about the chaos they had caused.[57] Though they'd sink another two ships during their patrol, nothing compared to being the first Japanese submarine to shell the U.S. mainland.

Nambu's parents would have been proud.

REPERCUSSIONS OF THE Ellwood attack* were far reaching and not just because it inspired the Steven Spielberg film *1941* starring John Belushi and Dan Aykroyd. The psychological impact of the bombardment caused many Californians to fear a Japanese invasion. This was exactly what Yamamoto had intended, though it was nothing compared to the fear he hoped to sow once the *I-400*s were complete.

U.S. historians would eventually pooh-pooh the attack, but 17 shells[†] were a small price for tying up U.S. Navy ships, manpower, and dollars. For the next three years, precious U.S. resources would be diverted to protecting the west coast, which was exactly what the Japanese intended. No ship could travel from San Francisco to Los Angeles, let alone Hawaii, without being escorted by a naval vessel. Not until 1945 was the Pacific coast considered safe enough that escorts were dispensed with.

The *I-17*'s message was swift and fast acting. The first widespread panic took place 32 hours later, when a remarkable story unfolded in the skies over Los Angeles.[58]

Just before two o'clock on the morning of February 25, U.S. air defense radar picked up a mysterious sea contact heading toward Los Angeles. When the contact was determined to be "unidentified aircraft," a yellow alert was issued. At 2:25 A.M., air raid sirens began sounding throughout the city. It was the second time that night that sirens had sounded, demonstrating just how on edge Los Angeles was. But when a red alert was declared at 2:30, people took it seriously. Ten thousand air raid wardens flooded the streets. By 2:32, antiaircraft guns were manned and ready as searchlights swept the skies. A citywide blackout went into effect from Santa Monica to Long Beach, which included radio silence.[59] Clearly, this was no drill.

---

* When I interviewed Admiral Nambu about the attack on the Ellwood oil refinery, I asked whether it had been his first visit to the United States. "No," he replied. "No?" I responded. "When was your first visit?" "Pearl Harbor." He smiled. I was soon to learn, it wasn't as a tourist.

[†] In his memoir, Nambu says they fired 17 shells. However Sato, in his history of the *I-400* submarines, quotes Nambu as saying 12 shells were fired.

The first antiaircraft (AA) guns opened fire at 3:16 A.M.[60] As the sound of AA flak filled the night, more batteries joined in. Pretty soon everyone was cutting loose. Some people saw Japanese planes; others saw bombs or parachutes.[61] A coastal artillery colonel spotted "twenty-five planes flying at 12,000 feet."[62] Another report sighted parachute flares over Santa Monica.[63] Twenty minutes later the 37th Coast Artillery headquarters in downtown L.A. received news that the Douglas Aircraft plant in Long Beach "had been bombed."[64]

Air raid wardens ran through the chilly night demanding people take cover.[65] As yellow tracer bullets raced into the sky, they were joined by sparkling ack-ack fire. AA debris began raining down on Santa Monica and Long Beach, and word spread that an enemy plane had crashed at 185th and Vermont.[66]

The Long Beach chief of police was on top of the local civic center using high-powered binoculars to report inbound planes heading toward Redondo Beach.[67] A reporter for the *Herald Examiner* saw 25 silvery planes in V formation moving slowly across the sky.[68] Other reports indicated the city was on fire.

An hour later it was all over.

By the time the skies cleared, more than 1,400 rounds of antiaircraft ordnance had been expended.[69] Unexploded shells and shrapnel fell in a 40-mile arc up and down the coast,[70] some of it landing on cars and rooftops.[71] A three-inch AA shell exploded in the backyard of Mr. and Mrs. Hugh Landis, blowing out their living room windows,[72] and shrapnel peppered the newly constructed bombers at the North American Aviation plant in Inglewood.[73] None of it hit an enemy plane, though.

The next morning the *Los Angeles Times* used four-inch headlines to tell the story:

L.A. AREA RAIDED!

JAP PLANES PERIL SANTA MONICA, SEAL BEACH,
EL SEGUNDO, REDONDO, LONG BEACH, HERMOSA,
SIGNAL HILL.[74]

But it wasn't Jap planes that menaced Los Angeles. It was Americans.

Five people died during the confusion, two of them struck by cars during the blackout[75] and three felled by heart attacks.[76] Sgt. Henry B. Ayers was one of the casualties. A 60-year-old California State guardsman, Ayers had a heart attack while driving an army truck full of ammunition.[77]

Most of the destruction was confined to AA shells damaging property. Of greater satisfaction was the efficient manner in which civilian defense officials swung into action only moments after being alerted. The only problem was, there'd been no attack.

Everything returned to normal when the all-clear sounded five hours later. Though newspapers reported employees were late for work the next day, the most unusual sight was people picking up shrapnel for souvenirs.

The day after the scare Secretary of War Henry L. Stimson said that as many as 15 aircraft, "possibly piloted by enemy agents," had flown over Los Angeles.

Navy Secretary Frank Knox disagreed. "As far as I know the whole raid was a false alarm . . . attributed to jittery nerves," he said.[78]

A congressional hearing was called, and even President Roosevelt raised an eyebrow over the comedy of errors.

There's no firm evidence of what triggered the SNAFU (situation normal, all fouled up), though it might have been faulty radar, which was still in its infancy. Whatever happened, confusion was probably amplified by searchlights illuminating AA bursts, which caused people to think they were seeing enemy planes.

As for what triggered the shooting in the first place, it's anybody's guess. One theory says that an AA battery using a weather balloon to measure wind conditions accidentally drew fire.* Others claim it was UFOs.

---

* Donald Young believes the cause may have been a weather balloon. As he explains, "With 3-inch guns ranging as high as 25,000 feet, it was necessary to keep anti-aircraft gunners up to date on current wind conditions in order to make any adjustments before any shooting started. This information was

If Nambu and the *I-17* had been ordered to create jitters along the west coast, they more than succeeded. Radio Tokyo reinforced the point when, on March 3, it broadcast: "Sensible Americans know the submarine shelling of the Pacific coast was a warning to the nation that the paradise created by George Washington is on the verge of destruction."[79] The English may have been fractured, but the intent was clear.

After torpedoing an American tanker,* the *I-17* sailed home to Yokosuka.[80] The sub had performed well, and Nambu was pleased. He was even more pleased when he received orders in Japan directing him to enter submarine school as a "class A" student. It was the moment he'd been waiting for.

Nambu was to become a sub captain.

----

gathered periodically by releasing meteorological balloons and then tracking them . . . At 3 a.m. on the morning of the raid, the 203rd launched two balloons, one from its headquarters on the Sawtelle Veterans Hospital grounds in Westwood and the other from Battery D, located on the Douglas Aircraft plant site in Santa Monica. So that the balloons could be tracked at night, a candle placed inside a simple highball glass was suspended under each balloon, whose silver color would reflect the light enough to be tracked to heights usually well above 25,000 feet. . . . According to [the officer in charge of the meteorological operations at Sawtelle, Lt. John E.] Moore, 'Our balloon continued up the coast, and the guns continued firing into the night. The next day the newspapers proclaimed "Japs Bomb Los Angeles."' " Donald J. Young, "Phantom Japanese Raid on Los Angeles During World War II," *World War II,* September 2003; online at http://www.historynet.com/phantom-japanese -raid-on-los-angeles-during-world-war-ii.htm.

* Though Captain Nishino heard the torpedo explode, the *William H. Berg* was not sunk and escaped.

CHAPTER 5

UNDERWATER AIRCRAFT CARRIERS

IF AT THE BEGINNING OF WORLD WAR II THE AMERICAN SUBMA-
rine force was "as nearly equal to Japanese submarine strength as
it was possible for coincidence to contrive,"[1] by May 1942 the Sixth
Fleet seemed invincible. Not only had Yamamoto's sub force tightened the noose around U.S. shipping on the west coast, it had successfully bombarded continental America between Santa Barbara
and Seattle. Add to this the attack on Pearl Harbor and Japan's
successful invasion of the Philippines, Malaya, Georgetown,* Thai-
land, Singapore, Hong Kong, Rangoon, Guam, Wake Island, and
the Dutch East Indies, and victory fever was at an all-time high.
Though June would prove a bloody month for both sides, there
seemed no stopping the Japanese in May 1942.

During this period, Japan's naval air corps was the finest in the
world. Mitsubishi's A6M Zero fighter (Allied code name: "Zeke")
was partly responsible, as were Japanese pilots, who were well
trained, battle hardened, and fearless. Some Japanese pilots were
so macho they even dispensed with their parachute. The naval air
corps, always a favorite of Yamamoto's, was on a roll, and it was
within this context that the architect of the attack on Pearl Harbor
came to expect the impossible.

When the question was raised of whether an attack plane that
would fit inside a submarine could be built, it was self-evident that
the sub design had to be agreed upon before any plane could be
specced. Otherwise how would anyone know how large, or small, to

_____
* Now called Penang.

make the aircraft, since it had to fit inside the sub's hangar? Once again Yamamoto was asking for a lot.

The *I-400*'s mission required a plane that had speed and range as well as the ability to carry the largest bomb possible. These features were contradictory. You can make a plane fast, or you can give it range—when you try to do both and make it carry the biggest bomb on your shelf, trade-offs begin.

Adding to the complexity was the need to design wings that could fold small enough for the aircraft to fit inside a sub hangar yet be unfolded fast enough for a quick launch. This meant fewer detachable parts. Attaching things takes time, and the more time a submarine spends on the surface, the more vulnerable it is to attack. Eliminating loose parts and automating assembly became especially important considering the limited deck space the launch crew had to work with. It was a complicated problem, one that required ingenuity to solve.

Some early IJN floatplanes could be launched from a sub in as little as seven minutes. But once fuel and hydraulic lines were threaded through a modern monoplane wing structure, detaching them became difficult. On top of this, the aircraft was so specialized, it couldn't be mass produced. This meant it needed custom building, which was slow and expensive.*[2]

The IJN had a history of outsourcing design and production of its aircraft to private sector manufacturers.[3] So while the Air Technical Bureau discussed the aircraft's specifications,[4] Naval Aviation Headquarters began secret talks with the Aichi Aircraft Company to design, test, and build the new plane.[5]

Aichi received a formal request to develop the world's first purpose-built attack plane to operate from a submarine on May 15, 1942.[6] Initially, the plane was named "17-*shi* Special Attack

---

* Squadron Leader Atsushi Asamura later said that the Aichi M6A1 cost 50 times more than a Zero fighter to build. Though it's almost impossible to substantiate this number, the *Seiran* was clearly an expensive airplane. See Atsushi Asamura, interview, *Rekishi Gunzou*, no. 85, October 10, 2007, pp. 154–59.

Bomber"[7] because 1942 was the seventeenth year of Hirohito's reign, and *shi* means "experimental." Aichi would apply its own utilitarian designation before the plane went into production.[8] But an even more glamorous moniker, *Storm from a Clear Sky*, would follow after the first prototype was built.

Aichi was an interesting selection to manufacture the plane. Founded in 1898 as the Aichi Clock and Electric Manufacturing Company, Ltd., the firm didn't get into the airplane business until 1920. By the early 1930s, Aichi had become the IJN's fourth major aircraft supplier. The IJN split its business among larger companies like Mitsubishi, Kawasaki, and Nakajima for efficiency's sake. But over time, Aichi became a "captured supplier," building aircraft exclusively for the IJN.[9] The company's most successful plane was the D3A dive-bomber (Allied code name: "Val"), which sank more Allied warships than any other Axis aircraft.[10] The plane's devastating record at Pearl Harbor probably contributed to the selection of Aichi to build the *I-400*'s attack bomber. Either way, Aichi had the necessary experience.

The company's design chief, Toshio Ozaki, was named project leader responsible for all aspects of the plane's design and construction. Ozaki was closely identified with the 17-*shi* program,[11] as were his two engineering assistants, whose job was to coordinate with the *I-400*'s design team to ensure that the sub's support equipment and environmental facilities met the aircraft's needs.[12] The humidity inside a sub is so great, it plays havoc with electrical systems. This was an important consideration, so Aichi paid close attention. Finally, Lt. Cdr. Tadashi Funada, the leader of Yokosuka's seaplane group and a member of the Naval Air Arsenal's Experimental Aircraft Department, worked closely with Aichi not only to design the aircraft but to serve as its chief test pilot as well.[13]

The 17-*shi* was conceived as a one-mission attack bomber,[14] no return, no deposit. Floats would be dispensed with (except for practice flights), not because a suicide mission was planned (those wouldn't become standard for another three years) but to maximize the plane's range and speed.*[15] After completing the mission, the aircraft's crew would rendezvous with the *I-400*, ditch the plane, and swim to the sub to be picked up. Presumably nobody thought a second act could top bombing New York and Washington.

The design called for two flight crew seated tandem style: a pilot in front, who acted as bombardier, and an observer in back, who acted as radioman, navigator, and tail-gunner, and made the calculations necessary to set torpedo depth. Since the aircraft not only had to get to its destination but had to defend itself along the way, the initial spec called for two machine guns: a fixed, front-facing 7.7mm gun and a rear-facing 13mm Type 2 gun.[16] The rear-facing machine gun was belt fed and handled 300 rounds.[17] Flexibly mounted, it folded down when not in operation and locked against the plane's starboard fuselage. When the gun was required, the observer swiveled his bucket seat 180 degrees to face backward and slid open the cockpit's overhead canopy, automatically raising the gun into firing position—a pretty neat trick.

It soon became apparent that the 17-*shi* would have trouble outrunning an enemy fighter. The plane's defensive armament wasn't satisfactory either. In the event of an attack, it would require luck or damn fine piloting skills to survive. But nobody was complaining. Early versions of the Zero fighter had neither armor plating nor self-sealing fuel tanks in the event of a puncture—both standard features on Allied aircraft. Since Japanese pilots were famous for their courage, neither speed nor lack of armor seemed a problem.

Like many planes of its day, the special attack bomber had an aluminum alloy airframe, with wood limited to the instrument panel and wingtips.[18] The control surfaces, namely the tail's rudder and elevator, were fabric covered, yet the overall plane was solidly constructed.[19] As one pilot who later flew the aircraft said, "It was the

---

* There is some controversy around whether the plane's floats were designed to be jettisoned in flight (to conserve fuel or to increase speed to avoid enemy attack). Sato suggests jettisoning was considered an option during the planning stages. However, if the idea was considered, it did not get past the early design stage. See Sato, *Maboroshi no Sensui Kubo,* p. 62.

most cutting edge plane of its time,"[20] and indeed, the special attack plane was destined to become not only Japan's most advanced and complex aircraft of the war[21] but its highest-performance floatplane in terms of payload and speed.

To keep things simple, Aichi looked at converting one of its own aircraft to do the job. The plane that made the most sense was the D4Y1 *Suisei,* a carrier-based dive-bomber (Allied code name: "Judy"). Aichi had recently begun mass production of the *Suisei,* and the company hoped it could be adapted for use aboard the *I-400* with few modifications; Aichi probably realized that the best way to save money was to share the major assemblies of two aircraft.[22] Unfortunately, the *Suisei* proved less adaptable as a sub-based plane. It may have been considered the IJN's best single-engine bomber of the Pacific war,[23] but it couldn't be made to fit in the *I-400*'s hangar.*

Research, design, and testing of the *I-400*'s aircraft would consume Aichi for the rest of 1942 and most of 1943,[24] and like everything else about the project, the schedule was ambitious. The *I-400* subs were designed to carry two attack planes each. Given 18 subs, this meant constructing a minimum of 36 planes.[25] But 36 planes were not enough, because trainers and replacement aircraft were also needed. The goal, then, was to construct a total of 78 planes, 44 in 1944 and another 34 in 1945.[26] The size of the order confirms just how important the IJN viewed the *Sen-toku* squadron.

But the first step was to develop a design that addressed the complex balance among size, weight, range, speed, and payload yet still allowed the plane to be folded into a small enough package to fit inside a sub hangar. That the hangar was only 11 feet 6 inches in diameter[27] made the job more challenging, since many propeller blades were longer than that. It wasn't going to be easy.

---

* According to Robert C. Mikesh in *Aichi M6A1 Seiran,* had the adaptation worked, the plane would have been named *Keisei.*

As MIGHT BE expected, the history of plane-carrying subs is an unusual one. At least six countries experimented with sub-plane combinations with varying degrees of success, but only Japan was able to carry the idea to fruition. Perhaps Japan's success was due to understanding the benefits of a sub-plane combo better than other nations, or perhaps she had the greatest need. Whatever the reason, Japan was to spend nearly 20 years perfecting the combination, when other countries had long since given up.

Both the British and Germans tested a floatplane-submarine combination during World War I. The Germans did it first in January 1915, when a floatplane pilot teamed up with a U-boat captain he'd met socially to conduct aerial reconnaissance of an English town.[28] The German High Command was not impressed, and no additional flights were made.

The HMS *E-22* was another early example. A British E-class submarine commissioned in 1915, she carried two Sopwith Schneider seaplanes on deck to intercept and destroy German Zeppelins.[29] The Admiralty had originally considered the idea of plane-carrying subs inhumane, but Zeppelin raids on London soon changed that notion. The first trial of the *E-22* was conducted in the North Sea on April 24, 1916. Submerging the boat in a calm sea, the Sopwith Schneiders floated free and took off for England, proving the concept worked. The trial was not repeated because two days later the *E-22* was torpedoed by a German U-boat. There were no survivors.

During the early days of sub-plane experiments, subs and floatplanes were used with a minimum of modification. The aircraft was carried on the sub's deck, but there was no means of housing it and no way of retrieving the plane once she departed.

The United States began experimenting with its own version of a plane-carrying sub in 1923. The *S-1* had a small on-deck storage container that housed a Martin MS-1.[30] Unfortunately, before the plane could be launched, 16 man-hours were required to put it together.[31] This made the Martin MS-1 about as popular as an unassembled toy on Christmas Eve. Once the aircraft was ready, the sub submerged enough to allow the plane to slip off its stern and take off in the water. The eventual launch must have been anticlimactic given the prep time.

The goal of the *S-1* was to use its plane to scout ahead of the fleet and report back on the enemy's position.[32] But as submarine expert Norman Polmar explains, "The U.S. had enough dirigibles and carrier planes that they didn't need to experiment with plane-based submarines."[33] It was no surprise then when the United States abandoned the program in 1927.

Britain picked up the gauntlet that same year with the *M-2*, also known as a "mutton boat" because its 12-inch gun and turret resembled a leg of lamb. The *M-1*'s first captain, Max Horton, was an early proponent of sub-borne airplanes. As a result, the *M-2* had its gun removed and was refitted with a floatplane hangar, a compressed air catapult, and a crane for loading and unloading aircraft.[34]

The *M-2* carried a Parnall Peto, which was a floatplane, but landing and recovering the aircraft in anything more than a force-two wind was nearly impossible.[35] Though it may sound impressive, a force-two wind is a light breeze accompanied by small waves—in other words, a nice day at the beach.

Launching a Peto from the *M-2* was an improvement over the time-consuming Martin MS-1, but not by much. Ten men had to crowd inside the tiny hangar to get the plane ready. They also had to wear waders and sea boots, because the hangar door was so close to the water, they often got soaked. The good news was that the Peto could be launched in under 12 minutes, a big improvement over the American *S-1*'s launch time. A Peto could also land, be recovered, disassembled, and stored with the *M-2* returning to periscope depth in less than 11 minutes. Given this capability, it's fair to say the *M-2* was the first submarine fully capable of carrying, launching, and retrieving an airplane.[36]

The *M-2* possessed an unfortunate design flaw, however. After the sub dove off England one January morning in 1932, the Royal Navy had to go looking for her. She was eventually found three miles off the coast in 100 feet of water. Her hangar door was open, as was the hatch leading from the hangar into the sub. Her entire crew of 60 had perished,[37] as did Britain's desire for further experimentation with plane-carrying subs. In the future, no submarine would have its hangar door placed so near the waterline.

Though Germany, Britain, the United States, and Italy "passed" on the plane-carrying-sub concept, France was next, and her commitment was big. Named the *Surcouf,* after Robert Surcouf, who made his career as a "licensed" buccaneer attacking British ships,[38] she was the world's largest, most powerful submarine when commissioned in 1934. At 361 feet in length, she was one of the longest subs ever built until the *I-400* class came along.

Surcouf's size was dictated by the need for a stable weapons platform that could both launch a plane and have range enough to reach the enemy. (This was also an issue that the *I-400*s faced.) The French wanted a commerce raider to do to Germany what the U-boats had done to France during World War I. The French weren't ones to stint on weapons systems either. As Richard Compton-Hall notes in *Submarine Warfare: Monsters & Midgets*: "The *Surcouf* had just about everything that could be crammed into a sub of the period,"[39] including a watertight turret, out of which extended twin eight-inch guns. Below the waterline, the sub boasted four bow-mounted torpedo tubes supplemented with 22 torpedoes.* And of course she carried a floatplane. In other words, this baguette really packed a punch.

Surcouf even had restraints to imprison 40 POWs from the ships she sunk,[40] a nice touch given Robert Surcouf's second career transporting slaves. But the French were more interested in commerce raiding than in floatplanes and soon dispensed with her aircraft. When the *Surcouf* disappeared without a trace in February 1942, French interest went with it.

Japan's interest in sub-borne aircraft was undeterred despite all this failure. In 1923 she purchased a Caspar-Heinkel U-1 seaplane from Germany[41] and began holding sea trials to learn the trade. Japan had good reasons for developing plane-carrying subs.

---

* "None of them reliable," Compton-Hall dryly reports.

First, subs played an important scouting role in the IJN's decisive battle strategy.[42] The enemy fleet had to be located and reported on while still distant from Japanese shores, and subs were ideal for this role. But subs don't handle scouting very well. If it's true that a submarine has a large scouting range, it's also true that it rides so low in the water that it has a restricted field of vision. And though a land-based aircraft has a much higher field of view, its scouting radius in the 1920s was limited to an hour or two. You could dramatically improve both the scouting area and the field of view if you built a submarine that effectively carried, launched, and retrieved an aircraft while at sea. The Japanese intended doing just that.

By 1925 Japan had developed her own prototype seaplane based on the Heinkel. Called the Yokosho 1-Go, she conducted tests using the *I-21* as her host sub.[43] Trials progressed enough by the fall of 1928 that the IJN was satisfied that a plane-carrying sub could serve a useful purpose.

In July 1932 the *I-5* became the first Japanese submarine to carry an aircraft in a watertight deck hangar.[44] When fleet maneuvers demonstrated that a sub-based reconnaissance plane could successfully find and report on the enemy, enthusiasm for the program grew. Assembling and disassembling the aircraft took too long, so the IJN continued pushing improvements.[45] The *I-6* followed in 1935. Built as an aircraft-carrying submarine from its inception (rather than modified later), the *I-6* was followed two years later by the *I-7* and a year after that by the *I-8*.[46] All of these boats had their floatplane hangar on their aft deck behind the sail, a design that changed over time to favor the forward deck for hangar and catapult placement. The *I-7*'s and *I-8*'s storage and catapult arrangements were an improvement because the subs were larger than their predecessors.[47] When it came to launching planes from a sub, bigger really was better.

By December 1936, Japan had withdrawn from the Washington and London naval treaties and began building submarines just as fast as she was able. Under the Third Fleet Replenishment Law, three new types of subs were planned, two of which, the Type A1 and B, carried a floatplane.[48] Twenty new *Junsen* Type B boats were laid down in January 1938,[49] followed by three new *Junsen* Type A1 boats laid down in January 1939.[50] They were among the best subs in the world at the time[51] and the only ones that carried airplanes.

Japan expected results from her aircraft-bearing submarines;[52] that's why plane-carrying subs were integrated into every major theater in which Japan's sub force operated, including the attack on Pearl Harbor. By the start of war there were 11 frontline I-boats with floatplanes,[53] and more were in the pipeline. By war's end, Japan had built 41 such subs.*[54] Because of this commitment, no other nation had so much experience building and operating plane-carrying subs.

But the Japanese were soon to encounter an important strategic issue related to sub-plane combat: Which weapon took precedence? A sub is intended to hunt its enemy, while a plane is intended to scout. What this meant in practice is that each one's mission interfered with the other. For example, before launching her scout plane, a sub would forgo attacking ships. This deterred combat operations. When her scout was returning, a sub was sometimes forced to give away her position to help the plane locate her. This ran counter to the sub's purpose as a stealth weapon.

Sub commanders weren't always happy subordinating their combat mission to reconnaissance, and the *I-400* class only exacerbated the situation. The *I-400*'s primary job was to deliver aircraft

---

* Hashimoto says in his book *Sunk!* that there were 11 aircraft-carrying subs at the beginning of the war. Orita notes in *I-Boat Captain* that there were 11 plane-carrying boats at Pearl Harbor; see Orita and Harrington, *I-Boat Captain*, p. 40. So it is reasonable to assume that the Sixth Fleet committed all its plane-carrying subs to the attack. Interestingly, these subs accounted for more than a third of the sub force deployed around Oahu (including Nambu in the *I-17*), which shows just how important plane-carrying subs were to the Japanese. Twenty-four additional plane-carrying subs were built as the war progressed, making for a total of 35. Hashimoto lists the plane-carrying subs at the start of war as including: the *I-7, I-8, I-10, I-15, I-17, I-19, I-21, I-23,* and *I-26.* These were followed by 19 boats numbered *I-27* through *I-45* as well as the *I-54, I-56, I-58, I-11,* and *I-12.* Of course, the *I-400, I-401, I-13,* and *I-14* should also be added to this list, which increases the number to at least 39. See Hashimoto, *Sunk!*, p. 36, for details.

to a set location. Attacking ships was now a secondary consideration. On the one hand, it was the next logical step in the evolution of sub-borne airplanes; yet it turned every conventional notion about submarines on its head. Which is why it's not surprising that the Naval General Staff took an intermediate step in July 1942 when it instigated a mission where the seaplane rather than its host sub would be the offensive weapon. The mission was the first of its kind. It would be launched before the *I-400*'s keel had even been laid, and it would proceed using an existing plane that required little modification.

But what was most surprising was that eight months into the war, the Naval General Staff wasn't just going to stand convention on its head—it was going to launch an aerial attack against the United States to prove that the idea could work. For Japan wasn't satisfied with just using submarines to shell the American coastline. She was going to use an airplane-carrying sub to bomb the American mainland for the first time.

CHAPTER 6

PROOF OF CONCEPT

WHEN THE CAPTAIN OF THE *I-25* HANDED WO NOBUO FUJITA a message summoning him to the Navy Ministry in Tokyo, Fujita was nervous. It was July 27, 1942,[1] and the *I-25* had recently returned from her third war patrol. Fujita had every intention of going on the sub's next patrol. He respected the sub's captain, Lt. Cdr. Meiji Tagami, and enjoyed flying her two-seater floatplane. He was in the middle of a much-deserved rest when he received the message, which was all the more unwelcome for failing to explain why he was being summoned.

It had been five months since Nambu shelled the oil facility near Santa Barbara and two months since the *I-400* subs had been approved for production. Unfortunately, the IJN had suffered a huge loss at the Battle of Midway in June. Yamamoto remained set on taking the war to the American mainland though. Shelling the west coast had been a start, and the *I-400*s might well prove the finish. In the meantime, the IJN was searching for a second act.

Certainly, Fujita was more than just a proficient seaplane pilot. During the *I-25*'s second war patrol, he had completed six successful reconnaissance missions over enemy ports in Australia and New Zealand.[2] But what could the Naval General Staff possibly want with him? He was just a pilot. They, on the other hand, were more akin to gods.

By the time he received the summons, Fujita had been flying for nine years. Born in 1911[3] and drafted into the navy in 1932, he had had extensive combat experience over China. After that he'd tested experimental aircraft,[4] always a sign of a respected pilot. Then he'd been promoted and assigned to the *I-23*, a plane-carrying sub. By the time the Pacific war started, Fujita had 3,500 hours of combat flight and a sterling reputation.

Fujita had the usual reserve of an experienced pilot. Calm, cool, and collected, he came across as serious, if withdrawn. He may have appeared cold to those who didn't know him, but he was popular among sub crews, who admired his courage and modesty. A simple man from a small farming village,[5] he had wide-spaced eyes and a handsome nose—the very picture of a dashing Japanese pilot.

Six weeks before Pearl Harbor, Fujita had been transferred to the *I-25*, a *Junsen* Type B class sub that carried a floatplane.[6] For the next month or so, he practiced night launches, then searched for a mock enemy fleet to report on. It wasn't the same as combat duty; still, Fujita understood the importance of his job. If the Yankees were to be defeated, they had to be found first.

Fujita had been aboard the *I-25* during the attack on Pearl Harbor. He'd even been in the same sentry arc as Nambu north of Oahu. Once the attack was finished, he wanted to be the first pilot to fly over the American naval base and report on the damage. But the storm-tossed crossing had so banged up his plane, it was unable to fly.[7]

Fujita smoothed out the message from the Naval General Staff and read it one more time to make sure he understood it correctly:

WARRANT OFFICER FUJITA IS INSTRUCTED TO REPORT TO
IMPERIAL NAVAL HEADQUARTERS AT ONCE.[8]

Fujita wasn't one to get involved in the politics at Naval Headquarters; he was more comfortable in a cockpit than a conference room. He assumed he'd be told why he was wanted once he appeared, but that offered little consolation. In the meantime, all he could do was worry.

THE MINISTRY WAS located in Kasumigaseki, the central part of Tokyo, where government offices were found. A well-polished plaque at its entrance indicated that the Naval General Staff shared the imposing edifice with the Navy Ministry, though relations between the two were sometimes strained. The four-story red brick building was surrounded by a tall iron fence and capped by a mansard roof, its Western influence clearly on display. It was also in the perfect location—only a block or so from the large wooded compound where the emperor resided.

Fujita took the morning train from Yokosuka for the hour-long ride to Tokyo. Even though he wore his best dress whites, it was hard not to be intimidated by the senior officers who walked the hallways.[9] His orders were to report to Cdr. Shojiro Iura, NGS, First Division. When he found the third-floor office, he entered the high-ceilinged room, came to attention, and called out:

"Warrant Officer Fujita, sir. Chief flying officer of *I-25*!"

"Thank you for coming," Commander Iura said, returning his salute.

At that moment another door opened, and a man wearing a commander's uniform walked in. He was instantly recognizable, especially since Fujita had seen his picture in the newspaper many times. It was the emperor's younger brother, Prince Nobuhito Takamatsu.

Fujita certainly hadn't expected to be meeting with someone as important as the emperor's brother. He felt so flustered, all he could do was come to attention again and repeat his name. Prince Takamatsu was gracious enough to overlook Fujita's nervousness. He had plenty of experience putting people at ease; a warrant flying officer was no problem.

The third son of Emperor Taisho, Prince Takamatsu had made a career of the Imperial Japanese Navy. He'd graduated from Etajima, served aboard a battleship, and attended torpedo, aviation, and gunnery schools.[10] After graduating from the Naval War College in 1936, he held various positions in the NGS, which was one reason, royal blood aside, the prince felt comfortable in the building. His presence also meant that whatever they wanted to discuss was far more important than Fujita had guessed.

History is unclear how many men were in the room that day. Besides Fujita, Commander Iura, and Prince Takamatsu, there may have been others. If there were, they didn't include Cdr. Tatsunosuke Ariizumi, the submarine staff officer destined to command the *I-400* squadron. Ariizumi had moved out of the NGS to a new assignment a few months earlier. Commander Iura was his replacement.

The presence of the emperor's brother required the most formal language possible. Rife as it was with honorifics, it was easy to make a mistake. It's safe to say Fujita kept his words to a minimum. After executing his lowest bow, Fujita was led to a table where several maps were spread out.

"We captured these at Wake Island," Iura explained. "They should prove useful."[11]

Fujita studied the topmost map. When he realized it showed the west coast of the United States, he couldn't believe his eyes. But what Iura said next surprised him even more.

"Fujita, you're going to bomb the American mainland."

Fujita was stunned. Bomb America? Which cities? San Francisco? Los Angeles? His mind raced with possibilities. This was big. But what Iura said next stunned him even more.

"You will bomb forests for us. Right about here." Iura pointed to an area just north of the California-Oregon border.[12]

Fujita was incredulous. Bomb forests? Why did they want to do that? Not only did it seem a waste of time, they didn't need a pilot of his caliber to fell lumber. A junior pilot would have done just as well.

Fujita couldn't hide his disappointment even from this august group, but at least he knew why they were meeting. It was to discuss an idea submitted almost seven months ago, an idea Fujita knew all about. Why did a junior officer in the IJN know about the first aerial bombing of the American mainland? Because Fujita had suggested the idea himself.

Fujita had first got the idea of turning a reconnaissance floatplane into an offensive weapon after the attack on Pearl Harbor. It was December 10, and the *I-25* had just received a position report on the USS *Enterprise*. The carrier was too far away for the *I-25* to catch it submerged, so Captain Tagami surfaced and pursued the flattop at flank speed. During the chase, *Enterprise* planes spotted the *I-25* and bombed the sub before she got close enough to attack. Tagami was forced under, and when he resurfaced, the *Enterprise* was gone. This started Fujita thinking.

Not long afterward the *I-25* received orders to attack a U.S. "transport fleet." Unfortunately, the fleet was too far away to reach in time.[13] This made Fujita ponder all the more.

Finally, on December 21, the *I-25* was ordered to attack a U.S. battle group that was soon to exit the Panama Canal.* On her way to intercepting the warships, the sub was spotted by an American destroyer and depth-charged so badly, Fujita and the crew barely escaped.

These experiences convinced Fujita that if sub-borne planes had the ability to drop bombs, they could attack targets that their subs couldn't reach. In the best case, a plane might sink an enemy ship or at least stop an attacking destroyer. Even if that wasn't possible, they might distract a ship long enough that subs like the *I-25* could catch up and finish the job.[14]

The more Fujita thought about it, the more benefit he saw to sub-borne planes acting as offensive weapons, and he soon found an advocate when he discussed his idea with the *I-25*'s executive officer.

"If our planes were armed with bombs, I could search far ahead of the submarine," Fujita explained. "I could not only locate enemy ships for the *I-25* but join in attacks to sink them."[15]

Lt. Tatsuo Tsukudo was enthusiastic. "You ought to put your ideas in writing and forward them to the high command, Fujita."[16]

This made Fujita laugh. Would Etajima graduates really listen to a farmboy?[17]

As the *I-25* headed toward Kwajalein, Fujita and Tsukudo continued to discuss the idea. They realized sub-borne planes could

---

* As we know from Nambu's memoir, this intelligence was faulty.

be used to attack both enemy ships and coastal targets such as aircraft factories and naval bases. They even discussed bombing the Panama Canal.[18]

As much as Tsukudo supported the idea, Fujita was reluctant to commit anything to paper. Still, Tsukudo believed Fujita was on to something, and insisted he write it down.[19] By the time they arrived at Kwajalein, Fujita had written a letter describing how to use a sub-borne plane as a weapon. When Captain Tagami read it, he appended his endorsement.

Tsukudo promised to forward Fujita's proposal to Sixth Fleet command. Fujita doubted anything would come of it though. Incredibly, someone had read his proposal, because now Fujita was meeting with the Naval General Staff, the most senior group responsible for Sixth Fleet planning and operations. And he wasn't just meeting the NGS's senior submarine staff officer—he was meeting the emperor's brother as well.

Fujita no longer wondered how he'd got there; still he was confounded by what they wanted him to do. Bomb forests in America? Why waste bombs on trees? It would be far better to bomb a major city like San Francisco. And if they chose to attack a west coast naval base like San Diego, it would really make a statement. But bombing trees was ridiculous!

Fujita's disappointment made for an awkward moment until Iura explained his thinking.

"The northwestern United States is full of forests. Once a blaze gets started deep in the woods it is very difficult to stop. Sometimes whole towns are destroyed. If we were to bomb some of these forests it would cause the enemy much trouble. It might even create large-scale panic once residents knew Japan could reach out and bomb their factories and homes from 5,000 miles away."[20]

Fujita listened thoughtfully. It made sense when explained this way. A forest fire could be a force multiplier, causing more destruction than one or two bombs. Still, it was an odd assignment. It seemed typical that a low-level officer would recommend Los Angeles as a bombing target, and the NGS would somehow turn it into trees. What happened to staff officers' brains once they were promoted past frontline duty? They seemed to forget what it was like and come up with all sorts of crazy plans.

But Fujita was a noncommissioned officer; he knew what orders meant. If he had any reservations, he kept them to himself. After all, the orders came from the emperor's brother. And there was nothing wrong with being the first pilot to bomb America.

The best part of the plan was that an attack on the mainland might force a redeployment of the Pacific Fleet. If Japan could get America to tie up vital warships, defending the west coast rather than using them in the Pacific against Japan, it would be a significant benefit to the empire.[21] Plus, Fujita had his own reasons for wanting to punish the United States. Three months before, the *I-25* had been berthed in Yokosuka next to the light carrier *Ryuho*.[22] When one of James Doolittle's B-25s dropped a bomb through the flattop's flight deck, many of the carrier's crew had been killed. The attack marked the first U.S. bombing of the Japanese mainland. It would give Fujita great satisfaction to return the favor.[23]

In fact, Doolittle's April raid accelerated a lot of things. Not only did it make the NGS more desirous of finding ways to attack the U.S. mainland, it increased the pace of their talks with Aichi about building the *I-400*'s special attack plane.[24] In retrospect, the two enemies seem to have been engaged in a tit-for-tat exchange. I shell Ellwood; you bomb Tokyo; I start forest fires in Oregon; you shell the emperor's summer palace. Both sides were struggling for psychological advantage. In Japan's case, there was an important strategic reason for striking the United States: the sooner America was forced into peace negotiations, the better. If the lack of certain weaponry stood in the way of shortening the war, then the IJN would build it. That's why the *I-400* construction program was under way.

Fujita and Captain Tagami were selected for the mission because their operational record was outstanding. The *I-25* had sunk a number of ships during her first west coast patrol, and Fujita had successfully conducted dangerous scouting missions over Australia and New Zealand. Additionally, Tagami was considered an aggressive skipper and had endorsed Fujita's idea. They were a natural choice to carry out the mission.

The plan was simple. Three missions dropping two incendiary bombs each would be made against three different locations in the dense forests of Oregon and northern California. Armed with a wind-spun propeller, each bomb contained 512 pellets that burned at 2,000 degrees Fahrenheit.[25] The bombs were small (weighing only 167 pounds each) because the *I-25*'s floatplane couldn't carry a large payload. What they lacked in size, however, they made up in firepower. Given the tinder-dry conditions of the Pacific Northwest in September, it would be more than enough to get a conflagration started.

The more Fujita listened, the more credible the plan sounded. The next few days proved difficult though. Just as Nambu hadn't been able to tell his family about the Pearl Harbor attack, Fujita couldn't tell his wife about his mission. Whenever he looked at their son, his heart sank thinking he might never see him again. It wasn't that Fujita lacked confidence. He knew his skills were strong. But surely some Yankee fighter would shoot his lumbering plane out of the sky.[26] He would just have to drop his bombs before that happened. Still, it hurt to think he'd never see his son again.

THREE WEEKS LATER Fujita sat on his bunk cleaning his sidearm. It was four o'clock on the morning of September 9, 1942, and the *I-25* was submerged off Oregon waiting for the weather to clear.[27]

Life on board a sub could be monotonous. Unlike a submarine's crew, pilots didn't have regular duties. Other than checking on his plane to make sure it received proper maintenance, there wasn't much for him to do. He'd gotten to know the *I-25*'s crew and liked many of them. Of course, Fujita stayed out of their way when they were working, and to his credit, he wasn't averse to pitching in. He certainly didn't consider himself better than the enlisted men, though the same couldn't be said for most IJN officers.

It's a bit surprising that the crew felt an attachment to Fujita, especially because his domain was the sky. A pilot's job is very different from a submariner's. Submariners work as a team, while a reconnaissance pilot flies alone (save for an observer), relying solely upon his skills for survival. Many sub crews looked up to their pilots as heroes. When they didn't return, it was a terrible loss.

Fujita must have felt restless waiting for the skies to clear. He tried to focus on the mission, but thoughts of his family probably intruded. Though it might seem odd to clean his gun at four in the morning[28] it helped take his mind off the waiting.

"Captain Tagami wishes you to report to the conning tower, sir."[29]

Fujita looked up and saw a crewman in front of him.

"Very well," he said, laying the pistol on his bunk. Maybe this time the captain would have good news.

When Fujita arrived in the darkened conning tower, Captain Tagami was gazing through the periscope.

"Take a look and tell me what you think," he said.[30]

Fujita grasped the cold metal handles and squinted through the eyepiece at the Oregon coast. It was dark out, but he could see the snow-covered hills behind Cape Blanco lighthouse. Amazingly, the Oregon coast wasn't blacked out.[31] What Fujita cared most about though were launch conditions.

After carefully studying the sea and sky, he turned to Tagami. "Captain, it looks good. I think we can do it today."

"Fine!" the captain responded. "In just a few minutes you'll make history, Fujita. You'll be the first person to bomb the United States of America!"[32]

Fujita returned to his bunk, where he put on his flight suit. As he zipped up the front, he thought, I'm finally going to bomb America. And it had all come about because he'd sent a letter up the chain of command.[33] It didn't seem possible.

Fujita placed several strands of hair and a few fingernail clippings into a small, light-colored box made of paulownia wood. If discovered on his mission, it was unlikely he or his navigator would return. The ossuary box would then be given to his family in place of his remains. Otherwise, his spirit could not be properly venerated.

Fujita went on deck after finishing his preparations. There seven technicians worked by starlight to ready his plane. First the hangar door was opened. Then the floatplane was rolled out on its dolly. Next, the wings, control surfaces, and pontoons were attached. When the plane was fully assembled, Fujita climbed into the cockpit and turned the engine over. The *Kugisho* E14Y spluttered to life.[34] Fujita had always loved the smell of oil fumes, and he found the plane's idling reassuring. When the engine was running smoothly, he reported to Captain Tagami.

"All ready, sir."

The captain nodded. "Good luck, Fujita."[35]

Seconds after Fujita saw a red-lensed flashlight waving from the sub's bow, his body slammed into the seat back, and he was launched into the sky. Turning toward the lighthouse, he flew toward the golden rays of the rising sun. His mission was finally under way.

If everything went well, this would be the first of many air raids over America.[36] The thought inspired Fujita. Still, he was concerned that his plane might be shot down before he'd dropped his payload. He mustn't let that happen.

S2c Ezra Ross was one of the first people to spot Fujita's floatplane as it neared the coast. Ross was standing watch at the Coast Guard station in Port Orford when he reported seeing an unidentified aircraft. Word passed quickly to the IVth Fighter Command, responsible for tracking incursions.[37] It was now official. Fujita's mission was no longer secret.

After he crossed the Oregon coastline, Fujita turned northeast and headed inland about 50 miles. It was a foggy morning with poor visibility, but U.S. forest rangers weren't just watching for fires on Mount Emily that day—they'd also been trained as air defense observers. Within minutes, two lookout posts heard Fujita's aircraft approaching.[38]

As he flew over Wheeler Ridge, Fujita ordered his observer to release the first bomb. The incendiary disappeared into the Oregon woods, its nose-mounted propeller spinning like a pinwheel. But the sudden change in weight distribution proved too great for the tiny plane, and Fujita found himself fighting a steep dive. Using the stick, he regained control just in time to see the first bomb explode in a brilliant white flash.[39]

Heading east, Fujita flew a few more miles before dropping his second bomb. Satisfied he'd made an important contribution to the war effort,[40] he leveled off at 100 feet and pushed his plane as fast as she could go.[41]

Fujita planned to rendezvous with the *I-25* at sea. However, as he passed Cape Blanco, he spotted two merchant ships directly in his path. Fujita didn't want the ships alerting American air defense, but he didn't have much choice. If he was going to meet the *I-25* at the predetermined location, he had to pass the two ships. The question was how to do it without being identified?[42]

The only answer was to fly between the ships at such low altitude, they wouldn't spot the insignia on his wings. His seaplane's silhouette was also a problem though, so Fujita flew so close to the wave tops that his floats nearly skimmed the water.

Unfortunately, his observer miscalculated their location. As soon as they were over the horizon, they realized they were too far south. Informed of the mistake, Fujita backtracked. Air defense officials were looking for him by now, so it soon became a race to see whether Fujita found his sub first, or U.S. fighter planes found him.

Fortunately for Fujita, he found his sub. After spotting the *I-25*, he executed a prearranged series of maneuvers like a scout bee signaling he was friendly.[43] When it was clear he'd been identified, he landed the plane, taxied alongside the sub, and was craned aboard.

Protocol dictates that officers behave in a calm manner when reporting to a superior, but Fujita could hardly restrain himself when he saw Captain Tagami. "Mission complete, sir. Both bombs exploded. Two large fires are spreading."

What excited Tagami more though was Fujita's news that two merchant ships were heading north at 12 knots. "Give me a course to intercept those ships!"[44]

As far at Captain Tagami was concerned, the *I-25* was still an offensive weapon, even if he'd just launched the first sub-borne airplane attack of World War II.

The technicians were still disassembling Fujita's plane when Tagami gave the order to pursue the freighters. Fujita was impressed by his captain's aggressiveness: attacking two ships after launching the first air raid on American soil demonstrated the proper fighting spirit. But the *I-25* was no match for U.S. air defenses. An American plane dove out of the sky and dropped two bombs on the sub just moments after the flight crew secured her hangar door.* Fujita had led the Americans right to the sub.

The *I-25* dove, leveled off at 250 feet, and rigged for silent running. As the crew listened to depth charges exploding overhead, it soon became apparent the detonations were moving farther away. Jokes were made about the accuracy of American fliers. An enemy had to be perfect to impress a Sixth Fleet crew.[45] Clearly, these were not.

The *I-25* remained submerged that day. Later in the evening when things were quiet, Tagami surfaced to recharge their batteries. Fujita was anxious to discuss the next attack, since they still had four incendiaries left. He was curious what the captain would do. Both men had recently heard an American radio broadcast describing the Japanese as capable only of repetitive behavior.

"The Americans will be expecting another sunrise [attack] . . . in the usual Japanese manner," Tagami said. "We'll make the next one a night attack [instead]."[46]

Fujita smiled at his captain's humor.

The *I-25* may have become the most wanted submarine on the west coast, but that didn't stop Tagami from attacking an American freighter.†[47] Fujita was anxious to make his next flight, of course. The plan was to launch off Cape Mendocino and torch California's

---

* This is how Fujita remembers it. Other Japanese accounts say the plane attacked the *I-25* the next day.
† The SS *Commercial Trader* was sunk on this date, but records indicate it was sunk not by the *I-25* as claimed but by the *U-558*, 75 miles east of Trinidad. Most likely, the *I-25* sunk a different freighter.

redwood forests. When seas proved too rough, Tagami returned to the scene of their first attack. Maybe the Americans wouldn't expect him after all.[48]

The *I-25* surfaced 50 miles west of Cape Blanco at midnight, September 29, 1942.[49] By now, the Oregon coast was blacked out, but a full moon helped guide Fujita into the sky. Once again he used the lighthouse to navigate and flew inland for half an hour before releasing his incendiaries into the old-growth forest below. Satisfied each bomb had exploded, Fujita turned round and headed back to the sub.*

Taking no chances on his return trip, Fujita passed north of Cape Blanco to avoid being spotted. He also cut power as he approached the coast and began a long, silent glide that took him over the ocean. Following a predetermined route, he flew west until he reached the rendezvous point. Unfortunately, the *I-25* wasn't there.[50]

Fujita knew the risks. The sub came first, his floatplane second. Though it was possible his observer had miscalculated, it was equally possible the *I-25* had been spotted and forced to submerge. Something similar had happened with the *I-36*'s floatplane. After flying over Pearl Harbor to report on damage, the aircraft hadn't been able to return without betraying the *I-36*'s position. The plane and her crew were never heard from again.[51]

Fujita banked steeply to get a clear look at the ocean. Locating a sub was like finding a particular feather in a barnyard, and it was even more difficult when it was dark. Though moonlight helped Fujita to see for miles, there was no sign of the *I-25*.

Fujita was willing to die on behalf of his country, but he wanted his death to mean something. To crash into an enemy ship was honorable. Even diving into the Cape Blanco lighthouse was acceptable so long as the enemy was hurt. But to run out of fuel and

---

* The U.S. Forest Service has no record of any fires in this area on this date. As a result, it's assumed that the bombs malfunctioned, or else, as in the previous raid, the unusually wet forest prevented a blaze from starting. However, unlike the first two incendiaries, no traces of these two bombs have ever been found. They're still out there somewhere.

crash into the sea was a waste.[52] Time was running out, however. Unless they found the *I-25*, they'd quickly run out of options.

Ironically, the thing that saved Fujita was the same thing that could have caused the *I-25* to be sunk: the sub was leaking oil. Much to his relief, Fujita spotted an iridescent slick on the ocean and followed the trail until it led him to the *I-25*. Then he landed alongside the sub and was craned back on board.

Fujita's two attacks were front-page news in Japan. The *Asahi Shimbun*, one of the country's largest-circulation newspapers, plastered the story in celebratory headlines:

INCENDIARY BOMB DROPPED ON OREGON STATE

FIRST AIR RAID ON MAINLAND AMERICA
BIG SHOCK TO AMERICANS[53]

Poor weather prevented Fujita from a third attack. Fortunately, it wasn't necessary—he'd accomplished his objective. Though unseasonably heavy rains dampened the forests enough to prevent Fujita's fires from spreading, fear was rampant on America's west coast. If this was the kind of reaction a few bombs could provoke, imagine what would happen when the *I-400*s launched their attack on New York and Washington. That had been Yamamoto's plan all along. They just needed time to execute it.

CHAPTER 7

CHALLENGES

CONSTRUCTION ON THE FIRST THREE *SEN-TOKU* SUBS BEGAN IN early 1943. The *I-400*'s keel was laid first on January 18 at the Kure naval arsenal, the *I-13* followed less than a month later in Kobe, and construction was set for April on the *I-401* at Sasebo.[1]

The *I-13* was the second-largest sub built by the Japanese Navy. Based on a modified version of the *I-9* sub, the *I-13* AM (for Type A Modified) was only 28 feet shorter than the *I-400* class.[2] Originally planned to carry only one aircraft in comparison with her larger sister, which carried two, the AM subs were hindered by a limited cruising range. Since the route from Japan to New York would pass either Africa's Cape of Good Hope or South America's Cape Horn, the *I-13* would have to be refueled by one of the *I-400*s during her return trip.[3] Seven AM Type subs were planned (*I-1*, *I-13* through *I-15*,[4] and 5094 through 5096[5]), along with 18 of the *I-400* class. Once their special attack bombers were included, the *Sen-toku* squad promised to cause significantly more damage than Fujita's lone plane over Oregon.

While sub construction was under way, Aichi made progress on the special attack plane. Nineteen forty-two was devoted to basic research,[6] with attention paid to wings and tail assembly. By January 1943 Aichi was ready to demonstrate the complex task of folding the plane's wings.

Aichi's skunkworks were located in a cold, cavernous hangar at its manufacturing plant in Nagoya. A select gathering of Naval General Staff officers were invited to tour a wooden mockup.[7] As the NGS officers gathered around the full-size model, they marveled at Aichi's engineering solution.

The 17-*shi* wasn't the first plane to have folding wings. That honor went to a British aircraft manufacturer in 1913. It wasn't until World War II that limited space aboard aircraft carriers significantly spurred the development of naval aircraft whose wings folded. It was no easy task, given the complexity of routing multiple fuel, hydraulic, and electric lines through a normally static wing structure, which is why neither the United States nor Japan had folding-wing aircraft at the beginning of the war. Perhaps the closest anyone came to matching Aichi's wing design was the Grumman F6F Hellcat, and even then there were significant differences.

As NGS officers watched, Aichi's staff carefully grasped the special attack bomber's wing and rotated it 90 degrees on its main spar, until the leading edge pointed downward. Then they walked the wing back until it lay flat against the plane's fuselage. The solution looked simple but was far from it. Aichi had thought of everything, including covering the folding parts of the wing assembly in luminous paint so they could be seen at night when prepping the plane.[8]

As for the tail assembly, it was decided that both the left and right horizontal stabilizers would fold down at their tip to avoid hitting the sides of the hangar. And since Aichi had selected a propeller 126 inches long,[9] there were still six inches of clearance between the prop tip and the hangar bulkhead.

Aichi's folding method worked so well, it was easy to see how the aircraft would fit within the narrow confines of a sub.[10] But the NGS had made an important change since the planning stages. The special attack bomber, originally designed for a one-way mission, was now to be reusable.[11] The change made sense. If the bombers could be concentrated against a target, then retrieved and redeployed against other targets, it would greatly increase their destructive capability. There was no point in losing all of them their first time out.

According to various reports, the design spec called for the floats to be jettisonable in midair.* This would increase the plane's speed and range in case of enemy attack.[12] If this feature existed,

---

* Though sources agree that *Seiran* floats could not be jettisoned, there appears to have been a discussion during the design stage about adding this feature.

it was only at the planning stage though. It was never incorporated into the final design.[13]

It was clear from the wooden mockup that the special attack bomber was handsome. She was well proportioned, with an attractive shape that looked streamlined. Later, when her air intake was added, she appeared to be grinning.

As Aichi's prototype made progress, the *I-400* construction program came under attack. A faction inside the Naval General Staff believed the subs were impractical and had become increasingly vocal about it. They argued that the *I-400* subs drew scarce resources from more important shipbuilding programs,[14] while also claiming the sub's size made her vulnerable to radar.

Every bureaucracy has its infighters. The chief opponent in this case was the NGS staff officer Cdr. Shojiro Iura. The man who'd briefed Fujita on burning Oregon forests wanted the *I-400* program reduced to two subs that targeted commercial shipping. "It would be different if they could have been finished right after the war started," Iura argued, "but the plans have only just been completed. It will take at least two years to build the subs. Even their planes have just begun testing. . . . They cannot be relied upon to have a substantial impact."[15]

It was a radical departure from Yamamoto's vision, and Iura was not alone. Several sub captains were also against the *I-400*s. They believed launching and retrieving sub-based aircraft in a combat zone was tantamount to "suicide."[16] Calls to scale back or cancel the program only increased.

Perhaps the most compelling argument for killing the program was the Battle of Midway. After Midway Japan increasingly fought a defensive war, and as the Japanese Empire focused on protecting its perimeter, there was less need for large-scale submarines to attack the U.S. mainland. Had the subs been completed shortly after Pearl Harbor, everything might have been all right. But the subs were at least a year from being finished. Time was running out.

Iura represented a formidable rear guard. But sometimes it's more dangerous to kill a project than to leave it alone. When it was suggested to Ariki Katayama that they stop production, the man responsible for building I-boats cunningly replied: "It may not be possible. . . . Material for four *I-400* subs has already been ordered and preparations are under way."[17]

It was a classically Japanese way of skirting the issue, no less effective for being indirect. After all, the *I-400* squadron was Yamamoto's idea, and though his recent spate of losses had humbled him, he was still commander in chief of the Combined Fleet. That is, until the United States miliary decided to kill him.

Yamamoto was on the island of New Britain preparing to fly from Rabaul to Bougainville when the United States made its move. It was a few minutes before six A.M., April 18, 1943, just two weeks after Yamamoto's fifty-ninth birthday. The morning was sunny and hot as his Mitsubishi twin-engine bomber lifted off the runway into the clear blue sky. Bougainville was only an hour and a half from Rabaul, yet Yamamoto's plane and an accompanying "Betty" bomber were escorted by six Zero fighters in case of enemy attack.

What Yamamoto didn't know was that U.S. cryptographers had broken the Japanese naval code and knew in advance exactly where he was going. Eager for revenge, 18 P-38s were sent to shoot down the architect of the Pearl Harbor attack. Yamamoto flew straight into an ambush.

The death of the Combined Fleet's commander in chief had devastating consequences. Talent was thin at the top of the Imperial Japanese Navy; replacing him would not be easy.[18] Importantly, everything Yamamoto had worked on was thrown into doubt, including the *I-400* program. It wasn't long before reactionary forces had their knives out. Now that Yamamoto was dead, they would have their day in the sun.

PART III

COMPLICATIONS

CHAPTER 8

REDUCTION AND REVIVAL

THE COMBINED FLEET WAS SEVERELY SHAKEN BY THE DEATH OF its commander in chief. Yamamoto may have had mixed success, but nobody expected him to be carried off the battlefield. The Japanese public wasn't informed of his death until more than a month after it happened. When it finally was announced, Yamamoto was awarded the Order of the Chrysanthemum First Class and posthumously promoted to fleet admiral. Still, it was just papering over the loss.

Rear Admiral Yamaguchi was supposed to succeed Yamamoto. But when he lashed himself to his sinking carrier at Midway, the IJN lost a competent replacement.[1] Adm. Mineichi Koga, Yamamoto's actual successor, was capable of bold thinking, but switching quarterbacks in midgame is tricky, especially when supporting players have trouble handling change.

Interestingly, the IJN didn't make a connection between Yamamoto's plane being shot down and the U.S. ability to read their naval codes. In fact, the Naval High Command believed it was impossible. Their stubborn refusal to believe that their codes had been compromised blinded them to what many sub captains already suspected. It would prove a crucial error.

Yamamoto had been dead less than a month when the jackals inside the NGS made their move. One of the *I-400*'s most powerful opponents was Shigeyoshi Miwa, chief of the Seventh Division, which had recently been created to oversee all aspects of IJN submarines.[2] Miwa had never liked the *I-400*s and was well positioned to kill the program.[3] There were other factors working against the *I-400*s as well. The Allied advance had so tightened the noose that by mid-1943 steel shipments were in sharp decline. It was senior NGS naysayers who most hurt the program though. They were against the underwater aircraft carriers on principle, and with Yamamoto gone, they cut back the number of subs from 18 to 10.[4]

Kurojima, Yamamoto's confidant, was determined not to give up the fight. After the death of his mentor, he had been moved to the NGS as Second Division chief. This meant the "weirdo officer" was ideally placed to defend Yamamoto's wishes. Like any good bureaucrat, Kurojima wanted to test the waters before deciding what to do, so he sent his staff officer, Lt. Cdr. Yasuo Fujimori, to investigate.

Fujimori was a good choice to gather intelligence since his job allowed him to move freely among the various NGS factions. Taking his role to heart, Fujimori set about convincing Miwa to support the program. But Fujimori faced an uphill battle. Twice he tried persuading Miwa, and both times he failed to change the stubborn officer's mind. The second time Miwa got so angry, he told Fujimori never to bring the subject up again.[5]

It's unlikely that Kurojima was surprised by Fujimori's failure. Miwa had never kept his feelings secret, and besides, Kurojima was only feeling him out before confronting the man himself. Fortunately, Kurojima had another card up his sleeve. When Fujimori reported his failure, Kurojima played his hand.

"Immediately following the start of war, Yamamoto told us we must reach the U.S. mainland," Kurojima explained. "This is why he ordered large-scale submarines that carry attack planes. [Given the war has changed,] we should now investigate how these can best be used to immediately revive their construction."[6]

Kurojima directed Fujimori to prepare a report on the number and types of submarines in the Sixth Fleet stable. This was a sound approach, given that most NGS officers agreed that too many different subs were being built. As one IJN officer observed, a Sixth Fleet shipyard was "like an exhibit at a submarine trade fair."[7] But knowing what to do and persuading a bureaucracy to do it are two different things.

It didn't take Fujimori long to demonstrate that the wide variety of Sixth Fleet subs hindered production efficiencies. The U.S. Navy had already consolidated sub design to realize the benefits of high-volume sub production. As a result, it was turning out high-quality, state-of-the-art subs before the war had even begun. But there were so many variations on Japan's *Kirai-, Kaidai-,* and *Junsen*-class subs, it was almost impossible to keep track.

Fujimori's analysis also revealed several important findings. First, enemy radar was responsible for the loss of many Sixth Fleet subs. Since Japan lagged in radar development, the imbalance wouldn't be corrected soon. This meant the Sixth Fleet needed to rethink how it used submarines, since its current strategy would only result in further casualties.

The Allied advance also necessitated a strategic rethink. Sixth Fleet sub requirements had changed since Pearl Harbor. They were no longer conducting war patrols off the American coast. In fact, they'd pulled so far back, they were at risk of losing control of the South Pacific. As the United States captured more territory, Japan was also having trouble resupplying army garrisons stranded on remote island outposts. Cargo subs were needed so that those currently engaged in underwater transport could be redeployed to fight the enemy.

Fujimori also acknowledged that the war in Europe had turned against the Axis. If Germany eventually lost, the Allies would redeploy their resources against Japan. It was a discomfiting thought. The U.S. Pacific Fleet was easily replenished, given America's production capacity. In comparison, Japan could ill afford to waste her limited resources. The Sixth Fleet had to fight smarter if it was going to survive.

Fujimori's analysis was as prescient as it was reality-based. Sixth Fleet sub production clearly needed to be consolidated, and it's to Fujimori's credit that he was so honest in the face of a bureaucracy not used to hearing the truth.

Fujimori's first recommendation was to focus production on three new types of subs. The first would be a state-of-the-art boat capable of achieving underwater speeds of 18 to 20 knots. These speeds were so fast, they were usually associated with surface travel, yet Fujimori had investigated the matter and believed a technical solution was possible.

He also called for the construction of dedicated cargo subs that could be used to transport supplies to areas where the surface fleet couldn't go. The number of combat subs currently being used in resupply operations was not only a poor use of their capability; it drove a high attrition rate. In other words, captaining a cargo sub was rapidly becoming a suicide mission.

Finally, Fujimori recommended that all 18 of the underwater aircraft carriers be built and that their construction be given the highest priority. "When striking a blow against a colossus like America, surprise attacks at vital locations are most effective," he wrote. "The *I-400* is the best [weapon] in the present arsenal for doing this."[8]

But Fujimori didn't stop there. He went on to argue for an increase in the *I-400*'s striking power to get America's attention. Specifically, he recommended enlarging the *I-400*'s deck hangar to house not just two but three special attack bombers. He also requested that the *I-13* and *I-14* hangar space be increased to include a second plane.*

Fujimori persuaded Ariki Katayama to finish the first two *I-400* subs plus the *I-13* and *I-14* within ten months,[9] less than half the time normally required to build a new submarine. Katayama felt it was possible if the project was made a top priority. Cancellation of the three remaining AM type subs originally planned (5094 to 5096) may have helped, but construction of the *I-1* and *I-15* would take longer.

Speeding up sub delivery certainly addressed one major concern: how soon the *I-400*s could be ready to attack. Any sweeping policy review is bound to step on toes though. Kurojima's persuasive powers may have been strong, but he didn't have Yamamoto

---

* According to Shizuo Fukui, the *I-13* and *I-14* had their aircraft-carrying capacity increased from one to two planes because of the reduction in *I-400* subs. Fukui, *Japanese Naval Vessels at the End of the War*, p. 36.

to back him up. This meant he couldn't throw Fujimori's proposal into the lion's den without socializing it first.

Kurojima worked hard to build consensus behind Fujimori's findings. Lobbying NGS decision makers before any official discussion occurred, he slowly made progress. By the time he met with Miwa, his fiercest opponent, it took only 30 minutes to convince him to support the program.[10]

A commonsense recommendation tied to a thorough assessment probably did as much to get the *I-400* program back on track as anything Kurojima said. Perhaps the smartest thing Kurojima did was to circulate the proposal for comment before bringing it up for official review. By the time he made his recommendation in August 1943, there were no serious objections.[11]

It was agreed that the *I-400* was to be finished before the end of 1943, followed by four subs in 1944, six subs in 1945, and seven subs in 1946.[12] Additionally, Aichi was urged to accelerate production of the special attack bomber to meet the new schedule.

Staggering production rather than finishing all 18 subs at once might have been a compromise, but it was necessary, given the need to redesign the expanded sub hangars and the increasing shortage of materials. Importantly, it showed that the program's opponents would compromise if its proponents were willing to get practical. Everything was smooth sailing—save for one important change.

New York City and Washington were no longer the targets.

WHEN JAPAN LOST Guadalcanal, she was gradually forced to withdraw from the Solomon Islands. Fujimori had witnessed the reality firsthand when he journeyed to Rabaul in August 1943.[13] From what he could see, the war situation was not encouraging.

Rabaul was one of the South Pacific's most important naval bases. However, now that Japan's defense perimeter was imploding, Fujimori could see it was just a matter of time until their southern defense collapsed altogether. But what if Allied supply lines could be cut? What if Allied resources could be squeezed the same way U.S. subs were squeezing Japan?

Fujimori first conceived of using the *I-400* subs to attack the Panama Canal while visiting Rabaul. Not only would such an attack starve the enemy's Pacific war machine, it would buy Japan much-needed time to regroup, resupply, and strengthen her perimeter. It was the same kind of bold, decisive thinking that Yamamoto had demonstrated when he decided to attack Pearl Harbor. Therefore, when Fujimori returned to Tokyo, he argued against attacking the U.S. mainland, recommending instead that the *Sen-toku* squadron be directed against the Panama Canal.

"The most effective way to cut U.S. supply lines is to attack the canal," he explained. "The underwater aircraft carriers are the most suitable weapon for the job."[14]

It's reasonable to ask why the Japanese hadn't already attacked the canal. The idea had been kicking around at least since the beginning of the war.[15] Nobuo Fujita had considered using a sub-borne floatplane to bomb the canal as early as January 1942. A flying boat had also been considered. When the Naval General Staff proposed attacking the canal, the Navy Ministry considered it a "novel idea" but rejected it as too difficult to execute.[16] Given the serious beating Japan was taking, the Panama Canal now seemed a logical target.

Not surprisingly, the NGS staff agreed.

CHAPTER 9

NAMBU UNDER FIRE

NAMBU COULDN'T BELIEVE HIS LUCK. THERE IN THE MIDDLE OF his periscope was every submariner's dream: ten Allied freighters intent on crossing his path. True, four Royal Australian Navy corvettes accompanied them, but from what he could tell, he hadn't been spotted.

It was late afternoon on June 16, 1943, and Nambu, now captain of the *I-174*, was on patrol between Sydney and Brisbane. Visibility was good, and the convoy was still 10,000 yards away, when he noticed that one of the ships was having trouble keeping up. Like a weak animal struggling to stay with the herd, it begged to be culled. Nambu ordered "down periscope" and began his attack approach.

Once he'd finished command school, Nambu was put in charge of a training boat. Teaching the next generation of submariners was important. Still, he was itching to get back to war.[1] He finally got his wish five months later, when he was named commanding officer of the *I-174*, a frontline fleet boat. Built in Sasebo and commissioned in 1938, the *I-174* was an excellent boat for the future captain of the *I-401* to learn his trade. A *Kaidai*-class submarine with four torpedo tubes in the bow and two in the stern, she was 345 feet long and carried 70 officers and crew. Her previous CO, Lt. Cdr. Toshio Kusaka, was one of the premier sub captains in the Sixth Fleet. Nambu would cross paths with him again when Kusaka was appointed commanding officer of the *I-400*. Until then, it was natural that he should follow in Kusaka's footsteps.

The *I-174* had departed Kure on May 5 after two months of training. Nambu flew a large paper carp from the sub's periscope in honor of Boys Day.[2] It was his first war patrol as CO, and Nambu wanted to inspire his crew. It was an appropriate symbol since the Japanese believed carp were strong enough to overcome any obstacle. He also hoped it would distract them from the nerve-wracking business of departure.[3]

Though he loved his role as commanding officer, Nambu found leavings difficult. His mind inevitably turned toward his family, whom he often talked about to his crew.[4] He never forgot the time his wife, Yukiko, had come to see him before the attack on Pearl Harbor. She had come to Kure with their one-year-old son, Masamichi. They'd stayed together at a *ryokan* near the Yokosuka naval base,[5] and though he'd been happy to see her, it was difficult as well.

Yukiko was expecting their second child at the time. Unfortunately, Nambu could tell her nothing about how long he'd be gone, or when he'd return. After three years of marriage, Yukiko was stoic; like many officers' wives, she didn't reveal her feelings. Nevertheless, the visit had been fraught with an undercurrent of emotion since their second child would be born while Nambu was at sea.

Few words needed to be spoken, since Japanese culture had taught husband and wife how to read between the lines. Yukiko wanted to be strong for her husband. This meant not burdening him with tears or the many worries she must have had. Nambu understood all this, but the visit wasn't easy.

When Nambu bade his pregnant wife farewell, she was framed in a doorway, their infant son cradled in her arms. He knew this might be the last time he saw his family, but it was his duty to fight for the emperor. As he walked away, it was difficult not to look back. Still, what would be gained by lingering?[6] It would only make things harder. Once he stepped outside the door, he resolved that only the mission would occupy his mind. This kind of leavetaking was not so much a hardening of heart as a focusing of purpose, and Nambu made a habit of it as the war dragged on. So much depended on how he performed that nothing could deter him. He had a job to do, and he'd trained long and hard to do it. There was no turning back.

Nambu's latest orders were to disrupt supply lines between the United States, Australia, and New Guinea. If he succeeded, the United States would have difficulty maintaining her perch in the South Pacific. For the past five months, Sixth Fleet subs had wreaked havoc off the Australian coast. Results were so encouraging that the *I-174* had been ordered to join the fight.[7] Nambu wasn't just on a hunting expedition—he'd been given a mission of strategic importance.

Nambu relayed the convoy's range, speed, and bearing to his executive officer, who began to plot a firing solution. The convoy was too far away to do anything, but at least they had time to set up. Of course, Nambu had every intention of eluding the corvette screen. Meanwhile, the sub's forward torpedo room prepared a reception.

When Nambu took his next sighting, he could see that in addition to the ten freighters, there were three American LSTs, or Tank Landing Ships. He kept the excitement from his voice as he informed his officers of this development. LSTs were the backbone of the Allied Pacific war effort because they delivered huge amounts of troops, cargo, and vehicles directly onto a beach. He couldn't have asked for a better target.

When Nambu had first arrived off the Australian coast, he'd been frustrated by a shortage of targets.[8] This probably had something to do with the successful number of sub attacks preceding his arrival. A crew's morale depends on their captain's ability to sink ships, though, and this made Nambu worry.

Just when he couldn't take it any longer, they encountered the *Edward Chambers*, a U.S. Army transport.* In his eagerness to score a kill, Nambu mistook the ship for a freighter and pursued it aggressively. Even though he couldn't get closer than 20,000 feet, he refused to let the opportunity slip by. Finally, when he'd run out of

---

* Nambu remembers it as a large, armed commercial vessel rather than a U.S. Army transport, but Allied records are more accurate in this instance; the *I-174* was probably too far away to accurately identify the type of ship.

patience, he ordered the *I-174* to "battle surface." Moments later the sub's gun crew began lobbing shells toward the army transport.*[9]

Nambu was certain at least one shell had struck the vessel. What he didn't count on though was a "freighter" firing back. Twelve rounds from the *Edward Chambers*'s three-inch gun forced the *I-174* to submerge.[10] It had been foolish to make a surface attack in broad daylight.[11] One well-placed shot into the sail, and the thin-skinned sub would have sunk. Nambu learned something important that day. He might have raised crew morale, but unless he set impatience aside, he wasn't going to last long enough to sink many ships.

Things went better after that. Nambu fired four torpedoes at a commercial vessel off Sydney, two of which he believed struck home.†[12] Now they were facing their largest convoy yet, GP 55 out of Sydney. Composed of 13 ships and five Australian corvettes,[13] the convoy was due in Brisbane on June 15.[14] It was Nambu's job to make sure it didn't arrive.

Two of the corvettes, the *Kalgoorlie* and the *Warrnambook,* patrolled the same side of the convoy as the *I-174*. The *Bundaberg* and *Cootamundra* patrolled the port side, while the *Deloraine* protected the straggler. Originally built as minesweepers, the Bathurst-class corvettes were too slow for convoy duty. Given the pressure that Sixth Fleet subs were exerting on supply lines, every available warship had been pressed into service.

As the setting sun outlined the convoy's silhouette, the *I-174* easily slipped inside the corvette screen. The convoy's weak link was the *Portmar,* a U.S. Army transport struggling to catch up. Nambu patiently waited for the transport to close the distance with another LST. When the two ships overlapped, he fired his first torpedo.

Two minutes later the stern of LST- 469 erupted in an explosion, killing 26 men and destroying her steering gear.[15] Nambu thought

---

* Though Nambu believed he'd hit the ship, there is no Allied record confirming a ship was attacked on this date at this location.

† Allied naval records show that Nambu fired upon the American Liberty ship SS *John Bartram*. All four torpedoes missed.

it a fatal blow* and turned toward the *Portmar* with a second salvo.[16] The ship's lookouts spotted his torpedoes and called for evasive action, but it was too late. A torpedo slammed into her number-one hold, igniting the ship's volatile cargo of gasoline and ammunition. Moments after the torpedo detonated, the *Portmar* was engulfed by explosions. Seven minutes later, the transport was gone.[17]

Cries of joy reverberated throughout the *I-174*.[18] Nambu had shown daring in sinking two ships. Unfortunately, the euphoria didn't last. The *Warrnambook* and *Kalgoorlie* immediately began searching for the sub as the *Deloraine* stayed behind to pick up survivors.

Nambu dove to 250 feet, the sub's safety limit, and was creeping out of the area when his sound operator reported approaching screws. Though the *I-174*'s crew did their best to remain silent, the *Warrnambook* found them anyway.

A depth-charge attack is terrifying for anyone who's experienced it. When a depth charge detonates close to a sub, the concussion rocks the boat like a hobby horse. Gear and food stores rocket every which way, and it's not unusual for paint chips to peel from the inside of a hull. Sometimes water or hydraulic lines burst, sending high-pressure jets spewing everywhere, and if they weren't sealed quickly enough, electrical equipment shorted out and caught fire. It was especially dangerous when a sub's cooling system was ruptured. Freon gas filled the interior, which could be fatal, and because Japanese hulls weren't welded, sea pressure popped rivets like rifle shots. Woe unto the crewman who stood in one's way.

The *Warrnambook* laid a pattern of depth charges perfectly mirroring the *I-174*'s escape route. Within moments they exploded with

---

* The LST-469, though damaged, remained afloat and was eventually towed back to Sydney. It belonged to MacArthur's newly formed Seventh Amphibious Force, which was short of ships. Loss of the vessel forced the last-minute elimination of troops and cargo from the assault convoy destined for MacArthur's first amphibious operation, the occupation of Kiriwina and Woodlark islands. See David Stevens, "The Naval Campaigns for New Guinea," Journal of the Australian War Memorial, n.d., http://www.awm.gov.au/journal/j34/stevens.asp.

all the fury of hell. Nambu's crew could do little except watch their gauges dance. Many removed their sandals or took to their bunks to avoid making noise while imagining the next explosion a direct hit. As the sub's interior temperature soared past 100 degrees, it became difficult to breathe, and the crew sweated profusely.

Water greatly amplifies sound, which means a depth charge explosion can deafen a crew if it is close enough. And nothing is more sickening than watching the hull flex inward every time a depth charge detonates. Many submariners swore that a detonation could convulse the hull as much as six inches. It wasn't the kind of story you wanted to personally verify.

Though Hollywood loves depicting a sub being sunk by a single, well-placed depth charge, the truth was most subs were sunk by cumulative damage sustained over a prolonged attack. Another Hollywood fallacy shows a depth charge sending huge geysers of seawater cascading into the sky. Unless a sub was near the surface, this was the least effective means of attack because it meant the depth charge's concussive pressure was vented into the air rather than against the sub's hull. Nevertheless, depth-charge explosions were a nerve-wracking experience and submariners dreaded them.

The *Warrnambool* and *Kalgoorlie* tracked the *I-174* for two hours, dropping 36 depth charges in four separate patterns. Finally, when they lost contact and saw oil on the surface, they concluded the sub had been sunk.[19] The Royal Australian Navy was wrong, however. The *I-174* had sustained damage, but Nambu had escaped and soon resumed combat operations.[20]

Nambu's success made him a hero to his crew. He'd attacked an escorted enemy convoy in broad daylight[21] and gotten significant results. In fact, Nambu's attack proved to be the most successful by a single Japanese submarine off Australia's east coast.[22] It also turned out to be the last two ships sunk in the region by a Japanese sub.[23]

As Japan's defense perimeter continued to weaken, I-boats were recalled to defend the South Pacific. This meant fewer combat subs were available to sink merchant ships off Australia. The *I-174*'s run was cut short for this reason. But Nambu wasn't just being recalled to defend the empire—he was being given the most despised assignment in the Sixth Fleet sub force.

Nambu was becoming a mole.

CHAPTER 10

NAMBU BECOMES A MOLE

THE HISTORY OF JAPANESE "MOLE" OPERATIONS BEGAN IN August 1942, when Admiral Yamamoto first ordered high-speed destroyers to ferry supplies to Japanese troops on Guadalcanal. Americans nicknamed the supply runs "The Tokyo Express" due to their speed and punctuality. Japanese destroyer captains had a different name for them. They called them the "Mouse System" because the enemy were like cats always waiting to pounce.[1] Eventually, the Allies so dominated the South Pacific that the Imperial Japanese Navy could no longer get supplies through via destroyers. That's when Yamamoto turned to Sixth Fleet submarines to take up the slack.

Underwater cargo duty was the most despised assignment in the Sixth Fleet, and Nambu hated it.

"Subs were meant to attack," he protested, "not to be deployed as cargo carriers."[2]

Disparagingly referred to as *moruga*, or "mole" ops,[3] it wasn't the kind of duty a combat sub captain took pleasure in performing. Though most submariners appreciated that they were on a humanitarian mission, turning combat subs into cargo ships—a purpose for which they were never intended nor especially well suited—created complications. One reason Nambu hated it so much was that transporting cargo was just as dangerous as combat ops without the satisfaction of attacking the enemy. The goal was to deliver supplies, which meant they had to remain hidden to successfully complete their task. Since a sub's crew is motivated by sinking ships, not ducking them, Nambu felt *moruga* ops hurt morale.[4] Of course, he did his best to maintain his crews' spirits, but the very nature of supply missions undermined his efforts.

U.S. Navy cryptographers presented another danger. Sixth Fleet radio traffic was being read by the Allies on a regular basis.[5] Consequently, U.S. naval forces knew a Japanese sub's destination as well as its arrival date and time. This significantly improved Allied antisub efforts, and Sixth Fleet losses increased commensurately. Just as bomber crews in England didn't expect to survive a set number of missions, Sixth Fleet submariners felt each *moruga* deployment would be their last. Even the soundest of men could crack under the pressure.

Worst of all, since every bit of space was needed for supplies,[6] combat subs had their torpedoes removed and their tubes used for storage.[7] Even a sub's deck guns were stripped to help offset the increase in cargo weight. This eliminated a sub's offensive capability, further depressing her crew.[8]

Despite the drawbacks, *moruga* ops would benefit the future captain of the *I-401* in ways he couldn't foresee. Stealthily transporting high-value cargo to a well-defended location was ideal training. Instead of carrying food and medicine, he'd be transporting three special attack planes to launch against the Panama Canal, but the skill set was the same. And though Nambu would continue yearning to attack the enemy at every opportunity, he would also learn the discipline necessary to carry out his mission.

By January 1943, as many as 20 subs were reassigned from combat to supply operations.[9] Typically, a sub would surface on a moonless night[10] and pass her cargo by hand to a waiting motorboat.[11] Allied naval dominance soon made it too dangerous though for subs to surface, and new methods had to be employed. First they tried ejecting supplies through the torpedo tubes, but cargo was damaged.[12] Next, supplies were secured to a sub's deck in rubber bags with just enough air sealed inside to allow them to float.[13] When the sub reached its destination, the bags were released and sprung to the surface, where marooned troops retrieved them.[14] Unfortunately, bags were occasionally contaminated by seawater or burst before reaching the surface. From January 1943 on, steel drums were used,[15] but problems remained. Storage drums were subject to tremendous variations in sea pressure. More than one supply mission arrived at its destination only to find its cargo had been lost along the way. Given the risks involved, it was a dispiriting lesson.

Rice and wheat were the chief supplies, though canned biscuits, salt, soy sauce, bean paste, plums, and dried bonito fish were also carried. Mail from home was especially appreciated, as were clothes, mosquito nets, medicine, small arms, and ammunition.[16]

One sub carried enough supplies to support 30,000 men for two days,[17] which sounds like a lot. It wasn't though, given how difficult it was for *moruga* subs to complete their mission. Despite the mole operations, Japanese troops were continually at risk of starvation. The use of combat subs to resupply them only shows how desperate the war had become.

NAMBU'S FIRST MISSION was transporting supplies from Rabaul on one side of New Guinea, to Lae on the other.[18] On August 17, 1943, he loaded food, ammunition, and fresh troops into his sub before departing. The troops at Lae were so hungry, they were eating grass. Nevertheless, every time an enemy ship passed overhead Nambu resented not being able to attack.[19] Sixth Fleet's commander in chief had made it clear that supply operations were to succeed no matter what,[20] which meant Nambu couldn't sink the enemy. No wonder he hated the job.

Three days later Nambu's crew offloaded supplies, replacing them with wounded soldiers for the return trip. The submarine was already so cramped that adding 40 casualties among a tightly packed crew made life miserable for everyone.[21] The moans of dying men frayed the crew's nerves and the smell was terrible. Somehow they returned to Rabaul without incident.

There were two more runs like this, the third being the worst. A B-24 dropped four bombs near them followed by an enemy sub sneaking up and firing three torpedoes. If Nambu hadn't reacted quickly, it would have spelled disaster. As it was, they barely escaped.

Nambu returned to Rabaul without completing the mission. He informed his command that it was impossible to deliver supplies when surrounded by the enemy. It wasn't that Nambu feared dying—he protested because he hated the thought of losing his crew in such a wasteful effort. The response was predictable. He was told to "force it."[22]

Nambu and his crew never got enough rest, partly because so many subs had been lost. Usually, they had only a few days in port before they were sent back out again. The loss of subs also meant a reduction in crew replacements. It was only a matter of time before an overextended crewman made a fatal mistake.

Nambu's fourth supply mission fared no better. Four times they were spotted by enemy planes, and four times they were forced under. They eventually made it to Lae, but on the return trip they faced a four-hour depth-charge attack, during which one of the soldiers they'd evacuated died of heatstroke. This left Nambu frustrated and depressed.

"I rely too much on my Japanese spirit," he wrote in his diary. "It is not enough. The enemy goes about freely . . . while we don't have a single torpedo . . . Do our countrymen know about our toils? We cannot win."[23]

Though a realistic assessment, it was uncharacteristically downbeat for Nambu. But the *I-174*'s captain had good reason to be depressed. He was notified in October that his sister, the only surviving member of his family, had died[24] (most likely of tuberculosis, which was rampant). Then Lae fell, despite his efforts to keep it resupplied. Finally, on November 20, 1943, Nambu received word that Masamichi, his firstborn son, had drowned. He must have felt his world was collapsing.

NAMBU KNEW LITTLE about his son's death, but what he did learn was crushing. His wife, Yukiko, had been invited on an outing to pick *mikan*, a type of orange, on the island of Kamakari. Fruit was a particular treat given wartime shortages, and Yukiko spent a pleasant afternoon wandering the orchard with her two sons Masamichi, now three years old, and infant Nobutaka. The navy wives gossiped while their children played among the orange trees. When it came time to return, two boats waited to take the families across the bay. The father of another family offered to take Masamichi, Nambu's oldest son, in a separate boat so Yukiko could focus her attention on the newborn. Yukiko resisted though. Her mother's instinct was to keep both children with her. When the man insisted, she gave in.

As she handed over her oldest boy to the helpful gentleman, she implored, "Please take care of my son."

"Don't worry. I will," he replied.

The boat carrying Yukiko and her baby arrived at the Kure beach first. But as the second boat approached, it overturned, casting Masamichi into the water. Nambu's wife immediately rushed to rescue him, but just as she reached for his tiny hand, a large wave swept him from her grasp.

It was a devastating blow. Nambu loved his family, but a sub captain can't show grief in front of his crew. As a result, he did his best to suppress his feelings. It was only through sheer will that he managed to function.

Finally, after completing seven supply missions, Nambu was promoted. He'd successfully delivered a total of 310 tons of matériel to the battlefield. Despite seven missions though, the *I-174* supplied no more cargo than one merchant ship could carry in a single voyage.[25] This problem would be partially addressed when the Sixth Fleet launched a new class of cargo subs later in the year. In the meantime, combat subs continued filling the gap.

CHAPTER 11

SEIRAN TAKES FLIGHT

WHILE THE SIXTH FLEET STRUGGLED WITH STRATEGIC ISSUES, the *I-400* construction program forged ahead. Production of the *I-403* began at Kawasaki Heavy Industries in Kobe on September 29, 1943;[1] keel laying for the *I-402* followed in Sasebo a few days later;[2] and construction on the fifth sub, the *I-404*, was set for February 1944.[3] This means at least five *I-400* subs and possibly six[4] were in varying stages of production by the end of 1943. When the *I-13* and *I-14* were included, a third of the squadron was under construction.

Meanwhile, the first test flight of Aichi's special attack plane was held on November 8 that same year.[5] Lt. Cdr. Tadashi Funada was her chief test pilot. A highly respected member of the Flight Technology Test Group at Yokosuka, Funada was probably the foremost seaplane pilot in the Imperial Japanese Navy. And because of his extensive experience, he was as much involved in the plane's design as in her flight testing.

Aichi's special attack plane must have created quite a stir when she first rolled out of her top secret assembly building.[6] For one thing, experimental aircraft were painted bright orange,[7] and the plane was so big, her cockpit stood more than 15 feet off the ground. She was the largest aircraft ever carried by a submarine.

Aichi's M6A1 was designed to do two mutually exclusive things: dive steeply to drop a bomb or come in low to launch a torpedo.[8] The first type of attack required "dive brakes," which slowed a plane enough that it didn't tear apart while diving. A torpedo attack, however, required a plane to fly low, straight, and fast. Each attack required different wing flap configurations and plenty of practice to master. In other words, Aichi's special attack plane was not for beginners. Then again, Funada was hardly a beginner.

It was a cold, gray day when Funada climbed into the cockpit. As he taxied down the nearby river, he looked forward to how the prototype would handle. But when he began climbing over Ise Bay,[9] he quickly realized something was wrong. The elevator controls on the plane's horizontal tail stabilizer, which controlled the plane's angle of climb or descent, weren't working.[10] A plane losing elevator responsiveness is akin to a car losing its steering. That's why Funada knew he had to make an emergency landing, and in a hurry.

The only way Funada could get the plane to descend was to throttle back her engine. As the plane's speed decreased, she began dropping through the snow-laden clouds. Careful not to stall, Funada became conscious of another problem as he made his approach. Floatplanes are notoriously difficult to land. They tend to be nose heavy, and if pilots aren't careful, they can easily flip over. Fortunately, Aichi had designed the aircraft to be less nose heavy than other seaplanes. As Funada eased back on the throttle, he felt the plane make contact with the waves. He had barely made it back alive.[11]

It might have been a successful landing, but it wasn't a successful test flight. The ailerons had to be redesigned,[12] one of several aerodynamic problems that plagued the prototype.*[13] Another of the plane's "x factors" was its floats. They were so large, the design team worried they'd create too much drag. The plane's wing area was increased to provide more lift,[14] but there were also problems with the plane's vertical stabilizer, which had to be lengthened to improve handling.[15] Unfortunately, the increased tail height meant the aircraft no longer fit inside the sub's low-ceilinged hangar. At first Toshio Ozaki, the plane's chief designer, considered making the tail assembly detachable.[16] But anything that had to be attached, like floats, required more time to assemble and launch the

---

* Funada recalls that it was the ailerons, or wing flaps, that were the issue. Other sources, however, suggest the problem derived from the length of the *Seiran*'s tail stabilizer, which led to overbalancing.

plane. Ozaki fixed the problem by hinging the vertical stabilizer's tip so it could be folded down, allowing the aircraft to fit inside the hangar. The plane's horizontal stabilizers were also hinged for similar reasons.[17] It was an ingenious if simple solution, leaving the floats the only detachable element.

One of the unusual characteristics of the attack plane was its water-cooled engine. Most Japanese seaplanes relied upon an air-cooled engine, but a water-cooled engine offered several benefits. First, it enabled the plane to warm up inside the sub. This not only reduced the plane's launch time—it minimized the time a sub had to be surfaced. Given that every minute increased the sub's risk of discovery, this was an important improvement. A water-cooled engine also lowered the aircraft's nose enough that it could fit inside the hangar. Additionally, it provided the necessary clearance between the propeller and the overly long torpedo the *Seiran* would have to carry, as well as better visibility from the cockpit,[18] an improvement *Sen-toku* pilots would come to appreciate.

The water-cooled engine was licensed from Germany's Daimler-Benz, further refined by Japanese designers, and named *Atsuta,* after a local Nagoya shrine. Based on Daimler's DB 601A engine, the *Atsuta* engine had 12 cylinders and delivered 1,400 horsepower at takeoff.[19] The *Atsuta* engine was not without problems, however. For one, lack of materials and poor metallurgy meant they required more maintenance than air-cooled engines. They also had a tendency to leak oil. As a result, it took a while before mechanics had the engine functioning properly, and even then it suffered from occasional problems. For now though, wing flaps, not the engine, were the main concern.

Aichi evaluated the special attack bomber against its own *Suisei,* since the plane was a naval dive-bomber too. Tests showed they had a similar rate of climb, but the combined weight and drag of the M6A1's floats reduced its cruising speed. Without floats, the plane was specced to achieve a maximum air speed of 345 mph, more than the comparable Curtiss SB2C Helldiver. With floats, however, the plane's performance was only 295 mph, comparable to the Helldiver's top speed but still a substantial decline. The attack bomber's range was almost a third less than the *Suisei*. Fortunately, since the plane would be launched from a submarine close to shore, range was less important.[20]

Despite problems with the maiden flight, the navy was satisfied enough to order 44 aircraft.[21] Given the importance of the mission, however, the plane needed a proper name. The Imperial Japanese Navy didn't always use utilitarian names when it came to its aircraft. Aichi's *Suisei* means "comet" in Japanese; *Saiun,* a reconnaissance aircraft, means "painted cloud." So, when Funada was asked by the Naval Air Command to come up with an appropriate moniker, he wanted something that did justice to the aircraft's special mission. He named it *Seiran*.

Composed of two kanji characters, *Seiran* can be translated as "storm from a clear sky." The name was inspired by an eighteenth-century woodblock print by Hiroshige.[22] Called *Seiran of Awazu,* the print shows the village of Awazu after a storm with mist rising from a nearby mountain. Funada hoped that the *Seiran* special attack planes would surprise the enemy by suddenly appearing "like a ninja out of the fog."[23] Therefore the name was not only inspiring because of its glamour, it accurately captured its purpose as well.

As far as Japan was concerned, the United States had turned a blind eye toward her aspirations for nearly 40 years. When America wasn't ignorning, belittling, or discriminating against Japan, she was seeking to hem her in. First the United States, Britain, Italy, and France had refused Japan a comparable-sized navy to limit her potential as a strategic rival; later the United States embargoed the precious oil that the IJN needed to function.

Nevertheless, the majority of Americans had been surprised by the attack on Pearl Harbor. Many of them had to look it up on a map to find out where it was. But if U.S. politicians had owned up to their machinations, they shouldn't have been surprised at all. America had consistently underestimated Japan—whether out of arrogance, ignorance, or ingenuousness, it was impossible to say. Now Japan would launch a surprise attack on the Panama Canal in the same spirit as the attack on Pearl Harbor. If everything went well, America would be caught off guard again, and the Imperial

Japanese Navy would strike just as Funada imagined it: like a storm from a clear sky. It wasn't just poetic, it was poetic justice.

The initial order for 44 aircraft included two trainers called *Nanzan*. Each *Nanzan* had hand-cranked landing gear rather than floats and dual controls for pilot training.[24] *Nanzan* were meant to replicate the *Seiran* flying experience, with several important differences. The *Nanzan*'s lack of floats meant the plane flew faster. Though the vertical tail stabilizer was shortened to compensate, it still handled differently.[25] *Nanzan* means "southern mountain," but one source claims the plane was jokingly referred to as *Serian-kai*, which translates as "difficult childbirth."[26] Whether this name referred to the training experience or the problem-plagued production process is unclear.

Despite troubles with his first test flight, Funada fell in love with the *Seiran*. In his postwar memoir, he wrote, "I piloted many kinds of aircraft . . . [but] the *Seiran*'s . . . responsiveness and controllability was unforgettable. To me, it was a masterpiece."[27]

This affirmation was to be echoed by many *Seiran* pilots, a testament to Aichi's design skills. Ozaki and his team had not only built the world's first sub-borne attack bomber, they'd built a plane that handled beautifully too.

CHAPTER 12

THE PANAMA CANAL

WHILE *SEIRAN* FLIGHT TESTS CONTINUED, FUJIMORI WAS BUSY at the Naval General Staff conducting research on the Panama Canal. Second only to Pearl Harbor, the canal was the most ambitious military installation the Japanese had ever targeted. But a lot of details were unknown, including the canal's design, construction, and defenses.

The first thing Fujimori did was to get his colleague, Technical Maj. Gen. Ariki Katayama, to assign him three of his most capable engineers. Their job was to analyze everything Fujimori could find about the canal. Information was understandably scarce; not only had the canal been built more than 25 years ago, it was on the other side of the world.

Fujimori's first bit of luck came when a Japanese engineer who'd worked on the canal provided him with a set of blueprints.[1] His next was when an NGS colleague told him about an American at the Ofuna prison camp who had guarded the canal. During questioning, the prisoner revealed that the canal had been heavily protected after the attack on Pearl Harbor, but once the war shifted in the Allies' favor defenses had been relaxed.[2]

Fujimori and his team worked in utmost secrecy as they gathered information and quickly had a stack of documents more than a yard high. Weekly meetings were held in the NGS strategy room to review the canal's topography and analyze its features.[3] One thing they learned was that the canal had been built to last. Hit by an earthquake only four days after it opened, the canal was undamaged, even though the quake was bigger than the one that had helped devastate San Francisco in 1906.[4]

It had taken 34 years and two nations to build the canal.* The largest engineering project ever undertaken at the time, the canal was considered a technological marvel along with the Pyramids and the Great Wall of China. It had two major lock systems: the Pedro Miguel locks on the Pacific side and the Gatun locks on the Atlantic.[†]

Fujimori realized that the locks were the most vulnerable part of the system and investigated attacking them from either the Pacific or the Atlantic side. A Pacific attack would offer an underwater strike force the best chance of concealment, since it was the most direct route from Japan. But Fujimori estimated it would take only a month to repair the locks on the Pacific side. However, if the Atlantic locks were destroyed, it could take up to six months to fix the damage.[5] Shipping would come to a standstill.

Destroying the Gatun locks wasn't going to be easy. They were as much fortress as transit system. The three chambers were each 1,000 feet long, with concrete walls 45 to 60 feet thick.[6] Also, the topmost lock was only 110 feet wide, less than three times a *Seiran*'s wingspan. Any plane coming in for attack would have a narrow margin for error.

But Fujimori wasn't as concerned about the locks, which appeared indestructible, as he was about their gates. It was their gates that had to be destroyed. Each lock contained double gates 65 feet wide, seven feet thick, and varying in height between 47 and 82 feet.[‡7] Built by a company specializing in steel bridge construction, the heaviest gate weighed 745 tons,[8] two to three times heavier than any lock gate ever built.[§] Load-bearing parts like hinges were cast from vanadium steel, a durable alloy used to make car engines.[9] It would take more than one bomb to destroy gates like this.

Additionally, each lock had not just one but two sets of gates—one

---

* The French began excavating the canal in 1880, the United States finished the construction, and the first ship navigated it in 1914.
[†] Excavation for the Miraflores locks did not begin until July 1940 and was suspended for the duration of the war in May 1942.
[‡] The tallest gates were on the Pacific side.
[§] This gate was on the Pacific side.

behind the other in case the first set failed.[10] Each lock also had an intermediate set of gates for smaller ships, and there was even an emergency dam that could be lowered in case the gates failed.

One fact that improved their chances was that the lock gates were hollow.[11] At least a bomb or torpedo wouldn't have to punch through seven feet of solid steel. Nevertheless, destroying them would be a daunting task. At minimum eight main gates, three interim gates, and an emergency dam had to be broached to offset the system's redundancy. Additionally, flying more than 30 attack bombers into such a narrow, well-defended area was asking for trouble. It would be hard enough getting the *Sen-toku* squadron within striking distance; concentrating all those bombers against three separate locks would be like Luke Skywalker flying against the Death Star.

Fujimori's breakthrough came when he realized two important things: first, they wouldn't have to destroy all the gates to put the canal out of commission, just the gates of the topmost lock. And second, the best way to destroy the lock gates wasn't by using just bombs or torpedoes, it was by unleashing the power of Gatun Lake.

Normally, it took 26 million gallons to float a ship 85 feet above the Atlantic.[12] All of this water flowed down from Gatun Lake, which sat behind the last set of gates of the topmost lock. If the Japanese could concentrate their forces against destroying the top gate, the gate opening onto Gatun Lake, then a torrential outpouring of water would drain into the Caribbean, destroying the other gates in its path. It was an elegant plan. At this time Gatun was the world's largest man-made lake;[13] it held millions of pounds of water pressure. The *Seiran* attack planes had only to release it.

Launching an aerial torpedo against a lock gate was a risky undertaking. Fortunately, static objects are easier to hit than moving ones, and nothing was more static than a 745-ton lock gate that was closed. With practice, they could learn to hit it accurately, but they'd have to get past the canal defenses first.

The Panama Canal was situated at one of the most strategic locations in the world, and the United States guarded it accordingly. Nearly 40,000 troops were based throughout the canal zone,[14] and the Atlantic approach was mined. Antitorpedo netting and mine-detecting equipment in each lock made it almost impossible for sabotage to succeed. Major fortifications were located at Colón, Margarita Island, and Toro Point. Fort Sherman, the primary military installation, boasted the largest artillery in the U.S. arsenal,[15] 16-inch cannons comparable to the fabled guns of Navarone. With a range of 25 miles, it was a good bet the 11-gun batteries would prevent any battleship from shelling the canal.

But the greatest risk in 1944 was aerial bombardment. Low-altitude barrage balloons hung over the locks, supplemented by 60 square miles of chemical smoke pots to obscure the canal from the air. Antiaircraft batteries were planted throughout the canal zone, and two long-range radar stations were set up on each coast. Finally, the United States had 634 searchlights to protect the canal from night attack and had built nine airbases and 30 aircraft warning stations, not counting newly constructed bases in Peru, Ecuador, Guatemala, Nicaragua, and Costa Rica.[16]

If that wasn't enough, a 1,000-mile defense perimeter extended from the canal into the Caribbean and was continually patrolled by U.S. planes and warships. Even if the *I-400* subs got close enough to launch an attack, it was unlikely the *Seiran* could reach the canal without being spotted.

As the weeks passed, Fujimori's team developed a plan for attacking the Gatun locks. Since ships transited only during the daytime, a dawn attack would be best, when the gates were closed and defenses lax. It also made sense to bomb the canal during the dry season (January through April), when it would take longer to refill Gatun Lake.[17] Finally, a combination of bombs and aerial torpedoes was proposed to destroy the lock gates.

Interestingly, the *Seiran* were to be abandoned after the mission, and their pilots rescued. This was not a suicide attack, however; the Imperial Japanese Navy wasn't that desperate.[18] Everyone would be coming home.

Fujimori reviewed his findings with various NGS officers to receive their endorsement. If anything, they wanted the mission hurried up. Though the final plan would be left to the *Sen-toku* commander, the attack was set for early 1945.[19] That meant they had a year to get ready. It wasn't much time, considering that none of the submarines were complete and that the *Seiran* weren't even in production, but time was of the essence. And there were other problems.

U.S. submarines had so clamped down on ocean routes that few essential materials were making it to Japan. Steel was particularly in short supply, and naval construction was affected. The *I-400* program was no exception. By October 1943 plans for 13 of the 18 *I-400* subs were canceled due to shortages.[20] This left only 5 subs: the *I-400*, *I-401*, *I-402*, *I-403*, and *I-404*, plus the *I-13* and *I-14*.* The fact that 5 out of 18 *I-400* subs survived the cutback signaled the importance of the mission. But it was still a blow to the program.

The rest of 1943 and early 1944 would be spent modifying and test-flying the *Seiran*. The planes had to be ready when the *I-400* subs were deployed in January 1945. The big question though was whether the subs would be finished by then. It was difficult to answer given that they were still on the building ways. Fujimori's job was to make sure they were finished on time no matter what.

Meanwhile, the *Sen-toku* squad's future commander was about to undertake the most important assignment of his career.

---

* The majority of accounts indicate that by October 1943, the *Sen-toku* squadron would be limited to five subs. Nevertheless, it appears that construction was begun on the *I-405*, which would have brought the fleet to six subs. This discrepancy has never been adequately explained.

CHAPTER 13

ARIIZUMI

When Cdr. Tatsunosuke Ariizumi first spotted the SS *Tjisalak,* the Dutch freighter was 600 miles south of Colombo, Ceylon (Sri Lanka). The 5,787-ton break bulk carrier was traveling unescorted, an invitation to trouble given Ariizumi's orders to disrupt Indian Ocean supply lines. It was early the morning of March 26, 1944, and the *Tjisalak* was 19 days out of Melbourne. As dawn broke, the day promised to be fair, with light winds and a gentle swell. Fortunately for Ariizumi, the Dutch cargo ship showed no interest in zigzagging to avoid enemy subs.[1]

It must have been a relief to be out from behind a desk. After serving two and a half years on the Naval General Staff and nearly two years as senior staff officer for SubRons 8 and 11,* the *Sen-toku* squadron's future commander finally had a sub of his own. It wasn't Ariizumi's first sub command; that had been the *RO-33* before the war had begun.† But after three staff jobs, he was happy to have a line officer assignment again. Unfortunately, necessity had as much to do with it as choice. The Sixth Fleet was running out of sub captains.

---

* There are historical discrepancies over Ariizumi's SubRon postings after he left the NGS. Ariizumi undoubtedly served as senior staff officer of SubRon 8 beginning in March 1942—it can be confirmed from multiple sources. However, Sato, who worked closely with Ariizumi, claims that his first SubRon posting after the NGS was SubRon 7, followed by SubRon 11 (but not SubRon 8). Nambu, on the other hand, says in his memoir that Ariizumi served in SubRons 8 and 2 (but not SubRon 11). The most reliable information suggests Ariizumi was a senior staff officer at SubRons 8 and 11.

† According to users.bigpond.net, Ariizumi held this position from 1937 until 1939. However, there is no corroborating evidence other than this reference.

Ariizumi's new command was the *I-8*, a frontline fleet boat tricked out with everything she needed to wage war against the Allies. A 2,231-ton *Junsen*-class Type 3 submarine,[2] she boasted a floatplane and a dual 5.5-inch gun mount.[3] One five-incher was standard on Japanese submarines, two was unusual. There was no more powerful configuration in the Sixth Fleet.

Ariizumi was familiar with the *I-8*. He'd served as senior staff officer for her squadron in Penang. It also didn't hurt that the Imperial Japanese Navy ran in his blood. The firstborn son of a lieutenant commander and a naval accountant,[4] Ariizumi had attended Etajima, Japan's elite naval academy.* Etajima had a profound effect on him. Both mentally and physically rigorous, it emphasized absolute obedience and left little room for individual initiative. It also made clear that there was no middle ground between victory and defeat, a lesson Ariizumi had absorbed.[5]

After graduating with Etajima's fifty-first class, he served his naval apprenticeship aboard a variety of ships, including the aircraft carrier *Akagi*.[6] Eventually, he enrolled in submarine school and worked his way up the ladder, including a stint aboard the *I-3*. When he showed promise, Ariizumi was admitted to Japan's Naval War College,[7] where only the top-performing officers were accepted. Attendance virtually guaranteed a senior position at the NGS and eventual command of an IJN warship.

After graduation, Ariizumi was assigned to the First Section, First Bureau of the Naval General Staff. First Section was considered the "brain" of the IJN.[8] Responsible for policy and strategic planning, it was a chance for Ariizumi to operate at a senior level where political acumen counted as much as smarts. Though serious in manner and autocratic in style, he had two years to familiarize himself with the labyrinthine workings of the Naval Ministry. Since Japan was already planning for war with the United States, it was an important position.

Ariizumi's most significant contribution as senior submarine

---

* Ariizumi is believed to have graduated in 1923, though some sources indicate 1924.

staff officer was championing the inclusion of five midget subs as part of the attack on Pearl Harbor. They'd been a last-minute addition to the plan.[9] Recently perfected, the two-man subs were to secretly navigate the entrance to Pearl Harbor, slip up its channel, and attack the U.S. fleet where it lay at anchor.

Yamamoto was not enthusiastic about the plan.[10] First, he insisted that all midget crews be rescued when the mission was over. Then he worried the midget subs would accidentally betray his surprise and demanded they not attack until after the aerial bombardment had begun.

Ariizumi waited all day December 8 for news of the midget sub attack, but Yamamoto's worst fears had been realized. At least one midget sub was detected before the aerial attack commenced. Though the Japanese maintained the element of surprise, Ariizumi's "special attack group" had made a poor showing. Only one midget sub penetrated the inner harbor and fired a torpedo. The rest either got lost or were discovered and sunk. Nine of the subs' ten crewmen were killed in the attack. The tenth was captured along with his sub, making him America's first Japanese prisoner of war.

Despite the debacle, Ariizumi lobbied to credit one of the midget subs with sinking the USS *Arizona* (BB-39).

"The world will scoff!" Mitsuo Fuchida, the leader of the aerial attack against Pearl Harbor, responded.[11]

It was obvious that a midget sub couldn't have sunk the *Arizona*, since she was shielded from torpedoes by another ship. This didn't stop Ariizumi, and a midget sub was credited with sinking the U.S. battleship. Ariizumi succeeded in having nine of his dead crewmen promoted twice in rank and enshrined as war gods at Yasukuni temple. It was an amazing accomplishment considering no one really knew how the midget subs had performed.

After the Pearl Harbor attack, Ariizumi became involved with Yamamoto's *I-400* subs. As senior submarine staff officer, he was responsible for shepherding them through the naval bureaucracy. Some people considered him the father of the *Sen-toku* squadron, an appellation he was proud of if not fully deserving of. Now, two years later, he was out from behind a desk and ready to do some torpedoing of his own.

Ariizumi launched his first "fish" when the *I-8* was a mile away. The torpedo struck the *Tjisalak*'s port side, just aft of her bridge. The freighter was rocked by a huge explosion, followed by a geyser of spray. Moments later the ship took on a sickening list. As the *Tjisalak* heeled over 20 degrees, Ariizumi launched a second torpedo. The situation deteriorated rapidly after that. The *Tjisalak* settled so quickly,*[12] her main deck was awash in no time.[13] Unable to send out a distress signal, the captain gave the order to abandon ship.

The last to leave the sinking freighter were her gun crew, who jumped into the ocean only when the water reached their ankles. Ariizumi had mistaken their cannon fire for depth charges and had kept the *I-8* submerged.[14] But once the *Tjisalak* went down, there was nothing left to fear.

Most times an I-boat slipped away after sinking an enemy ship. It was a bad sign if one lingered. When Ariizumi surfaced his sub, he spotted lifeboats in the water and decided to investigate.[15] Once the sail cleared the waves, he scrambled onto the bridge and ordered the machine guns manned. The *I-8*'s 25mm antiaircraft guns had been swapped out for 7mm guns while the sub was in Kure.[16] The change had surprised the crew, which wondered why anyone would want to downgrade their armament.[17]

Ariizumi turned to Lieutenant Honda, his executive officer, and told him to muster all off-duty personnel on deck.[18] Then speaking to his translator, Jiro Nakahara, Ariizumi directed him to address the lifeboats.

"Where's the captain?" Nakahara called using a megaphone.

The *Tjisalak*'s crew stared in silence.

"Where is your captain?"

When there was no response, Nakahara tried again:

"Where-is-the-captain!"

---

* Various accounts suggest between three and six crewmen were killed by the explosions.

Finally, the *Tjisalak*'s master, Capt. C. Hen, stood in his lifeboat and shouted: "I am the captain! What do you want?"

"You must come alongside and report!"[19]

Captain Hen didn't have much choice, so he did what he was told. After everyone in his lifeboat climbed aboard the *I-8*, the *Tjisalak*'s senior officers were identified, their hands were tied behind their back, and they were pushed through a hatch in the sail. The remaining crew were held at gunpoint, stripped of their life preservers, and thoroughly searched.

None of the *I-8*'s crew were prepared to take 102 prisoners, resulting in considerable confusion.[20] One thing was clear, however— they all wanted souvenirs. One of the *Tjisalak*'s survivors had his knife confiscated, while another lost his watch. Money, jewelry, official papers, and personal photos were also taken.

After the survivors were searched, their hands were tied, and they were led one by one to the sub's foredeck, where they were made to sit cross-legged with their heads bowed. When the last lifeboat was emptied, Nakahara began shouting from the bridge.

"Do not look back because that will be too bad for you."

The officers on deck joined in: "Do not run! Do not run! Suppose you run? You will be shot."[21]

The clumsy English was less about communication and more about intimidating the *Tjisalak*'s crew. But some of the prisoners ignored the threat and looked anyway.

The sun was brutally hot as the sub rocked with the motion of the waves. After the last lifeboat was cast adrift, the *I-8*'s machine guns opened up and filled it with holes. Then the sub's diesel engines sprang to life,[22] and the *I-8* headed east.[23]

Lt. (jg) Sadao Motonaka, the sub's gunnery officer, had been told to use his sword if anyone tried to escape. Motonaka had little experience wielding such a weapon and had already embarrassed himself by accidentally breaking its tip off when he stuck it into the deck. But when a Chinese deckhand tried escaping, Motonaka didn't hesitate to slash him.[24] When another Chinese deckhand jumped into the sea, the *I-8*'s crew were ready. Competing to see who could score the first bull's-eye, they laughed as they fired into the water.[25] A third prisoner, naked from the waist up, also dove overboard and was shot in the back. Blood could be seen spurting from the wound before the man disappeared in the waves.[26] When his body failed to reappear, he was presumed dead.

It was clear that Ariizumi intended to kill his prisoners though the method he chose was a surprise. Assembling two rows of crewmen on either side of the *I-8*'s aft deck, Ariizumi armed them with guns, swords, and iron bars taken from the ship's railing.[27] He intended each one of the *Tjisalak*'s survivors to pass through this lethal gauntlet, where they would be shot, bayoneted, clubbed, or cut with a sword.[28] It was a laborious method to be sure, but a more certain way of eliminating prisoners than strafing with a machine gun.[29]

Not all of Ariizumi's crew liked the idea of killing prisoners. Motonaka thought it disgusting. Still, he had to comply: "A captain's order was the same as God. If the captain made up his mind to [destroy his] sub, we had to obey."[30]

Even the *I-8*'s dive control officer found Ariizumi's behavior excessively "brutal."[31]

The *Tjisalak*'s fifth engineer, hardly more than a boy, was struggling to contain himself when two of the *I-8*'s crewmen motioned for him to stand.[32] After the three men disappeared behind the sail, there was a brief silence followed by a gunshot.

The *Tjisalak*'s first mate was next. He considered jumping overboard, but a quick death seemed preferable to drowning. After rounding the sail, he found a Japanese crewman waiting for him with a revolver. The first mate stopped, expecting to be executed, but the man waved him toward the stern instead. As he stood above the *I-8*'s churning propellers, a bullet was fired into his head. Moments after tumbling into the sea,[33] the first mate disappeared from sight.

As the murderous gauntlet continued, Ariizumi went below deck to question the prisoners. The interviews took place in the *I-8*'s wardroom with Nakahara serving as translator. The first person Ariizumi interrogated was the Dutch freighter's only female passenger, an American woman named Mrs. Brittan. Pretty with soft eyes and wavy brown hair, Mrs. Brittan remained calm throughout her interrogation. Nakahara recognized her accent as American, but it didn't take long to determine that she held little intelligence value. Her chief novelty, being a woman, soon passed. When Ariizumi finished, Mrs. Brittan was sent forward for confinement.

Next was Captain Hen. When he entered the wardroom with his hands tied,[34] he complained to Ariizumi that it was against international law for a captain to be confined in such a manner.

"Stupid fool!" Ariizumi shouted. "This is war!"[35]

Hen pleaded leniency for his crew,[36] but it was too late. After two hours of slaughter, Ariizumi had sped up the attrition by tying the prisoners who remained on deck to a rope and ordering the *I-8* submerged.[37] It doesn't take a man long to drown when he is tied to a submarine. The force of water easily squeezes the air from his lungs, and if that doesn't kill him, the sub's rapid descent will.

After Nakahara assisted in questioning several of the *Tjisalak*'s officers, he went to the forward crew compartment to see if Mrs. Brittan needed anything. When she asked for some water, Nakahara was happy to fetch it for her.[38] Then they got to talking.

Mrs. Brittan was a former Red Cross worker who'd lived in Japan before the war. Nakahara, a Nisei born in Hawaii, listened sympathetically to her recollections. When Lieutenant Honda appeared informing him the American woman would have to be executed, Nakahara didn't have the heart to look her in the eye. He suspected Mrs. Brittan already knew her fate, but that only made it more difficult.

Later that night, Lieutenant Honda came for Mrs. Brittan. She was remarkably composed given the situation. When asked whether she wanted a blindfold, she calmly declined. When her turn came to go on deck, she bowed to the crew and politely offered a "*Sayonara*."[39]

It was dark as Ariizumi waited for the prisoners to emerge from deck hatch number three. The first to be executed was either the

Tjisalak's chief engineer or radio officer, who let out a bloodcurdling scream.[40] Ariizumi had instructed his dive officer to kill the man, but he made such a botch of it that Ariizumi was forced to take over.[41]

The second prisoner to appear was Mrs. Brittan. Some crew accounts say Ariizumi used a sword; others claim it was a pistol.* Whatever the method, Ariizumi quickly dispatched the American woman, followed by another *Tjisalak* officer.

Captain Hen was last to be killed. Perhaps it was Ariizumi's way of honoring a fellow captain, or perhaps it was just a matter of chance. But before the *Tjisalak*'s master could be executed, he jumped overboard.[42] Since his body was never recovered, his escape amounted to a death sentence.

Later that evening Lt. (sg) Motohide Yanabe was heading to his bunk when Ariizumi called him into his cabin. Holding out his bloody sword, Ariizumi asked Yanabe to clean it for him. He could give it to an orderly, he explained, but Yanabe could keep a secret.[43]

Yanabe was washing Ariizumi's sword when Nakahara entered the compartment. When he saw what Yanabe was doing, Nakahara made a disapproving grimace. Yanabe didn't feel like explaining himself; after all he was under captain's orders.[44] When he finished, he washed his hands[45] and left without saying anything.

Nakahara wasn't surprised by what he saw. He'd heard Ariizumi had beheaded some of the prisoners.[46] But Nakahara was angry. It had been wrong to massacre the survivors, and he wasn't the only crewman to feel this way. Motonaka was also upset. The *I-8*'s gunnery officer was angry that people he'd shared a meal with had been executed. Killing a woman was especially heinous. Now Motonaka wanted off the *I-8* at the first opportunity.[47]

---

* According to Nakahara during the Tokyo War Crimes Tribunal, Ariizumi used a sword. Jiro Nakahara, statement, October 13, 1948, p. 5, Macmillan Brown Library (MBL). Additionally, Yanabe admitted cleaning Ariizumi's bloody sword after the *Tjisalak* massacre. Motohide Yanabe, statement, Sugamo Prison, August 30, 1948, MBL. Nevertheless, some accounts cite a pistol being used to execute the high-priority prisoners, so it's possible that both implements were used but on different prisoners.

Feelings about the massacre ran high among the crew. Even the sub's second in command, Lieutenant Honda, had difficulty talking about it.[48] Clearly, they'd committed an atrocity, but under whose authority?

The answer came the next day when Ariizumi told Lieutenant Honda that the Naval General Staff had ordered all survivors of sunken merchant ships to be killed.[49] Whether Ariizumi felt guilty or thought his senior officer deserved an explanation is impossible to know. What's clear is that Ariizumi wanted his direct report to understand that he hadn't ordered the prisoners killed on his own authority; he was carrying out the wishes of the high command. As the *Tjisalak*'s 98 victims had already learned, massacre was official policy.

Four of the *Tjisalak*'s officers, including the first mate and an Indian lascar, miraculously survived the slaughter. After swimming nearly eight hours, they found one of their ship's damaged lifeboats and managed to stay afloat long enough to be rescued by a passing American Liberty ship. Though their ordeal was over, I-boat massacres in the Indian Ocean were not. Four SubRon 8 sub captains, three of whom would soon join the *Sen-toku* squadron, were determined to kill as many merchant mariners as possible.

Ariizumi's reign of terror had only just begun.

CHAPTER 14

ARIIZUMI UNDER FIRE

THE *I-8* SANK ANOTHER FREIGHTER AFTER THE *Tjisalak*. Inexplicably, Ariizumi failed to kill the crew. It's possible he was prevented from doing so by an Allied patrol. It's also possible he gave the crew a free pass. If so, the reasons are unclear. But Ariizumi returned to his former methods on his second war patrol, when the *I-8* encountered the SS *Nellore,* an Australian freighter out of Bombay.

It was June 29, 1944, when the *I-8* sank the 6,942-ton *Nellore* with a combination of torpedoes and deck gun fire. Armed Japanese crewmen boarded one of her lifeboats to question survivors. After a half-hour interrogation, a European woman; a Javanese husband, wife, and their child; two French soldiers; and the *Nellore*'s gunner were taken prisoner.[1] Seventy-nine of the *Nellore*'s 209 passengers and crew died in the sinking or were lost at sea.[2] The rest either made it to Diego Garcia or were rescued. Of the seven prisoners taken aboard the *I-8,* only the Javanese woman and her son survived.[3] The rest were never heard from again.

When Ariizumi sank the American Liberty ship *Jean Nicolet* three days later, it was a repeat of the *Tjisalak* massacre, right down to the murderous gauntlet and submerging with survivors tied to the deck. Ninety-nine passengers and crew were taken aboard the *I-8.* Everyone was killed save for 24 survivors who were later rescued by the Indian Navy.[4] Of the three Americans taken prisoner, only one survived the war.[5] Not long afterward the British began calling Ariizumi "the Butcher."[6]

THE *I-8*'S CREW grew increasingly unhappy after the second patrol.[7] Ariizumi warned them not to talk about the killings,[8] but the wear of so many atrocities affected morale.

Lieutenant Honda, the boat's executive officer, confided to an underling that he was "not happy regarding the actions taken by the CO." It was a startling admission for a second in command. Honda obviously knew atrocities couldn't be covered up. They'd "only cause trouble at a later date."[9]

Ariizumi must have known his crew was distressed because he called Yanabe, the *I-8*'s engine room officer, to his quarters for a candid conversation. Yanabe was an Ariizumi loyalist. He was the first person the captain turned to when he needed his sword cleaned. Yanabe spent his time overseeing the sub's engines, which meant he may not have been as involved with the massacres as other crewmen.

We have only Yanabe's side of the story, given during the Tokyo War Crimes Tribunal. We know from his testimony though that he spoke openly to his captain about the crew's distaste for the "atrocities."[10] What Yanabe says has the ring of truth about it, especially since Ariizumi tended to curb his temper when talking to a loyalist.

As Yanabe explained the crew's discomfort, Ariizumi listened quietly. Once again the *I-8*'s captain confided that his hands were tied; he was acting on orders from the Naval General Staff. Yanabe took the incautious step of pressing further, always a danger given Ariizumi's temper. He mentioned that U-boats had caused an international incident during World War I when massacring prisoners. The *I-8* might face a similar uproar. Ariizumi already knew about this and told Yanabe he'd killed the prisoners only after a great deal of thought. Nevertheless, he realized he was in a difficult situation. Committing atrocities was "not good," he admitted.[11]

Even "the Butcher" felt guilty.

THE MORALITY OF submarine warfare had been troubling the "five great powers" almost from the invention of the first submersible. Unrestricted warfare means attacking enemy merchant vessels without warning. (Warships were always fair game.) But it had not always been so. The first attempt to restrict submarines came shortly after World War I. Germany had targeted both merchant and passenger ships during the war, nearly defeating Great Britain. The British Admiralty pushed for the abolition of submarines during the 1921 International Conference on Naval Limitation in Washington, arguing they were immoral like poison gas.[12] Since the United States and France objected to this position, no limitations were set.

U.S. Senator Elihu Root was one of the first to propose that a merchant ship's passengers and crew be put in a place of safety (such as lifeboats) before a submarine sank a vessel. But the U.S. Navy opposed the Root Resolution, arguing it would limit the effectiveness of a legitimate weapon.[13] The 1930 London Naval Conference tried reviving the resolution, including a "visit and search" policy for merchant ships. After much back-and-forth, Japan, the United States, and Britain finally agreed to Article 22, the first comprehensive ban on unrestricted submarine warfare. Though the intent was high-minded, the practical implications proved unworkable. Any commercial ship with a radio could call for help, thereby endangering an attacking submarine. Since it took time for a crew to evacuate their vessel, the sub was left dangerously exposed. Once war was declared, Article 22 went out the window.

Within hours of the attack on Pearl Harbor, the U.S. chief of naval operations sent a notice to all submarine commanders that they were now free to engage in "unrestricted warfare" against Japan.[14] The United States had signed the 1930 London Naval Treaty outlawing such warfare, but given the devastation in Hawaii, it was quick to abandon the agreement.[15] It also didn't hurt that unrestricted warfare boosted the morale of sub crews.[16]

An argument can be made that forbidding unrestricted submarine warfare was impractical. Merchant crews were destined for slaughter as a by-product of war, be it from torpedoes, machine guns, or drowning. Ironically, the strategic focus of the Sixth Fleet was attacking warships, not merchant ships,[17] while U.S. sub policy concentrated on eliminating as many Pacific merchant vessels as possible. Yet it was Japan that would be held accountable for massacring crews, not the Allies, even though in a few notable cases like the USS *Wahoo* (SS 238), U.S. sub crews also killed survivors.*

But the question remains, who issued the order to massacre merchant crews in the Indian Ocean, and what did Japan hope to gain by it?

ARIIZUMI WASN'T LYING when he told his executive officer he'd been ordered to kill prisoners. The order had come from the Sixth Fleet via the Naval General Staff and can be traced to a meeting in Berlin between Adolf Hitler, his foreign minister Joachim von Ribbentrop, and Japan's ambassador to Germany, Hiroshi Oshima.[18] Among the topics discussed during the January 1942 conference was Hitler's belief that no matter how fast the United States built merchant ships, she would always be short of qualified seamen. The IJN knew that every merchant ship the Sixth Fleet sank would disrupt the Allied war effort, which is why Ariizumi's mission was to destroy enemy supply lines in the Indian Ocean.[19] Since a typical Liberty ship could be built in 42 days, it was impossible to sink enough of them to keep pace with production. That's why Hitler sought to redress this imbalance. The result was an agreement not only to sink Allied freighters but to massacre their crews, in the interest of discouraging recruitment for the merchant marine. Hitler made it clear that since Germany and Japan were fighting for survival, there was no room for humanitarian practice. Oshima concurred and conveyed the conversation to the Japanese naval attaché.[20] Two months later the Sixth Fleet issued the following directive:

---

* The USS *Wahoo* (SS 238), under the command of Lt. Cmdr. Dudley "Mush" Morton, machine-gunned approximately 1,000 Japanese afloat in the ocean after sinking a troop transport on January 26, 1943. This was only one of many atrocities that U.S. military personnel committed in the Pacific theater.

DO NOT MERELY SINK ENEMY VESSELS, BUT POSITIVELY
ANNIHILATE THE SURVIVORS. AS FAR AS CIRCUMSTANCES
PERMIT, INTERN THE PRINCIPAL PERSONNEL OF SUNKEN
ENEMY SHIPS AND ENDEAVOR TO OBTAIN INFORMATION.[21]

The order to eliminate survivors originated from the Navy General Staff in Tokyo and was verbally issued to the Sixth Fleet by an NGS officer around March 1943. In turn, the Sixth Fleet issued written orders to the commander of SubRon 8 in Penang later that same month.[22] Ariizumi was already familiar with the order, since he'd served as SubRon 8's senior staff officer previous to captaining the *I-8*.[23] When he returned to Penang in February 1944, the order was still in effect though it had not been acted upon.

Although Ariizumi was not involved in formation of the policy, he was determined to set a good example. When he was still an NGS staff officer, he'd been overheard saying, "To win a war, you must exhaust [the enemy's] human resources."[24] The new policy was hardly a departure from his own thinking.

Not all sub captains thought this way, of course. Of the nine captains in SubRon 8, five refrained from massacring merchant crews. Of the four captains who did kill survivors, three (Ariizumi, Kusaka, and Shimizu) would go on to oversee, or captain, *Sen-toku* subs. Nambu and Ohashi would be the only *Sen-toku* captains with no blood on their hands.

At least one Penang-based sub captain was reprimanded for being too lenient in his treatment of survivors.[25] Given Japan's historical animosity toward POWs, Ariizumi's disdain for taking prisoners should come as no surprise. Though it doesn't excuse his actions, which were heinous, it does explain them. It wasn't just a case of Ariizumi following orders; he was adhering to a code he'd been raised to believe in, a code that hundreds of years of history reinforced and that his education and training had taught him to serve. That's why Ariizumi was the first to carry out the order more than a year after it was issued.

Japanese treatment of POWs may have been barbaric, but it wasn't crazy. It not only had historical precedent—it had its own indisputable logic as well. If killing merchant crews meant fewer men for supply lines, then so be it. Of course, the *Tjisalak* survivors had no difficulty differentiating between the horror of drowning from a torpedo attack and being bludgeoned to death aboard a Japanese sub. The resulting hue and cry confirmed as much.

The British government was first to protest. In a letter to the Japanese Foreign Ministry dated June 5, 1944, the British demanded "immediate instructions to prevent the repetition of similar atrocities and to take disciplinary action against those responsible."[26]

The British protest was delivered to Japan's foreign minister by the Swiss foreign minister in Tokyo. No reply was received; nor was anything heard in response to a follow-up message.[27] On July 28 the Dutch government also complained about the *Tjisalak*'s sinking.[28] Finally, two months after the Swiss foreign minister had sent a reminder, the Japanese Foreign Ministry issued an official response.[29]

> *My Dear Minister*
>
> *I have the honor to acknowledge the receipt of your Excellency's letters . . . concerning a protest by the British Government which pretends that in the Indian Ocean some Japanese submarines torpedoed British merchant vessels and unlawfully attacked the survivors of the vessels.*
>
> *Concerning this matter I have caused the competent authorities to make strict investigations of each case indicated, and it is clear that Japanese submarines had nothing to do with the facts alleged in the protest.*
>
> *I have the honor to ask your Excellency to forward this reply to the British Government.*
>
> *I take this opportunity,*
> *Mamoru Shigemitsu, Minister for Foreign Affairs*[30]

British, Dutch, and American protests eventually forced an inquiry into the massacres, resulting in a Kafkaesque investigation where the Japanese military conducted interviews about a policy it had sanctioned and now denied. When the investigation eventually reached SubRon 8, Ariizumi was called in for questioning. Asked about the massacres, he could hardly disguise his anger. The duplicity of being questioned for something he'd been ordered to do so sickened him, he refused to answer questions and turned his head away in disgust.[31]

Ariizumi may have been nicknamed "the Butcher," but his failure to answer questions didn't harm his career. A few weeks after the *I-8* returned to Yokosuka, he was given the most important assignment of his life: command of the *Sen-toku* squadron.

Meanwhile, his future nemesis, the USS *Segundo*, was heading his way.

CHAPTER 15

THE *SEGUNDO* (SS 398)

THE PORTSMOUTH NAVY YARD WAS BITTERLY COLD WHEN THE USS *Segundo* launched stern first into the icy waters of the Piscataqua River. Richard "Fox" Binkley, seaman first class, stood on deck that winter's day along with 20-plus crew members assigned to the *Segundo*'s fitting out.[1] It was so freezing outside, it must have seemed like the wife of the assistant secretary of the treasury was taking her sweet time breaking a champagne bottle across the bunting-draped bow. But finally the air horns screeched their jubilant message, and the half-finished sub began moving down the building ways.

Somewhere a naval band played "Anchors Aweigh" as Binkley, locked in salute, stood firm on the *Segundo*'s deck. The sub moved amazingly fast for an object weighing 2,500 tons. Nevertheless, Binkley rode her all the way down into the slack tide, ending in a roiling ocean of foam. It was February 5, 1944, and the *Segundo* was nearing completion.

The USS *Segundo* (SS 398) was a Balao-class submarine. Named for a fish in the cavalla family that includes yellow jack and pompano, she was one of 44 Balao-class subs built by the Portsmouth Navy Yard during the war. After Congress approved a massive fleet expansion in 1940, Portsmouth had found itself at the center of the greatest sub construction program in history. U.S. submarine forces had come a long way since the start of war, and the navy was now producing boats at a record pace.

Portsmouth built more subs during World War II than any shipyard in America. New London's Electric Boat Company came next, followed by Mare Island Navy Yard in San Francisco, the Manitowoc

Shipbuilding Company in Wisconsin, the Cramp Shipbuilding Company of Philadelphia, and the Boston Navy Yard. Still, none compared to Portsmouth.

Portsmouth built a total of 80 subs during the war, more than half Balao-class.[2] Electric Boat may have produced better-finished subs, but Portsmouth subs had the latest equipment that captains hungered for.[3] Portsmouth subs also had a more angular silhouette than those of Electric Boat. Edward Beach, author of *Run Silent, Run Deep* and a sub commander himself, described Portsmouth boats as looking like "sleek, streamlined monsters."[4]

Since Portsmouth was a government yard, it didn't have to worry about profit margins. Designers could concentrate on construction techniques that reduced time on the building ways. Some sub sections were prefabricated before a keel was even laid. This modular approach shortened the time from keel to commission. The fastest Electric Boat ever built a sub was 317 days. By the time the *Segundo* was commissioned in May 1944, Portsmouth had reduced that time to a record 173 days.[5]

Interestingly, Portsmouth's construction methods stood in stark contrast to Japanese methods. Though Japan would eventually lead the world in automotive assembly techniques, she had not yet learned the fine art of mass production. One reason Japan's sub construction faltered was that the Imperial Japanese Navy never consolidated behind a standardized fleet boat design. Instead, they built almost as many sub variations as General Motors built car models. This approach took longer to produce subs, cost more, and hampered quality. When material shortages struck, Sixth Fleet sub production further declined.

The key to American success was building one submarine design at a time. Once the United States had standardized behind the Gato-class design, shipyards could concentrate on increasing sub production.[6] It was exactly this replacement capacity that Hitler feared. Portsmouth was the first shipyard to build the Balao-class sub. Balaos were the successor to the Gatos and were virtually identical, with one important difference. They could dive 100 feet deeper. This was crucial because Japanese depth charges were often set to explode at 150 feet.[7] Since Balao-class subs could dive twice that depth, they stood a better chance of surviving an attack.

The secret to their increased depth was a thicker hull design using high-tensile steel. This enabled the sub to reach a depth of 925 feet before collapsing.[8] Sub designers, conservative by nature, set an operating limit of 400 feet. This may have been playing it safe, but it was still an improvement over Gato subs, whose safety depth was capped at 300.

For obvious reasons, submariners referred to Gato boats as "thin skins" and Balao boats as "thick skins." In the beginning, some feared the Balao's thicker hull might reduce flexibility, causing her to rupture when depth-charged. This did not turn out to be a problem though. In fact, many sub commanders felt comfortable enough to take their subs down to 600 feet in an emergency, well below the prescribed "safety depth."

The Balao sub's depth limit was so important, it was labeled top secret.[9] If Japan were to learn of it, American subs would lose their advantage because Japanese depth charges would be set to explode deeper. One hundred and nineteen Balao subs were built between 1942 and 1945.[10] In keeping with her lead role, Portsmouth built the first, laying her keel on June 26, 1942. When Congress authorized the 1943–44 Combatant Building Program, hull numbers 381 through 410 were assigned to Portsmouth. Hull number 398 would eventually become the *Segundo*.

The *Segundo* was a typical Balao-class sub. She was 312 feet long and 27 feet wide with a draft of 15 feet. She ran on four Fairbanks-Morse diesel engines (the most reliable sub engines of the war), was rated at a top surface speed of 20 knots (9 submerged, which she could only maintain for a limited time), and had a cruising range of 11,000 nautical miles. Additionally, the *Segundo* was operated by ten officers and 70 enlisted men, could patrol for up to 75 days, and could remain underwater 48 hours albeit at very slow speed (12 hours was more typical). And she was by no means small. Displacing 1,525 tons surfaced and 2,415 tons submerged, she was one of the largest submarines the United States had to offer.[11]

Because of her hull number, a Portsmouth worker called the

Segundo a $3.98 sub knocked down from four dollars. He meant it as a joke, of course. Brand-new fleet boats were regularly called "gold-platers," mostly out of envy.[12] They were state-of-the-art combat subs and every commanding officer wanted one, especially if he had something to prove.

When the *Segundo* launched in February, she still required four more months of construction. Not surprisingly, her commanding officer, Lt. Cdr. James D. Fulp, Jr., was concerned that if his boat wasn't finished soon, the war might end without him. By mid-1944 the United States was flooding the Pacific with so many submarines, Japanese naval targets were becoming scarce, which is probably why Fulp and his crew were eager to get back to the action. For the meantime, they'd have to wait until the *Segundo* was finished.

THIRTY-FOUR-YEAR-OLD FULP WAS an experienced submariner when he was named commanding officer of the *Segundo*. If a sports team is nothing without a winning coach, then the same can be said for the crew of a combat sub. Fulp began shaping his men two months before the *Segundo* even touched water, and his influence would continue well beyond the four patrols he would captain. In many ways, Fulp did more to shape the future of the *Segundo*'s crew than his successor, Capt. Stephen L. Johnson, which would turn out to be both a blessing and a curse.

When the war began, Fulp was executive officer of the USS *Sargo* (SS 188) based in the Philippines. It was a baptism of fire because the U.S. Asiatic Fleet was outgunned, outmanned, and virtually obsolete compared to the Japanese navy. When hostilities commenced, the *Sargo* was one of the first U.S. subs to go on war patrol. By the time Fulp finished seven patrols, he was already a hero.[13]

James Douglas Fulp, Jr., was born August 27, 1910, in Ridgewood, South Carolina. Known as Toots to his family and J.D. to his friends, Fulp had brown hair, blue eyes, and a mouth full of crooked teeth. His mother was named Daisy, and his father, J. D. Fulp, Sr., had served in the army during World War I. Fulp's ancestors had come from Scotland and, according to the 1790 census, were already established in what was to become North Carolina. A staunchly Presbyterian family whose relatives had fought in the Revolutionary War, the Fulps had a strong military heritage. If J.D., Jr., learned anything growing up, it was respect for the military.

Fulp was raised in Greenwood, South Carolina, where he played softball, football, basketball, and track, excelling at each sport. He transferred his junior year in high school to the Bailey Military Institute, where his father, "Colonel" Fulp, was superintendent. The institute was a modest affair. The school's main barracks consisted of a three-story brick building with a front portico and side porches. Cadets wore uniforms and, for special occasions, jodhpurs, boots, Sam Browne belts, and a dress sword. Precision drilling took place on the school's broad lawn, while its brass band paraded regularly through town.

Records show that J.D. was one of Bailey's best athletes, especially in football, where he excelled. His grades were consistently in the high eighties and low nineties, and when he graduated with honors in 1928, he was fourth out of a class of 42. It's unclear how much slack if any J.D.'s father cut him at Bailey. One area where he may have received help was getting appointed to the U.S. Naval Academy. When J.D. passed the entrance exam, he was still short a physics credit. As a result, he didn't report until July 1, 1929,[14] three months after Nambu had started at Etajima.

Fulp was well liked by his peers. They considered him a natural leader, though like a lot of midshipmen, he struggled his freshman year. Within the first few months of his arrival, he was deficient in math and physics and failed the school's swimming requirement, a surprising lapse for a midshipman. Matters grew worse when Fulp spent the better part of October in the infirmary due to a football injury.

A December 1929 letter from the secretary of Annapolis's academic board to Colonel Fulp explained: "It is difficult to state just what has been the cause of your son's deficiencies . . . the course here is an intensive one and boys quite frequently have a bit of difficulty in adjusting themselves to their new surroundings."[15]

Fulp had to forgo Christmas leave and spend it at school

undergoing remedial instruction. He was probably still "adjusting to his surroundings" when he was given 50 demerits for "conduct to the prejudice of good order and discipline."[16] Records indicate Fulp was returning from the city on Christmas Eve when a commander, suspecting he was drunk, escorted him to the officer of the watch. On reaching Bancroft Hall, Fulp made a run for it.[17] It was poor judgment, typical of boys his age, but that didn't help his case. Fulp "bilged out" of Annapolis a month later.

Despite this record of failure, Fulp was encouraged to reapply. When he was admitted for the 1930 fall term, he never looked back. By the time he graduated four years later, Fulp had gone from being a somewhat doughy, awkward-looking teen, into movie star handsome. Annapolis had not only fixed his teeth, it had turned him into a serious young man ready for responsibility. Fulp may have felt more at home on Farragut Field than with academics, but his classmates considered him "a true southern gentleman" for his good looks and polite behavior.[18]

Upon graduation, Fulp was commissioned an ensign in the U.S. Navy and posted to the USS *Tuscaloosa* (CA-37). He was soon promoted to lieutenant (junior grade) and transferred to the USS *Winslow* (DD-359), where he won distinction as a gunnery control officer.

Fulp's life changed dramatically in January 1939 when he enrolled in the basic officer class at the Submarine School in New London, Connecticut. Classmates included Chester Nimitz, Jr., son of the famous admiral, who six months later graduated second out of a class of 26. Fulp graduated sixteenth. Soon afterward he was assigned to the *Sargo*.

Fulp found time to marry in between war patrols, and in August 1943 he entered command class at the New London Sub School. Enrollment in the six-week course was for only the most promising candidates. Lt. Cdr. Nobukiyo Nambu had entered a similar program in Japan the previous year and emerged a full-fledged sub captain. Fulp hoped for a similar result. Continuing his mixed academic performance, he graduated tenth out of a class of ten. In

January 1944 Fulp was transferred to the Portsmouth Navy Yard to fit out the *Segundo*. If all went well, the new sub would be his first command.

THERE'S NO UNDERESTIMATING the complexity of a Balao-class sub, even if it operated on basic principles. There were miles of piping, a rat's nest of wiring, and complex ballast tank arrangements to understand. Emergency valves hung from bulkheads like mushrooms after a rainstorm, and there were so many systems to comprehend, it could be intimidating to the uninitiated. In addition to propulsion, ventilation, refrigeration, and air-conditioning systems, there were trim and drain systems, as well as water-distillation and waste-removal systems (all with their own plumbing), not to mention hydraulics, steering, bow and stern plane mechanisms, anchor handling gear, and fuel and oil lubricating systems. Many of these were necessary to keep a sub not only habitable but a functioning war machine as well.

The sheer mechanical intricacy of a World War II sub was so overwhelming, it required an understanding of math, geometry, science, chemistry, physics, biology, mechanics, and engineering. And if that weren't enough, whenever a sub was at sea, the very environment she operated in threatened to flood her at any moment. It was a never-ending battle that put a sub crew on their guard, and this was before they'd even encountered a single enemy.

In terms of sophistication, a Balao-class sub was the space shuttle of its day, only safer. And though low-earth orbit may be a hostile environment, at least it didn't have enemy ships whose sole purpose was to sink you with a depth charge. One way sub designers managed risk was to build redundancy into every system. If steering failed in the conning tower, there was another steering station in the control room. If bow plane hydraulics failed, they could go to manual. If the sub was having trouble surfacing because a main ballast tank was ruptured, they could always blow the safety.

It was this emphasis on redundancy that made submariners

check and double-check everything they did, because one mistake could cost them their lives. Safety extended even to the way submariners spoke, with each command crafted to ensure accuracy and clarity. Nothing was left to chance.

IT WAS A major challenge to forge a group of sailors into a functioning crew. You couldn't just take 80 guys, plop them in the middle of Portsmouth Navy Yard, and hope they'd form a team; a captain had to work at it. But training a crew while a sub was under construction was "like training a racehorse locked inside the barn."[19] Fortunately, Fulp didn't have to do it alone, he had an executive officer (XO) to help him.

Lt. John E. Balson had a sharp mind and an unflappable manner. He also had a sense of humor so dry, it could run a sub aground in the middle of the Pacific. Balson didn't talk much, which led Fulp to nickname him "Silent Joe." But if Fulp calling Balson quiet was the pot calling the kettle black, there was no mistaking Balson's aptitude. He was the same kind of XO Fulp had been aboard the *Sargo*. The two were well matched.

One important way Fulp shaped his crew was by not playing games with them. He might not have talked much, but what he said counted for a lot. A man always knew where he stood with Captain Fulp. Best of all, he radiated the kind of quiet confidence sub crews just lapped up.

Fulp taught his crew how a "hot running" boat operated, and they learned to take pride in a job well done. Fulp's legacy left a lasting impression aboard the *Segundo*, a legacy his replacement would rely upon when it came time to face the *I-401*.

THE *SEGUNDO* WAS finally ready for commissioning on Tuesday, May 9, 1944. Fulp officially assumed his first command in a formal ceremony lasting only ten minutes. At the rate Portsmouth was turning out submarines, there wasn't time for anything longer.

Ten days after he took command, Fulp took the *Segundo* out for the first time.[20] Five days later the navy's Board of Inspection and Survey officially accepted the boat into the U.S. submarine force.

Fulp spent the next few weeks running battle station exercises and torpedo-firing simulations. As his crew grew proficient, he progressed to high-speed maneuvers, including collision drills and dive alarms. Soon, the *Segundo*'s crew developed the speed and confidence Fulp was looking for.

The men weren't beyond getting in trouble though. Some of the more curious wondered what the colorful buoys were in the harbor. When they hauled one up and discovered it was a lobster trap, they began nightly raids to supplement their dinner. Only when they learned that lobster thieves are treated in Maine the same way cattle rustlers are in Texas did the practice stop.[21]

Finally, the *Segundo* departed Portsmouth for the Naval Torpedo Station near Newport, Rhode Island. After taking on a load of "fish," Fulp's fire control party practiced their attack approach in Narragansett Bay, launching 30 torpedoes in two days. As a reward, half the crew was given leave to enjoy themselves in Middletown. Unfortunately, they got into a brawl with the locals and returned to the sub with a variety of shiners. When Fulp learned his remaining crew planned revenge, he restricted all hands to ship.[22]

After the *Segundo* spent a week at New London, she was ready to head south to the Panama Canal. Transiting the eastern seaboard promised to be uneventful. U-boat sinkings had been a problem at the start of the war, but by June 1944 the situation was under control.

There were surprises along the way though. One evening while the *Segundo* was surfaced, one of her senior officers spotted a half dozen torpedoes heading for the sub. When he saw their wake, he cried out an alarm. The torpedoes turned out to be nothing more than playful dolphins. Needless to say, the officer took a ribbing.

Another day Ens. Rod Johnson had the four-to-eight-A.M. watch. Johnson was scanning the horizon when a sudden flash caught his eye. Training his binoculars off the port bow, Johnson saw the feathered wake of a long, thin periscope a few feet above water. No sub was supposed to be there, so Johnson immediately called for a dive. Moments later the *Segundo*'s sound man tuned in to the receding vibrations of a sub screw. So much for being in safe waters. After that the *Segundo* began zigzagging.[23]

IT TOOK THE *Segundo* only eight hours to cross the Panama Canal. By the evening of July 5, she was moored at the sub base in Balboa.[24] The crew marveled at the Pacific's 18-foot tidal spread, but they didn't have long to relax. Fulp conducted sound tests the next day to check on their noise-reduction efforts. When it came time for torpedo attack simulations, he pushed his men even harder.

Balboa wasn't all work and no play, however. When he wasn't busy spotting periscopes, Ensign Johnson spotted a five-foot-long stuffed iguana in the Balboa officers' club. Deciding it would look perfect in the *Segundo*'s wardroom, Johnson smuggled the reptile on board, along with a case of Old Grand-dad.[25]

Fulp left Balboa for Pearl Harbor on July 9. Drills were a daily routine along the way as he strove to build a proficient crew. It was slightly before noon on Tuesday, July 25, when the *Segundo* finally arrived at the submarine base at Pearl Harbor. After minor repairs, she underwent three more weeks of training. Finally, Fulp received orders for his first war patrol as captain of the *Segundo*.

In accordance with ComSubPac Odord 268–44, the *Segundo* was ordered under way as a member of "Wilkins' Bears," one of three wolf packs bound for patrol between Mindanao, the second-largest island in the Philippines, and the Palau Islands, 500 miles east. Admiral Halsey's plan was straightforward: deploy ten subs in three wolf packs to sink any Japanese warships that interfered with the American invasion of Palau.[26]

It was time to see what Fulp's crew had learned. They were finally going to war.

CHAPTER 16

DECLINE

BY THE TIME THE *SEGUNDO* LEFT PEARL HARBOR ON HER FIRST war patrol, Japan's Sixth Fleet was so decimated, it threatened to disintegrate as a cohesive fighting force. During the three-month period the *Segundo* crew underwent training, Allied antisub patrols sank 25 Japanese subs.[1] This was practically half of all remaining Japanese subs, which left only 26 fully operational boats in the entire force. Considering there had been more than twice as many subs at the start of war, the Sixth Fleet was rapidly declining.[2]

May 1944 was an especially horrendous month. While Captain Fulp was preparing the *Segundo* for shakedown trials, the USS *England* (DE-635), accompanied by the USS *George* (DE-697) and USS *Raby* (DE-698), used ULTRA intelligence and a new weapon called a Hedgehog to locate and sink six Japanese subs in a row.[3] The boats were stationed in a picket line 30 miles northwest of New Ireland when the destroyer escorts found them.[4] The *England* had already helped sink the *I-16* on May 21. The next day they located the *RO-106* and sunk her as well. Using the Hedgehog, which launched contact-exploding depth charges in a circular pattern, the three escorts worked their way down the Japanese sentry line. Later that same day they found and sank the *RO-104*, followed by the *RO-116*, the *RO-105*, and the *RO-108*. By this point, Japanese intelligence had picked up so many U.S. naval messages boasting of a clean sweep that they hurriedly signaled the last two boats to disperse.[5] Later U.S. naval forces concluded that the six-sub sinking was the most brilliant antisubmarine operation in history.[6] If lost crews could speak, they might have found *brilliant* an infelicitous word choice, but it certainly exemplified shortcomings in Sixth Fleet sub tactics.

As far as Nambu was concerned, sentry lines turned subs into sitting ducks. He'd even protested against them during a January 1944 conference at Truk. The loss of six subs had proved him right, but at great cost.

Unfortunately, the loss in May was nothing compared to the disaster that followed in June. The IJN was still preparing for the decisive naval battle, even though the location kept shifting closer to Japan. The situation worsened when the IJN High Command made a stupendous miscalculation by predicting the final battle would occur near Palau in the Caroline Islands. Instead, U.S. naval forces invaded Saipan, Tinian, and Guam nearly a thousand miles to the north, taking Japan completely by surprise.

The Allied assault on Saipan began on the morning of June 11, 1944, and Vice Adm. Takeo Takagi, CINC of the Sixth Fleet, immediately ordered his subs to head north to the Mariana Islands. Unfortunately, by the time they arrived, U.S. antisub forces were waiting. Eight more subs were lost due to the efficacy of Ultra intelligence and disorganized dashing about at the behest of Sixth Fleet higher ups.[7]

Additionally, the U.S. invasion took a devastating toll on the Sixth Fleet command structure, which happened to be located on Saipan. Admiral Takagi had based his headquarters on the island, thinking it an ideal location from which to direct his sub squadrons' southern arm. Now Takagi found himself under attack by Allied invasion forces. Abandoning his headquarters, he and his staff fled into Saipan's mountainous jungle. This brought an abrupt halt to sub operations, which had to be transferred to Truk, where SubRon 7's Rear Adm. Noboru Owada took over. Owada immediately called for the rescue of his commander in chief, so subs were sent to evacuate Takagi. They never stood a chance. Saipan's surrounding waters were so choked with Allied forces, it was impossible for a boat to approach the island, let alone effect a landing.

Takagi called off his own rescue on July 2. Four days later he sent his final message:

I AM PLEASED TO HAVE DEFENDED SAIPAN TO THE DEATH
AND TO HAVE WITNESSED THE BRILLIANT ACHIEVEMENTS
OF THE SUBMARINES UNDER MY COMMAND. COMMANDING
ALL SIXTH FLEET PERSONNEL REMAINING . . . I AM GOING TO
CHARGE INTO AN ENEMY POSITION. BANZAI![8]

That was the last anyone heard from Takagi. The Sixth Fleet's commander in chief, the third CINC in three years, was presumably wiped out along with the rest of his staff in the ensuing charge. Three thousand Japanese soldiers, sailors, and airmen fought to the death on Saipan. The enemy bloodbath was so remarkable that even the U.S. Marines were impressed.

After the Sixth Fleet's humiliating defeat, the IJN's image reached an all-time low. Vice Adm. Shigeyoshi Miwa assumed command of sub operations in mid-July. Losses were so catastrophic, he didn't have much to work with. The fall of Saipan, Tinian, and Guam meant Japan would now be in range of the B-29 Superfortress, a high-altitude bomber developed specifically for attacking Japan.

Miwa had served as a Sixth Fleet squadron commander at Pearl Harbor. He was experienced, pragmatic, and under no illusions as to what he'd inherited. To anyone else, the situation would have seemed hopeless. Nevertheless, Miwa, like the IJN High Command, was determined to fight.

One reason Allied naval forces were having such success in the Pacific had to do with Ultra intelligence. The other reason was radar. By 1943 every U.S. sub was equipped with radar, but Japan didn't begin installing the new invention until 18 months later, and even then it was an inferior version. U.S. radar was able to detect Japanese planes, ships, and submarines at a far greater distance than Japan could spot U.S. forces. And when Americans applied radar to fire control, its effectiveness was devastating.

The loss of Saipan had major repercussions beyond crippling the Sixth Fleet. The Allies had called for unconditional surrender. Now it wasn't just a case of playing defense; Japan's survival as a nation was at stake. This contributed to a dramatic change in strategy. Whereas Japanese naval forces had bravely defended the homeland by engaging the enemy with an array of modern subs, planes, and ships, these forces, and the well-trained men needed to guide them, were in increasingly short supply. What had seemed unthinkable to many in the high command six months ago would now become the strategy of last resort.

The impact of this change would be enormous for the *Sen-toku* squadron. Though still under construction, the *I-400* subs faced a seemingly impregnable Panama Canal; meanwhile the Allies were moving so close to Japan that Imperial military forces were being either methodically destroyed or hopelessly left behind. Importantly, the advent of radar combined with the use of Ultra intelligence meant the Allies knew virtually every move a Japanese sub would make. Though construction of the *I-400* subs and their *Seiran* cargo remained a secret, it didn't take a psychic to guess that all would become known once the subs were operational.

Sixth Fleet activity dropped nearly to zero in late summer 1944, while Japanese subs were finally equipped with radar. This meant the chances of the *Segundo* meeting an I-boat on her first war patrol were small. Miwa wanted his subs in the safety of Japanese waters while he used the waning summer to develop a new strategy. How much longer Japan's home waters would remain safe was an open question. Regardless of the answer, Miwa needed time. By September, the Sixth Fleet was again ready to prosecute the war with a new strategy that would unnerve the Allies. Japan was preparing to launch her first wave of suicide attacks. Sixth Fleet subs would be the tip of the spear.

UNFORTUNATELY FOR NAMBU, it was back to being a mole. After a brief time captaining a combat sub, during which he'd nearly been sunk several times, he'd been reassigned to outfitting the *I-362*. It was the exact same role Fulp had had at Portsmouth, except that the *I-362* wasn't a combat sub—it was the first in a new line of underwater cargo carriers that Fujimori had recommended.

Nambu left Kure on the *I-362*'s maiden voyage. It was August 23, 1944, just days before the *Segundo* left Pearl Harbor for the South Pacific. The first thing Nambu noticed, once he'd gotten under way, was just how shoddily built his new sub was. The bridge vibration was so strong that a lookout using high-powered binoculars couldn't see a thing because his body shook so much. This was a serious problem, since lookouts were as important to a sub's survival as radar and often more reliable.

Nambu knew the problem could be solved by adding steel plate to the bridge, but he might not have appreciated just how little steel plate there was to be had. U.S. submarines had cut off Japanese supply routes, and few ships bearing raw material were getting through. The situation was bad enough that by 1944 the Japanese government was taking metal coins out of circulation and melting them down for reuse as war matériel. A decree had even been issued declaring all metal pots, pans, and utensils property of the state, and they were collected as part of a national scrap drive.[9] Since Japanese shipyards were running low on steel, they had no choice. They had to cut corners.

Nambu had only a month to train his crew, far less time than usual. A shortage of men and boats, and the increasingly dire fate of stranded troops, demanded he get under way as soon as possible. Nambu's crew weren't green only from inexperience; they were green from seasickness as well. He intended to overcome their deficiency through intensive drilling, but an inexperienced crew wasn't his only handicap. Compared to the *I-174*, the new sub was a "tortoise,"[10] built for transport rather than speed. If that wasn't bad enough, the sub's radar was faulty.[11] Nambu tried not to let it bother him—he swallowed the bitterness and pressed on. Every time he turned around, however, something seemed to break down. It was not an auspicious beginning for a new sub.

Nambu couldn't help but wonder about the wisdom of the Japanese High Command. At the beginning of the war, the IJN had performed well and achieved much. But did Imperial forces really have to be spread so thin? Had anyone ever thought how to supply such a vast network of men? The obvious lack of planning disturbed him. A submarine was best suited for cutting enemy supply routes, not for transporting cargo. He couldn't forgive those in the Sixth Fleet who preferred to use a submarine as a mole rather than to attack the enemy.[12] Something was wrong.

After resupplying the 4,000 stranded troops on the Micronesian island of Nauru, Nambu sailed for Truk, where things were not much better. Once home to the Sixth Fleet and Yamamoto's principal headquarters, Truk was eerily quiet. Nambu could see that the island had been left to wither on the vine. The emptiness was chilling.[13] The message from Tokyo was that they could still win the war. For anyone in the field the evidence was in stark contrast.

The truth of the matter was that by the fall of 1944, the mortality rate for Sixth Fleet submarines was astronomical. By the end of the war, nearly 100 subs would be sunk, virtually the entire Japanese sub force. Even by September 1944, many of Nambu's colleagues were dead, and given the way things were going, he could expect to join them soon. It was Nambu's duty to show courage in the face of despair. Though outwardly he maintained his resolve, inwardly he had his doubts.

By the time Nambu returned to Kure, Japanese military strategy had radically changed. The loss of Saipan, followed by the successful U.S. invasion of Ulithi, put U.S. fighting forces in uncomfortable proximity to Japan. Ulithi, a previously unknown backwater in the Caroline Islands, boasted the world's fourth-largest lagoon. It was a natural staging area for the U.S. invasion of the Philippines and Japan. Combined Fleet Headquarters decided that the best way to delay an invasion would be to launch an attack on Ulithi. Two Sixth Fleet subs were charged to carry out the mission. While Nambu awaited orders, modifications began on a new breed of suicide sub.

After spending two months outfitting the *I-361* (yet another cargo carrier), Nambu was relieved of command and ordered to Sasebo.[14] He was finally getting his wish. He was being made captain of an offensive submarine, a brand-new boat so secret that nobody knew its designation. It was no ordinary sub. It was the *I-401*, the flagship in a new series of boats called the *Sen-toku*, or "special submarine" squadron. Conceived by Admiral Yamamoto to attack New York City and Washington, thereby changing the course of the great Pacific war, the *I-400*s' current mission was to bomb the Panama Canal.

But Nambu wasn't the only Sixth Fleet officer entrusted with this game-changing assignment. A commander had been put in charge of the attack squadron. He was so well regarded that many considered him the only officer to be reliably entrusted with such an audacious task, a mission so freighted with importance that the top naval command were the only ones who could green-light it.

As Nambu would soon learn, his new commander, fresh from the Indian Ocean, was Tatsunosuke Ariizumi. It was a personnel appointment that would change his life.

SHIP SIZE COMPARISON CHART

IMPERIAL JAPANESE NAVY *I-401* SUBMARINE - 400 FEET

IMPERIAL JAPANESE NAVY *I-14* SUBMARINE - 373 FEET

U.S. NAVY FLETCHER-CLASS DESTROYER - 376 FEET

U.S. NAVY BALAO-CLASS SUBMARINE - 312 FEET

PART IV

THE MISSION

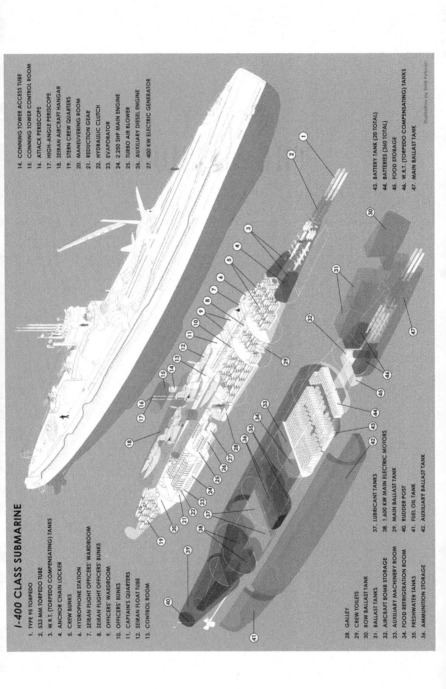

I-400 CLASS SUBMARINE

1. TYPE 95 TORPEDO
2. 533 MM TORPEDO TUBE
3. W.R.T. (TORPEDO COMPENSATING) TANKS
4. ANCHOR CHAIN LOCKER
5. CREW BUNKS
6. HYDROPHONE STATION
7. SEIRAN FLIGHT OFFICERS' WARDROOM
8. SEIRAN FLIGHT OFFICERS' BUNKS
9. OFFICERS' WARDROOM
10. OFFICERS' BUNKS
11. CAPTAIN'S QUARTERS
12. SEIRAN FLOAT TUBE
13. CONTROL ROOM

14. CONNING TOWER ACCESS TUBE
15. CONNING TOWER CONTROL ROOM
16. ATTACK PERISCOPE
17. HIGH-ANGLE PERISCOPE
18. SEIRAN AIRCRAFT HANGAR
19. STERN CREW QUARTERS
20. MANEUVERING ROOM
21. REDUCTION GEAR
22. HYDRAULIC CLUTCH
23. EVAPORATOR
24. 2,250 SHP MAIN ENGINE
25. TURBO AIR BLOWER
26. AUXILIARY DIESEL ENGINE
27. 400 KW ELECTRIC GENERATOR

28. GALLEY
29. CREW TOILETS
30. BOW BALLAST TANK
31. BALLAST TANKS
32. AIRCRAFT BOMB STORAGE
33. AUXILIARY MACHINERY ROOM
34. FOOD REFRIGERATION ROOM
35. FRESHWATER TANKS
36. AMMUNITION STORAGE

37. LUBRICANT TANKS
38. 1,400 KW MAIN ELECTRIC MOTORS
39. MAIN BALLAST TANK
40. RUDDER POST
41. FUEL OIL TANK
42. AUXILIARY BALLAST TANK

43. BATTERY TANK (20 TOTAL)
44. BATTERIES (360 TOTAL)
45. FOOD STORAGE
46. W.R.T. (TORPEDO COMPENSATING) TANKS
47. MAIN BALLAST TANK

Illustration by Emils Petersic

Chapter 17

NAMBU AND THE *I-401*

The *I-8* docked at Yokosuka Naval Base on October 9, 1944.[1] The *Sen-toku* squadron was in the final stages of construction when Ariizumi left his sub for the last time and hurried to Tokyo to be briefed by Yasuo Fujimori of the Naval General Staff.[2]

Ariizumi knew the *I-400* subs were a career-making assignment. Many in the Imperial Japanese Navy considered attacking the Panama Canal to be as important as the latest suicide weapon, a human-guided torpedo called a *kaiten*. Executed properly, the *Sen-toku* attack might help Japan fend off defeat. Ariizumi felt honored to be given responsibility for such an important mission.

The *I-400* subs were to be organized into Submarine Squadron 1 (SubRon 1) and based in Kure. SubRon 1 was the only Sixth Fleet squadron consisting entirely of subs—no surface flagship or tender would be needed for their mission. Initially, SubRon 1 would consist of four subs: the *I-400* and *I-401* and the *I-13* and *I-14*. If all went well, three of the four subs would launch before the end of the year, with the *I-14* following shortly thereafter.

As Fujimori described it, the amount of men and matériel allocated to the program was nothing short of incredible. Nearly 600 submariners would man the four subs. The *I-400* and *I-401* alone accounted for more than half that number. This didn't include their *Seiran* pilots and observers, or the maintenance technicians, ground crew, and armorers needed for land and sea assignment. In other words, the underwater aircraft carriers and their support personnel totaled nearly 1,000, almost as many men as were found in the average Japanese infantry battalion.

The amount of manpower necessary to construct the *Sen-toku* squadron was equally enormous. So great were the resources required to build four submarines that three separate naval yards were employed, both military and civilian. Supplying steel created such a drain on Japan's shipbuilding program that naval higher-ups constantly complained about the shortage.

And that wasn't all. There were four additional subs in various stages of completion: the *I-402* would be ready by July 1945, and the *I-404* (the next furthest along) would follow later in the year. As for the *I-403* and *I-405*, the former was in the early stages of construction, while the latter hadn't been built yet. As for the 12 remaining boats *I-406* through *I-417*, they were paper subs only. They'd never got past the planning stage.

The resources devoted to the *Sen-toku* subs were astonishing given the damage the Japanese war machine had sustained. It signaled just how strongly the NGS believed in the mission.[3] Japan's defense perimeter may have been crumbling, but if the subs could destroy the Panama Canal, thereby stopping war matériel and reinforcements, they just might prevent compliance with the Allied demand for unconditional surrender.

Ariizumi was glad to hear that his subs were nearing completion, but he must have felt concern as to whether there would be enough time both for sea trials and for a full training schedule. The earliest he could start would be around the New Year. Given how poorly the war was going, his squadron would have to rush to get ready.

After meeting with Fujimori, Ariizumi went to Shizuoka to spend a few days with his wife, Matsu, and their five children.[4] It's reasonable to assume he was glad to see them after such a long absence. Ariizumi may have been a war criminal, but he still loved his family. Not much is known about this visit except that he drank heavily during his stay.[5] Whether it was to relieve the stress of the Indian Ocean massacres, to celebrate his new appointment, or just because he liked to drink, we can't know for sure.

Ariizumi could be touchy, though. On a previous home visit, Matsu had served grilled sea bream the night before his sub was to leave. When Ariizumi ate only the bottom portion, she made the mistake of serving him the remainder for breakfast. When Ariizumi saw what she'd done, he erupted.

"I'm about to go on a boat!" he shouted, throwing his plate on the floor. "It's bad luck to serve fish with no bottom!"[6]

Meanwhile work continued on the *I-400* subs.

LESS THAN A month later, Nambu arrived at the Sixth Fleet Submarine Base in Sasebo. It was November 1, 1944, and a chilly wind blew off Mount Eboshi.[7] Sasebo was a Pacific-facing port located on Kyushu, Japan's southernmost island. Nambu's experience captaining mole operations would prove useful in commanding the *I-401*. Instead of transporting food to remote islands, he'd be carrying three special attack planes to bomb the Panama Canal. It was definitely a step up. Not every sub captain had the discipline necessary to hide from the enemy. Nambu might have thought it a pathetic skill, but he soon learned just how handy it could be.

As Nambu strode across the naval yard, sparks rained down in a hellish waterfall while the pounding of hammers assaulted his ears.[8] When he finally saw the *I-401*, he was shocked—nothing had prepared him for her overwhelming size. The boat was so huge, you could easily stack one of his former subs on her deck.[9] And that wasn't all. The *I-401* was so secret that many of the guards didn't know her true identity.[10]

A World War II sub was a lot more complicated than it looked. It wasn't just a single hollow tube with a conning tower on top—it was three separate components welded together. The largest component was the sub's pressure hull, which contained her habitable spaces such as the engines and control room. Next came her ballast and fuel tanks, which wrapped around the outside of the hull. These were filled with seawater, air, or fuel depending on the need. The third element was the sub's superstructure, which sat atop the pressure hull. On the *I-401*, the superstructure supported the sub's teak decking and was semipermeable to allow water (or air) to flow underneath; that's why, when a submarine submerged, water could be seen spouting into the air. There was essentially nothing between a sub's pressure hull and her deck except emptiness.

TOPSIDE

BRIDGE   The next thing Nambu would have noticed was the *I-401*'s sail, also called a fairwater, sitting atop her hull like a castle turret. It was offset from the sub's centerline nearly seven feet to port,*[11] to compensate for the weight of the aircraft hangar.[12] Wrapped around the top of the sail was the bridge, the preferred location for surface attacks. It was a spartan affair, open to the elements, that could be used only when the sub was above water. The bridge was like an oversize crow's nest. It contained five 20X pressure-proof binoculars;[13] a repeater compass; a set of collision, dive, and battle station alarms; and a single Type 96[14] 25mm antiaircraft gun mounted on her aft section.[15] When the dive alarm sounded, as many as eight officers and lookouts had to clear the deck in under a minute. Jumping through the narrow bridge hatch, they slid 25 feet down a ladder,[16] like firemen down a pole. Less-experienced submariners burned their hands on the long slide down.[17] At least there was a three-foot-thick canvas hassock to absorb their landing at the bottom.[18] Occasionally a crewman lost his grip and plunged down the ladder, taking everyone with him.[19] In that case not even a hassock could cushion their fall.

The sub's two periscopes (attack and high angle) towered above the bridge, along with various radar and radio antennas. Additionally, there was a watch station on the air search radar column.[20] The added height enabled a lookout to see farther than at deck level. This was important because a sub sat so low in the water, it couldn't see the horizon 12 miles away. The *I-401*'s extraordinary

---

* The actual distance was six feet ten inches.

height made this less of a problem, every foot helped. Of course, most subs lurked at periscope depth waiting for a ship to pass. Nevertheless, lookouts were crucial when the sub was on the surface, especially for spotting aircraft or smoke from an enemy ship's stack. The *I-401* may have had the latest surface and air radar, but no captain relied on it 100 percent. Sub lookouts were as important during World War II as they had been during the glory days of sail.

GUN DECK Just beneath the bridge was the 100-foot-long gun deck. Sitting on the roof of the aircraft hangar, it was exaggeratingly described as a promenade worthy of the Queen Mary.[21] Three waterproof triple-mount AA guns took up most of the area, one forward and two aft. Each gun required two men to operate and had its own ammunition scuttle. A pointer controlled windage from the left seat, while a trainer controlled elevation from the right.[22] The target was framed in an open-ring gunsight, and the pointer fired the weapon by operating a foot pedal. Since each gun spat 220 rounds per minute and a single 25mm shell weighed five and a half pounds, they were a healthy defense against aircraft.[23]

Gun crews liked fighting it out on the surface: looking your enemy in the eye while doing something about it was preferable to waiting for the explosion of a torpedo. One problem with surface fighting, however, was that the motion of the sea made it difficult to fire accurately. Additionally, a single hit from an enemy shell could easily hole a conning tower, rendering a sub unable to submerge. Since a submarine's true purpose is to destroy its enemies with a torpedo, most sub captains preferred a quick dive to a surface shoot-out, Hollywood movies not withstanding.

DECK The most obvious feature on the *I-401*'s deck was the 102-foot-long aircraft hangar.[24] Stretching over a quarter of the sub's length, the hangar was only a few inches shy of 12 feet in diameter[25] and was capped by a massive cone-shaped door. The hangar was ribbed like a whale inside, and there were racks for spare parts, maintenance tools,[26] and one set of *Seiran* pontoons. The hangar was so large, it presented a serious risk if flooded. A two-inch rubber gasket kept the door watertight, but there was always a chance the enemy might hole the hangar. In that case, the sub could release 220 tons of fuel to offset the lost buoyancy.[27] Britain's *M-2* had taught the Japanese well.

CATAPULT AND CRANE   The *I-401*'s catapult was custom built and, at 85 feet, 4 inches in length,[28] longer than any catapult in the IJN. It was also the most powerful catapult the Japanese built during World War II.[29] Using compressed air, it could launch a four-ton plane every four minutes at a speed of six knots.[30] Catapult rails extended from inside the hangar and ran the length of the foredeck. As they approached the bow there was a three-degree incline to help give the airplane lift. There was also a collapsible crane located on the port side of the foredeck just in front of the hangar door.* When not in use, the crane lay flush with the deck.

ADDITIONAL DECK ARMAMENT   In addition to the bridge's defensive armament, the *I-401* carried a Type 11 140mm gun on her after deck. The largest submarine gun in use, it was the same type as found on the battleship *Nagato*. Better described as a cannon than a deck gun, it was capable of firing an 84-pound projectile 16,400 yards at 2,789 feet per second.[31] After the *Seiran* and Type 95 torpedoes, the *I-401*'s deck gun was its most dangerous weapon.

---

* Nambu recalled that the crane was able to lift 3.5 tons, but he was probably wrong about this. A *Seiran* weighed approximately 7,300 pounds without pilot, observer, or fuel. Fully loaded, she weighed close to 10,000 pounds. As a result, the lifting capacity of the *I-401*'s crane was probably at least 5 tons and may have been as much as 12 tons. See Nobukiyo Nambu, *Beikidoukantai wo Kishuseyo: Sensuikuubo I-401 Kanchou No Shuki* [*Surprise Attack on the American Fleet! Memoir of the I-401 Aircraft-Carrying Submarine by Its Captain*] (Tokyo: Fuami Shobo, 1988), p. 180.

HATCHES   Nambu's sub had seven deck hatches, which granted access to important areas like the torpedo and engine rooms.[32] Twenty-five inches in diameter, they were a comfortable fit for the Japanese.[33] Each hatch, plus the sub's two main induction valves and hangar door, was wired to a board in the control room that indicated whether they were open or shut. You never knew when the sub might need to dive in a hurry, so close attention was paid to this board to avoid accidental flooding. Occasionally, when the sub was cruising on the surface, a high wave swept over the main induction valve, causing a fluctuation in the boat's internal pressure. When that happened, ears would pop and the engines would backfire, filling the sub with fumes. In addition to feeding the diesel engines with oxygen, the main induction provided battery and hull ventilation as well as some of the only fresh air the crew ever breathed. Everyone knew when the main induction was open because fresh oxygen (as good as sunshine) filled the boat.

STEALTH COATINGS   Being the largest sub in the world had its drawbacks. One of them was a huge radar signature. To compensate, the sub's sail was indented at its base, to reflect radar waves back into the sea. In case this wasn't enough, the *I-401* had two anechoic coatings on its hull, one above the waterline, the other below.[34] According to Japanese navy personnel, the coating above the water absorbed radar waves, while the coating below the water was for "sound [echo ranging] protection."[35] Though the ability to fool sonar is questionable, there is some indication that the below-the-line coating helped dampen any sound emanating from the sub.[36] This helped the sub avoid detection from anyone listening for her with a hydrophone. The coatings were black, lumpy, and easily abraded. They also reduced the *I-401*'s speed by a knot.[37] If anyone questioned their efficacy, Nambu wasn't one of them. Anything that increased his sub's stealth factor was welcome, especially since the Panama Canal was so heavily guarded.

INTERIOR

It's impossible to get lost aboard a submarine—all compartments are on the same horizontal axis, save the conning tower, and each compartment is sequential, one leading to the other. This means only a fool can't find his way. But the *I-401* easily made fools out of newcomers.

The first thing Nambu would have found confusing is that instead of each compartment having only two hatches, one leading forward and the other aft, four of the sub's eight compartments had an additional hatch in the hull, leading into what appeared to be a second sub running alongside.[38] This gave the impression that the *I-401* was two subs welded together, with hatches connecting the starboard and port halves. There was an important reason for this twin hull configuration: it provided a more stable launch platform for three fully loaded attack planes. Still, two interconnected subs lying side by side would have disoriented Nambu, just as it would any submariner who was used to moving only forward or aft. Port or starboard had never been an option until now.

NO. 1 COMPARTMENT: TORPEDO ROOM   The *I-401*'s torpedo room was located in the bow compartment. Most submarines have only one forward torpedo room, while the *I-401* boasted two, one stacked on top of the other in a duplex arrangement. It was an unprecedented configuration for a World War II sub and immensely gratifying for any captain eager to sink ships.

A typical Balao-class sub carried six bow tubes, while the *I-401* had eight, four in the lower compartment and four in the upper.[39] Though a Balao sub also had four tubes in her stern while the *I-401* had none, and carried 24 torpedoes to the *I-401*'s 20, no convoy or antisub patrol relished a sub that could launch eight of the war's best torpedoes nearly all at once.

In truth, U.S. subs were at a disadvantage when it came to torpedoes though this would change as the war progressed. The Mark 14 was most accurate when fired from less than a mile away.[40] As Japanese naval tactics improved, this became increasingly difficult, forcing U.S. subs to launch from a greater distance. Japanese subs faced no such hindrance. Their Type 95 torpedoes had a range of five to seven miles.[41] It was like bringing a lance to a knife fight.

Each of the *I-401*'s torpedo tubes had two sets of doors, an inner set for loading and an outer set for exiting. The inner doors were strong enough to withstand the crushing force of the sea, and neither door could be opened at the same time, to prevent flooding. Spare torpedoes sat on racks just behind the loaded tubes and took up so much room, the crew slept on top of the ordnance.[42]

One detail Hollywood movies rarely got right was the sound a torpedo made exiting a sub. In the case of the *I-401*, a hissing of compressed air, followed by water flowing back into the tube, could be heard, though only in the torpedo room, since the compartment's watertight doors were shut during battle. Japanese torpedoes were quieter than their noisy American counterparts, but a slight shudder could still be felt in the torpedo room whenever a "fish" launched.

NO. 2 AND 3 COMPARTMENTS (STARBOARD): FORWARD CREW BERTHING   Directly aft of the torpedo room was the first of three crew compartments for enlisted men. The *I-401* carried 174 crew and 21 officers,[43] though the total number exceeded 200 once pilots and aircraft technicians were counted.* There were never enough berths for enlisted men. Officers and CPOs may have merited their own bunk, but third-class ratings slept wherever they found space,[44] including on rice sacks.

The two forward crew compartments extended aft for nearly a quarter of the sub's starboard side. Each compartment had a three-tiered bunk configuration similar to the *Segundo*. Despite the *I-401*'s size, however, conditions were just as cramped, with one

---

* According to Nambu, the *I-401* had 204 officers and crew. Nobukiyo Nambu, *Beikidoukantai wo Kishuseyo: Sensuikuubo I-401 Kanchou No Shuki* [*Surprise Attack on the American Fleet! Memoir of the I-401 Aircraft-Carrying Submarine by Its Captain*] (Tokyo: Fuami Shobo, 1988), p. 221. The *I-400* carried fewer crew.

important difference: Nambu's sub carried almost three times as many men.

Each bunk hung suspended on chains and could be folded up as necessary.[45] The crew's gear was stored in floor lockers beneath the bottommost bunk.[46] "Hot bunking," or sharing a bed, was also common: when one man was on duty, another man slept in his bunk, and vice versa. Beds were often used as dining tables,[47] and the forward crew quarters also had a section for toilets, or heads. The facilities were standard squat-style openings connected to a sanitary tank. Heavy usage and excretory inaccuracy caused by rough seas guaranteed that no one lingered.[48] Some sub captains allowed their crew an occasional shower,[49] but fresh water was in such short supply that bathing was the first luxury dispensed with once war commenced. Officers were limited to one cup of water per day for washing.[50] Some used sake to wipe themselves down,[51] though it didn't help much since officers were limited to a single hand towel.[52]

NO. 2, 3, 4 COMPARTMENTS (PORT): OFFICERS' QUARTERS AND WARDROOM   On the port side of the no. 2 compartment was the officers' galley. Some captains enjoyed special meals, but Nambu tended to waive this privilege.[53] There was also berthing for six warrant officers and space for the hydrophone room. Sound is the most important sense a sub can have below periscope depth. It enables her to locate an enemy or, if she is too noisy, betrays her own position. Sound heads located outside the sub's hull picked up underwater noise and relayed it to the hydrophone operator. The sea might have been noisy, but an experienced sound man could read it like a book. He could tell the difference between snapping shrimp and the click of a depth-charge detonator. He could even tell whether a ship was approaching or receding, as well as what type it was.

The officer's wardroom was on the port side, opposite the crew's quarters. It was capacious compared to that of the *Segundo* and doubled as a dining room or off-duty lounge for the flagship's officers. The wardroom featured a pair of wooden tables in its center with bench-style seating and sleeping berths along both sides.[54] The berths were double-stacked, sat upon a chest of wooden drawers, and had privacy curtains like a sleeper on a Pullman car. The wardroom also had a fan and was trimmed in wood, most of it varnished—something you'd never find aboard an American sub.[55] Part of the officers' quarters sat next to a bomb magazine though, so not every aspect was luxurious.

Dolls softened the surroundings of many Sixth Fleet subs. The *I-401* had one in her wardroom.[56] A demure, white-faced Japanese woman dressed in an exquisite kimono, she was a sentimental item intended to remind the officers of home. Though no Betty Grable pinup, many officers found comfort in her.

Ariizumi's and Nambu's cabins were located next to one another near the control room. Both cabins were small with a tiny desk, bed, and hardly enough room to change one's mind. Nevertheless, they provided the privacy necessary for command.

NO. 4 COMPARTMENT (STARBOARD): CREW'S BERTHING No. 4 was the last crew compartment in the forward half of the boat. Enlisted men were segregated from their officers aboard Sixth Fleet subs, just as they were in the U.S. Navy. But sealing 200 men inside a cramped combat sub bred an informality that softened differences in rank. Even the dress code was relaxed. An enlisted man's uniform consisted of a short-sleeved shirt, shorts, socks, rubber-soled shoes, and a short-brimmed cap.[57] Just as there was leeway in what U.S. enlisted men wore aboard a fleet boat, the *I-401*'s men exercised similar sartorial discretion. Some went shirtless, limiting themselves to shorts and straw sandals; others wore only a *fundoshi*, or loincloth, when working in the hotter parts of the sub. Officers were more regular in their dress, but the longer the patrol, the quicker they dispensed with formality.

Nothing affected submarine fashion like high temperatures. Some days it was so hot, men slept naked.[58] The *I-401* had air conditioning, but South Seas heat easily overwhelmed her cooling plant. Humidity was also a problem. A *Seiran*'s avionics were particularly vulnerable, as was the sub's electronic equipment. The airplane hangar was packed with desiccant to reduce humidity,[59] but for the men inside the sub, it was a dripping steam bath.

Not much attention was paid to the habitability of Sixth Fleet subs.[60] Creature comforts were few, and crews didn't receive the rest they needed after each mission. Add to this a shortage of trained men, and efficiency declined as the war progressed.

The crew offset their grim industrial setting with a few personal touches. Some of the most popular were Japanese keepsake dolls. Mothers, sisters, and girlfriends made *imon ningyo* for their sons, brothers, and boyfriends to keep them company on their long, lonely voyages. They were a familiar sight in the crew quarters, and it wasn't unusual to hear a man bid his companion good night before turning in.[61] At least he knew he wouldn't die alone.

Sub hygiene was also questionable. Though there was water for brushing teeth,[62] many men chewed gum instead.[63] Most grew beards,[64] but haircuts were given to those who wanted them,[65] especially since a shaved head helped prevent lice (a constant problem in close confines). Submarine living conditions were undeniably tight. Still, Japanese home life had prepared crews for close quarters and they quickly adapted.

One of a crew's few personal luxuries was smoking. Favorite brands included *Kinishi, Homare,* and *Cherry,*[66] and most men were heavy smokers. Smoking was allowed in many parts of the sub, but cigarettes were in such short supply they were considered a treat.

Another problem affecting the *Sen-toku* subs was rats: it was impossible to keep them off the boats. This wasn't unusual.[67] U.S. subs were plagued by cockroaches. One Sixth Fleet sub set up a rice feeder for their rats; others adopted them as pets.[68] Inevitably, there was the odd sailor who trained them for his personal enjoyment. But having rats wasn't all bad. Sixth Fleet crews often joked, "Safely returning subs have rats. Sinking ones don't."[69] They had a point.

NO. 5 COMPARTMENT (PORT): CONTROL ROOM Though relations on a sub could be informal, that didn't extend to the control room, where only the strictest protocol prevailed. The control room was the sub's nerve center. It was where diving, surfacing, and navigation functions were managed as well as where every important environmental system was monitored. Though the conning tower duplicated many of these stations, they were generally limited to combat use.

The *I-401*'s control room was far larger than that of a Balao-class sub. (There was even a head for the convenience of those on duty.) Controls included the hydraulic vent manifold, which flooded a sub's ballast tanks, enabling it to submerge; the high-pressure blow manifolds, which emptied the ballast tanks of water so the sub could surface; the trim manifolds, which pumped water from one ballast tank to another (or into the sea) to help a submerged sub achieve equilibrium; the air and ventilation systems, which kept the crew breathing; and the main distribution panel, which managed the sub's electrical supply. The sub's radio shack, radar room, ship's office, engineer's log room, and access to one of its main ammunition scuttles were also located in the compartment. In fact, the only vital systems not found in the control room were the physical propulsion systems, torpedoes, defensive armament, and food prep. Nevertheless, the control room kept close tabs on all of them.

Although a sub's operating principles were basic in nature, her engineering was not. Every inch of space in the control room was covered by a bewildering array of dials, levers, valve wheels, gauges, meters, circuit breakers, and control knobs. Nothing made sense unless you'd been to sub school. The piping schematic alone would have confounded anyone unfamiliar with sub design. Crew members might have preferred sinking enemy ships, but the truth of sub life was more prosaic; much of their time was spent protecting against the sea's invasiveness.

BALLAST TANKS   Just as controlling altitude is vital to a plane's operation, maintaining buoyancy is critical to a sub's survival. Unsurprisingly, the *I-401* had four types of ballast tanks. The first were the main ballast tanks, which wrapped around the underside of her pressure hull. When a sub wanted to submerge, she filled these tanks with seawater, which entered through flood ports located near her keel. Once flooded, the tanks grew heavy, pulling her downward. When the sub needed to surface, compressed air was used to blow seawater out through the main vents, increasing her buoyancy.

The main ballast tanks did the heavy lifting of surfacing the boat, but other ballast tanks were necessary for specific maneuvers. For example, when a sub needed to dive in a hurry, the negative tank was flooded. Located underneath the forward part of the sub, it quickly gave the boat the descent angle she needed to dive. The negative tank was especially helpful when the sub was on the surface and had to escape a fast-approaching enemy. In turn, when a sub needed to surface in a hurry, the safety tank was emptied, or "blown." Located amidships to help maintain the sub's balance, "blowing the safety" was the fastest way to restore buoyancy in an emergency.

Variable ballast tanks were considered "variable" because they could be used to store either fuel or seawater. This was necessary because when a sub consumed fuel, it lost weight and became more buoyant. To compensate, seawater was pumped into the variable tanks to make up the difference.

Surfacing, submerging, and maintaining equilibrium were three critical tasks that took up much of the control room's focus. Given their importance, one of the most common expressions aboard a Japanese submarine was "Blow the main tank!" *Blowing* means using compressed air to force water out of the tank, thereby improving buoyancy and allowing the sub to surface. On a somewhat amusing note, Nambu used a Japan-ized version of the order: *"Men tanku burou!"* which was phonetically equivalent to the English.

HELM AND DIVE PLANES   A sub constantly had to switch between the two-dimensional world on the surface and the three-dimensional one below. To help with this, the control room had three "steering" stations. The first was the helm, a large metal wheel used to control the rudder in the stern. The helm directed the forward motion of a sub both when surfaced and submerged. The helm wasn't enough for steering underwater, however—a sub required dive planes as well.

The dive planes were two sets of fins located on the outside of the *I-401*'s hull, one set near the bow, the other near her stern. The dive planes enabled her to ascend or descend depending on their angle. When operating on the surface, the *I-401* kept her dive planes rigged in an upward position. She only lowered them to navigate underwater. At first glance, the *I-401*'s bow planes hardly seemed large enough to control the sub,[70] but Nambu found them more than adequate.[71]

Two dive planesmen stood side by side at separate steering stations, one controlling the bow, the other the stern. An array of gauges stared them in the face, including a depth gauge, a speed indicator, and a bubble indicator, which showed the boat's up-or-down angle. An experienced planesman could keep the boat so steady, the sub's depth gauge never budged an inch.

NAVIGATION   Since the central helm station and master compass were located in the control room, much of the sub's navigation was done there. It had a small table for manually plotting the sub's position and tracking enemy targets. Secondary firing solutions were also developed there, to reconfirm those made in the conning tower.

Sub navigation was not very sophisticated during the war. If a sub knew her position within 50 miles of her actual location, it was considered accurate. Celestial navigation was common, and many a navigator scrambled onto a sub's bridge at night to read the stars. Plotting a sub's position was as much art as science.

RADAR   The *I-401* carried three different types of radar, all of which had a station in the control room and outlets on the aft part of the sail. The Mark 3 Model 1 air search radar was used to spot planes, while the Mark 2 Model 2 was used to find surface ships. It also had a nondirectional antenna for passive radar detection as well as an omnidirectional antenna, a direction finder, and a target-detection antenna.[72]

The principle behind radar was almost magical. The *I-401* would send out a radio wave that "bounced" off an object, like a ship or plane, and returned to the sub, providing the target's range (distance) and bearing (direction). If the *I-401* tracked the target long enough, it was also possible to deduce its course and speed. The distinctive circular scope and secondhand sweep of light were intended to ensure that the enemy never approached the sub without warning. That was the theory at least. But Japanese radar was still in its infancy and prone to break down. It might have been an improvement over binoculars, especially in poor weather, but it was frequently frustrating.

RADIO ROOM   The radio room, where the *I-401* connected to the outside world, was located on the port side of the control room. It would soon become a favorite place for *Seiran* pilots to loiter while the sub was under way.[73] The communications officer responded to a plethora of messages via shortwave radio—much to Nambu's annoyance, since he preferred radio silence. Orders from Japan were transmitted at night, when a sub was surfaced, but the *I-401* could also receive messages at periscope depth via a special antenna mounted on her bridge.

NO. 5 (STARBOARD): AUXILIARY ROOM   Opposite the control room on the starboard side of the sub was a special compartment, which at least one source claims was used to overhaul *Seiran* engines. A hatch 31 inches in diameter connected the compartment to the control room.[74] There was also an overhead access tube leading to the aircraft hangar.*[75] *Seiran* engine maintenance was usually conducted in the hangar, which is not surprising, since it is hard to imagine how they fit an *Atsuta* engine into the auxiliary room even on a sub as large as the *I-401*.

Two of the sub's supplementary generators were located in the auxiliary room, as was the sub's turbo blow, which was used to

---

* The access tube was 20 inches in diameter and had both upper and lower hatches.

empty the main ballast tank when the sub was surfaced and (God forbid given how high she sat in the water) required more freeboard.

GALLEY   Every sub has a galley. The *I-401*'s was located adjacent to the auxiliary generators.[76] One can imagine the difficulty in preparing three meals a day for 200 men. Somehow, the *I-400* cooks managed. Three freezer lockers below the galley deck kept food cold,[77] and four[78] oversize steam kettles turned out large quantities of rice to provide the crew with the much-cherished staple.[79]

Food was the best part of life aboard the *Sen-toku* subs. It was far better than anything the Imperial Japanese Army received, and there was plenty of it. Rice was served at every meal, and the galley even managed delicacies like cow tongue, boiled eel, and sweet bean paste. Staples included broiled fish, shrimp or vegetable *tempura*, beefsteak, pork cutlets, eggs, pickled horseradish, dried seaweed called *nori*, chestnuts, fresh oranges, canned peaches, pears, and pineapples, fruit juice or sodas, and *miso* soup for breakfast.[80] Green tea was consumed in vast quantities, and coffee less so, though it was available. Evening snacks included noodles, or biscuits with milk.[81] Some Sixth Fleet subs even had ice cream, though it was usually reserved for special occasions like the last meal before a dangerous mission.[82] In fact, after a few weeks at sea, one of the *I-400* cooks yearned for simpler fare, such as brown rice and pickled plum.[83]

An onboard nutritionist planned every meal[84] even though fresh vegetables ran out by the tenth day at sea. After that it was canned food morning, noon, and night,[85] with onions thrown in for variety. Tinned vegetables were especially unpopular, since they tasted like sand and ashes.[86] There were only so many canned sweet potatoes a crew could eat before complaining set in. Bottled vitamins were available at each meal, since it wasn't unusual on longer voyages for mild cases of beriberi to develop.[87] The real problem with the *I-401*'s food supply though was that the sub's size greatly reduced the number of flying fish that jumped on her deck. This limited a much-appreciated supplement to the standard fare—yet another consequence of being big.

CONNING TOWER Immediately above the control room was the *I-401*'s conning tower, which was used for combat operations. It was a dark, cramped space 8 feet in diameter and 20 feet long,[88] only 2 feet longer than the *Segundo*'s conning tower. When nine men squeezed in during battle stations, the compartment became impossibly tight. Nambu could make a ship or aircraft sighting through one of two periscopes, calculate firing solutions, and launch torpedoes from the conning tower. There were also duplicative sound, radar, and helm stations, a further example of how redundancy was a central design feature in submarines.

One of the worst things a sub could face was its conning tower being flooded, either by accident or by an enemy blowing a hole in its plating. The situation was especially dangerous aboard the *I-401*, because the sail's offset position could easily heel the sub onto her side.[89] The sail had extra steel plating to protect against such an event,[90] but it was still a risk.

NO. 6 COMPARTMENT: PORT AND STARBOARD ENGINE ROOMS
The *I-401*'s engines were located in two compartments aft of the control and auxiliary rooms. Unlike the *Segundo,* where the engine rooms were sequential (one forward, one aft), the *I-401*'s engine rooms flanked each other with a hatch connecting the port and starboard compartments. The sub's four diesel engines were the only ones of their kind in the Sixth Fleet,[91] but their defining characteristic, besides their unusual size, was how temperamental they could be. Each engine was rated at 2,250 shp and was connected to one of two propeller shafts via reduction gears in the aft section of the compartment.[92] With a clean bottom, the *I-401* could generate a top speed of 20 knots surfaced and up to 7 knots submerged (though not for long).[93] She might have been big, but she was by no means slow.

Up to four engines could be used on the surface to power the

I-401, though one engine was usually delegated to charging her batteries. However, her diesels couldn't operate below periscope depth, so batteries were used to drive an electric propulsion system.

Nambu's sub carried approximately 500,000 gallons of diesel oil, enough to fill 15 railway tank cars.[94] Fuel was in such short supply that the Imperial Japanese Navy cut it with soybean[95] and pine oil.[96] This means it burned dirty and left a black exhaust cloud for enemies to follow. Unfortunately, nothing could be done about it.

The engine compartment also housed several vapor-compression stills. Each still (called an evaporator) turned the ocean into fresh water by boiling it. Their output was never as advertised, so there was little water for personal use and none for showers.[97] This partly accounted for the sub's unmistakable smell of grease, diesel fumes, hydraulic fluid, male sweat, cigarette smoke, and whatever was being cooked for lunch. After a while, nobody cared.

NO 7. COMPARTMENT: PORT AND STARBOARD MANEUVERING ROOMS Just aft of the main engine rooms were the sub's port and starboard maneuvering rooms. If Nambu wanted to increase speed, the information was relayed via engine annunciators from either the conning tower or the control room to an electrician's mate in the maneuvering cubicle. There he manipulated a set of long metal levers to power the sub's electric motors either up or down, depending upon Nambu's order.

The *I-401* had two 1,200 shp electric motor-generators, one for each propeller shaft. The electric motors drew electricity from storage batteries used to drive the sub when submerged. If the engine room was defined by noise, the motor room was defined by heat. In fact, the electric motors generated so much heat, the men worked shirtless. The sub's humidity also shorted out the compartment's electrical distribution panels, making for constant problems.[98]

NO. 8: AFT COMPARTMENT The last compartment inside the *I-401* was her largest. Located in the stern, it was the crew's aft berthing compartment. Here the sub's interior hull gave way to a 61-foot-long space, the widest in the sub and second in size only to her aircraft hangar. U.S. subs usually reserved their aft compartment for a stern torpedo room, but the *I-401*'s held sleeping quarters, a head, various steering mechanisms, and an emergency signal ejector to let rescue ships know where the sub had gone down.[99]

The aft compartment was slightly more relaxed than the rest of the sub, in part because it was the area least likely to be visited by an officer. Crew members entering the compartment removed their shoes before stepping onto a raised wooden deck. So many feet rubbed the wood planking that it soon became as polished as a dance floor.[100]

BATTERY COMPARTMENT   Below the *I-401*'s habitable space was a second world, where the sub's inner workings were housed. It was a dark, dank place that included the pump room, the ventilation exhaust blowers, the lubricating and freshwater tanks, the anchor chain, ammunition storage, and a considerable number of valves and piping: it was no place for a man suffering from claustrophobia.

The *I-401*'s life-giving battery cells were located here. Made of lead and containing sulfuric acid, each cell weighed more than 100 pounds. These cells were used when the sub was submerged to power the electric propulsion system. Batteries could prove a liability, however, especially if contaminated by saltwater, which produced fumes that could overwhelm a crew. There was also a chance, when the batteries were recharging, that hydrogen might build up and ignite. Not surprisingly, batteries were checked as often as a boat's powder magazine, since an explosion in either could scuttle the sub.

U.S. subs were hardly five-star hotels, but they were downright luxurious compared to the *I-401* and a lot more reliable. For example, the *Segundo* had three showers, four heads, and more than half a dozen sinks for 70 men, while a typical I-boat would have considerably fewer bathroom facilities for more than twice the crew. A Balao-class sub not only had what a Japanese I-boat cap-

tain would have considered an impressive number of bathroom facilities, it also had a top-notch air-conditioning plant. And if that
didn't ensure a crew's comfort, there were an ice cream freezer, a
film projector, a sunlamp in the engine room, steak on the menu,
and a washing machine that used too much water. There was even
an escape hatch in case the sub went down, although most submariners had little faith it would work and insisted its only purpose
was to placate their mothers. These were inconceivable luxuries for
a Japanese sub captain like Nambu. Sixth Fleet submarines were at
war—sunlamps had nothing to do with it.

IT WOULDN'T HAVE taken long for Nambu to conclude that his
sub's huge size reduced her maneuverability. Anything that increased a sub's dive time or diminished her operational capacity
was frowned upon. So though the *I-401* was fast both above and
below the surface, her dive time (not to mention her ability to stop
promptly) was compromised.

Another problem was the sub's sail. The fact that it was offset
to port created an unbalanced form of drag when the sub was submerged. It was as if the front wheels of a car were permanently out
of alignment. A helmsman had to steer a seven-degree starboard
course at two knots submerged just to follow a straight line. Additionally, the offset tower meant the sub required a larger starboard
turning radius when underwater.[101] Nambu would shrug off these
difficulties, but they'd be constant worries for his helmsmen.

After Nambu's inspection of his new sub, he likely drew the following conclusions: the *I-401*'s high freeboard, broad beam, and
deep draft would make her a comfortable boat in a seaway; her hull
shape would naturally reduce roll and pitch, and her bridge would
remain dry under most weather conditions; and though her safety
depth was only 328 feet (82 percent of her overall length), she was
fast and well armed.[102] Yes, size reduced dive time and maneuverability, which made her lumbering, but she could certainly defend
herself.

When Nambu finally exited the *I-401*, his heart pounded with a sense of expectation. He would soon command a sub that the Imperial Japanese Navy had staked everything on.[103] That he would lead her on a top secret mission designed to change the course of the war only added to his pride. Though he knew his chances for success were slim, Japan's future rested on his shoulders. He would complete the mission or die trying. There was no turning back.

CHAPTER 18

THE 631ST

AS 1944 DREW TO A CLOSE, THE *I-401* REMAINED UNFINISHED. Nearly two years had passed since the sub's keel had been laid. Katayama's timeline had proved optimistic. Although the Sasebo naval yard was working around the clock, the flagship was still behind schedule.[1]

It was important to maintain crew morale in the face of such a delay. To this end, Nambu commissioned a ship's song. Usually, individual vessels didn't have an anthem. The *I-401* was an unusual case.[2] Nambu asked his crew for lyrics. Then, after editing their contributions, he had the Sasebo Naval Band set them to music. When it came time to rehearse, his crew lustily sang their flagship's new song.

Symbolic rituals required a surprising amount of Nambu's attention. They were necessary though to preserve IJN tradition. For example, every IJN ship had an onboard shrine where the crew prayed for success. The *I-401*'s primary shrine was in the control room. But a statue of Ise, the spirit who watched over submariners, was needed to fill the niche. Fortunately, the Grand Shrine at Ise, one of Japan's most sacred Shinto sites, was nearby. Nambu also needed a written fortune for the sub, to reassure the crew about their future. Too busy to get it, he sent his chief navigator to fetch one instead.[3] Sometimes superstition was more comforting, especially when logic suggested something less satisfying.

The Imperial Japanese Navy officially organized the *Sen-toku* subs into SubRon 1 on December 15, 1944.[4] The next day the *I-13* was completed.[5] Captained by Cdr. Katsuo Ohashi, the *I-13* immediately departed for her shakedown cruise in the waters off Kobe.[6]

Ohashi was the third *Sen-toku* captain to have served in the Indian Ocean. It's not clear whether he knew Ariizumi personally. Still, he'd sunk a fair number of Allied merchant ships as skipper of the *I-56* (later the *I-156*). Interestingly, when he came across Australian airmen in a lifeboat in 1942, he declined to massacre them despite his officers' entreaties.

"The war situation won't be affected," Ohashi told them. "Let's not partake in any senseless killing."[7]

Fourteen days after the *I-13* was commissioned, the *I-400* was also handed over. It was just two days before the New Year,[8] and the *I-401* still wasn't ready. Nambu could only wait enviously as his sister subs headed out to sea.[9]

AT THE SAME time SubRon 1 was being organized, the 631st *Kokutai*, or air group, was formed with Ariizumi in command. Ten *Seiran* bombers, three for each of the two *I-400* subs and two for the *I-13* and *I-14*, respectively, would form the heart of the unit, with additional *Seiran* for training and replacement. It was a much-reduced force compared with Admiral Yamamoto's original vision. Yamamoto's plan had called for 18 subs and 44 *Seiran* before the underwater aircraft carriers had been reduced in number. By June 1944 Aichi had completed a measly four *Seiran*, with a production capacity limited to one per month.[10] This meant that only ten *Seiran* would be ready by the end of the year, far short of the modified goal.[11] And two of these weren't even combat aircraft, they were trainers. As a result, when the *Sen-toku* subs began launching in December, not one *Seiran* was ready for assignment. They were still undergoing flight testing.[12]

Engine problems were partly responsible for the slow pace of *Seiran* production.[13] You couldn't do anything without a reliable engine, which led to a cascading series of consequences. Shortage of aircraft meant flight tests were delayed, which in turn meant fewer planes were available for pilots to qualify in. Additionally, more and more pilots were being transferred to Yokosuka in anticipation of the 631st being formed. When new pilots arrived, they had to make do with alternative floatplanes like Aichi's *Zuiun,* which they disparagingly referred to as a "toy."[14] Frustrations mounted.

The situation was further complicated by the surface fleet, which got first dibs on experienced pilots.[15] There were so few aviators with combat experience this late in the war that many of the 631st's pilots were green. Almost none of the new arrivals had the dive-bomb experience necessary to attack the Panama Canal.[16] Though specialized training could make up for the shortfall, they had to have planes to train in, and that continued to be an issue throughout the winter months.

Ens. Kazuo Takahashi was one of the first pilots to show up for *Seiran* instruction. Confident and handsome, Takahashi had been a seaplane instructor when the war started and later became a floatplane pilot aboard the *1–37.*[17] It probably wasn't a coincidence that he'd been assigned to the 631st, since he'd known Ariizumi when they'd served together in SubRon 8.

Takahashi had never even seen the ocean before enrolling in the navy's Junior Pilot Training Course,[18] yet by the time he arrived at Yokosuka Naval Air Station, he was a veteran pilot. His seaplane experience made him an ideal choice for a *Seiran* pilot. When Takahashi arrived at Yokosuka on August 24, 1944, he was given a *Seiran* instruction manual and told to read it. A week later he donned his flying helmet lined with rabbit fur and flew his first *Storm from a Clear Sky.*[19]

Takahashi began flying *Seiran* in September. He measured takeoff, landing, ascent, and cruising speeds, as well as fuel consumption and descent rates. There was also some formation flying. What Takahashi liked best though was testing the *Seiran*'s responsiveness. The plane handled so well, he soon fell in love.[20]

By mid-September, Takahashi was flying the *Nanzan,* or land version of the *Seiran.* He found the plane lighter and faster than the sea-based version.[21] He especially enjoyed its acrobatic abilities, finding it handled as well as a Zero fighter,[22] high praise considering the plane was merely an attack bomber.

Come October, Takahashi was ready to begin torpedo training.

After learning how to operate the bombsight, he took to the air over the Otake target range carrying a torpedo. Dropping to an altitude of only 100 feet, he skimmed across the ocean at breakneck speed. Centering the target in his bombsight, he pressed the drop activation switch just below the grip on his control stick. When the torpedo fell, a miniature light verified its release.[23] Takahashi already knew that it had dropped though—because his plane leaped 60 feet into the sky.[24]

Takahashi watched with anticipation as his torpedo raced toward the target. After 300 feet it inexplicably slowed, veered to the left, and began emitting smoke. He was crestfallen—he'd expected it to explode. He didn't realize it was a dummy.[25] Takahashi had one more chance to practice dive-bombing that month, but he would need a lot more training before he became an expert.

By November 15 engine production had improved enough that Takahashi was sent to collect another *Seiran* from Aichi's factory.[26] Aichi's skunkworks were in a stand-alone building separate from its main plant.[27] *Seiran* were built in a large steel-framed hangar with a curved roof, floor-to-ceiling windows, and metal support columns that looked like bridge trusses. Built one at a time, it was a customized approach compared to the assembly lines favored by the United States. It was the best Aichi could do given the specialized nature of the aircraft.

When Takahashi arrived, Aichi's assembly facility had a poster on the wall reading, "Let's pull together!"[28] High school students were building much of the plane by hand. The Ministry of Education had suspended classes so students could work in war production.[29] Many of the workers were girls 12 to 15 years old,[30] which resulted in some unexpected consequences. One *Seiran* fuselage was found to have a drawing of a Japanese woman scratched in its surface—not exactly regulation markings for a combat aircraft. The system worked though and to prove it, two new *Seiran* stood ready for Takahashi to fly.

Lt. Atsushi Asamura arrived at the Yokosuka seaplane base in November 1944. Twenty-two years old and small for a pilot,[31] he had no trouble fitting into a cockpit. He was already a seasoned flyer—his specialty was twin-seater seaplanes. Like Ariizumi, he was an Etajima graduate,[32] but he was more senior and had taught at Kashima Naval Air Station. Most recently he'd been an aircraft officer aboard the cruiser *Aoba*.[33] When the *Aoba* was severely damaged during the Battle of Leyte, Asamura was transferred to Yokosuka. There were never enough experienced seaplane pilots to go around.

Asamura was on the tarmac when he noticed a bright orange aircraft buzzing in the sky overhead.[34] The color designated an experimental plane, which naturally piqued his curiosity.

"What's that?" Asamura asked Lt. Cdr. Tadashi Funada, the *Seiran*'s first test pilot.

"It's the most secret of secret planes. It's called *Seiran,* and we only have two so far. Once we've manufactured thirteen, we'll load them onto submarines and bomb the Panama Canal. You're going to be the flight leader."[35]

Asamura's chest swelled with pride. Finally, the bantam pilot was getting a mission commensurate with his desire.

Asamura may have been a talented pilot, but he was a difficult personality. A stickler for protocol, he angered easily when someone crossed his imagined boundaries. This keen sense of "correctness" meant he followed orders with exceptional dedication. It also meant he was rigid and unyielding. Whereas Takahashi was arrogant and critical, Asamura could be petty and vindictive. Their differing personalities would eventually clash. In the meantime, they focused on flying.

Seiran flight-testing was far enough along that by November 24, the plane was officially accepted by the IJN.[36] Aircraft production was dealt a blow, however, when a December 7 earthquake shook Nagoya. The quake lasted five minutes, killed 1,000 people, and caused heavy damage. Though no *Seiran* were destroyed, their wing jigs were twisted like taffy, even though some metal pipes were 12 inches thick.[37] *Sen-toku* personnel were rushed to the plant to assist in the cleanup.[38] Meanwhile, production was brought to a standstill.

When the 631st was officially formed eight days later, no *Seiran* were available for the unit.*[39] They were still being tested. Asamura may have been proud to be assigned to the air group, but Takahashi wanted out of sub-borne airplanes. One reason was that he wouldn't be flying in the relative safety of the Indian Ocean but deep in the heart of enemy territory. While Asamura was grateful to die for his country, Takahashi took a more jaded view. Since he considered defeat inevitable, little would be gained by his death in battle. In other words, being assigned to the 631st was "the worst possible news."[40]

FINALLY, ON JANUARY 8, 1945, the *I-401* was commissioned under the cloudy skies of Sasebo. Since the sub was top secret, few people attended the ceremony. When it was over, Nambu sailed the *I-401* quietly out of the harbor.[41]

Although 60 percent of the *I-400*'s crew had limited experience aboard a sub,[42] Nambu felt he had few greenhorns among his men.[43] Forty percent of experienced submariners is low for a combat boat. It was certainly fewer than a U.S. sub was comfortable carrying.

Nambu didn't linger in the waters off Kyushu.[44] So many U.S. submarines were in the area that there was a saying: You could walk across their periscopes from Singapore to Japan without getting your feet wet.[45] Nambu was right to be concerned. U.S. subs considered the sea lanes around Kyushu to be prime hunting ground, and the *I-401* made a tempting target.[46]

Nambu quickly headed for the safe waters of the Inland Sea with Ariizumi onboard. They met up with the *I-400* and *I-13* near

---

* According to Takahashi, the 631st had six *Seiran* and five *Zuiun* by February 1, 1945. See Takahashi, *Shinryu Tokubetsu Kogekitai*, p. 176.

Kure, where they conducted dive and surface drills, practiced trimming the boat, and did underwater navigation exercises.[47] After repeated practice, the *I-401* could crash-dive to periscope depth in just under a minute—a significant achievement given the size of the boat but almost twice as long as the *Segundo* required.

ACCEPTANCE TRIALS FOR the underwater aircraft carriers were carried out separately from *Seiran* flight training.[48] While Nambu's sub underwent its shakedown period, the *I-400* and *I-13* assembled near Kure Naval Base to test the unloading, launching, and stowing of *Seiran*.[49] It was the first important step in the marriage between submarine and aircraft, and success would lead to joint tactical training.

The catapult test was especially important. Meant to determine the maximum payload a *Seiran* could carry and still be launched from a sub, the test involved adding sand to a hollowed-out practice bomb, attaching it to a rack underneath the *Seiran*'s belly, and launching both from the sub. The bigger the bomb, the better the bang, but safety considerations played an important role. They discussed removing the plane's floats, or reducing her fuel to accommodate the bomb load if the catapult tests failed. As it was, Takahashi successfully flew from the *I-400*'s deck carrying a 1,760-pound practice bomb, the heaviest ever launched from an IJN catapult.[50]

ARIIZUMI MADE HIS first appearance in the 631st's command room on January 11, 1945. Many of the air group's officers were nervous, having never met him before. Takahashi wasn't one of them. He'd seen Ariizumi drunk in Penang and wasn't the least bit intimidated. The same couldn't be said for his fellow officers, though, who awaited their boss with trepidation.

Everyone fell silent when Ariizumi entered the room. He greeted each of his officers individually; then in a monotone devoid of emotion, he gave a short motivational speech. Takahashi felt the commander's speaking skills left a lot to be desired.

He was in for a surprise though when Ariizumi asked him to stay behind.

"When I look at the personnel chart I see there are only four or five pilots with combat experience and only two with experience on submarines," Ariizumi noted. "There's going to be a lot that comes up, so please don't hesitate to give your opinion. I ask you in particular because I think it will be the quickest way to success."

Takahashi was pleased. It was unusual for a commanding officer to ask his subordinate for an opinion. Then again, they were so short on experience, Ariizumi needed all the help he could get.[51]

Ariizumi departed for Tokyo the next day. While meeting with the Naval General Staff, he ordered his assistant to visit the NGS reference room and collect everything he could find about the Panama Canal. It took the better part of a day to sort through all the books and naval charts. When the assistant finished, he had filled two parachute bags with documents.[52] The material would prove critical for planning the mission.

ANOTHER S*EIRAN* WAS ready on January 13, 1945. But while Takahashi was on a train bound for Nagoya, a second earthquake struck leaving disaster in its wake. If the December quake had been bad, the *Mikawa* tremor was worse. The first thing Takahashi noticed was that the heavy doors to Aichi's airplane hangar had been toppled. *Seiran* production was also impeded.[53]

As if the program weren't bedeviled by enough problems, B-29 raids had begun in December. The Nagoya region generated more than half of Japan's aviation production, so the U.S. Army Air Force had targeted the area for destruction. Fifty-six air raids followed over an eight-month period, burning the city to a cinder. Workers spent so much time huddled in air raid shelters that little got done. This meant the 631st had only five *Seiran* and six

Zuiun for training.[54] Additionally, problems with the *Atsuta* engine persisted. It was a constant battle keeping the few *Seiran* they had operational.[55]

On the morning of January 20, 1945, a *Zuiun* piloted by Warrant Flying Officer Suzuki was scheduled to fly a navigation exercise. Before he could take off, however, Suzuki's observer reported in sick. Warrant Flying Officer Sasaki was on the reserve list, but nobody wanted him to fly since it was his wedding day. Sasaki volunteered anyway feeling there was enough time to complete the exercise before his bride arrived at the Kure train station.

When the exercise was over, Takahashi watched Sasaki return. The Kure mountains could make landing difficult and Sasaki's *Zuiun* circled the bay four times. When it crashed behind a hangar, Takahashi jumped into an ambulance and raced to the scene.

Sasaki's plane had smacked nose first into the front yard of a girls' school. The crash site was surrounded by students, whom Takahashi warned to stay clear, since he feared a fire. Ambulance attendants worked more than an hour to free Sasaki from the wreckage, but to no avail; he was already dead.

It was the 631st's first casualty. Nevertheless, Takahashi was more concerned about the bridal party, which was due to arrive at any moment. Sasaki's in-laws were understandably shocked when told the news, and the bride wailed so uncontrollably, Takahashi felt responsible. Unfortunately, there was still the matter of the wedding to deal with. The shrine was understanding and canceled the ceremony, but the restaurant refused to refund any money. After consulting with Takahashi, the bridal party changed the wedding reception to a wake.

Takahashi wasted no time in preparing an altar, rounding up photographs of the two airmen, and arranging for sutras. When everything was ready, he called his colleagues together: "The purpose of tonight is to mourn our friends. It's also important to console the family, particularly Sasaki's bride. Do not forget this even if you get drunk!"

The guests lit slender sticks of incense as they arrived, and placed them in front of the altar. Two young airmen, handsome in their naval uniforms, looked out from the photographs. When the reception began, Takahashi offered a few words in honor of their fallen comrades.

> When we pilots board our plane, we . . . lead the way to victory without concern for life or death. The battlefront holds no profit for us. Our fellow crew members are killed one after another . . . If I die in action, it won't be surprising particularly now that *tokko* attacks are being carried out as a regular part of combat. Survival is but a dream. Today, Suzuki and Sasaki gave their lives. They went to that other world earlier than the rest of us. No matter how bad things get though, Japan will not surrender. In the end, there is no path for us but death. We will follow comrades, so please, wait for us.

Finally, the reception got under way. Sake was dispensed; military songs were sung, and there was even dancing. When the bride suddenly smiled, Takahashi felt relieved. Her family expressed gratitude for his efforts.

Unexpectedly, two officers appeared and began haranguing them. "What is the reason for this commotion?" one shouted. "Two of our comrades have died! Shame on you!"

Seeing that the outburst shocked the bride's family, Takahashi lost his temper. "You may be our superiors, but I can't stand you lecturing us. Tonight's reception is held at the request of the bereaved. If you have a problem with that, tell it to the Commander."

The officers knew Takahashi had a close relationship with Ariizumi and left, but Takahashi doubted that was the end of it. After all, he'd publicly rebuked two senior officers. They wouldn't let him off lightly.

A memorial service was held a few days later for the airmen. Ariizumi attended the ceremony, which took place in an aircraft hangar on the Kure naval base. When the service was finished, he sent for Takahashi.

Assuming he was to be reprimanded, Takahashi defended his behavior at Sasaki's wake.

"Don't give it a second thought," Ariizumi said. "That's not why I called you here."

Takahashi was surprised, but what came next surprised him even more.

"Have you ever launched a torpedo from an airplane?" Ariizumi asked.

Takahashi's grin was the only answer the commander needed.[56]

CHAPTER 19

FULP ON PATROL

WHILE THE *I-400* SUBS WERE STILL UNDER CONSTRUCTION, THE *Segundo*'s first war patrol got off to a shaky start. Captain Fulp and his crew were in the Surigao Strait near the Philippines when two friendly aircraft appeared out of nowhere and strafed the surfaced sub.[1] Though the shots fell short, it wasn't a good omen for Fulp's first patrol. Then three-quarters of the way through their deployment, a Japanese aircraft dropped two bombs on them. It was the morning of Friday, October 6, 1944.[2] Fulp had just been promoted to commander and was eager to show his acumen, when a Japanese plane was reported six miles distant. Forced to sound the dive klaxon, Fulp cleared the deck and ordered the sub's watertight hatches closed. The *Segundo* had only a few inches of water overhead when the first bomb struck. A loud explosion rocked the sub, followed by a second blast.

"That's all for him," a veteran submariner remarked. "He only carries two."[3]

Had they been depth charges instead of bombs, the damage could have been fatal. As it was, the explosions damaged the *Segundo*'s deck gun, blew one of the four mufflers off her engine exhaust, and broke the foundation mounts on the generator powering her torpedo data computer.[4] Worse, was not finding any targets. The *Segundo* was patrolling in support of the Palau invasion, but since the IJN didn't oppose the American landing, Fulp had nothing to shoot at. As one officer put it, "We were there— it was the enemy that didn't show up."[5]

After ComSubPac released the *Segundo* from her responsibilities, Fulp made a beeline for the Luzon Strait. Located between the northern tip of the Philippines and Formosa (now Taiwan), the deep-water passage was the perfect place for a sub to attack. The majority of Japanese shipping passed through the bottleneck, which was nicknamed "Convoy College." Unfortunately, the Philippine invasion temporarily curtailed enemy shipping. Once again, Fulp found nothing to sink.[6]

Finally, the *Segundo*'s wolf pack had modest success. The USS *Seahorse* (SS 304) sank an 800-ton escort, while the USS *Whale* (SS 239) sank a 1,200-ton tanker.[7] The *Segundo* came up with a big, fat goose egg.

Approximately 70 percent of all ComSubPac patrols came home without sinking a single ship during this period,[8] slim pickings compared to what an aggressive skipper hoped for. Sixty days at sea was just long enough for the *Segundo*'s oranges to go bad. Fulp ended his first war patrol without having fired a single shot.

The *Segundo* docked at Majuro in the Marshall Islands on October 21, 1944. A relief crew from the USS *Bushnell* (AS-15) came aboard, while Fulp and his men went to Myrna Island rest camp for two weeks of relaxation. Meanwhile the *Segundo* went into dry dock to have her badly nicked propeller blades fixed.[9]

A little R&R helped the *Segundo*'s crew to forget their failure. The men played volleyball, swam in the ocean, and wrote long letters home. One pastime that proved popular was Gilly ball. It was played just like baseball, except that a coffee can filled with Gilly juice was placed at each base. Gilly juice consisted of 180-proof ethyl alcohol (normally used for torpedo fuel) cut with fruit juice. When a player came to bat, he took a swig of Gilly juice. If he made it to base, he got another swig. Pretty soon a high-scoring team began to falter, giving the other side a chance to catch up. When a Myrna Island rest officer happened by, he was invited to join the game, but when he saw the inebriated condition of both teams, he gave it a pass. Gilly ball was fun to play, even if no one remembered the score.[10]

Wallace Karnes had an atypical experience at rest camp. Told he had to check his .45 sidearm during his stay, Karnes complied. Unbeknownst to Karnes, however, Chief "Doggy" Downs signed the gun out, and carried it to the mess tent. When Downs couldn't get a waiter's attention, he pumped six rounds into the air. It didn't improve the service, since the waiters were cowering under a table, but it was good for a laugh. After that a new regulation was issued: submariners shall refrain from discharging firearms in the mess tent.[11]

The *Segundo*'s crew returned from rest camp recharged if hung over. Combat subs experienced personnel turnover of 10 to 25 percent at the end of a patrol, so it wasn't unusual to pick up new crew members. Victor Horgan was one of them. A scrappy little ensign from Portland, Oregon, Horgan had been skiing on Mount Baker when he first heard the news about Pearl Harbor. His NRTOC commander, a former sub captain, had inspired Horgan to apply to sub school. A year later he was assigned to a sub relief crew on Majuro.

Horgan wasn't quite sure why he'd been selected for the *Segundo*. Some of the guys in his relief crew had been working as long as a year without permanent sub assignment. In contrast, he'd only been there a single day before being assigned. There was something special about Horgan, though. He might have described himself as a slow learner, but he was determined. One incident stood out in particular.

During a class on approach technique, Horgan's sub school instructor chose him to perform an exercise on the attack simulator. Informed his sub was at 300 feet, Horgan was tasked with bringing her to periscope depth without the benefit of several ballast systems his instructor had deemed inoperable. Horgan's peers chuckled at his predicament. None of them believed he could solve the problem. Horgan wasn't sure he could either. Still, he wanted to do his best.

Careful not to make a mistake, he slowly worked his sub toward the surface. His timidity only convinced his classmates that he was inept, and they ribbed him all the harder. It was a while before Horgan brought his sub to periscope depth. When he did, his instructor was impressed. Grace under pressure was a highly valued quality in a sub officer and Horgan hadn't cracked despite his classmates' abuse. Later, when Horgan graduated from sub school, the same instructor asked what assignment he'd gotten.

"Relief corps," Horgan said, disappointed.

"What did you want?"

"Combat sub."

Nothing more was said. When Horgan arrived at Majuro, he moved to the head of the line and was assigned to the *Segundo*.[12]

Fulp's sub left for Saipan on November 16, 1944. After topping off his fuel tanks, Fulp joined a three-sub wolf pack called "Roy's Rangers."[13] The pack, which was led by the USS *Trepang* (SS 412) and included the USS *Razorback* (SS 394), had orders to prevent Japanese reinforcements from reaching the Philippines. When the *Segundo* arrived on station December 1, she immediately began patrolling the Luzon Strait.[14]

Fulp's luck was better this time, but not by much. He had multiple ship contacts in the early part of his patrol, but couldn't launch an attack. December was typhoon season, which hampered his ability to operate. Every time the *Segundo* surfaced, she was swamped by heavy seas. It was difficult enough finding enemy targets, let alone launching torpedoes, in such conditions. Finally, on the evening of December 6, the *Trepang* spotted seven Japanese merchant ships with three escorts.[15] It was the biggest shooting gallery Fulp had ever seen.

The *Trepang*'s commander might have been called the "praying skipper" for his religious beliefs, but Fulp would be damned before a God-fearing zealot stole his glory. With high seas and an overcast sky, conditions were poor for a surface attack. Fulp chanced it anyway.[16]

Hiding in front of Luzon's dark background, Fulp crept along the surface. But as gale force winds whipped the sea into a frenzy, what had begun as an advantage soon turned against him.[17] Though Fulp managed to close the distance without being spotted, conditions were so rough, he worried they'd impede the accuracy of a surface-fired torpedo. He also had to be careful not to sink one of his own subs—always a danger when operating in close proximity.

Picking what appeared to be a troop transport, Fulp ordered the torpedo gyros set nearly at zero and launched six Mark 18s from the *Segundo*'s bow tubes. Given the storm-tossed seas, it was a wonder the torpedoes ran true. A few minutes later the first of three fish slammed into the ship's engine room. A massive eruption of water, flame, and molten metal leaped into the sky, followed by two more explosions. As the ship lay smoldering, her escort began circling like a calf around its wounded mother.

Fulp was confident the transport was disabled, so he took the opportunity to attack a second vessel. Using the cover of darkness, he wove between two escorts, one of which was only 400 yards away.[18] It was such an audacious move that Fulp's officers were wide-eyed in disbelief. One of the defenders was the *Kuretake*. More than 20 years old, she wasn't exactly a state-of-the-art destroyer.[19] But she was accompanied by the CH-33, a modern sub chaser.[20] Either ship could have had radar. Still, Fulp was undeterred.[21]

After dashing through the defense perimeter, Fulp ordered engines to one-third to give the torpedo room time to reload. When all six tubes were ready, he maneuvered into firing position.

Most subs fire from a range of 1,800 to 2,000 yards. But Fulp had had such bad experience with navy torpedoes, he didn't trust them. He'd fired 11 Mark 14s on the *Sargo*'s first war patrol, some at point-blank range, and none had detonated. Torpedo failure had plagued the sub's next six war patrols. Now Fulp had his chance to make up the misses.

While Fulp conducted his attack approach from the bridge, Ens. Rod Johnson operated the torpedo data computer (TDC) in the conning tower. The TDC performed the trigonometric calculations necessary to compute a target intercept course for a torpedo. Inputs for the primitive computer included the enemy's range, speed, and bearing relative to the *Segundo*. Once the calculations were complete, the TDC estimated a moving target's constantly changing position and provided the correct angle settings for a torpedo's gyroscope.

Johnson hadn't had much experience in the conning tower and was probably cautious working with Fulp. He had a good idea though of what a comfortable distance for an attack was. An overcast night might have been ideal for up close and personal fighting, but once the *Segundo* closed to within 1,800 yards, Johnson's confidence began to slip.

"Fifteen hundred yards, captain."

"Proceed," Fulp replied.

"Thirteen hundred," Johnson reported.

"Closer."

"Twelve hundred."

Johnson's voice betrayed his concern. Fulp remained unmoved. As they passed the 1,000-yard mark, Johnson protested they were too near the target.[22]

Fulp responded calmly: "We're gonna get close enough to throw stones at 'em."

Fulp finally fired at 900 yards. Keeping the spread small, he launched three torpedoes, at least two of which hit home.[23] The target wasn't an ordinary freighter though; it was a giant Japanese ammunition ship.

The first explosion was so powerful, it knocked the *Segundo*'s chief torpedoman out of the conning tower and into the control room.[24] When wreckage began raining down upon the sub, one of the lookouts panicked: "Oh my God, they're firing at us!"[25]

But the ship wasn't returning fire. It was too busy disintegrating.

The concussions were so immense, those on deck had to grab the railing to keep from falling. When the heat wave reached their faces, it felt like their eyebrows were being singed.

Since water conducts sound faster than air, the experienced hands inside the sub knew what they were hearing. "Ammunition ship," one remarked.[26] Seconds later the smell of cordite wafted through the bridge hatch.[27]

As explosions consumed the ship, bright yellow flames lit up the night, and tracer ammo arced into the sky. Strangely, the ammunition ship continued plowing a path through the sea, even as she was being ripped apart.[28] Then in an instant she was gone.

A sub's patrol report is not known for exaggeration, yet the *Segundo*'s entry states: "the quickest . . . most devastating explosion imaginable [tore the ship apart] . . . it just did not seem possible that anything could be obliterated so instantaneously."[29]

Indeed it was remarkable that so large a ship could vanish into thin air. Even the *Segundo*'s radar man had to look twice after a final massive explosion blew the ship to kingdom come. The only thing left was her outline burned into the lookouts' retinas.[30]

Fulp wasn't finished, though. One of his torpedoes had hit another vessel, which was rapidly sinking.[31] A few minutes later she too was gone.[32] Fulp now returned to the first ship he'd hit, ablaze from stem to stern.[33] Before he could polish her off, however, the *Razorback* finished the job.[34] It was a disappointment for the *Segundo*'s fire control party,[35] even though the crew was pleased with the overall results. They'd sunk two, possibly three enemy vessels in one night. Success made them feel indomitable.

The next morning the *Segundo* was surrounded by wreckage.[36] It was hard to know for sure who had sunk which ship in all the confusion. In addition to sinking the ammo ship, it appeared the *Segundo* had holed both the *Yasukuni Maru*, a 5,794-ton freighter that was later abandoned, as well as the *Kenjo Maru*. Though the *Kuretake* managed to escape, she didn't remain free for long. The *Razorback* sank her three weeks later,[37] while the *Segundo* continued on patrol.

A COMBAT HIGH pervaded the sub for several days. Though it eventually passed, one thing that didn't let up was the weather. Typhoon might be just another name for a Pacific-born hurricane, but weather conditions made life impossible for Fulp and his crew. Come December 9, winds were running at eight on the twelve-point Beaufort scale, making it difficult for the *Segundo* to travel on the surface.

Wallace Karnes was in the control room when Fireman First Class G. H. Saunders arrived to relieve the last watch of the day. Karnes didn't know Saunders well.[38] Like Horgan, he was a new recruit who'd come aboard at Majuro. He'd been with the *Segundo* less than 30 days.

It didn't help that Saunders said so little. He might have seemed calm as he donned his foul weather gear, but Karnes was glad he wasn't the one going topside on such an ugly night. The crew was sick of being tossed around by the storm, and a bridge watch marred by gale force winds and heavy seas wasn't anyone's idea of a cakewalk. Saunders thanked Karnes after he finished dressing, and disappeared into the conning tower. Though there was no better experience than on-the-job training, the new guy was about to get a full dose.

When Saunders climbed out the bridge hatch, he was immediately drenched by spray. Even the heartiest sailor would have felt seasick on such a miserable night. It's hard to imagine a new recruit feeling any different atop the periscope shears.

When the *Segundo* suddenly lurched to port two hours later,[39] the darkness made it impossible to see what was going on. A giant wave had broached the sub's starboard side, tipping her over at a 35-degree angle. A lookout heard a cry,[40] and moments later Karnes heard a thud strike the hull.[41] An alarm sounded, and the engines stopped. A float light was thrown overboard.

The waves were so enormous, it was impossible to see where Saunders had gone. Fulp circled back, but all the search light illuminated besides good intentions was a driving rainstorm and mountainous seas.[42] Thirty-seven minutes later Fulp called off the search. It wouldn't take long to attract enemy notice with their signal light blazing. Besides, finding a man in the middle of a typhoon was next to impossible, especially at night.

Nobody was sure what had happened. The lookouts had a bar to tie into while standing watch. Whether Saunders failed to hook in, or he accidentally unlocked himself, or his line failed was never reported. Whatever happened, Saunders was probably knocked out by his fall. Even if he was conscious, it wouldn't have taken him long to drown in a typhoon.

Fulp held a short memorial service.[43] After reading from the Bible,[44] he asked for a moment of silence and hung his head in prayer.[45] Despite being stoical, Fulp felt an emptiness that night.[46] It was tough losing a crew member, nor could it have helped that Saunders was the *Segundo*'s first casualty. They had finally been blooded.

THE PATROL WAS subdued after that. The weather remained so poor, lookouts were ordered to wear a whistle around their neck in case they fell overboard. When their watch finished, brandy was served to revive them.

An even more violent typhoon swept down unexpectedly on December 17. Sustained winds of 145 mph were recorded, with gusts up to 185.[47] The *Segundo* submerged during the worst part, but the ocean was so turbulent that Fulp had difficulty maintaining depth control.[48] Once the sea calmed around Christmas, everyone hoped to sink a Japanese warship, but the holidays brought an unpleasant surprise.

The seas were again running high on December 26, with 40-foot crests. Vic Horgan was resting in his bunk while the *Segundo* made 12 knots on the surface.[49] Feeling the ocean's peaks and valleys, Horgan realized the sub was getting out of sync with the waves.[50] Moments later the *Segundo* plunged into the trough of an enormous roller. Before she could recover, a second wave broke over her sail, forcing water down the bridge hatch. So much saltwater poured through the main induction valve that the forward engine room was flooded, sweeping away a machinist's mate struggling to close the valve. An avalanche of ocean also cascaded into the control room, knocking Wallace Karnes into the pump room, where he landed in three feet of freezing water.

The quartermaster quickly dogged the bridge hatch, while the engine room secured the main induction valve. Before they could do anything else, a powerful wave drove the *Segundo* 36 feet underwater, smashing instrument panels and thoroughly shaking up the crew. Meanwhile, Fulp fought to gain control.

It didn't take a damage report to reveal an inch of water carpeting the control room. A few short feet away, Karnes was having little success draining the pump room. The *Segundo*'s ventilation system had siphoned seawater into several parts of the sub including the radio shack, which was partially flooded, and the after battery compartment.

Karnes plunged his arms into the pump room's icy brine, searching for the strainer. When he found it blocked, he cleared it of the obstacle, which brought the water level down. Despite the crew's quick action, however, the master and auxiliary compasses were knocked out, leaving only the magnetic compass for navigation.[51] Luckily seawater hadn't contaminated the batteries; otherwise there might have been an explosion. As it was, the radio was on the fritz and navigation unreliable.

The most important question, once the *Segundo* surfaced, was whether the lookouts were still alive. Fulp doubted it.[52] It would take more than a whistle to survive two monster waves and a five-fathom dunking.

Turning to the officer of the deck (OOD), Fulp ordered the bridge hatch opened and an inspection made. When the OOD gave his report, Fulp must have felt relieved. All lookouts were present and accounted for.[53]

The quartermaster's quick action in dogging the bridge hatch had saved the sub.[54] Nevertheless, it was the nearest the *Segundo* had come to being sunk.[55] Regrettably, it dulled the shine of their earlier accomplishments.

The rest of the patrol was uneventful.[56] Fulp encountered so few targets, it seemed like the Imperial Japanese Navy had gone home. When orders arrived to head for Guam,[57] they were happy to go.

Fulp might have sunk more than three ships if the weather hadn't proven a far worse enemy than the Japanese. The cigar-smoking captain was still put in for the Navy Cross. The recommendation stated: "The fighting spirit and exceptional skill displayed by the Commanding Officer . . . were particularly outstanding and merit special recognition." Fulp may have been credited as an inspiration to his men,[58] but Vice Adm. Charles A. Lockwood, commander of the Pacific submarine force, didn't agree, and turned him down for the Navy Cross.[59] In its place, Fulp was awarded the Silver Star for valor, the military's third-highest decoration given to a U.S. serviceman. It was still an important acknowledgment of what he had done.

By the end of the *Segundo*'s second war patrol, Fulp was doing an excellent job shaping his men into a high-functioning combat unit. His coolness under fire, combined with his undeniable competence, demonstrated he could take his crew into battle, rack up victories, and bring them home safely.

It was a strong start for Fulp, who remained eager to engage the enemy. All signs might have pointed to the war winding down, but as far as the *Segundo*'s skipper was concerned, their fight had just begun.

CHAPTER 20

KURE

THE *I-14* WAS THE LAST UNDERWATER AIRCRAFT CARRIER completed. Captained by Cdr. Tsuruzo Shimizu, the sub was commissioned during the first half of March 1945. Shimizu was a veteran sub commander—he'd captained three boats before the *I-14*.[1] But there was another reason Shimizu skippered a *Sen-toku* sub. He already knew Ariizumi.

Shimizu had first met Ariizumi when they were stationed at Penang. A 1930 graduate of Etajima's fifty-eighth class, Shimizu had served aboard four subs before receiving his first command.[2] In May 1943 he was named captain of the *I-165* and assigned to SubRon 8, the same sub squadron as Ariizumi.[3]

Shimizu was an impressionable young officer when he burst uninvited into Ariizumi's quarters one night. It was a serious breach of etiquette even though Shimizu was just seeking advice on becoming a better skipper. Instead of scolding Shimizu, the normally stern commander chose to mentor him. Ariizumi was strict when it came to official business, but he could be big-hearted when it came to junior officers wanting guidance. As a result, Shimizu felt nothing but respect and affection for the commander.[4]

The square-jawed officer with narrow eyes and thinning eyebrows almost didn't make it to Penang, however. While en route, an Allied sub fired three torpedoes at him, all of which missed.[5] The next month, while operating in the Indian Ocean, he sank a 10,286-ton British freighter on its way to Calcutta. The ship's radio operator managed to get an SOS off, and her crew escaped unharmed, despite the ship's cargo of ammunition.[6] The freighter, however, was a total loss.

Ariizumi and Shimizu had something else in common besides captaining Indian Ocean subs. Two weeks before Ariizumi sank the *Tjisalak*, Shimizu torpedoed the British merchant ship *Nancy Moller*. The *Moller* was hauling coal from South Africa to Ceylon when Shimizu put two torpedoes into her.[7] It was March 18, 1944, as the *I-165* surfaced 50 yards from the *Moller*'s lifeboats and took six survivors on board. A Japanese officer gave orders to shoot two of the survivors, both of them Chinese. One died instantly, while the other suffered a chest wound. Next, the *I-165* partially submerged, leaving two Indian lascars to be washed overboard. One of the *Moller*'s lifeboats rescued the lascars as well as the wounded Chinese. But the sub didn't leave the scene. Instead, Shimizu took a page out of Ariizumi's book. When he was only 200 feet from the *Moller*'s lifeboats, Shimizu's bridge guns opened fire. Thirty-two out of the *Moller*'s 60-plus crew were killed in the fusillade,[8] putting Shimizu in the select group of sub captains who massacred survivors. Four days later the HMS *Emerald* pulled 31 castaways from the sea.[9]

In July 1944 the *I-165* was diverted to mole operations ferrying supplies in the Pacific. Shimizu didn't like mole ops any more than Nambu did. He'd even come close to losing his sub during one mission. Finally, in November 1944, Shimizu returned to Japan.[10] He was assigned the *I-14* in March 1945, the last sub captain to join Ariizumi's squadron.

Before the *I-14* departed Kobe in March,* Shimizu raised the *Hirihokenten* banner. Designed to inspire warriors going into bat-

---

* Dates for the *I-14* departing Kobe vary. For example, Nambu recalls the *I-14* "being completed" on March 10, 1945; see Nambu, *Beikidoukantai wo Kishuseyo*, p. 206. Tsugio Yata and Tsugio Sato both say the *I-14* departed Kobe on March 14, or the day before the Allies launched a B-29 raid against the city. See Sato, *Maboroshi no Sensui Kubo*, p. 147. The U.S. Naval Technical Mission to Japan, *Reports of the U.S. Naval Technical Mission to Japan*, Series S: *Ship and Related Targets*, Index no. S-17, *Japanese Submarine Operations* (Washington, D.C.: Operational Archives, U.S. Navy History Division, 1946), chap. 2, states that the *I-14* departed Kobe on March 14. However, if the *I-14* left Kobe *the day before* the Allied bombing raid, it must have left on March 16, since the raid took place on March 17.

tle, the flag quoted an ancient Chinese text: "Right Triumphs over Wrong, Law Triumphs over Right, Power Triumphs over Law, and Heaven Triumphs over Power."[11] Clearly, Shimizu was determined to triumph.

Since the *I-14* was delivered late, Shimizu had little time to train his crew. Forced to rely on his experience, he devised a schedule condensing everything he knew into an intensive training program.[12] With Japan's air and sea capability diminishing by the day, and Allied strength growing exponentially, the crew of the *I-14* would have to perform flawlessly to complete their mission. Long-term survival wasn't even a consideration.

Shimizu wasn't just an experienced sub captain—he was lucky, too. The day after the *I-14* departed Kobe, B-29 bombers attacked the harbor. The *I-15*, a *Sen-toku* sub that was 90 percent complete,[13] was severely damaged, while the *I-14* escaped unharmed.[14] Luck was to become Shimizu's defining characteristic.

THE 631ST AIR group also continued training. Takahashi got some additional dive-bomb practice, despite Kure's ever-present mountain hazard. But when a midair collision resulted in two more casualties, Lieutenant Asamura was dispatched to find a safer place to train.[15]

There are so many islands dotting Japan's inland sea that at times it seems more like the land of a thousand lakes than an open waterway. Yashiro Island was one of them and was quickly deemed a suitable location for training. The island was accessible by floatplane and ferry and even had private homes for rent. A base was constructed, and flight operations were ready by mid-March.[16]

The 631st had ten *Seiran* by now. Engine malfunctions were still a problem, though flight time was increasing.[17] *Seiran* were pulled out of their hangar sheds every morning by tractor. Each plane rested on a steel-framed dolly that could be towed to shore, where the aircraft was floated off into the sea. When they returned from training, saltwater was carefully hosed from their fuselage and wing joints to minimize contamination.

Nobuo Fujita, who had dropped incendiary bombs on the Oregon forest, was busy training seaplane pilots at Kashima during this period. Some postwar accounts claim he was a *Seiran* pilot as well. Though Fujita's teaching skills would undoubtedly have been needed, he was never officially a member of the 631st. It is possible that he taught *Seiran* pilots as a member of the 634th air group, which lent *Zuiun* to the 631st for training, but he was never officially part of the mission.

Once the air group was established at its new location, Ariizumi called NGS Staff Officer Fujimori: "We've built a new base on Yashiro Island. I want you to come down and watch the training."

Fujimori agreed and even hitched a ride in a *Seiran* for the last leg of his trip. After a day of observation, he expressed some concern. "The water landings look pretty bad," he said candidly.

Ariizumi laughed. Takeoffs were more important than landings. "Obviously, they can't be flipping over, but don't worry. We'll carry the mission out in style."[18]

Rough-water landings weren't the only problem though. Yashiro's sandy beaches quickly fouled the *Seiran* engines and jammed the wing joints, making it difficult to open and close them.[19] Before long the 631st needed to move again.

Takahashi grew increasingly unhappy with the situation. He doubted the ability of their current officers to pull off a raid on the Panama Canal. His skepticism can be viewed either as pragmatic or as characteristically negative; either way it held a kernel of truth. For example, Asamura, the *I-401*'s air group leader, had the necessary seaplane experience but no experience launching from submarines. Yamamoto, Takahashi's observer, had limited hours in the cockpit and no combat experience.[20]

But Takahashi reserved his most withering scorn for the 631st's executive officer, Lt. Cdr. Masayoshi Fukunaga. As far as Takahashi could tell, Fukunaga had no experience with submarines, *Seiran*, or air combat. Furthermore, Takahashi had never even seen him fly. When Fukunaga didn't show up for night training, Takahashi began a whispering campaign accusing him of collecting hazardous duty pay without flying. As far as Takahashi was concerned, Fukunaga was a thief and a coward. How could the 631st expect to succeed with this kind of leadership?[21]

Takahashi's "take no prisoners" attitude was typical of his personality, which was one reason he had difficulty getting along with Asamura. Competitive feelings, bad chemistry, and Asamura's seniority also played a role—as the Chinese say, two tigers cannot share the same cave. Not even Ariizumi was exempt from the ensign's harsh assessment. The commander had extensive experience in submarines, but when it came to overseeing an air group, Takahashi felt he was a neophyte.[22] Though not entirely fair (there'd been a floatplane aboard Ariizumi's *I-8*), nobody had ever commanded anything like the *Sen-toku* squadron. No doubt Takahashi thought he could do it better.

THOUGH TRAINING FOR the Panama Canal attack continued apace, Vice Adm. Jisaburo Ozawa, vice-chief of the Navy General Staff, had other plans for the *Sen-toku* subs. Nicknamed "the Gargoyle," Ozawa was considered one of the ugliest flag officers in the Imperial Japanese Navy.[23] That didn't stop him from being creative, and his plans for the *Sen-toku* subs were just that.

Ozawa proposed sending the underwater aircraft carriers to the American west coast, arming their *Seiran* with biological weapons, and unleashing germ warfare against a populous U.S. city.[24] The idea had first surfaced in December 1944, when the *I-400* subs were beginning to deploy. The navy soon took it up, establishing a room in NGS headquarters for planning the operation. But the navy's biological weapons program was uncooperative,[25] forcing Ozawa to turn to the army for help. Relations between the army and navy were never cordial. Nevertheless, the army appointed Capt. Shirou Hattori to help with the program. The person Hattori turned to for advice was the infamous Dr. Shiro Ishii.

Dr. Ishii was Japan's top virus expert. He'd commanded the army's notorious 731 Unit near Harbin, Manchuria. Organized in

1936, the secret laboratory had conducted germ warfare experiments on Chinese and American prisoners, infecting them with various diseases, including cholera and typhus.[26]

The joint army-navy undertaking was named Operation PX. Ishii recommended that aircraft drop fleas infected with bubonic plague, something he'd already tested with some success in China. Several cities were considered as targets, including San Diego, Los Angeles, and San Francisco. One source suggests east coast cities might have been considered as well.[27]

The navy approved Operation PX in early March 1945.[28] Arizumi was probably unaware of the change, since target selection was the provenance of naval higher-ups. Meanwhile, he continued preparing for the Panama Canal attack.

Approval was only momentary, however. In a March 26 meeting to discuss the operation, one of the army's most senior officers, Yoshijiro Umezu, chief of the Imperial Japanese Army General Staff, rejected the plan.

"The operation is unpardonable on humanitarian grounds," Umezu declared. "If a virus is used, war between Japan and the U.S. will escalate to war against all humanity and Japan will be the subject of derision."[29]

Naval authorities opposed Umezu's decision,[30] but once the army had withdrawn its support, there was nothing they could do. Operation PX was killed before the *Sen-toku* squadron was any the wiser.

Given their respective historical roles, it's ironic that the Imperial Japanese Navy proposed such an Armageddon-like attack while the army counseled restraint. Obviously, fighting had become so desperate there was nothing Japan wouldn't do to prevent defeat. Though the navy had its share of harebrained schemes, including swimming tanks; human torpedoes; rocket-powered suicide planes; and some might even add the *Sen-toku* subs, the navy usually took a conservative path. But by 1945, Japan's strategy of choice was to mobilize every means possible to resist surrender. If this meant organizing suicide attacks by *kamikaze* and *kaiten,* or training women and children to use bamboo spears to repel an Allied invasion, so be it. Operation PX fit right into this mindset.

BY THE START of 1945, the Sixth Fleet was a shadow of its former self. Only 20 modern combat subs were left, including the *Sen-toku* squadron. Many of the remaining subs were being refitted to carry *kaiten*, which meant combat subs were no longer considered offensive weapons as much as transport vessels for suicide torpedoes. Add to this a few surviving cargo subs and obsolete boats suitable only for training, and the Sixth Fleet was virtually extinct.[31]

Nambu's former command, the *I-362*, soon joined the list. The cargo-carrying sub had been scheduled to arrive at Mereyon Island on January 21. When she was reported missing, Nambu had no choice but to mourn his comrades.[32] And the *I-362* wasn't the only sub missing. Ariizumi's Indian Ocean boat, the *I-8*, had been lost as well. The *I-8* had been pursuing an American convoy on the surface southeast of Okinawa[33] when a lookout sighted the USS *Stockton* (DD-646). Part of the convoy's screen, the U.S. destroyer tried contacting the Japanese sub using a megaphone.[34] Ariizumi's replacement, Lt. Cdr. Shigeo Shinohara, had no interest in listening, and ordered a crash dive.

As the *I-8* approached the 100-foot mark, depth charges began exploding near her stern.[35] Since the *Stockton* easily determined the sub's position from the sound of her propellers, the accuracy of the attacks improved and their frequency increased. Minutes later a depth charge exploded, holing the crew's quarters, and water began flooding the compartment. The sudden loss of buoyancy forced the sub down near the 450-foot mark, dangerously close to crush depth. The cascading seawater concentrated in the sub's stern exacerbated her plunge and tipped her bow upward at a 25-degree angle.[36] It was like climbing the Matterhorn for anyone inside.

The crew did their best to make repairs, but the sub's main power plant was offline, and the concentration of water in the stern meant the sub continued to sink. The only thing Shinohara could do was give the order to blow the after tanks. Though this stopped the sub from imploding, the air bubbles betrayed her position, causing the *Stockton* to send down another wave of depth charges.[37]

The attack lasted four hours. All the *I-8*'s crew could do was silently await death.[38] The *Stockton* made seven attacks in all. When her depth charges were exhausted, she was joined by the USS *Morrison* (DD-560), which dropped 11 more patterns.[39] Finally, Captain Shinohara gave the order for battle surface. It was a brave if desperate move, because the *I-8* had no more torpedoes left with which to defend herself.[40] The only thing Shinohara could count on was darkness. After the *I-8* blew her tanks, another mass of bubbles rushed to the surface, marking her location. When she broke the waves at 2:00 A.M., the enemy was waiting.

The *I-8*'s gun crew crowded into the conning tower while the sub cleared the waves. The moment the bridge hatch opened, the men sprang into action. There was a strong wind and a big swell as Petty Officer Takamasa Mukai ran barefoot to his station. The moon hung in the sky like a pale searchlight while Mukai loaded the 140mm gun.[41]

The *Morrison* was only 900 yards away when the *I-8* surfaced. The destroyer spotted the sub off her starboard bow and immediately tried to ram her.[42] The *I-8*'s 25mm antiaircraft gun was first to open up.[43] Mukai also got a round off before enemy gunfire began smacking into the deck around him.[44] A moment later a metal splinter pierced his foot.

Mukai ran to the bridge for help, but just as he approached, one of the enemy's five-inch shells blew it apart.[45] Stumbling back to his post, he resolved to make a stand. The two destroyers pounded the sub for half an hour.[46] Finally, after multiple hits[47] the *I-8* rolled over[48] and went down by the stern. Mukai was thrown into the ocean. When he awoke, he found himself in the sick bay of an American destroyer,[49] the only *I-8* crewman to survive.

These were but two examples of the fate that awaited the fast-dwindling number of Sixth Fleet submarines. Lost sub commands, inexperienced flight officers, harsh water landings, and sandy hydraulic fluid were only some of the problems bedeviling the *Sen-toku* subs. Vice Adm. Marc A. Mitscher was about to significantly add to them. This time it was Kure's turn to feel the pain.

KURE WAS A navy town. The IJN had been there more than a hundred years, bringing a measure of culture and sophistication to what otherwise would have been a sleepy little fishing village. Now one of Japan's "big eight" cities, Kure was home to approximately half a million people, many of them connected with the IJN. Navy paychecks had enabled music, theater, and the tea ceremony to flourish, in addition to bringing running water and flush toilets to the city.[50] The most important aspect about Kure was that it was home base to the principal units of the Japanese fleet. This made it a tempting target for Vice Adm. Marc A. Mitscher's Task Force 58. Suddenly, it was payback time for all those islands America had wrested from Japan.

The *I-400*, *I-401*, and *I-13* were anchored at the Kure Naval Base when dawn broke the morning of Monday, March 19. The *I-401*'s crew had just returned from a five-day pass. Chin-Ji Inouye, the *I-401*'s sonar operator, was eating breakfast and thinking about his family when the air raid sounded. Sprinting to the *I-401*, he took up a defensive position alongside his crewmates. Time stood still as they craned their necks toward the empty sky. As sirens wailed in the background, they nervously awaited the arrival of the enemy air armada.[51]

Satoru Fukuoka, a *Seiran* ground crew member, was carrying ammo to an antiaircraft battery halfway up a mountainside when American aircraft first appeared. As he watched the enemy's attack leader dip his wing, Fukuoka prepared for the worst. One Grumman Hellcat after another swooped down in a power dive and, leveling out a few feet above the naval base, opened up with their 20mm cannons. The effect was devastating.[52]

Fukuoka's AA battery found it difficult to shoot down the enemy planes. The mountains shielded the aircraft until the last possible moment, and once their power dive began, it was too late.

Lt. Tsugio Yata, the *I-401*'s 22-year-old chief gunnery officer, had joined the sub just before her commissioning. An Etajima graduate, Yata was young and energetic but had never experienced battle.[53] The attack happened so quickly, he had little time to organize the *I-401*'s defenses. As Helldivers and Corsairs began diving out of the sky, Nambu guided his gunnery officer: "Wait, wait, not yet, gunnery chief." Then: "Now *Teppo*! Shoot!"[54]

The roar of the *I-401*'s triple-mount antiaircraft guns was so great, Yata couldn't hear his own commands. His gun crew discharged at least 10,000 rounds defending their sub, but the enemy planes were so thick, it was like shooting a swarm of bees.[55]

The *I-400* was nearby in number-two dry dock and unable to move.[56] The crew had been warned of the attack, so her guns were manned and ready when the first planes appeared[57] at 7:30 A.M.[58] Though trapped, she put up a good fight. Koshimoto, one of her many engineers, lugged ammo as fast as the gun crew could expend it.[59] Brass casings piled on deck like New Year's confetti, their delicate clinking lost in the cacophony.[60] One enemy aircraft scribbled a smoke trail across the sky before exploding in midair.[61] Another lost a wing and turned upside down before crashing nearby.[62] Although a few planes were shot down, it was the IJN that took a beating that day. U.S. aircraft were targeting four battleships anchored in the harbor:[63] the *Yamato*, *Ise*, *Haruna*, and *Hyuga*.[64] Normally, a battleship would try to escape an air attack, but that wasn't possible in this situation—their fuel tanks were empty.[65] Nevertheless, the battleships fought back with everything they had. Turning their cannons skyward, they blasted away with tremendous force.[66] Though the sound was deafening and the fury impressive, it was a waste of ammunition. The nimble attack bombers could easily evade cannon fire.

Inouye felt as if every antiaircraft weapon, machine gun, and sidearm was being used to repel the attack, but from Takahashi's position atop Yashiro Island, the air base seemed unable to defend itself.[67] Takahashi had been in Kure that morning. When he heard that carrier-based aircraft were heading their way, he jumped in his *Seiran* and flew it to the island for safety.[68]

Takahashi watched awestruck as enemy planes turned aircraft hangars into sieves. It was dispiriting.[69] The real battle wasn't taking place on the airfield though—it was happening in port. U.S. naval intelligence may not have known about the *I-400*'s mission, but it was hard to miss three gigantic submarines anchored in the harbor.

As wave after wave of enemy planes descended, Nambu hurried to get the *I-401* under way.[70] Meanwhile, huge water geysers erupted nearby as the sub pulled away from the pier. Yata had no doubt they'd been spotted and were now the focus of attack.[71] Though the sub's triple-mount batteries chased the enemy across the sky, it was pointless to remain. The *I-401* had put up a good fight, but she was being raked by machine-gun fire, and enemy bombs were closing in. The *I-400* might have been stuck in dry dock, but the *I-13* had already escaped. Nambu had to follow.

The *I-401* was fueled, so all Nambu had to do was find deep water and submerge.[72] But as the sub backed away from the dock, an enemy plane released a bomb overhead. Inouye watched it tumble toward the sub as if in slow motion. He could feel in his bones it was going to hit them.[73] But instead of striking the *I-401*, the bomb landed on the pier next to them.[74] The explosion was only 100 feet away,[75] so Inouye was close enough to see a gunner on the *I-400* get his face blown off. It only took a second, but the image burned into his brain forever.[76] Captain Kusaka was also injured, hit by shrapnel in the head and thigh,[77] as was the *I-400*'s chief navigator. By the time the explosion dissipated, at least six men were dead, two of them *Sen-toku* crew members.

So much smoke blanketed Kure that Nambu used it as cover.[78] It was still a shock though when he passed the *Oyodo*. Rolled onto her side, her decks awash, the cruiser's guns were blazing into the sky. Her fighting spirit made Nambu proud.[79] Nevertheless, as soon as the *I-401* cleared the harbor, he submerged to periscope depth and waited out the rest of the attack underwater.

As the *I-401* sat on the bottom of the Inland Sea, Nambu must have questioned his future. The Imperial Japanese Navy had just experienced a devastating attack, forcing the *I-401* to cower in the waters of her home port. They still had three months of training left, yet the *Sen-toku* squadron had barely survived. It was up to Ari-izumi to move things along, but the Allies weren't going to make it easy. Time was running out.

CHAPTER 21

ADVERSITY

THE *SEN-TOKU* SUBS WERE LUCKY TO ESCAPE LARGELY UN-harmed. The *I-400* and *I-401* sustained minor damage; the *I-401* was hit by machine gun bullets,[1] and the *I-400*'s fuel tank was punctured by shrapnel. Additionally, two crewmen were killed,[2] and Kusaka, the *I-400*'s captain, would need time to recover from his wounds. Surprisingly, the *I-13* had escaped unscathed and the *I-14* hadn't even been there—once again, Captain Shimizu had been lucky. Taking the *I-14* on a ten-day training mission, he'd departed Kure on March 18, missing the attack by a single day. It was the same fortuitous timing that had saved him from the Kobe air raid.[3] Clearly, Shimizu had good karma.

Takahashi inspected the Kure air base for damage. Empty cartridge casings littered the tarmac, and many of the structures were riddled by cannon fire. The decoy planes were so shot up, they barely resembled aircraft.[4] The important thing was that none of the *Seiran* had been damaged. The IJN could hardly afford to lose more *Seiran* with the aircraft in such short supply.

B-29s had already bombed Nagoya.[5] The results weren't quite as spectacular as the Tokyo firebombing the previous day. Still, the incendiaries burned enough of the city that Aichi's Eitoku facility was damaged, further slowing *Seiran* production.[6] Allied air raids and recent IJN losses dealt the Combined Fleet such a devastating blow, it ceased to function as anything more than a self-appointed suicide squad. The U.S. Navy still wasn't happy with the results though, and B-29s were diverted from bombing cities to parachuting aerial mines into the Inland Sea.[7] Operation Starvation commenced on March 27, when nearly a thousand mines were dropped, many of them in the waters around Kure, where the *Sen-toku* subs were training.

Aerial mining took the IJN by surprise.[8] The Kure Naval District did its best to remove them, but there was a shortage of minesweepers.[9] Furthermore, the new-model magnetic mines were difficult to dispose of. A training sub hit one mine while practicing off Kure and was lost. The *I-53* hit another and was severely damaged.[10] Overnight, a significant portion of the Inland Sea became unsuitable for naval operations.[11]

Operation Starvation didn't just curtail IJN fleet movements; it also increased the danger of *Sen-toku* sub training. The *I-400* subs had just begun practicing with their *Seiran* when the mines were laid. Their goal was to assemble, catapult, retrieve, and stow their aircraft with special attention paid to launching them. All three *Seiran* were supposed to be launched in under 30 minutes, but as training began, it took at least 45 minutes to get them into the air.[12]

Launching three planes in quick succession would be critical to the mission. The longer a sub remained on the surface, the more likely she'd be discovered. But mechanical difficulties hampered a sub's three *Seiran* from being operational at the same time.[13] Even when the planes were working properly, it never lasted; one always broke down.

The situation especially worried Nambu. Only once had the *I-401* managed to launch all three of her aircraft one after the other.[14] And now that the waters had been mined, it was unlikely they'd get more practice in the Inland Sea.

There was tremendous complexity in launching a *Seiran*. While the sub was still submerged, the plane's maintenance crew climbed up an access tube that led into the hangar.[15] Once inside, mechanics pumped coolant and heated lubricating oil into the plane's engine.[16] This facilitated a faster launch by reducing the warm-up time a *Seiran* required on the surface. As the maintenance crew prepared the aircraft, another team waited in the conning tower. The minute the sub broke the surface, they dashed on deck to open the giant watertight door leading to where the planes were stored. Once the door was open, the hydraulic whine of the exterior catapult rails could be heard as they rose to join the rails inside the hangar.[17]

Seiran were stored sequentially in a sub, nose to tail, with their wings and stabilizers folded. Each plane sat on a rail cart in the hangar. The carts were kept in the lowered position to prevent the plane's propeller from hitting the ceiling. Before the *Seiran* were wheeled on deck, their bombs were attached.[18] Once the first two planes were moved out of the hangar, their rail carts were raised, tilting the *Seiran* toward the sky. Finally, a team connected a high-pressure hydraulic hose to begin unfolding the wings.[19]

When Nambu saw how a *Seiran*'s wings were cranked into place, he thought it amazing.[20] Indeed, it was remarkable how elegant the process could be when the aircrew got everything right. But almost nobody got anything right the first few times they launched the planes. Worse, assembly would be a lot more difficult on the wave-tossed ocean than on the relatively calm waters of the Inland Sea. They'd need to practice until everything became second nature.

Hidden mines, maintenance problems, and fumbling aircrews weren't the only issues, though. *Seiran* flights were becoming increasingly hazardous as the United States began to dominate Japanese skies. Whenever Takahashi and Asamura flew, they had to be on constant lookout for enemy fighters. It was bad enough that the sea was unsafe; now Kure had proven the skies were equally dangerous.

Still, nothing was more hazardous than an inexperienced pilot. A senior pilot like Asamura could execute a smooth-water takeoff after only three attempts, while a junior pilot required at least ten takeoffs to master the practice.[21] Takahashi certainly appreciated the junior pilots' eagerness. But when it came to flying a state-of-the-art aircraft, technical skill outweighed enthusiasm every time.

And then there was mastering dive-bomb techniques. Takahashi didn't think it would be especially difficult to hit a lock gate since it was stationary, but low-altitude bombing was a skill acquired only after weeks of training. The junior pilots would need lots of it before they'd be effective.[22]

On April 10 ten *Seiran* took to the air over Fukuyama to simulate attacking the city. After repeated diving from 16,000 feet, Takahashi's air group finished for the day and headed back to base. Since a storm was coming, Takahashi landed in a river rather than the gulf, where the water was choppy. Two more *Seiran* landed without incident. When it came time for Second Lieutenant Ichiyoshi to put down, he ignored Takahashi's example and chose the gulf instead. Takahashi held his breath as he watched Ichiyoshi's plane make its approach.

Boy, that's dangerous, he thought. *I'll have to reprimand him.*

As he watched Ichiyoshi's *Seiran* bounce across the waves, Takahashi grew increasingly concerned. When one of the plane's pontoons broke off and the aircraft flipped over, he couldn't stop himself from shouting, "You idiot!"

A rescue boat rushed to the scene, but Ichiyoshi's head had smashed into the cockpit windshield, killing him instantly. His observer was luckier. Thrown clear of the plane, he survived the crash.[23]

It was the third accident and fifth fatality for the 631st. Though not unexpected, given the high-risk nature of their training, the casualties were beginning to add up.

As IF EARTHQUAKES, aerial mines, aircraft accidents, and enemy fighters weren't bad enough, the *Sen-toku* subs soon found themselves out of fuel. Vice Adm. Charles A. Lockwood, commander of the Pacific submarine force, knew Japan's fuel was running low. His subs had sunk 76 oil tankers with just such a goal in mind.[24] What Lockwood couldn't have known, was just how little oil was left.

Normally, an I-boat would have enough fuel to spend three months searching for targets. But fuel was now so scarce, Japan's few remaining subs had to take the most direct route to a shipping lane and wait for something to cross their path.[25] The IJN's fuel shortage was further compounded when the super-battleship *Yamato* drained the tanks at Kure's Tokuyama storage depot in April.[26] The *Yamato* was heading to Okinawa to repel the U.S. invasion. Even if she survived the sortie, she would have only enough fuel for a one-way trip.[27] Some have speculated that the *Yamato* was sacrificed in order to preserve fuel for the *I-401*'s mission.[28] There is no evidence for this claim. The IJN started the war with six million tons of oil,[29] enough to last two years. But Tokuyama, despite being one of the largest oil facilities in the IJN,[30] only had 2,000 tons left.[31]

The *I-400* and *I-401* each required 1,700 tons of fuel to complete their missions,[32] and priority was traditionally given to the surface fleet. Attacking the Panama Canal might have been important, but Ariizumi had to compete with the rest of the navy for his fuel allotment. There just wasn't enough to go around.

The 631st faced similar problems. So little aviation fuel was available that the *Seiran* squads barely had enough for training. Low in octane, the fuel had been blended with turpentine and alcohol to make it go farther, but it was such poor quality, the pilots jokingly called it "Marianas gas."[33] The IJN was aware of the problem and planned to use submarine tankers to import two million gallons of fuel from Singapore and Formosa. The *I-402* fell prey to this initiative, along with seven I-class and four HA-class subs. Instead of being completed as an underwater aircraft carrier, the *I-402* was converted into a giant underwater tanker, with a fuel capacity of 182,000 gallons.[34]

Given the fuel shortage, Ariizumi faced a difficult choice. Kure had only enough fuel for one *I-400* sub. Without fuel there was no training, no mission, and no hope of staving off defeat. Unfortunately, the Combined Fleet could not give what it didn't have. Ariizumi would have to go elsewhere.[35]

The only place where fuel could still be found in any appreciable quantity was at the IJN naval bases in China and Korea. And so Ariizumi decided to sail his flagship to the port of Dalian in Manchuria to get oil from the stocks located there.

It wasn't going to be easy. To reach China, the *I-401* would have to sail south through the Inland Sea to one of two exits, the Shimonoseki Strait on Japan's west coast, which led to the Sea of Japan, or the Bungo Strait on Japan's east coast, which led to the Pacific. Both exits were heavily mined, and each had its own set of problems. The

Shimonoseki Strait was a ten-mile doglegged channel whose narrowest point was only 800 yards wide. It would be nearly impossible to thread it without encountering a mine. On the other hand, American subs were posted outside the Bungo Strait, just itching to sink any I-boat entering the Pacific.

Ariizumi had no alternative. If he didn't try for China, he'd never get enough fuel to continue training, let alone embark on his mission. But if he braved the mine-infested waters, there was a good chance he'd never reach China. Ariizumi finally decided on the Shimonoseki route. Yes, it was heavily mined, and there was always the chance the U.S. Navy might attack in the Yellow Sea. Nevertheless, it was the shortest distance between Kure and Dalian. Additionally, the *I-401* had a degaussing mechanism, six cables snaking their way the length of the outer hull. They not only prevented the sub from rusting, they helped shield it from mines by dampening its magnetic field. They would just have to risk it.

Since traveling on the surface was the fastest way to Dalian, Ariizumi had a wooden smokestack added to his flagship to disguise her identity.[36] Given her size, the *I-401* could easily pass for a surface ship. Whether the deception would save her from attack was debatable, but it certainly masked her aircraft-carrying secret.

The *I-401* departed Kure on April 11.[37] She had just left the harbor when a swift current ran her aground. Nambu dumped ballast and quickly refloated her,[38] but it was an unlucky start. The next day the *I-401* was again traveling on the surface. It was 8:50 in the morning, and they were off Hime Island in the Inland Sea. Nambu was on the bridge, and since they had only a short distance to go before reaching the entrance to Shimonoseki, he made it a point to warn his sonar operator to keep a sharp lookout.[39]

Both Ariizumi and Yata, the chief gunnery officer, were in the wardroom having coffee.[40] A moment later both men felt an explosion lift the sub's stern into the air. Ariizumi's coffee cup hit the ceiling before spilling its contents.[41] Moments later the crew began sealing the sub's watertight doors.

In the split second it took Nambu to register the explosion, he knew they'd hit a mine. Was it survivable? Until the damage reports came in, he was at the mercy of his imagination. In the meantime, the sound of water gushing into the sub was not reassuring.[42]

Chapter 22

ATTACKING THE CANAL

THE *I-401* WAS IN 160 FEET OF WATER WHEN A MAGNETIC MINE released its anchor and floated toward the surface.[1] The ensuing explosion may have shaken the whole boat, but it was the stern that bore the brunt of the damage.

A white haze enveloped the aft deck as a churning mass of ocean boiled around the stern.[2] Had the *I-401* been traveling any slower, the mine would have hit amidships, possibly sinking her. As it was, the *I-401*'s twin propellers and their respective shafts were also vulnerable, as were her stern planes. A mine explosion in the stern could just as easily sink them.

Initial reports indicated that a fuel tank had been ruptured,[3] and a Kingston valve (which regulated the flow of seawater into the ballast tanks) was damaged.[4] It didn't take long for Nambu to ascertain the *I-401* would survive. Even so, she was in no condition to travel to China. Traveling with an oil leak was like laying down breadcrumbs for the enemy to follow. As for the gushing water, the explosion had ruptured a sake tub, sending its contents spouting into the sub.[5] Everyone had a good laugh about that.[6] It had been a close call though. All they could do now was limp back to Kure.

Unfortunately, Ariizumi was no closer to obtaining the fuel he required. With his flagship in need of repair, he had no choice. He had to send the *I-400* in place of her. Kusaka's sub was virtually identical to the *I-401*, save for a few cosmetic differences. She also had the same large fuel capacity, which meant she was a more logical choice than the smaller-capacity *I-13* or *I-14*. The one thing the

I-400 did have that the other subs in the *Sen-toku* fleet lacked was Cdr. Toshio Kusaka.

Kusaka was a highly skilled captain, as evidenced by his commander title and three previous sub commands.[7] He'd also recovered enough from the minor wounds he'd sustained during the Kure air raid to resume skippering his sub. Born in a small village on the island of Shikoku in June 1904, Kusaka had wanted to be a fighter pilot but was steered toward submarines because of his small stature.[8] Like Nambu, he was an Etajima graduate. He had also been at Pearl Harbor, captaining the *I-74*. When Doolittle's Raiders bombed Tokyo in April 1942, it was Kusaka's sub that had been sent to intercept the USS *Hornet* (CV-8).

It's likely Kusaka and Nambu knew each other before joining the *Sen-toku* squadron. Kusaka had turned command of the *I-74* (later designated the *I-174*) over to Nambu in November 1942. Kusaka had also captained war patrols off the Australian coast and transported ammunition and supplies, just like Nambu. Although their résumés were similar, Kusaka was more experienced than Nambu, which is probably why he had his own command while Nambu had to captain under Ariizumi's watchful eye.

Kusaka had also served in the Indian Ocean at roughly the same time as Ariizumi. He'd commanded the *I-26* and sunk two tankers between December 1943 and March 1944. One of his most memorable missions involved landing Indian revolutionaries near Karachi to promote an uprising against the British. Though most of the nationalists were captured or killed, it was the kind of old-fashioned spy caper that only happened in novels.

Three days after Ariizumi massacred the SS *Tjisalak*'s crew, Kusaka followed suit, using the *I-26*'s deck guns to riddle the lifeboats of an American Liberty ship, the SS *Richard Hovey*.[9] Kusaka killed eight survivors,* making him one of four SubRon 8 sub captains implicated in killing prisoners. By August 1944, Kusaka was named chief equipment officer for the *I-400*.

---

* Accounts vary in the number of survivors killed, ranging from four to eight.

"Kusaka was the best captain anyone could ask for," Lt. Kazuo Nishijima, the *I-400*'s chief navigator, noted.[10] Since Nishijima was the sub's second seniormost officer after Kusaka, it was no small compliment.

Kusaka's many years of combat experience, combined with his unquestionable ability and good judgment, earned him the respect of his crew.[11] Importantly, he radiated the same kind of confidence as the *Segundo*'s Captain Fulp. Not surprisingly, Kusaka's crew would do anything for him.[12]

Dalian, located near Port Arthur on the Yellow Sea, was an important commercial port. When Russia lost its war with Japan, it had conceded Dalian in 1905. Since then, the IJN had made significant investments in the port, which was now home to a large stock of diesel fuel.

The *I-400* left Kure for Dalian on April 14 disguised as a frigate.[13] Barrels were placed on the catapult rails and covered with a canvas tarp, while dummy cannons and machine guns were added to complete the ruse.[14] Kusaka navigated the Inland Sea at reduced speed to avoid triggering mines. As he approached Himejima, the island where the *I-401* had nearly been lost, he encountered some good luck. Two Japanese merchant ships were also heading through the Shimonoseki Strait. Kusaka joined the middle of their single-file procession, using the lead vessel to shield his sub from any mines in his path.

As Kusaka followed the first ship into the narrow strait, the *I-400* proceeded slowly on the surface. The channel was quiet save for the seagulls overhead, whose shrill cries sounded like a warning not to proceed. From his position on the bridge, Kusaka could see the red-bellied bottoms of capsized ships as the *I-400* passed by. Those that had rolled over revealed the ugly puncture wound of a mine explosion against their hull. Other ships had simply settled on the canal floor, their bottoms ripped out by 1,200 pounds of high explosives. With their decks awash, and masts poking above the waves, Shimonoseki looked like a graveyard for ships.

Suddenly, the freighter ahead erupted in an explosion as a

mine tore out its keel.* The ship was so close that the smoke pouring from her hold made Kusaka's eyes water. Though he could see the ship's crew jumping overboard, he could not stop to assist them. Everyone was on their own in a situation like this. The shore was not far away, and rescue stations had been established for just such an occasion. The explosion had been so violent though that many of the ship's crew probably never made it above deck. It was a chilling reminder that the odds of survival were no more than a coin toss.

After Kusaka navigated past the expiring vessel, he found himself in the lead. Without a buffer, he worried the *I-400* would be sunk next. As anyone who's ever been trapped in a minefield knows, the anticipation of destruction is excruciating. Lookouts can scan the water all day, but they are unlikely to spot a mine beneath the waves. What's more, sonar was useless in a narrow channel riddled with wrecks. Even so, Kusaka never considered turning back. The channel was too narrow, there was a ship following him, and Ariizumi would have condemned him. His only escape was forward.

To Kusaka's surprise the ship behind him was next to hit a mine.[15] After an enormous explosion, the freighter quickly filled with water. Kusaka must have felt that the spirit Ise watched over him that day, since the *I-400* was the sole survivor of a three-ship convoy.

After successfully navigating the rest of the strait, the *I-400* arrived in Dalian on April 20.[16] Kusaka released his crew for shore leave, which included a Chinese banquet hosted by the Manchurian Railway, and the company of "comfort women" from Korea, China, and Japan.[17] In the meantime, the *I-400* took on 1,700 tons of fuel made from liquefied coal[18] as well as a cargo of soybeans,[19] iron,[20] peanuts,[21] and molybdenum.[22] When Kusaka departed for Kure, the return trip proved uneventful.[23]

---

* Kazuo Takatsuka remembers the two ships sinking on the *I-400*'s way to Nanao Bay, not Dalian. However, since both Nambu and Sato recall it as happening during the *I-400*'s trip to Dalian, I've done the same.

WHILE THE *I-401* was undergoing repair, Ariizumi used the time to adopt what he hoped would be a game-changing technology. The device he wanted to use was called a snorkel, and the reason he wanted his flagship to have one was that he believed it would help her to remain hidden underwater longer.

The device was simple enough. Two pipes, one for air intake, the other for exhaust, were mounted on the periscope shears. Both pipes connected to the sub's auxiliary engines, supplying oxygen and venting toxic gas. When the sub was at periscope depth, it could hydraulically raise its snorkel above the surface,[24] and because each pipe had a self-sealing valve, water couldn't flood in.

The small size of the pipes made them invisible to radar and difficult to spot at a distance. Radar itself was a game-changing innovation that put Sixth Fleet subs at a disadvantage. Since Japan adopted the technology late, Ariizumi was betting the snorkel could help level the playing field. Being able to use their auxiliary engines while submerged might give them just enough extra time to escape undetected.

Ariizumi's hopes for the snorkel were not unreasonable. If the *Sen-toku* subs could remain hidden underwater a little bit longer, they could slip past the U.S. Navy to launch a surprise attack.[25] Interestingly, American subs didn't use snorkels. The U.S. Navy felt their cost, weight, space requirement, and reduction in engine performance outweighed any benefits.[26] It didn't hurt that the Pacific sub force was so strong, it had little reason to hide. U.S. subs wouldn't adopt the technology until after the war. When they did, Portsmouth was the first shipyard to add them.[27]

After the *I-400* returned to Kure, Ariizumi ordered his three other submarines outfitted with snorkels, making them one of the first Sixth Fleet subs thus equipped.[28] Installation took most of May,[29] but the lost time was worth it, especially if it created an advantage Ariizumi could exploit.

Next, the squadron commander called a meeting to brief the

officers of SubRon 1 and the 631st air group on the Panama Canal attack. Held at Kure Naval Base on or about April 25,[30] the meeting included among others: the 631st's seniormost officer, Lt. Cdr. Masayoshi Fukunaga; two of its most senior pilots, Asamura and Takahashi; and SubRon 1's four sub captains: Nambu, Kusaka, Shimizu, and Ohashi. Given the importance of the mission, representatives from the Naval General Staff and Sixth Fleet also attended, including Commanders Shojiro Iura and Yasuo Fujimori.[31]

The meeting began promptly at 9:00 A.M.[32] Chairs had been set up in the briefing room, and a large board diagrammed the route to Panama.[33] Ariizumi arrived, looking tan from all the time he'd spent on the *I-401*'s bridge. When all relevant personnel had gathered, the 631st's XO, Fukunaga, called the meeting to order.

"Based on the latest map exercise," he said, "I would like to explain SubRon 1's strategic plan and decide our training goals going forward."[34]

The plan was as easy to articulate as it was difficult to carry out. First, the *Sen-toku* squadron, comprising the *I-400*, *I-401*, *I-13*, and *I-14*, would travel the same course as Nagumo's carriers had on their way to Pearl Harbor.[35] After passing north of Hawaii, Ariizumi's subs would then head southeast until they reached the coast of Ecuador.* When they were 100 miles off Ecuador, the subs (separated by 50 miles) would surface and launch their ten *Seiran* aircraft at 3:00 A.M.[36] To accommodate the maximum bomb load, the *Seiran* would be stripped of their floats. Once launched, the aircraft would rendezvous, then fly northeast across the top of South America, passing over Colombia. To avoid radar contact, they would fly at low altitude. Once they reached the Caribbean, they would double back and head toward the Atlantic entrance to the canal.

---

* Sato indicates that the original plan was for the subs to mass off the coast of Colombia, which would have put them slightly closer to the Panama Canal. Tsugio Sato, *Maboroshi no Sensui Kubo* [*Phantom Submarine Carrier*], (Tokyo: Kabushiki Gaisha Kojin-sha, 1989). However, since Takahashi was at the actual attack plan meeting, it seems more accurate to use his account. Kazuo Takahashi, *Shinryu Tokubetsu Kogekitai* [*Divine Dragon Special Attack Unit*] (Tokyo: Koujinsha, 2001).

Ariizumi was counting on the destructive force of ten *Seiran* payloads to destroy the lock gates. Given the fact that Gatun was the largest manmade lake in the world, he had a good chance for success if his planes got through. If for any reason the *Seiran* didn't completely destroy the upper lock gates, the massive outward pressure of the lake would finish the job.

After the *Seiran* destroyed the gates, they were to rendezvous with their mother subs in the Gulf of Panama. Ditching their planes in the ocean, the aircrews would swim to their respective subs, climb on board, and return home to Japan.

Several important questions remained, however. One of the biggest was which ordnance to use to destroy the lock gates. Fujimori's team at the Naval General Staff had researched this question and come to the conclusion that a combination of torpedoes and bombs would be most effective,[37] but more research was required.

After his presentation, Fukunaga opened the floor to questions. Takahashi knew most of the pilots wouldn't know what to ask, so he was first to raise his hand. Standing as he addressed the 631's XO, Takahashi asked what phase the moon would be in when the *Seiran* launched from the submarines.

"Out of consideration for the submarines' safety, you will fly on a moonless night," came the reply.

Takahashi was taken aback. "Just flying my plane at night with a full tank of gas and a torpedo will be difficult enough. For ten airplanes to find one another in the dark, then fly in formation, will be impossible. What's more, flying over Colombia at low altitude means the chance of being discovered is extremely high."

"We'll look into that and respond," Fukanaga said dismissively.[38]

Takahashi wondered if the attack had been thought through properly. Yes, it was only a draft plan; still, success depended on the details, and Commander Ariizumi was nothing if not detail oriented. Takahashi took some consolation in knowing Ariizumi had listened to his question. The "map exercise" may have ended before the tactical issues were resolved,[39] but at least Ariizumi knew further study was required.[40]

AFTER THE ATTACK briefing, Ariizumi went to Yokosuka Naval Air Base to personally investigate the right ordnance for destroying the lock gates. Once again he confirmed that a combination of torpedoes and bombs was ideal. Unfortunately, a torpedo attack by floatplane bombers required a level of skill that the 631st air group hadn't yet developed. After discussion, Ariizumi, Fukanaga, and Asamura agreed that all ten *Seiran* planes would carry the largest bomb in the navy's arsenal, a 1,760-pound behemoth—the same kind that had sunk the USS *Arizona* at Pearl Harbor. They also agreed that the planes would fly at low altitude before slamming into the lock gates. It was the only way to ensure the canal's destruction, but it meant that none of the *Seiran* pilots would be returning. It was also the opposite of Admiral Yamamoto's original intention. Yamamoto didn't believe in sacrificing men unless he had to. Rescuing the *Seiran* aircrew had always been a priority. NGS Staff Officer Fujimori, who had guided development of the *I-400* subs after Yamamoto's death, shared this view. Given the current level of pilot training, however, the only way to ensure a successful mission was to crash the planes into the lock gates.[41] And so it was decided, if not explicitly stated, that the Panama Canal attack would become a *tokko,* or suicide mission. It was hardly a surprise given the lamentable state of the war. Now, stakes had been raised to the highest possible level.

Asamura wasn't afraid of dying. He'd been reconciled to a suicide mission almost from the start.[42] If destroying the canal meant sacrificing 20 men, so be it; Asamura feared failure more than death.[43] He'd stop at nothing to achieve success.

Not everyone shared Asamura's enthusiasm, especially since the unit wasn't informed of the change. When a mechanic found a workman tinkering with the *Seiran* bomb release mechanism, he immediately informed Takahashi.

"What are you doing?" Takahashi demanded of the workman.

"I've been ordered to fix the *Seiran* so the bombs remain attached to their undercarriage."

"Do the aircrews know about this?"

The answer was no.

Takahashi immediately went in search of Fukunaga. When he found him, he lit into him with a vengeance: "It's unforgivable to tell us we aren't on a suicide mission and then go behind our backs with secret preparations for a *tokko* attack."

Fukunaga responded coolly, "Given the war situation, airplanes are assigned to *tokko* missions. No air groups can avoid it. All *Seiran* are to participate in a suicide attack."

"I'm not saying I won't go on a *tokko* attack," said Takahashi. "I know planes are flying suicide missions every day. But don't lie to us. Why can't you be honest and tell us you want us to go on a suicide mission? That would be the dignified thing to do!"[44]

Fukunaga was not used to being reprimanded by a subordinate, and he shouted back at Takahashi, "Vice Admiral Onishi decided at an NGS meeting that all *Seiran* will ram the Panama Canal! It was agreed by our unit's leading officers to keep it secret so as not to stress the aircrews."[45]

Surprised at the news, Takahashi turned abruptly and left. Before the day was over, everyone knew the mission had changed.[46]

Takahashi wasn't alone in questioning the suicide attack. Nambu was also against it: "I don't care what Commander Ariizumi or the Sixth Fleet think. As captain, I will find a way to retrieve my *Seiran* crews."[47]

Several of the *Sen-toku* captains thought it a waste to send such highly trained pilots on a *tokko* mission. When Takahashi later learned it was Fukunaga who'd insisted on the suicide attack, he became furious all over again.[48]

The 631st aircrews accepted the decision with equanimity. Nevertheless, their attitudes subtly changed. Some pilots began staying in Fukuyama overnight, even though it was against regulations. Takahashi was one of them. He didn't care if he was court-martialed. He was going to enjoy what little life he had left. The mission was only a month away. They could hardly afford to dismiss him.[49]

Training proceeded smoothly despite the discord. The 631st now had ten pilots and ten observers skilled in flying *Seiran,* with additional pilots in reserve. Though engine trouble continued to force emergency landings, the *Seiran* crews were becoming proficient.[50] In a few weeks, they'd be ready to attack.

CHAPTER 23

GREEN LIGHT

WHILE TRAINING CONTINUED, ARIIZUMI REFINED THE ATTACK plan. In early May he submitted a draft to Sixth Fleet command who, after reviewing it, forwarded it to the Navy General Staff for approval. It was agreed to launch the *Seiran* on a moonlit night, presumably in deference to Takahashi's wishes. The upper Gatun lock gates were also confirmed as the target, including the mechanism for opening and closing the doors.[1] Finally, it was agreed that all ten planes would attack the upper gate one after the other, to ensure its destruction.[2] A mid-June departure date was set for Panama.[3]

Squad assignments for all four subs were announced on May 20.[4] Asamura was named squadron leader for the *I-401;* Takahashi was put in charge of the *I-400*. The last stage of *Seiran* training involved attacking a full-sized mockup of the Gatun gates. But mining had virtually closed Japan's Inland Sea, so Ariizumi ordered SubRon 1 and her *Seiran* squads to transfer to Nanao Bay, on Japan's west coast.[5] It was hoped that the sheltered waters of the Noto Peninsula would provide refuge from mines and enemy planes. Attack training could then proceed unhindered.

The *Sen-toku* subs were ready for departure by the end of May. Snorkels had been installed on all four subs, and familiarization training was complete. Since the *I-400* was fully fueled, the *I-401* would get what was left in Kure's tanks.[6] The *I-13* and *I-14*, however, would have to tap the fuel tanks in Chinkai, Korea, before meeting up with their sister subs in Nanao Bay.

The two smaller subs departed on May 27.[7] Even the *I-13* and *I-14* were unable to escape the dangers of Shimoneski though. While the subs overnighted at Moji, a short distance from the strait's entrance, the port came under attack from B-29s. Both subs got away, but the difficulties were increasing.

The 631st's four *Seiran* squads flew to Nanao Bay shortly thereafter. The majority of planes transferred to their new base at Anamizu, while a few planes remained at Fukuyama for future missions.[8] Once again private homes were rented for accommodations, and weather and communication functions were established.[9]

The *I-401* prepared to leave for Nanao on June 1, with the *I-400* following the next day.[10] Many people at Kure Naval Base turned out to see the huge sub off. As a brass band played, officers crowded alongside enlisted men gaping at Ariizumi's flagship.[11] Asamura must have burned with pride as he watched the dockside gathering. Their mission might have been secret, but he knew what the cheering crowd could only guess at: the *I-401* was Japan's last best hope for survival. That is, if they got through Shimonoseki first.

The last thing Nambu wanted to do was transit the strait. It was just too dangerous.[12] He'd already tried it once and nearly lost his sub. He'd rather take his chances with the Bungo Strait, work his way along the bottom of Kyushu, and then head north. But Ariizumi insisted on the shortcut.

The route seemed reckless to Nambu. Kusaka had just barely managed to get through, and the *I-13* and *I-14* had been attacked not far from its entrance. To make matters worse, Nambu would have to cross the strait at low tide.[13] Low tide meant mines were closer to the surface. Since the *I-401* had a 24-foot draft it made her even more vulnerable.[14] It wasn't a pretty picture.

Nambu tried persuading his commanding officer to take the Bungo Strait, but Ariizumi insisted the direct route was best. The Bungo Strait had its own problems, he noted. It might have been wider and deeper, but it took longer to navigate than Shimonoseki, and transiting the bottom of Kyushu would leave them open to enemy attack. Plus passing through the Tsushima Strait into the Sea of Japan would be dangerous, since it too was mined. Time was of the essence. They had only a few weeks before the mission; they could afford no further delay. Nambu backed down.[15]

There was often tension between Nambu and his commanding officer. Both men had strong personalities, and both believed their way was best. Part of it was command style, part of it chemistry.[16] One problem was Ariizumi's tunnel vision. Rigid and unyielding, he refused to give in. The mission was everything, and he knew best. Nambu, on the other hand, was more flexible. Though the mission was important, the welfare of his crew also mattered. His men might die in battle, but he wasn't going to sacrifice them needlessly. Ariizumi, however, would destroy the canal no matter what the cost. If men had to be sacrificed, well, that was war. A man's life was a small thing compared to serving the emperor.

Nambu must have swallowed his anger at the rashness of Ariizumi's plan. He was ready to die in pursuit of the mission, but what was the point of dying before they'd even left Japan? Nevertheless, Nambu instructed the navigator to plot a course for Shimonoseki, and went about his business.

It was customary for large warships to leave port at night to avoid Allied detection. Since the *I-401* was the world's largest sub, she left that evening under the cover of darkness. When they arrived at Shimonoseki the next day, the view from the bridge reaffirmed Nambu's concern.

There were so many sunken ships, their masts looked like a forest of iron trees.[17] It seemed impossible that a sub could pass through all that and still avoid a mine. Nambu cut the engine's RPMs to prevent any sound-activated mines from being triggered and slowly entered the strait.[18] Next, he began gingerly weaving his sub through the forest of sunken masts.[19] If he could skirt close enough to a wreck, he might be able to hide in its magnetic field and avoid triggering a mine. It was a risky tactic, but the masts would serve as his guide.

Nambu sweated freely as he navigated the slow-motion slalom course.[20] There was nothing more disconcerting than watching a sunken ship slip by, each wreck a testimony to the impossibility of their task. While the *I-401* glided quietly on the surface, individual crew members visited the sub's shrine to ask Ise for protection.[21] The snail's pace of their journey, combined with the visible failure of all those who'd gone before them, only made the crew more nervous. While the lookouts held their breath, Ariizumi remained silent and unreadable.

Fortunately, Ise watched over them that day. When the *I-401* emerged into the Sea of Japan, Nambu felt relief. He was also in for a surprise. There were a shocking number of shipwrecks along the coast[22]—evidence that enemy mines weren't just confined to the Inland Sea. The wrecks also suggested U.S. subs might be operating in the area, which would make training a lot more hazardous.

As the *I-401* headed northeast toward Nanao, the attack on the Panama Canal entered its final stage of preparation. Only a few weeks more, and they would be on their way. Nambu's successful navigation of the Shimonoseki Strait had proved the gods were still on their side. They had come too far not to succeed.

CHAPTER 24

FULP'S LAST PATROL

WHEN THE *SEGUNDO*'S SECOND WAR PATROL FINISHED, CAPTAIN Fulp headed for Guam. The patrol had been successful—sinking three ships and surviving a flood were no small accomplishments, despite losing a man. Nevertheless, when Fulp sailed into Apra Harbor on January 5, 1945,[1] Guam came as a relief.

Fulp released his crew for two weeks of rest and recuperation at Camp Dealey. Dealey had been open only six weeks[2] and was still a rude collection of Quonset huts and tents. The Marines had recently recaptured Guam, killing more than 18,000 Japanese in the process. Still, the island wasn't as quiet as it looked. The United States might have regained control of the shell-cratered speck, but a handful of Japanese remained hiding in the mountains. Some sub crews hunted Japs for pleasure.[3] The practice ended in December, however, when five submariners were ambushed and killed.[4] The *Segundo* arrived shortly thereafter, and though most Japanese holdouts had been reduced to carrying spears, Guam was still not secure.

Ens. Lewis Rodney Johnson learned this the hard way his first night at Dealey. Johnson was fast asleep, about 200 feet from the cook's tent, when he was awakened by popping noises.[5] Jumping out of bed, Johnson was surprised to see Japanese soldiers running past him. The holdouts regularly stole food at night, and the camp's cooks were chasing them off with rifle fire. Johnson was probably in more danger of being shot by a chef than injured by a hungry Japanese soldier. Still, it was impossible to get a good night's sleep knowing the enemy was near.

The problem persisted throughout their stay. One afternoon a *Segundo* crewman waiting for chow noticed a gap in the line ahead of him. When the crewman took a closer look, he saw a man standing in the gap with no one around him. Realizing it was a Japanese soldier, he gave the man a wide berth. Others in line did the same. The Jap wasn't a threat, he was just hungry,[6] but it was another sign of just how poorly the war was going for Japan. The Japanese soldier was taken into custody shortly afterward, but at least he got a free meal.

THE *SEGUNDO* LEFT Guam on February 1, 1945, for her third war patrol. Destined for the East China Sea, she was accompanied by the USS *Razorback* and USS *Sea Cat* (SS 399).[7] The East China Sea could be dangerous. Known for its shallow water and poor sonar conditions,[8] it was a tough place for a sub to hide. Of more concern was the shrinking number of enemy targets. Of the 87 war patrols mounted from Pearl Harbor between January and March 1945, almost 70 percent returned without sinking a single enemy ship.[9] In fact, Japanese targets were so scarce, Pacific-based subs were reduced to attacking smaller vessels like fishermen and coastal merchants. If Fulp didn't know the exact statistics, he certainly knew it was difficult to find the enemy. The *Segundo*'s third war patrol would be no exception.

A month went by without Fulp sinking a ship. Aside from the accidental triggering of a fire extinguisher, which "considerably bolstered the boat's CO_2 content,"[10] the only other notable event came while the sub was off Nagasaki. Seas were calm, and Ensign Johnson had the watch, when the *Segundo*'s periscope punctured the waves and spotted an I-boat on the surface. It's tempting to think the Japanese submarine that Johnson saw was the *I-401*, since Nambu was conducting shakedown training in the area at this time. We'll never know for sure because the I-boat turned and headed into Sasebo harbor before Captain Fulp could get off a shot.[11]

Eventually, the three U.S. sub captains became so frustrated at the enemy's absence, they broke up their wolf pack. They hoped to improve their chances of finding a target by patrolling individually.[12] But aside from spotting two Japanese hospital ships, the *Segundo* continued to lack enemy contact.

Fulp had already radioed ComSubPac requesting an extension to his patrol when he finally encountered the enemy. It was March 6, and the *Segundo* was in shallow water off the Korean coast. Normally, Fulp would have let the ship go (she was that small), but they'd been out for a month with nothing to show. He was desperate for action.

Fulp closed the target to within 1,300 yards before letting loose with four torpedoes. If it was overkill, he wasn't taking any chances. Incredibly, all four missed. Errors related to the torpedo spread were responsible, which just goes to show what happens when you get the math wrong. Fulp considered a gun attack, but the sea was too rough to be accurate.[13] Consequently, the first real target of their patrol escaped without a scratch.

Fulp's luck improved the next evening. It was nearly three in the morning when radar identified a target at 16,000 yards. The ship was the *Shori Maru*, a smallish freighter weighing 3,087 tons. Fulp remained on the surface as he made his approach, despite the sea being so phosphorescent it seemed white. Thirty-six minutes later he launched the first of four torpedoes.

His lead fish ran erratically, so Fulp aimed for the middle of the target. The second one blew the ship's stern clean off, while the third struck amidships. It didn't matter that the fourth went missing because two minutes later the *Shori Maru* was gone.[14]

Fulp intended to pick up survivors but called it off when radar reported a convoy nearby. Two transports accompanied by two destroyers were too juicy a target to pass up. Japanese warships were always more desirable than merchants, and though destroyers were dangerous, Fulp hoped to make a clean sweep of them.

With three torpedoes remaining in the bow and a full nest aft, Fulp made for the convoy. As dawn broke, the *Segundo* was still 4,100 yards away. Since the transports would soon reach the safety of a nearby island, he had to act fast. Unfortunately, one of the escorts, sensing the *Segundo*'s presence, closed to within 2,400 yards, forcing Fulp to break off the attack.

Two weeks later the *Segundo* was ordered to Pearl for refit.

THE *SEGUNDO* LEFT on her fourth war patrol on April 26, 1945.[15] When she arrived in Saipan on May 8, a dinner was held to celebrate her one-year anniversary. Germany's recent surrender must have contributed to the good cheer. Certainly, the newly installed ice cream freezer didn't hurt. U.S. forces continued to face a daunting enemy though. Germany had been defeated, but the Japanese showed no inclination to surrender. And though enemy targets were in decline, the *Segundo* was still in danger from sea mines or a Japanese destroyer bearing a grudge.

Once again Fulp headed for the East China Sea. It was his eleventh war patrol, fourth as captain of the *Segundo*. Though eleven patrols were a lot for a submariner, Fulp showed no sign of fatigue. He'd worked these waters before, and even though he knew they were dangerous, he was eager for action.

As proof, a crewman spotted an untethered mine bobbing on the surface. The sub's 40mm guns quickly dispatched it.[16] On May 18 they passed two cadavers floating in the sea, "one Jap, one Yank."[17] It was a grim reminder of the war's toll on both sides.

On the afternoon of May 29, Fulp encountered six Chinese junks destined for Korea.[18] Junks (also called sampans) were small wooden sailboats used for coastal transport. They had a large mast aft, a smaller one forward, and a jib. The Japanese had come to rely on them as their merchant fleet was destroyed. There was something suspicious about an identical fleet of junks all heading in the same direction, so Fulp surfaced for a closer look.

As the *Segundo* passed the first vessel, Fulp reduced speed and ordered the .50 caliber machine guns manned. After closing to within 50 yards, he looked each junk over, then let them pass—until somebody noticed a Japanese insignia on one of the last boats. Fulp ordered a warning shot, intending to sink the vessel, but instead of abandoning the sampan, her crew scurried below deck. It was strange behavior, which didn't deter Fulp. He sank the ship anyway.

The *Segundo* inspected 14 junks that afternoon.[19] It wasn't difficult to guess which ones were the enemy. As the *Segundo* approached, the Korean crews bowed and smiled at the passing sub. The Japanese crews, however, changed course, trying to hide their bow markings. As the *Segundo*'s patrol report noted, the enemy crews appeared "stalwart, surly and unbending as you would expect Japanese to be."[20]

Ens. Vic Horgan was topside when a *Segundo* crewman charged up on deck waving a .45-caliber sidearm. When the man began shooting at the Japanese crews, Horgan felt disgust. He could understand blowing a ship out of the water. But shooting individuals? That wasn't what they were about.[21]

A total of 60 junks appeared that afternoon,[22] which must have given Fulp pause, since he was outnumbered. He still managed to sink seven of them though, demonstrating just how granular the Pacific war had become.

As the days passed, the *Segundo* continued reaping small rewards. On June 3 she encountered a four-masted schooner from an earlier age. Over 200 feet long, she was fully rigged with great billowing sails and classic lines.[23] Fulp launched two torpedoes at 500 yards, both with zero angles and a 90-degree port track. Thirty seconds later the explosion from the first torpedo broke the schooner in two. The second torpedo missed due to a bad gyro angle, but it didn't matter. The ship was destroyed.[24]

The only significant opposition Fulp encountered on the *Segundo*'s fourth war patrol came late on the evening of Friday, June 8. Near Port Arthur, China, the sub spotted a good-size tug. Fulp suspected a trap, since the Japanese were known to use heavily armed Q-boats disguised as freighters to lure U.S. submarines to their doom. The tug appeared to have a ship in tow, but it was pitch black, and Fulp wasn't sure what he was seeing. He prepared to attack anyway.[25]

The *Segundo* closed to within 600 yards before letting two torpedoes go. The target immediately turned to confront them. It might have been a tug, or it might not; Fulp had no way of knowing.* Unfortunately, both torpedoes missed, and whatever it was set course to ram them. Fulp ordered full speed ahead to avoid a collision. Even then the "tug" missed by only 100 yards. Fulp was in no mood for retreat, so he called for a "down the throat" shot, the most difficult kind to make. He slowed the *Segundo* to ten knots before letting loose with a torpedo from his aft nest. Even at a "kissing distance" of 580 yards, it somehow missed.

Embarrassed at having wasted three good torpedoes, Fulp took a moment to consider his options. The night was too dark for effective gun action, and the water too shallow to dive. His only choice was to risk a high-speed surface attack.[26] Hiding in front of an island's black silhouette, he gave his gun crew 20 minutes to adjust their eyes to the darkness. Then, at 22 minutes past midnight, he began his charge.

The *Segundo* raced at flank speed, maintaining a small angle on the bow to keep her profile at minimum.[27] At first Electrician's Mate Bud Quam, the pointer on the five-inch gun, found it so dark, he couldn't see what he was shooting at. The target was out there though because whatever it was, was firing back at him.[28] Once the *Segundo*'s deck guns opened up,[29] their tracer ammunition provided all the illumination Quam needed.[30] Twenty-four minutes later both targets were destroyed.

Naturally, a crew wanted to celebrate an enemy being sunk, but nothing was supposed to be "dryer" than a sub on war patrol. Fortunately, this wasn't always the case. Fulp kept a shower filled with Greasy Dick, a Pittsburgh-brewed beer. It was broken out only with the captain's permission, usually on Sundays to and from war patrols, or after a successful enemy engagement. Crewmen were limited to one can each, which they could drink off duty and never

---

* Some of the *Segundo*'s crew suggest it was two Japanese "whale killers," patrol craft similar to a PT boat.

during battle stations.[31] No one recalls whether they drank a Greasy Dick that night. It wouldn't have been surprising if they had. A seaman and his booze aren't easily parted, and sinking two ships was reason to celebrate.

FULP PRIDED HIMSELF on taking calculated risks. He knew how to analyze a situation, finding the right balance between aggression and winding up dead at the bottom of the sea. Some sub captains wouldn't attack in less than 180 feet of water. Fulp wasn't one of them. The *Segundo* spent a lot of time in shallow depths, since that was where coastal shipping was found. He wasn't foolish, though. When the sun came up, he knew to head for deep water.[32]

You couldn't always depend on Fulp's brand of courage, however. One of the few times Fulp's instincts let him down came in the Yellow Sea. He'd just sunk a Japanese freighter and was being pursued by her escorts into shallow water when the enemy inexplicably broke off their attack. Fulp couldn't understand why until he realized they'd chased him into the middle of a minefield.[33]

Unable to see what lay in his path, Fulp had to maneuver with tremendous care. It was all too easy for the sub's bow or stern planes to snag a cable pulling the attached mine against the hull where it would explode. And at that close range it only took a single mine to sink a sub.

Fulp spent the better part of a day working his way through the obstacle course.[34] Once or twice his crew heard the terrifying sound of a steel cable scrape the length of the *Segundo*'s hull.[35] The noise alone was enough to make your knees buckle. But Fulp managed to shimmy his way out of trouble. It wasn't an episode he wanted to repeat, however. Perhaps that's why his patrol report never mentioned it.

The final attack of the *Segundo*'s fourth war patrol turned out to be Fulp's last. It began on Sunday, June 10, while the sub was still in the Yellow Sea. Once again Fulp found himself in only 90 feet of water. It was 10:35 in the evening when SJ radar picked up a contact at 14,000 yards. The target proved to be the *Fukui Maru No. 2*, a Japanese freighter accompanied by two escorts.

It was a poor night for an attack. Fog reduced visibility to 500 yards, and the sub's radar wasn't working properly. A submerged approach would be preferable. Unfortunately, it was out of the question. But a surface attack was also dangerous, especially if the escorts had radar.

The night was so dark, Fulp couldn't see the freighter at 600 yards. Using target bearing transmitter bearings to make his calculation, he launched four torpedoes shortly after midnight. Forty seconds later three explosions could be heard. Three minutes after that the *Fukui Maru* was gone.

The next day the *Segundo* was ordered to Midway. Her fourth war patrol was over.

THE SUB'S REFIT lasted more than a month. There were problems with the main motors, and rust was found in the torpedo tubes.[36] Nobody was disappointed, though. The *Segundo* had won her fourth battle star and added ten more enemy ships to her battle flag.

The crew loved Midway. A nineteenth-century coaling station about a third of the way between Hawaii and Japan, the island was a welcome break. The monk seals were so tame, you could walk right up and scratch their belly, and the gooney birds provided hours of entertainment.

Fulp was awarded a Gold Star in lieu of a second Silver Star for conspicuous gallantry in his penetration of "shallow enemy-controlled waters and . . . skillfully executed gun and torpedo attacks which resulted in the sinking of 14,000 tons of enemy shipping."[37] But the glow didn't last.

On June 29, in a brief formal ceremony, Cdr. James Douglas Fulp, Jr., in accordance with Commander Submarine Force Pacific Fleet, Subordinate Command, Navy No. 1504, Serial 403, was relieved as commanding officer of the USS *Segundo*. Having completed his duty as sub captain, Fulp was returning to Pearl Harbor, for a staff job. In other words, he was being kicked upstairs.

The *Segundo*'s crew were sorry to lose their captain.[38] Fulp had proven both capable and reliable, attributes they'd come to appreciate. Importantly, he'd shaped them into a fighting machine that could handle just about anything thrown their way.

Unfortunately, their new captain, Lt. Cdr. Stephen L. Johnson, didn't make the same impression. Instead of coming across as calm, cool, and collected, Johnson seemed young, arrogant, and impetuous. It was not a good combination.

What kind of skipper have we got now? the crew wondered.

They would soon find out.

Chapter 25

NANAO BAY

The day after the *Segundo* sank its second four-masted schooner, Nambu's *I-401* arrived in Nanao Bay. The *I-13* and *I-14* were already there waiting. The *I-400* was due to follow the next day.[1] Finally, all four submarines would be together, with a full complement of *Seiran* to practice attacking the canal. Considering that three of the four subs had been commissioned by early January 1945, it was late in the game to be fully operational.

Nanao Bay is located in the crux of the Noto Peninsula. Extending into the Sea of Japan like a curled index finger, the peninsula stands halfway up the west coast of Honshu opposite Korea. Noto was sparsely populated in comparison with Kure. Except for the town of Anamizu, there was hardly anyone about. It was perfect for secret training.

Ariizumi's hope was that the region's deep water and hidden coves would protect them against enemy air raids. Still, the trip there had been discouraging. Everywhere they looked, they'd found America's handiwork. Sunken ships littered Japan's shoreline, and what traffic continued to ply the waters hugged the coast. The enemy had never seemed closer.

They didn't have to look far for an explanation. Once Germany surrendered, America no longer had to split her forces between the European and Pacific theaters. Japan could now expect the full force of the United States military focused against her. If the *Sen-toku* subs didn't close the Panama Canal, tens of thousands of men and countless tons of ships, planes, tanks, bombs, and ammunition would flow uncontrollably into the Pacific. Ariizumi had to put a stop to these reinforcements, otherwise Japan would be invaded before the year was out. Destroying the Panama Canal was the only action left that could prevent defeat.

After successfully refueling at Chinkai, the *I-13* and *I-14* had arrived at Nanao. It was June 1, 1945, and the bay was covered in fog, forcing them to wait for it to clear.[2] Three days later, while the rest of the fleet was still in transit, the *I-14* craned her two *Seiran* on board. It was the first time Captain Shimizu had his full complement of aircraft.[3] The *I-14* was finally fully operational.

The 631st air group had already established a new base. While Nambu had been making his way up Japan's west coast, the *Seiran* pilots had settled into their headquarters. They didn't have long to wait. Joint training began on June 6.[4] The subs practiced rapid surfacing and *Seiran* assembly, followed by a swift catapult launch and crash-diving to escape detection. When the drill was complete, the subs resurfaced; the *Seiran* landed in their wake, taxied up their port side, and were craned on board, where the process was repeated all over again.

Perhaps the most labor-intensive part of *Seiran* assembly was attaching the floats. Everyone knew when the time came that the *Seiran* would launch without them. They needed them for training though. There was no way for a seaplane to land safely and be retrieved without them. Securing the floats took a ten-man team at least two and a half minutes[5]—one reason *Seiran* launchings didn't go as quickly as Nambu would have liked. Of course, eliminating the floats would reduce precious launch time, but that was reserved for the mission.

While the floats were being attached, the rest of the team swarmed over the planes completing their prep work. As soon as the first *Seiran* launched, its rail cart was removed, the surrounding area was cleaned up, and the second plane maneuvered into launch position. The real problem came after the second plane was catapulted into the sky. The *I-400* subs had originally been designed to accommodate only two aircraft. When the third *Seiran* was added, the resulting design changes did not allow for the same kind of smooth launch process as the first two planes. One reason was that the sub's deck could only accommodate two planes at a time, leaving the last plane stranded in the hangar. This meant both planes had to be in the air before the launch crew could turn their attention to prepping the third. Considerable time was lost.*

Ariizumi made his sub captains drive their crews relentlessly. He had to. The *Sen-toku* subs were so far behind schedule and Japan was so badly losing the war, there was little time left. This meant training was around the clock. The subs left port every day between two and three in the morning and often didn't return until ten that night.[6] Training in darkness was critical, since it simulated the conditions under which the *Seiran* would launch. Still, the schedule was grueling. The mechanics had the most difficult time. Up all night launching planes, they'd spend the morning performing maintenance to make sure the *Seiran* were ready for the next practice. They got little sleep, no time off, and even less sympathy, since they were under pressure to speed up the launch process. At one point, the stress became so great, Nambu heard a maintenance man shout, "I will never be a mechanic on a submarine again!"[7] Maybe he was kidding—Nambu wasn't sure. Either way, he admired their determination.

At first it took the better part of a day to launch three planes.[8] But as aircrews became more adept, they managed to get it down to 45 minutes, then a half hour. Finally, after six weeks of training, they were able to catapult the first two planes in as little as four minutes.†[9]

The problem was the third plane, which took up to 20 minutes to launch.‡[10] That was nearly three times longer than the first two planes combined. They may have cut total launch time to 28 minutes, but that was a lifetime in enemy waters.

---

* According to some accounts, it took almost twice as long to prep the third *Seiran*.

† Robert Mikesh says seven minutes were required to launch each of the first two planes. See Mikesh, *Aichi M6A1 Seiran,* p. 13. Nambu, however, says all three planes could be launched in ten minutes.

‡ Sato, in *Maboroshi no Sensui Kubo,* says the third *Seiran* required 15 minutes to launch (p. 143). Nevertheless, it was a considerably longer period than for the first two aircraft.

Despite the complaints of a few mechanics, the *Sen-toku* crew were in high spirits.[11] After so many delays, they were finally training without interruption. Nambu felt proud to lead these men. They'd been called upon to save their country and would selflessly heed that call. But he harbored no illusions. He knew their chances of survival, let alone success, were shrinking by the day. Still, he'd overcome any obstacle, suffer any deprivation, in order to succeed. The mission was everything.

And so the *Sen-toku* squadron practiced over and over again. As Nambu reduced launch times, a symphony of coordination began to take shape. Despite his best efforts though, the *Seiran* continued to be plagued by problems.[12] Sometimes an aircraft's wing would be damaged during launch preparation, leaving the pilot to fume while repairs were made. Other times the engine didn't work as designed. *Seiran* engines tended to overheat at full throttle, and there were still many oil leaks.[13]

One day shortly after takeoff, Asamura was surprised by hot oil geysering into his cockpit.[14] The *Seiran*'s canopy was so obscured by the viscous black liquid that he was forced to make an emergency landing near his sub. Asamura's piloting skills saved him from disaster, but he was lucky. Some *Seiran* pilots were forced down so far from their sub that precious time was lost retrieving them.

Not every mishap was easily remedied. It was bad enough that the maintenance crews had to operate in darkness, sometimes the sub's pitching and rolling threw them overboard. Timing the catapult launch was also a challenge. A *Seiran* had to be launched into the wind to ensure enough lift for it to climb. Nambu did his best to steer accordingly, but wind and wave direction could change without notice, putting the *Seiran* in jeopardy.[15] Furthermore, *Seiran* pilots needed to see the horizon when launching, which was difficult at night.[16] It was easy to get disoriented and crash upon takeoff, which was one reason the pilots received six-yen hazard pay each time they launched.*[17]

---

* The pilots called hazard pay *pong roku* because *pong* was the sound the catapult made during launch and *roku* means "six." Interestingly, the hazard

Taking off from a sub was always dramatic. The catapult was noisy,[18] but the actual launch was smoother than what Asamura was used to.[19] Its concussive force still slammed him into his seat back though. As the *Seiran* hurled down its track toward the tapering bow, the giant sub must have seemed not quite long enough to successfully launch an airplane. There was a sickening dip at the end, when the *Seiran* shot over the water and its engine clawed hungrily for altitude. An experienced pilot knew to gun the throttle for the lift he needed. For Asamura, it was the greatest ride he'd ever experienced.

The *Seiran* was one of the most cutting-edge planes of its day. Asamura was especially impressed by its gyro compass. Not even IJN surface ships had such a modern device. Though the initial *Seiran* were well made, quality dropped off as production fell. But as far as Asamura was concerned, the *Seiran* rivaled the best bombers the IJN had to offer. He just couldn't get enough of that plane.[20]

As launch times improved, the 631st turned to bombing the Panama Canal mockup. The workshop at Maizuru Naval Base had built a full-size wooden version of the Gatun gates, based on blueprints Ariizumi had provided. When the mockup was complete, it was towed on a raft by tugboat to Nanao Bay, where it was anchored between two buoys.[21]

The *Seiran* were dwarfed by the immensity of the structure. They were like flies dive-bombing a bowling alley. Skimming across the ocean surface at high speed takes skill, something many of the pilots still lacked. Nevertheless, they flew toward the mockup in a shallow attack hitting a top speed of 184 mph before breaking off at the last second and repeating the exercise.[22]

There would be no turning back from the lock gates, regardless of how quickly their flying skills improved. It would be virtually impossible to ditch a seaplane without floats and a bomb attached. No matter what happened, the *Seiran* pilots were heading for destruction.

---

pay was capped at five launches no matter how many launches a *Seiran* pilot undertook.

The secrecy about the suicide mission sickened Takahashi. There was no reason the air group couldn't carry out an attack and return safely to the subs. Bombing a stationary target was far easier than attacking a moving ship, which was why Takahashi had lost all confidence in his commanders. If Ariizumi wanted to throw his life away on a mission that could succeed without the sacrifice, he wasn't going to stand in his way—he'd already lost 120 classmates.[23] One more death wouldn't matter, not even his.

Training conditions continued to prove difficult. Night training was particularly hazardous, with weather their biggest problem. June is Japan's rainy season, and the weather was so poor, the *Seiran* pilots were often grounded by rain or fog.[24] A pilot can't improve if he doesn't fly, and every day that Asamura and his men spent sitting in their barracks was another day lost.

The *I-14* was especially hard pressed to catch up. The last of the four *Sen-toku* subs to be commissioned, the *I-14* had the least amount of training. Captain Shimizu pushed his men hard to make up for lost time, but there was only so much he could do. Once his sub's engine broke down, costing them part of a day; another time a float on one of the *Seiran* was damaged. These incidents hurt his crew as much as the pilots, since both needed training.[25] Practice was the best way to avoid mistakes. Without it, you were asking for trouble.

Finally, training progressed enough that the bay became too confining and Ariizumi moved them into the Sea of Japan.[26] The launch crews benefited from the open water, but with pilot inexperience, mechanical problems, and poor weather, it wasn't surprising when another *Seiran* crashed.

It was the morning of June 13, and Lt. Masuo Egami and his observer, WO Hisayoshi Kimoto, were ferrying a newly completed *Seiran* from the Aichi factory to Nanao. Weather over the Noto Peninsula had deteriorated to the point where the ceiling was 500 feet and visibility less than six miles. Given the poor conditions, Egami and Kimoto crashed into a nearby mountain. The plane disintegrated, and both men were killed.[27] The 631st's casualties were continuing to mount.

The two men were promoted posthumously, and a memorial service was held at a local Anamizu school. Ten *Seiran* flew over the ceremony to honor their sacrifice.[28] Takahashi thought it a shame the two had died. He'd known Egami from Penang and had admired his modesty. He understood they had felt urgency to deliver their plane, but he wished they'd turned back instead of fighting the weather. The old saying was true after all: the good died young.[29]

The day after the funeral Lt. Yasuo Kishi and his observer, Takeshi Tsuda, went missing.[30] Darkness had settled on the last day of flight training, as their *Seiran* flew over Toyama Bay. When Kishi and Tsuda failed to return to base, a search was organized. The *Sen-toku* subs scoured the surrounding waters for four days without finding evidence.[31] Later, the two men's bodies washed ashore on a nearby island.[32] Theories were rife over the cause of the crash. One crewman speculated the plane was shot down by U.S. aircraft.[33] Another thought changing wind conditions might have been responsible.[34] Whatever the reason, the loss was problematic. Nine men had died in five crashes, destroying three *Seiran* and two *Zuiun*. Additionally, another man had been killed when the *I-400*'s high-pressure tank had blown.[35] The mission could not afford many more losses.

IF ARIIZUMI HAD any luck during this period, it was maintaining the secrecy of his goal. The *Sen-toku* subs were one of the most confidential weapons programs in the Imperial Japanese Navy. They had been carefully camouflaged during construction, and their existence was so secret that when a new crewman reported for duty, he was told no such sub existed.

Historians have claimed that U.S. naval intelligence knew nothing about the underwater aircraft carriers and little about their *Seiran*. Though it's true that the United States knew nothing about the Panama Canal strike, they did know something about the *I-400*s. For example, in a U.S. naval intelligence document titled "Japanese Ship List: Know Your Enemy!" a description of the *I-400* and *I-401* appears on page 11. Since the document is dated December 18, 1944, it means the U.S. Navy knew about the *Sen-toku* squadron at about the same time they were commissioned. But there was knowledge of the subs even before then.

When the United States invaded Saipan in July 1944, it captured authorizations issued by Japan's Navy Ministry detailing ship and submarine construction. In May 1945, while the *Sen-toku* subs were still bottled up in Kure, U.S. Naval Intelligence released a translated version of these documents, which listed where and when the *I-400* subs were being built.[36]

A June 1945 naval intelligence report also described the subs as carrying an airplane and potentially playing an offensive role. "These units may be used for long range supply and combat operations," the reports states. "[And] it is believed that a scout observation plan is carried for reconnaissance patrol."[37] The subs might have been operational by the time the United States learned of them, but their existence was certainly known, if not their intended purpose.

The same held true for the *Seiran*. Though the United States never assigned Aichi's M6A1 a code name, Naval Intelligence was aware that the plane existed. A 1944 report from the Allied Air Technical Intelligence Center indicates that the plane was of unusual design, flew 220 mph, and was intended for use with a submarine. The report even translates the plane's name as "clear day."[38] Though U.S. Intelligence failed to identify the *Seiran*'s purpose as a special attack plane or its intended target, it's clear the United States knew of its existence, even if the details of Ariizumi's mission were unknown.

This means the *Sen-toku* subs were at risk, especially since U.S. code-breaking efforts rendered the entire Sixth Fleet vulnerable to attack. Once Ariizumi began reporting his sub's coordinates, it would be easy to find and destroy him.

Unfortunately for Ariizumi, he counted on his underwater aircraft carriers remaining a secret.

Chapter 26

THE TASTE OF PERSIMMON

Ariizumi considered the Sea of Japan to be safe because it had been for three years. But U.S. submarines had recently begun penetrating the Tsushima Strait's mine-laden barrier. On June 9, while Nambu trained in the waters of Toyama Bay, the USS *Skate* (SS 305) entered the Sea of Japan along with eight other subs. The next day the *Skate* torpedoed and sank the *I-222* a short distance from where the *I-401* was practicing.

Inouye, the *I-401*'s sonar operator, happened to be on deck that day when a huge column of water rose into the sky.[1] Nambu assumed that an enemy sub trying to enter the bay had hit a Japanese mine and sunk. He soon learned the truth though when the *I-222* failed to arrive at Nanao.[2]

The *I-222* was an antiquated sub. Commissioned in 1927, she'd eventually been withdrawn from combat and used for training ever since.[3] Filled as she had been with green recruits, the consequences were both sad and predictable when she crossed paths with the USS *Skate*. There was little an unarmed sub could do against an experienced predator. The incident also demonstrated that the United States could kill Japanese "chicks in their nest." Had the *I-401* been operating a bit farther north, it could have been her rather than the *I-222* that was sunk.[4] As it was, the *Skate* and her colleagues destroyed 28 ships during the next two weeks.

Clearly, the endgame had finally begun. The Sea of Japan was no longer safe.[5] Fortunately, the *Sen-toku* squadron's departure for Panama was only a few days away. Importantly, *Seiran* launch times had improved significantly. Some accounts suggest all three planes could be launched in as little as ten minutes, though this was probably without floats (if at all).*[6] Twenty to 30 minutes is a more realistic assessment, and even then it was only when everything went right. It was significant progress though. The special attack fleet had not only reduced their launch time, *Seiran* pilots were proficient enough to attack the Gatun lock. They were ready to embark on their mission.

If the *Sen-toku* squadron had reduced its window of vulnerability, its mission still relied upon surprise. As at Pearl Harbor, it had to reach the enemy undetected, or the mission would fail. Considering that four subs would have to travel the width of the Pacific, surface near where U.S. defenses might reasonably expect them, launch their planes in the middle of the night, and attack at dawn without being discovered, stealth would play a crucial role in their success.

Unfortunately, stealth was the only card they had left, because Ariizumi was about to receive some shocking news from the Naval General Staff.[7] The fall of Iwo Jima and the impending loss of Okinawa meant the enemy was on their doorstep. The war had passed the point where bombing the Gatun lock would make a difference. As a result, the mission to attack the Panama Canal was being scrapped. Instead, the *Sen-toku* subs were being assigned a completely new target.

WHEN THE ATTACK on the Panama Canal was canceled, Ariizumi was furious.[8] The *Sen-toku* subs had been training for six months, they'd overcome every conceivable obstacle placed in their way, and they were finally ready to bomb the canal. Furthermore, the purpose of the attack was to prevent the invasion of Japan. How then could it be canceled? The nation's future was at stake. The news was too bitter to accept without a fight.

NGS Officer Shojiro Iura journeyed from Kure to Maizuru to fill Ariizumi in on the details. Sometime in early June, while the

---

* Nambu in his memoir says it took 20 minutes to launch all three aircraft.

Sen-toku squadron was training, a meeting had been held with the Navy Ministry. NGS Senior Officer Yasuo Fujimori had made a presentation to Navy Minister Mitsumasa Yonai and other attendees, reviewing the attack plan. Shortly after Fujimori finished, he was told:

"Cancel it, we don't have time."

Fujimori probably expected some resistance. The mission's usefulness had been questioned before. But it's doubtful he expected the attack to be canceled. Fujimori had devoted several years of his life to chaperoning the Panama Canal mission through the naval bureaucracy. Ariizumi had even called to tell him they were finally ready. Now, everything they'd worked for vanished in one meeting.[9]

There was one person, however, who refused to accept the verdict: Ariizumi. He continued to champion the attack despite Iura's efforts to dissuade him. He made all the necessary arguments. His fleet was ready; the pilots had trained on a special mockup of the canal; they could leave immediately. But the plan to attack the canal was officially over. In its place, Ariizumi proposed attacking San Francisco or Los Angeles.[10]

At first the idea seemed foolish. What was the point of attacking an American city this late in the war? Ten *Seiran* bombers could hardly do enough damage to hurt the Americans. Ariizumi wasn't crazy though. He was angry—angry and proud. Attacking Los Angeles might only inflict one ten-thousandth of the damage that American bombs had inflicted upon Japan, but it would demonstrate the Sixth Fleet's resolve.[11] Even a single arrow shot in the heart of an American city was worth the risk if it proved the fighting spirit of Japan's submarine force.[12]

As Ariizumi viewed it, bombing the American people would be payback for the mayhem American B-29s were inflicting on Japan. It was also a way to show that his *Sen-toku* subs were a force to be reckoned with. After all, Ariizumi's honor was at stake. And if everyone died on the mission, well, what a glorious finale it would be.[13]

Ariizumi gained some support among Sixth Fleet officers for

attacking a west coast city. First, Chief Staff Officer Hanku Sasaki signed off. Then the Sixth Fleet's sixth and final commander in chief, Tadashige Daigo, gave his assent. Since the Naval General Staff also had to approve, Ariizumi headed to Tokyo to plead his case.[14]

The historical record is muddled when it comes to the debate over target selection. According to Captain Nambu, Ariizumi was unwilling to abandon the Panama Canal mission and went to Tokyo to fight for its resurrection.[15] Tsugio Sato, who seemed to know Ariizumi as well as anyone, says the issue of attacking San Francisco or Los Angeles had been settled before Ariizumi went to Tokyo. Whatever the sequence of events, attacking the Panama Canal versus American west coast cities was probably discussed after the Ministry and Navy General Staff votes, even if only for a short while.

Interestingly, there has been speculation that the *Seiran* were to be replaced by manned, jet-propelled suicide rockets.[16] Such a weapon, the Model 43A, with folding wings for submarine launch, was in development at the end of the war. Though there is no evidence it was specifically intended for the *I-400*s, it's possible it was considered, given the extreme thinking the Japanese High Command was capable of. There's also been speculation that if Ariizumi had been permitted to launch a west coast air attack, his *Seiran* air group would have carried a "dirty" bomb.

The theory can be traced to a German U-boat, the *U-234*, which departed Kiel, Germany, in March 1945 destined for Singapore.[17] The sub carried a special cargo in her mine storage area: ten lead-lined boxes containing uranium oxide.* Destined for the Japanese Army, the radioactive material

---

* Uranium oxide is not radioactive, therefore does not require lead-lined packaging. Nevertheless, the material is believed to have been radioactive and may have been something other than uranium oxide. The exact nature of the material continues to be classified.

was allegedly paid for by a shipment of gold sent to Germany aboard the *I-52*. The two tons of gold were in exchange for Nazi weaponry, including the Me 262, the world's first jet-powered fighter, and the *U-234*'s uranium shipment.[18] Some historians claim the radioactive material was destined for a dirty bomb to be dropped by *Seiran* aircraft over San Francisco or Los Angeles.[19] The claim is based largely on conjecture, and supporting evidence is thin at best. It doesn't help that the gold payment never reached Germany. The *I-52* was sunk off the west coast of Africa, taking the gold shipment with her. In any event, Hitler died while the uranium was in transit, the two Japanese officers guarding the material committed suicide, and the *U-234* surrendered to the U.S. Navy.[20] In other words, the uranium never reached Japan. It's conceivable (though unlikely) that the material could have arrived in time for Ariizumi to launch a west coast attack, if indeed this was even its purpose. But as events transpired, Ariizumi didn't need to make dirty bombs. The Naval High Command had other plans for him.

THE SUMMER OF 1945 was exceptionally hot in Japan.[21] The air was so humid, it felt like a wet woolen overcoat, and the relentless buzzing of cicadas made the atmosphere seem even more oppressive.

Ariizumi boarded the *Shinetsu* train accompanied by Lieutenant Funada for the long, convoluted trip to Tokyo.[22] Even though military personnel were given travel priority, the carriage was crowded.[23] The train was traveling under blackout conditions, and Japan's narrow-gauge tracks made for a bumpy ride. As if a hot, swaying train carriage weren't enough, Allied bombs threatened the trip every step of the way.[24] When Ariizumi finally reached his destination, he must have been tired indeed.

By June 1945 few buildings were left in Tokyo. Curtis LeMay's bombing campaign had nearly wiped the city off the map. Hotel accommodations were especially scarce, so Ariizumi stopped in

Shizuoka to spend the night with his family. Unfortunately, an incendiary raid the day before had reduced the town to ashes.

When he arrived at Shizuoka station, Ariizumi must have wondered whether his house was still standing. Smoke filled the air, and the burned-out ruins of the largely wooden city lay collapsed in the streets. Ariizumi's house was near the army parade grounds; there was little reason to expect it had survived. When he arrived at his street corner though, the house was still standing.[25] It was a miracle.

Ariizumi's mother and his wife, Matsu, greeted him at the entranceway, along with his five children. It was a glorious homecoming. Ariizumi had not seen his family for some time, and he missed them terribly. Matsu expressed her deep appreciation for her husband's safe arrival, even if it was only for one night. While she attended to his every need, Ariizumi's children scampered about, excited by their father's return.

That night Matsu prepared a sumptuous dinner.[26] As Ariizumi ate his fill he probably contemplated the family garden a few feet away. A persimmon tree grew there. The Japanese describe the bittersweet flavor of its fruit as tasting like the memory of first love, a poetic if somewhat sentimental association. Persimmons were popular in Japan. They were looked forward to like summer corn in America or the first apples of the fall season. One wonders whether Ariizumi expected to live long enough to taste its fruit, especially since persimmons didn't ripen until the fall. He'd certainly had his share of bittersweet experience. Given the way his war was going, it was unlikely he'd live to see his persimmon tree bloom.

Matsu knew her husband was likely to die. She probably suspected this was the last time she'd see him. This was one reason why so much emotion ran beneath the surface of their reunion. But Matsu didn't even get 24 hours with her husband. Early the next morning Ariizumi left for Tokyo. It was the last time they would ever see each other.

Considered the father of the *Sen-toku* submarine squadron, Admiral Isoroku Yamamoto wanted the *I-400*s to launch a surprise attack against New York City and Washington, DC, forcing America to sue for an early peace.

Yamamoto's air raid against two of America's most important cities was intended as a follow-up to his surprise attack on Pearl Harbor. By driving the United States to the negotiating table early, he hoped Japan would be able to keep her South Pacific conquests. An attack similar to what Yamamoto planned was later depicted in Makoto Aida's six-panel sliding screen *A Picture of an Air Raid on New York City,* 1966. *Photograph by Hideto Nagatsuka. Courtesy of Mizuma Art Gallery, Tokyo.*

The *Sen-toku* subs' squadron commander, Tatsunosuke Ariizumi, not only had a taste for drink, but was also called "gangster" by his crew for his ruthlessness in prosecuting the war.

The *I-401*'s officers and crew knew their commanding officer, Nobukiyo Nambu, had their best interests at heart, though they couldn't always say the same for Commander Ariizumi.

Kazuo Takahashi, one of the *I-400*'s *Seiran* pilots (*far right*) with Cdr. Toshio Kusaka, commanding officer of the *I-400* (*in foreground*). Takahashi was highly critical of his colleagues, but he was one of the few *Seiran* pilots with extensive combat experience.

Lt. Atsushi Asamura, the *I-401*'s *Seiran* squadron leader, was prepared to die if that's what it took to complete their mission. *Courtesy of Lt. Atsushi Asamura*

The *I-401*'s officers assemble in front of the aircraft hangar door on the sub's foredeck with Lt. Cdr. Nobukiyo Nambu (in dark uniform).

At 400 feet 3 inches long, the *I-400*s were the largest submarines ever built until the nuclear-powered *Ethan Allen* class in 1961. Each sub carried a two-hundred-man crew and three special attack planes, and could travel one and a half times around the world without refueling.

The *I-401's* biggest challenge was launching all three of its *Seiran* in under half an hour; the longer she remained on the surface, the greater risk she ran of being sunk. Seiran, *painting by Jack Fellows, jackfellows.com*

Opposite: The *I-400's* enlisted men are shown gathered on the sub's deck with the *Asahi* naval ensign flying above them. While the *I-401* carried a crew of 204, including officers, enlisted men, and pilots, the *I-400's* crew was smaller in number.

The *I-400*'s wardroom was far larger than that of a typical U.S. combat sub. Trimmed in wood, it served not only as a gathering place for the sub's officers, but also as their dining room, briefing room, and sleeping quarters. *U.S. Navy*

According to official accounts, all blueprints for the *Sen-toku* subs were destroyed at the end of the war. However, the author discovered the last complete set in a closet at a Japanese naval facility. *Courtesy of the author*

Aichi's M6A1 attack plane was the world's first, purpose-built, sub-borne aircraft designed solely for offensive purposes.

Seiran were not only handsome-looking aircract, but were also the most advanced planes built by the Imperial Japanese Navy during World War II.

Lt. Cdr. Tadashi Funada gave Aichi's M6A1 attack plane its poetic name, *Seiran*, named after Hiroshige's woodcut print showing the village of Awazu enshrouded in mist after a storm. It was an appropriate moniker because Aichi's M6A1 were designed to appear over New York City without warning, like "a storm from a clear sky."

The USS *Segundo*'s commanding officer, Lt. Cdr. James D. Fulp Jr., demonstrated the kind of confidence and command authority that inspired his crew. *Bachrach Photography; courtesy of Lynne Fulp*

Lt. Cdr. Stephen Johnson replaced Fulp as commanding officer of the USS *Segundo*. His habit of playing dice with his men combined with his brash talk worried some of his officers. It also didn't help that his nickname "Slick" wasn't always meant as a compliment. *Courtesy of Suze Comerford*

The *Segundo*'s executive officer, Lt. John E. Balson, was nicknamed "Silent Joe." Nevertheless, his sense of humor was so dry it could run a submarine aground in the middle of the Pacific. *Courtesy of the Balson family*

The *Segundo* was launched at the Portsmouth Navy Yard in February 1944. It would be four months before she was commissioned, and another four months before she embarked on her first war patrol. *U.S. Navy*

Between January and March 1945, nearly 70 percent of all ComSubPac subs returned from patrol without having fired a shot. Nevertheless, the *Segundo* (*above*) saw more than her fair share of action. *U.S. Navy*

On his fourth war patrol, the *Segundo*'s skipper, Commander Fulp, encountered a fleet of sampans. When several turned out to be the enemy, he had no choice but to sink them. *Photograph by Lt. Rodney L. Johnson, formerly of the USS* Segundo

After the rigors of the *Segundo*'s second war patrol, Commander Fulp was put in for the Navy Cross. He is shown here receiving a battle ribbon at Midway in June 1944 after the *Segundo*'s fourth war patrol. *U.S. Navy*

Shown here at Midway, the officers of the USS *Segundo* proudly display their sub's battle flag in June 1944. Commander Fulp is standing, third from right; his executive officer, Lt. John Balson, is standing, second from right.

In this previously unpublished sequence of images, the *Segundo* faces off against the *I-401*. This photograph was taken from the *Segundo*'s foredeck. *Photographs by Lt. Rodney L. Johnson, formerly of the USS* Segundo

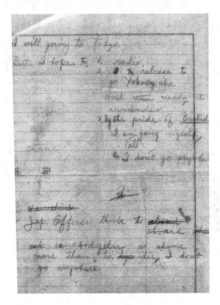

Accurate communication was a problem during the *I-401*'s surrender talks, making an already tense situation even more fraught with danger. Shown here is a page from the notes Lt. Muneo Bando used to negotiate the surrender to the USS *Segundo*.

The *I-401*'s chief navigator, Lt. Muneo Bando (*at center*), approaches the *Segundo* in a rubber raft to discuss surrender terms.

The *I-401*'s Lieutenant Bando, negotiates surrender terms with Lt. Cdr. Stephen L. Johnson aboard the *Segundo*.

Captain Johnson and Lieutenant Bando confer over a map aboard the *Segundo*. Johnson insisted on escorting the *I-401* to Yokosuka while Bando wanted to divert to Ominato in hope of escape.

The bridge of the *I-400* with the black, triangular flag of surrender flying next to the Rising Sun naval ensign.

The USS *Blue* (DD-744), *left,* circles the *I-400* to cut off any possible escape. *U.S. Navy*

Cdr. Hiram Cassedy, who insisted on capturing the *I-400* "twice," stands with hand on holster while eyeing Japanese war booty with obvious interest. *U.S. Navy*

The *I-401* (or possibly the *I-14*) arrives in Tokyo Bay under the watchful eyes of the *I-400*'s crew in the waning days of August 1945. *U.S. Navy*

The U.S. Navy sailed the *I-400* to Pearl Harbor, where she was put into dry dock so her unusual design could be studied in more detail. *Photograph by John M. Johnson GM3, I-400 prize crew member; courtesy of David Johnson*

In March 2005, the Hawaii Undersea Research Laboratory found the *I-401* near where the U.S. Navy torpedoed her. Ariizumi's flagship is easily recognizable, including her bridge with a still-open hatch. *Hawaii Undersea Research Laboratory*

Today, the *I-401*'s triple mount antiaircraft gun are clearly visible on the ocean bottom. Lt. Tsugio Yata used these guns to repel American fighters during their March 1945 air attack on Kure Naval Base. *Hawaii Undersea Research Laboratory*

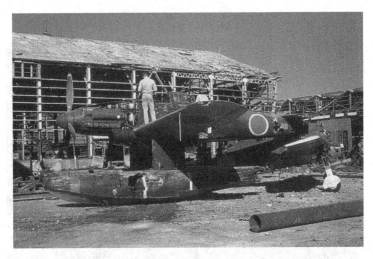

After the war ended, the U.S. Navy brought a captured *Seiran* to the United States for inspection. It spent nearly twenty years at California's Alameda Naval Air Station, falling prey to souvenir hunters and sun exposure before being shipped to a storage facility at the National Air and Space Museum in 1962.

The Smithsonian Institution spent nearly $1 million and several years lovingly restoring the only surviving Aichi M6A1 *Seiran*, which can be seen today at the National Air and Space Museum's Steven F. Udvar-Hazy Center in Chantilly, Virginia.
National Air and Space Museum, Smithsonian Institution

ARIIZUMI HEADED TO Hiyoshidai, where the Imperial Defense Command was headquartered. Hiyoshidai, or Hiyoshi for short, was a warren of deep underground bunkers named for the town on the outskirts of Tokyo where it was located. Lying nearly 100 feet beneath the newly built Keio University, Hiyoshi boasted 16,000 feet of tunnels designed to survive the impact of a one-ton bomb.

The command bunker was lined in concrete with rounded ceilings and miles of wires strung along its walls. It was so damp, the tunnels dripped water even in summer, and a small groove was carved into the floor for runoff. Junior personnel lived in the tunnels. Although it was a good place to avoid the summer heat, the accommodations were hardly luxurious. Most command personnel chose to sleep in aboveground dormitories where a hot bath was available.

The Japanese military subscribed to a certain amount of delusional thinking right up until the end of the war, but not even the most optimistic naval officer could ignore the evidence staring them in the face. The dark, cavelike atmosphere of Hiyoshi perfectly fit the siege mentality that dominated the Combined Fleet. Suicidal naval offensives were ordered one after the other. Despite little chance of success, their practical result was to reduce the Imperial Japanese Navy to nothing.

Unifying Japan's military command at Hiyoshi in April 1945 was an obvious step in defense of the homeland. Still, it only demonstrated how far the Imperial Japanese Navy had fallen. Moving to Hiyoshi meant that the Combined Fleet's flagship headquarters had to be abandoned. In other words, Japan's naval command was no longer safe in its own waters. Working out of a rabbit's burrow only underlined how far the navy had fallen.

When Ariizumi arrived at Hiyoshi, he presented himself to the Naval General Staff.[27] He explained that the *Sen-toku* subs were ready, and he passionately defended attacking the canal. Nothing could inflict more damage on the enemy than destroying their entrance to the Pacific, he proclaimed.[28] He wanted the higher-ups to change their mind.

Ariizumi was not one to buck the system; he knew his place in the command structure, which is why it's so surprising he traveled to Tokyo to lobby his superiors. A Japanese officer did not argue with orders unless he was sure he was right.[29] All of his hard work, combined with his rigid personality, must have warped his judgment. His position was understandable though, courageous even. From the late delivery of the subs, to their thwarted training in the Inland Sea; from fuel shortages to air raid attacks; from earthquakes to incendiary attacks, exploding mines, and the loss of five aircraft and nine *Seiran* crewmen, Ariizumi had overcome overwhelming odds to achieve the impossible. It was bad enough that he faced the full force and fury of the U.S. Navy; having his own command turn against him was more than he could bear.

Ariizumi viewed bombing the Panama Canal as the pinnacle of his career. It represented everything he and his men had worked for, trained for, fought for, and died for. To cancel the attack when they were so close to being ready would be shortsighted, and worse, it would endanger the future of Japan.*

After presenting his case, Ariizumi sat stone-faced awaiting a reply.

"I agree with (your) opinion," an NGS officer told him. "However, we must break the deadlock of war. . . . U.S. task forces are menacing the Japanese mainland. It is of utmost importance that we annihilate them first. Rather than attack the canal, we should attack enemy carriers at Ulithi. This will achieve better results."[30]

Ariizumi's petition was denied.

It's unlikely that Ariizumi let the matter drop. It was certainly within his character to press a point. At least one report suggests he was scolded for continuing to insist the Panama mission should proceed.

---

* The content of Ariizumi's plea is speculative. Nevertheless, one can reasonably deduce from the information available that Ariizumi briefed the NGS on the state of his squadron's readiness as well as his contention that the Panama Canal attack should go forward.

"A man does not worry about a fire he sees on the horizon when other flames are licking at his sleeve!" he was told.[31]

Ariizumi might have been hard-headed,[32] but he was also realistic. He'd made his appeal and lost. His only choice was to return to Nanao and inform the squadron of their new target.

It was time to rally his men.

CHAPTER 27

JOHNSON TAKES COMMAND

THE *SEGUNDO*'S NEW CAPTAIN, LT. CDR. STEPHEN L. JOHNSON, had his work cut out for him. Captain Fulp was beloved by his crew. He'd sunk 17 ships during four war patrols and had brought them back safely each time. Meanwhile he'd shaped his men into a high-functioning combat unit. It was a tough act to follow.

It didn't help that Johnson made a poor first impression. A sub captain's job was to prosecute the war, not win a popularity contest. Still, Johnson's behavior put his men on edge. For example, Fulp never dove the sub before confirming that all the hatches were sealed. Johnson just dropped them in the hole without ever checking.[1] The *Segundo*'s crew didn't take such differences lightly. Johnson's claim that they'd soon be tossing medals down the bridge hatch didn't help matters. The last thing a crew wanted was to take unnecessary chances, especially with the war winding down. Was Johnson the guy who'd get them all killed? Nobody knew for sure.

If a sports team can't succeed without a winning coach, the same can be said for a combat sub. Johnson's lack of command presence made his crew uneasy. Some skippers were born with it; others instilled command presence through fear. Age had something to do with it. At 34, Fulp was confident and mature, while Johnson, four years younger, was still unformed. Fulp didn't speak much, but what he did say counted for a lot. On the other hand, Johnson's brash talk made him seem impetuous—not a good sign in a sub captain.

Johnson's biggest battle though was being an unknown. More than one of the *Segundo*'s officers guessed it was his first command.

It was his third.* These shortcomings meant the crew's respect wouldn't be given freely; Johnson would have to earn it. He might have been as tall as Captain Fulp, but no one thought he could fill Fulp's shoes—at least, not yet.

It's UNCLEAR WHETHER Steve Johnson understood that his crew had doubts about him. If he did, he probably didn't care. He had always done things his way regardless of what people thought. Whether by design or accident, one thing was clear: Steve Johnson had been raising hell almost from birth.

Stephen Lobdell Johnson was born in Chicago on August 10, 1915. The second son of John and Corrine Johnson, he'd lost both his father and his older brother to the 1918 influenza epidemic, when he was only three.[2] His mother eventually remarried. David Callahan was a dry goods wholesaler in his forties when he asked Corrine for her hand. Not much later he moved the family to Lafayette, Indiana, to be near his business.

Johnson was an adventurous kid with a daredevil streak a mile wide. One family story recalls him spitting into an open manhole, losing his balance, and falling in. That was Steve Johnson all over, doing something he shouldn't and getting into trouble for it.

Having an active stepson was a big change for Callahan, who had been a bachelor most of his life. This probably explains why Johnson was shipped off to a military academy in Peekskill, New York. Johnson was only an average student though and required a postgraduate year at an Annapolis feeder school. It must have worked, because he passed the entrance exam and enrolled at the academy just one month shy of his nineteenth birthday.

For all their differences, Johnson and Fulp had some things in common. Like Fulp, Johnson was found to be academically deficient in his first term and bilged out of Annapolis. He was readmitted a year later, but unlike Fulp, his academic record continued

---

* It was also Johnson's eighth war patrol in total.

to decline. Importantly, Johnson's fondness for breaking the rules put him in constant hot water. He received 39 demerits his first year. The next year this number increased to 44, including 20 for "hiding in closet . . . to skip drill."[3] His third year was no better. He earned 53 demerits for various infringements and spent seven days "confined to ship."[4] The trend was clearly heading in the wrong direction. By January of his senior year, Johnson had 56 demerits when he was caught returning from leave under the influence of alcohol.

The medical officer examining Johnson found the midshipman so inebriated, he couldn't walk a straight line. The doctor also noted, somewhat damningly, that Johnson was in a jocular mood—further evidence he didn't take things seriously.[5] Johnson received 100 demerits for his transgression,[6] which, combined with the 56 he'd already earned, put him over the permissible limit. He was immediately placed on probation for the remainder of the academic year. Johnson had bigger problems than unsatisfactory conduct, however. The academy's new superintendent, Rear Adm. Wilson Brown, had it in for him.

Corrine Johnson pleaded her son's case in a letter to the superintendent. "I do so deeply regret this whole affair . . . the finest citizens of Lafayette know [my son] to be honest, straightforward and worthy . . . if you would be so kind as to allow him to graduate with his class, I shall be truly grateful to you."[7]

The superintendent was not reassuring. "Your son's future as a naval officer depends entirely upon himself," Brown responded. If that was the case, Johnson's goose was cooked.

That same day Superintendent Brown sent a memo to the acting secretary of the navy arguing Johnson be given a diploma but denied a commission. "There is doubt as to his . . . general dependability," the superintendent wrote. Fortunately for Johnson, the request was denied, and he received both a bachelor of science degree as well as a commission in the U.S. Navy, despite earning three more demerits for being late to formation.

Johnson boasted of being his class's "anchor man," but, though he graduated near the bottom of 581 midshipmen, he wasn't last. There were five academic offenders with worse records behind him. He spent the next year and a half serving aboard the USS *Oklahoma* (BB-37) and the USS *Anderson* (DD-411).[8] Then he applied to the officer's basic course at the U.S. naval sub school in Groton, Connecticut. As he later noted, "Many former friends consider the fact that I completed the course to be newsworthy."[9] It should come as no surprise that Johnson graduated thirtieth out of a class of 43.

It wasn't until he was assigned to the USS *Shad* (SS 235) and became a full lieutenant that Johnson began to distinguish himself. His characteristic aggressiveness helped. Good grades don't necessarily make for a good sub captain. Many COs excelled academically, only to be dismissed during the war for excessive caution. Johnson understood excessiveness, but caution usually failed him. After the *Shad*'s sixth war patrol, he was awarded the Silver Star for conspicuous gallantry in "render[ing] invaluable assistance to his CO in conducting aggressive torpedo attacks."[10] It was just the kind of thing he excelled at.

During this period, Johnson married an admiral's daughter, which certainly didn't hurt his career any. After serving aboard the *Shad,* he returned to sub school to qualify for command and was eventually named executive officer of the USS *Tunny* (SS 282).

Johnson spent seven months aboard the *Tunny,* during which time his aggressiveness paid off. Earning a Gold Star (in lieu of a second Silver Star), Johnson was cited for his "coolness and high devotion to duty" as well as his "excellent judgment and thorough knowledge of attack problems."[11] After his stay aboard the *Tunny,* Johnson finally received orders for his own sub command. In June 1945 he replaced Fulp as captain of the *Segundo.*

Despite seven war patrols under his belt, Steve Johnson could still lose his temper. A future crew member nicknamed him "Screaming" Steve Johnson for his profane outbursts.[12] The *Segundo*'s crew had yet to experience a Johnson tirade. He might have captained two old-fashioned S-boats and been XO of the *Tunny,* but the *Segundo* marked the first time he'd ever captained a frontline submarine.

Perhaps it was Johnson's enthusiasm for commanding his first combat sub that made him so gung-ho, or perhaps it was his gunslinger disposition. Whatever the reason, it made his crew nervous as they prepared to depart on the *Segundo*'s fifth war patrol.

It would also be their last.

CHAPTER 28

OPERATION STORM

CANCELING THE PANAMA CANAL MISSION MADE SENSE UNDER the circumstances. If the special attack force left immediately, it would take until the end of August before it was in position to bomb the canal. By that time, Japan feared, the U.S. invasion could be well under way, rendering a canal attack moot. Additionally, the Allies were sending European theater ships into the Pacific, either by circumnavigating Africa or by transiting the Suez Canal. Destroying the Panama Canal would do nothing to stop these ships from reaching the Pacific; nor would it impede the considerable number already there.

The anchorage at Ulithi had been an important staging area for the U.S. invasions of Iwo Jima and Okinawa.[1] Presumably it would remain so for the invasion of Japan. It could easily handle 1,000 ships, more than Pearl Harbor, and additional ships were on the way. Given the declining war situation, it made sense for Japan to destroy as many of these ships as possible rather than close the route for those coming later.

Additionally, an immense amount of fuel would be required for four underwater aircraft carriers to make the round trip to Panama. The Naval General Staff knew there wasn't enough left in Japan to support such a mission. However, if Ariizumi's special attack force was redirected against Ulithi, they might slow down, if not prevent, an impending invasion.[2]

Bombing raids had recently burned the navy ministry to the ground.[3] Nagoya had taken another pounding, further disrupting *Seiran* production, and even Nanao had been hit. By June, U.S. incendiary raids had become such milk runs that ComSubPac had forbidden submariners from hitching rides on B-29s to view the destruction.[4] When Allied raids struck Kure on June 22, two more Sixth Fleet subs were lost.[5] Although accuracy had improved between January and June 1945, it still didn't qualify as "precision bombing," and many Japanese cities suffered the same fate as Dresden.[6]

While Ariizumi met with the Naval General Staff, he ordered his assistant to collect all the materials he could find on Ulithi.[7] The fires inside the Naval Ministry had grown so intense, the safes inside had melted. As a result, the most important documents, including maps, navigation charts, and files, had been hidden in a nearby bomb shelter for protection. But the surviving papers had been moved in such a hurry, they were in complete disarray. When Ariizumi's assistant searched for documents related to Ulithi, he found nothing and returned to Nanao empty-handed.[8]

WHEN THE *I-13* and *I-14* abruptly left Nanao, Takahashi became suspicious. The whole point of their training was for subs to practice with their aircraft. When the two subs left their *Seiran* behind, it suggested something was up.[9] Takahashi asked around, but nobody knew why they'd departed. As it turned out, his instinct was right.

Ulithi had been a thorn in the side of the Imperial Japanese Navy ever since it became the primary anchorage for the U.S. Pacific Fleet. A circle-shaped coral atoll in the Carolina Islands, Ulithi was about halfway between Palau and Guam. The Imperial High Command was convinced that Ulithi's harbor, with its enormous armada of ships, aircraft, and troop transports, was the main staging area for the Allied advance on Japan. Such an advance had to be stopped if Japan were to remain a sovereign nation.

The IJN had begun attacking Ulithi in November 1944. First, it launched *kaiten* against the defended anchorage, with middling results. A second *kaiten* attack in January 1945 fared no better, and a third attack, which included *tokko* aircraft, was only slightly more successful. Of the 24 Japanese bombers sent to attack Ulithi in March 1945, only two survived the long journey. It was dark when they arrived, but the anchorage was illuminated. U.S. sailors were watching a movie when one bomber dove into the starboard side of the USS *Randolph* (CV-15). There was so little fuel left in the plane's tanks that when she hit the carrier, she failed to catch fire. Her bombs exploded though, igniting the planes on the hangar deck. Despite being badly marred, the *Randolph* was soon repaired and served as Task Force 58's flagship, the same task force that would soon run rampant up and down the east coast of Japan. As for the second Japanese bomber, she mistook a nearby island for an aircraft carrier and dove headfirst into its baseball field.[10]

The Ulithi attacks were strong on bravery if short on results, but that didn't stop Ariizumi. As soon as he returned to Nanao, he gathered his officers to brief them on the new target.*

"I would like to attack Panama," he said stiltedly, "but Okinawa has already fallen. The final mainland battle is near. . . . The U.S. military's advance base is Ulithi [which includes] aircraft carriers and troop transports. We need to sink [those] ships!"[11]

ATTACK ORDERS WERE issued on June 25 by Vice Adm. Jisaburo Ozawa, commander in chief of the Combined Fleet. The Ulithi mission was divided into two phases. Phase one was called Operation Light (*Hikari*) and called for the *I-13* and *I-14* to transport four high-speed reconnaissance aircraft named *Saiun* to Truk. The two subs were to arrive at Truk by the end of July, where the four planes would be uncrated, assembled, and flown over Ulithi to determine the disposition of enemy ships.[12] Once the information was col-

---

* There is some confusion around when and where Ariizumi briefed his men about the Ulithi mission. According to some accounts, he did so before he left for Tokyo, when the *I-13* and *I-14* were still present with their full complement of *Seiran*. If this is the case, it seems unlikely he would have pleaded to continue the Panama Canal mission when he met with the NGS. Since Ariizumi clearly fought the decision to cancel the Panama Canal mission, he probably waited to brief his men until he returned from Tokyo. If he briefed them upon his return to Nanao, part of his fleet might well have been missing. However, if he waited until he reached Maizuru, the *I-13* and *I-14* had already departed for Ominato. The dates provided by the historical record are contradictory, confusing, or incomplete.

lected, it would be relayed by radio[13] and used by the *I-400* and *I-401* to finalize their attack.

Phase two of the mission was called Operation Storm (*Arashi*). It was appropriately named, since *Seiran* means "storm from a clear sky," and they were responsible for leading the surprise attack on Ulithi. The order specified that the *I-400* and *I-401* were to rendezvous near the U.S. anchorage in late July or early August and then, using the information gathered from *Saiun* reconnaissance, launch their six bomb-carrying *Seiran*. The planes would depart on a moonlit night, fly the short distance to Ulithi, and crash into the largest American ships they could find, preferably a battleship or an aircraft carrier.[14] Another sub employing *kaiten,* or human torpedoes, was scheduled to attack Ulithi at the same time.[15] If all went well, the Japanese would materialize out of nowhere. It would truly feel as if U.S. naval forces had been struck by a storm out of a clear sky.

The plan was both desperate and dangerous. The route from Japan to Ulithi passed Okinawa, Saipan, Guam, and the Marshall Islands. Not only did the U.S. military control these islands, the shipping lanes connecting them were a major route for the U.S. Navy. Additionally, security was hardly lax at Ulithi, especially after three enemy attacks. There were regular air and sea patrols, an anti-submarine net across the harbor entrance, and military forces on round-the-clock alert. Despite all the security, it was decided that Ariizumi's strike force would rendezvous south of Ulithi.[16] Though Japanese intel suggested American security was weakest there, the mission would not be easy. They would surely encounter the enemy. As usual, Ariizumi was undeterred.

THE *I-13* AND *I-14* spent ten days in Maizuru loading supplies.[17] Meanwhile the *I-400* and *I-401* continued training in Nanao Bay. Once Takahashi learned the target was Ulithi, he recommended a change in their training regimen. He wanted to practice flying at low altitude to avoid radar, reasoning it would be difficult for U.S. fighters to spot a *Seiran* only 100 feet above the water. Even if they were discovered, it would be nearly impossible for a fighter to attack them without the risk of crashing into the ocean. Asamura agreed, and training changed accordingly.[18]

Additionally, Takahashi had come to accept the necessity for suicide. He hadn't believed in sacrificing aircrews to attack the Panama Canal, but now that they were sinking a capital ship, there was no alternative. The only way to ensure success was to turn his plane into a giant bomb and crash it headlong into an aircraft carrier. Given that most flights were *tokko* by this time, he really had no choice.

When aircrews from the *I-13* and *I-14* came to say goodbye, Takahashi couldn't help but notice their guilty expressions.[19] Their sub's new reconnaissance role meant they were no longer going to die, a Truk-based aircrew would fly in their stead. As the *Seiran* pilots crowded around Takahashi, they tried cheering him up. "We're praying for your success," they told him, adding, "We'll be following you soon."[20]

The parting proved so difficult, Takahashi thought he'd prefer dying than having to say goodbye again.[21] It was an uncharacteristically sentimental feeling for a man known to be critical. Then again, they'd trained so closely, the pilots seemed more like brothers than colleagues. He couldn't help but feel emotional.

AFTER TRAINING WAS complete, the *I-400* and *I-401* left Nanao Bay for Maizuru, keeping a lookout for U.S. subs along the way. It was July 13, and Takahashi was confident that their skills had improved enough that the Ulithi mission stood a chance of success.[22]

When the *I-400* arrived at Maizuru, Captain Kusaka pulled Takahashi aside and gave him 300 yen and a four-day pass. Considering that a pilot's monthly salary was 122 yen, this was a large sum of money. Kusaka told him the pass and extra pay had come from Vice Admiral Daigo, commander in chief of the Sixth Fleet.

Takahashi knew why he was getting them. *Might as well have a good time,* he thought.[23] After Maizuru, it would be too late.

Four days later, when Takahashi returned from shore leave, he noticed a *Seiran* being repainted. The plane wasn't just receiving a touch-up coat of green—its fuselage was covered in silver, to re-semble an American fighter. When Takahashi saw Japan's red sun emblem being replaced by the blue and white naval star insignia of a U.S. aircraft, he became indignant.

"Who is responsible for such a cowardly act?" he demanded.[24]

Painting the *Seiran* to look like American aircraft was a blatant violation of international law. It wasn't so much this violation that infuriated Takahashi—it was the disgrace of flying such an impor-tant mission in aircraft disguised to look like the enemy. It was downright shameful.

Takahashi knew it was useless to complain. No one was going to pay attention to the inflamed sensibilities of a pilot. In the spirit of protest, he drew a picture on the prop spinner showing a heart with an arrow through it and the words "Hit to Kill."[25]

Asamura didn't share Takahashi's concerns about the ruse. They only had one shot at attacking Ulithi, and the odds were against them. Yes, it was a "dirty play," but if U.S. fighters mistook the *Seiran* for friendly aircraft it might buy enough time for him to crash into a ship. There was no point in worrying about interna-tional sensibilities.[26] They needed every advantage they could get.

THE *I-400* AND *I-401* spent seven days at Maizuru loading three months' worth of supplies.[27] Enough food, ammunition, and fuel were boarded to get them to Ulithi and, assuming everything went right, to Hong Kong and Singapore after that.[28] So many crates, canned goods, and rice sacks were stacked in the corridors that traversing the sub was difficult. To ease the congestion, wooden planks were laid on top so the crew literally walked over their food.[29] It raised the height of the deck so much, the planks were almost even with the bottom bunks in the crew quarters.

Though wartime food was deplorable, the *I-401* didn't lack for delicacies. Among her stores were bread, Inari sushi, *sekihan* (red sticky rice), dried squid, hindquarters of lamb, curry powder, on-ions, canned spinach, parsley, soy sauce, whiskey, and straw-covered flagons of sake. Staples such as canned sweet potatoes and white rice were loaded in great quantity, since they made up a significant part of the crew's diet.

As the day of their departure grew near, everyone made preparations for their death. Asamura entrusted a dagger with a note stating "Stake everything you have" to a friend for delivery to his parents in Osaka.[30] Nambu led a delegation of the *I-401*'s officers to pray at Shiraito Shrine. When they finished, they received inspirational headbands to wear into battle.[31]

Unknown to his officers, Nambu invited their families to say goodbye.[32] When their mothers, fathers, and wives suddenly appeared in Maizuru, there were moments of tear-filled joy. Nambu made it clear that this was the last time they were likely to see their son, husband, or brother. Japan's position was so desperate, he even feared America would invade while they were away. Nambu could only guess what would happen to his family if they fell into enemy hands. He hoped his wife would hide in the mountains.[33] In the meantime, he preferred not to think about the consequences.

Yata had written a farewell note to his mother, but when she surprised him by coming to say goodbye, he chose not to send it. She assumed that Yata, her only child and last living relative, would not be returning from his mission. What Yata didn't know was that his mother planned to hang herself after they said goodbye.[34]

The *I-400* and *I-401* finished their preparations by July 19.[35] That night 12 members of the *Seiran* aircrew were invited to a farewell banquet with the head of the Sixth Fleet, Admiral Daigo.* Ariizumi, Nambu, and Kusaka, the *I-400*'s captain, arrived at Shitairo, a traditional Japanese restaurant, at 6:00 P.M.[36] Senior Staff Officer Shojiro Iura, who had briefed Fujita on bombing Oregon, attended as well. Geishas kept the cups filled, as toasts were drunk in honor of the 12 brave men. It was a solemn occasion, and a poem recognizing their sacrifice was recited. As the night grew late alcohol flowed freely and the men indulged in camaraderie and sentimental song.[37]

---

* Both Nambu and Sato recalled that the farewell dinner in Maizuru was held on July 19. Takahashi, however, said it was July 18.

The high point came when the *Seiran* aircrews were invited to approach Admiral Daigo. One by one each man came forward and stated his rank, name, and sub designation. Daigo then handed him an empty cup, which a geisha filled with sake. After the pilot had drunk his share, he returned the cup and thanked the admiral for his support.[38]

Daigo could see the determination written on each man's face.[39] These were the finest young men Japan had to offer. Ariizumi's four subs represented a quarter of all the operational combat subs left in Japan. Surely, those present felt the ultimate sacrifice would soon be shared by everyone around the table.

THE NEXT MORNING the *Seiran* aircrews assembled on deck alongside the *I-401*'s catapult.* Nambu wore his dress uniform for the ceremony. The senior officers of the Maizuru Naval Base wore the same. The crew of the *Sen-toku* squadron also gathered to watch as Commander Ariizumi presented each member of the *Seiran* aircrew with a short sword, a parting gift from Admiral Daigo.[40] The scabbard of each sword was engraved with the words "Divine Dragon Special Attack Unit."[41] Ariizumi had come up with the designation based on the first character of his name.[42] It was a bit of bravado, since the unit had not received any official designation. By this point Ariizumi was more concerned about inspiring his men than about navy protocol.

The *Seiran* crews stood at attention as Ariizumi stopped in front of each man and presented him with his sword. No written order had been issued declaring the mission a suicide attack, but no such order was necessary. The men knew what the sword implied. It meant fight to the death.[43]

Heiji Kondo watched from the *I-401*'s bridge as Asamura was handed his sword. The little *Seiran* pilot quivered with emotion

---

* Nambu says the ceremony took place on July 20, as does Sato. However, if the *I-401* arrived in Maizuru on July 13 as Sato suggests, it means the sub remained in Maizuru for eight days, not the seven days he claims.

as he grasped its hilt. But it wasn't Asamura's shaking that moved Kondo, it was the expression on his face. Conflict was written there, the conflict between seriousness of purpose and the will to live. Although Asamura was overcome with emotion, he did not hesitate. He'd vowed in his heart to die for the mission, and though he couldn't speak for the other pilots, he knew what he must do.[44]

Takahashi felt the blood drain from his face as Ariizumi handed him his sword. *Is this finally the end?* he wondered.

After the ceremony was over, public relations officers flocked around the *Seiran* crews, handing them thick squares of expensive paper on which to write their last words. The results would appear in a future issue of Japanese newspapers and be preserved at Etajima for posterity.

Takahashi thought for a moment before dipping his brush into a pool of black ink. When his words had dried, he thought they'd captured his feelings, perfectly.

"I do not regret giving my life for my country," he'd penned. "But what will become of my mother?"[45]

RACE AGAINST TIME

CHAPTER 29

DEPARTURE

THE *I-400* LEFT MAIZURU NAVAL BASE ON JULY 21, 1945.[1] LED BY a minesweeper, the sub motored slowly on the surface, while a reserve *Seiran* aircrew ran along the shoreline shouting encouragement.[2]

Takahashi had no more stomach for tearful goodbyes. "Get out of here, you idiots," he shouted at his comrades. "I don't want to see your face."[3]

Kusaka's sub was heading for Ominato,[4] a naval port near the northern tip of Honshu. Ominato was the final departure point for the *Sen-toku* force. Situated on Mutsu Bay, a day's journey, the port provided access to the Pacific Ocean through the well-guarded Tsugaru Strait. It was virtually the only exit from the Sea of Japan that the Sixth Fleet could still use.

Before Nambu followed in the *I-401*, he raised a banner on the bridge.[5] Meant to inspire his crew it proclaimed in large, bold characters, "Japan, land of the gods."[6] But it seemed like the gods had abandoned Japan. An increasing number of bombing raids had taken place since the first attack in November 1944, and the recent addition of carrier-based attacks only increased the pressure. Every night U.S. Armed Forces Radio filled the airwaves with a Japanese-language broadcast listing the cities to be destroyed by morning. As one submariner noted, in terms of propaganda "it sure beat 'Tokyo Rose.' "[7] For those who didn't have radios, B-29s dropped leaflets. "Read this carefully as it may save your life," one pamphlet explained. "In the next few days, four or more of the cities named on the reverse side will be destroyed by American bombs."[8] Japanese records estimated that by the end of July 1945, at least half a million civilians had been killed in nationwide air strikes, with another million injured. B-29s were hammering the civilian population so often, they were being driven to the point of insanity.[9]

If Japan's civilians were terrified, her military remained unmoved. To get the point across, Allied forces launched air strikes against naval bases at Yokosuka, Kure, and Sasebo. By the end of July, little remained of the Imperial Japanese Navy except smoking hulks.

The raids had an impact on the *I-400* subs still under construction. The *I-402*, which had been converted into a gigantic fuel carrier, was unharmed, but the *I-404*, which had been moored off Kure awaiting completion,[10] was sunk by U.S. carrier planes.[11] And though work had commenced on the *I-403* and *I-405*,*[12] it had since been abandoned along with the underwater aircraft carriers *I-406* through *I-417*.[13]

The *I-13* and *I-14* were first to arrive at Ominato on July 4.[14] The subs were there to load two *Saiun* aircraft each, which were partially disassembled, crated, and waiting dockside.[15] The Nakajima C6N *Saiun* was a single-engine, carrier-borne reconnaissance aircraft, but by the time Ariizumi needed the planes, there were no Japanese carriers left for them to fly off of.

Built by Nakajima, the *Saiun* carried a pilot, a navigator (who doubled as an observer), and a radio operator (who doubled as a gunner when the plane came under attack). The *Saiun* could outrun a Grumman F6F Hellcat, and Nakajima was so confident in the plane's speed, it had built a night fighter version.[16] Her Allied code name was "Myrt," but *Saiun*, which means "Painted Cloud," was far more poetic.

The *I-13* and *I-14* had conducted live-fire exercises while in Mutsu Bay. Using their largest deck gun, they had fired long distance to perfect their aim.[17] And since the war had reduced shipping traffic

---

* There is some dispute as to how much work was done on the *I-403*. Some Western historians claim the sub was canceled before its keel was laid. However, since both Nambu and Sato, members of the *Sen-toku* squadron and the 631st, respectively, state construction had begun on the *I-403*, it seems reasonable to assume that it had.

to almost nothing, there was little chance of hitting anything they didn't want to.

The *I-14* was scheduled to leave Ominato first, followed by the *I-13*,[18] but the bearings[19] in the *I-14*'s prop shaft[20] overheated, requiring repair. As a result, the *I-13* left Ominato on July 11.*[21] The crew's friends and family were invited for the sendoff. Since it was the last time they were likely to see one another, the parting was emotional. The crew lined up on deck wearing white headbands with the characters for "Certain Victory" spelled out.[22] As the surrounding mountains bore silent witness to the painful parting, the *I-13* got slowly under way.

U.S. battleships had already begun shelling northern Honshu and Hokkaido by then.[23] It was the first time U.S. naval gunfire had been directed against the Japanese mainland.[24] The Kaminishi ironworks, south of Ominato, were reduced to scrap metal,[25] and railyards and harbors were targeted as well. Ominato was also on the list.

During the time it took to repair the *I-14*, Allied air raids repeatedly forced her to the harbor floor. It must have been frustrating to constantly crash-dive as carrier planes attacked, yet that didn't prevent the *I-14* from riding out the raids on the bay's bottom. Captain Shimizu guessed they'd be spending most of the voyage to Truk submerged; a little more underwater time wouldn't hurt.[26]

Despite being attacked day after day, the *I-14* managed to depart Ominato on July 17.[27] It's remarkable that any of the *I-400* subs managed to escape during this period, especially since Maizuru and Ominato were on the receiving end of several significant attacks. Large in size and slow to submerge, the subs were sitting

---

* Dates for when the *I-13* left Ominato for Truk vary (depending on source) from July 2 to July 15. In *Sunk!* (p. 139), Mochitsura Hashimoto says both subs left Ominato on July 15, while Orita (p. 300) says it was July 2. Both accounts seem wrong because we know the two subs left on separate days. Additionally, in *Undersea Victory* (p. 473), W. J. Holmes says the *I-13* left Ominato on July 5, which also seems too early, since most accounts have the subs arriving at (not departing) Ominato around this time. Though it's impossible to know for sure, it seems the *I-13*'s departure was closer to July 11.

ducks when anchored in a harbor. Nambu's former sub, the *I-361*, had been sunk earlier in the month. Only three of her crew had survived.[28] Every submarine Nambu had served on since the beginning of the war had now been destroyed. The *I-401* was the last one left.

NAMBU REACHED OMINATO on July 22.[29] It was early evening, and there was a drizzling rain as the *I-401* sailed into the harbor.[30] Kusaka's sub had arrived a few hours earlier. Since the *I-401* had been replenished at Maizuru, her stay at Ominato was brief. Nambu gave half his crew permission to go ashore, while the other half remained to load perishables.[31] It would be their last chance to enjoy such delicacies as mackerel and the other fresh foods that were available in Ominato.

Takahashi was one of the lucky ones granted shore leave. He knew it would be the last time he'd set foot on land, so he savored the few hours he had. First he enjoyed a hot bath. Then he sat down to write his will. There were many things he wanted to say to his mother. Unfortunately, everything he wrote sounded sentimental or whiny, so he kept the letter simple. When he was finished, he gave it to two junior officers to deliver, along with the short sword Ariizumi had presented him and the 100 yen in bonus pay he had left. Stripped of his belongings, Takahashi felt relieved.[32]

While Takahashi spent the evening arranging his personal affairs, Ariizumi dined with a friend. Dinner was a sedate affair compared to Ariizumi's last evening at Maizuru. He enjoyed two extra helpings of his favorite dish, accompanied by his usual intake of liquor.[33] This seemed a more fitting way to spend his last night ashore than singing drinking songs and giving emotional toasts.

Kondo, one of the *Seiran* mechanics, enjoyed a cup of sake that night. After the day he'd had, he deserved it. Kondo had been detailed to paint one of the *I-401*'s *Seiran*. For some reason, the planes hadn't been disguised in Maizuru, and Kondo was assigned to rectify this. He didn't have strong feelings about the task; he was just carrying out orders. Regardless, there was no denying how strange a *Seiran* looked disguised as an American plane.[34]

Kondo had been painting the fuselage earlier in the day when a Japanese patrol craft appeared overhead. The plane took Kondo by surprise. There were so many American fighters around that the Japanese aircraft could easily have mistaken the newly disguised *Seiran* for the enemy. Kondo rounded his back in an awkward attempt to hide the American markings. As the patrol craft circled, he stood frozen, his face only inches from the wet paint. Fumes filled his nose and his eyes began to water as Kondo maintained the uncomfortable position. The situation would have been funny if it hadn't been so dangerous.

The air patrol eventually lost interest and flew away.[35] If Kondo had been attacked, there was nothing he could have done but run. The irony alone would have been enough to kill him. As it was, he managed a sigh of relief.

The *I-400* left Ominato the next day at 2:00 P.M. Two hours later the *I-401* followed.* The rain had finally stopped, making for a beautiful afternoon.[36] The sun was beginning to set, and the Shimokita Mountains loomed green and lovely in the background.[37] Since Nambu expected this to be his last view of Japan, he seared it into his memory.[38] He had no way of knowing the *I-401*'s mission would be the Sixth Fleet's final offensive of the war.

There was constant fear of enemy subs penetrating the Tsugaru Strait, and of course Halsey's Third Fleet was not far away. Fortunately, the only things Nambu passed as he sailed through the strait were fishing boats. Then at two in the morning, a water spout erupted behind the sub's stern.[39] It was followed seconds later by a loud report.[40]

A bridge lookout pointed at a flash from the Hokkaido coastline. Moments later another shell smacked into the sea, this time off their port side. The *I-401* was under attack.[41]

"Submerge immediately!" Nambu cried.[42]

A Japanese shore battery had spotted the sub's silhouette and,

---

* Both Sato and Takahashi say the *I-401* left two hours later. However, Nambu remembers it as only one hour later, while Asamura says there was a six-hour interval.

thinking her the enemy, opened fire. Nambu dove his sub before the shore battery had a chance to improve its aim, but it had been a close call.

The *I-401*'s captain was so disturbed by the incident, he kept repeating "Dangerous, dangerous" under his breath.[43] Ariizumi was incensed enough to fire off an angry radio message scolding the army for its trigger-happy response.

It's no surprise that friendly fire almost sunk Nambu's sub, especially since it was operating in secret. At least Japan's coastal forces were paying attention. This might have been cold comfort, but if Ariizumi's mission failed, a strong defense would be necessary.

It was up to the *I-401* to see that it wasn't needed.

Chapter 30

UNDER WAY

THE DAY AFTER THE *I-401* LEFT FOR ULITHI, AICHI'S NAGOYA facility was bombed again, causing extensive damage. It was the second such attack in July, so when Aichi rolled its twenty-eighth *Seiran* out the hangar door, it was its last.

Aichi wasn't alone in this problem. The entire Japanese war machine had ground to a halt. The U.S. sub embargo was squeezing Japan for all she was worth. Meanwhile, Admiral Halsey's armada was closing in.

Ariizumi knew his special attack force was surrounded, but he had two tricks he was counting on to escape undetected. The first was the snorkels he'd installed in May. The longer they helped him hide beneath the surface, the better they could avoid radar. The second trick was the two special anechoic coatings on the outside of each sub designed to improve their stealth factor. The U.S. Navy didn't need snorkels or stealth coatings, but Ariizumi believed them to be one of the few advantages he possessed besides the courage of his crew.

By the time the *I-401* left Ominato, so much of Japan's sub force had been destroyed that SubRon 1 was the Sixth Fleet's only full-strength unit. Operation Storm was a brave undertaking, given its limited chance for success. No sacrifice was too great to protect the homeland.

After nearly being sunk in Tsugaru Strait, the *I-401* spent most of the next two days underwater. The U.S. Navy wasn't the crew's only source of fear. Japanese patrol craft could easily mistake a *Sen-toku* sub for American and bomb it, so Nambu kept his sub submerged until he was safely out of range of Japan. It wasn't until

July 25 that he felt secure enough to surface in daylight. He then
headed south at 19 knots, to make up for lost time.[1]

The attack plan was straightforward. The *I-400* and *I-401* would
proceed independently of each other, minimizing the chance of
both subs being sunk. The *I-401* would navigate south past Saipan,
Guam, and Truk.[2] She would then meet up with the *I-400* on August 12 near Ponape Island,[3] where they would review the *I-13*'s and
I-14's aerial intel. The two subs would then proceed to the southern waters off Ulithi, to rendezvous one last time before launching their attack.[4] It was a convoluted route, made necessary by
U.S. dominance of the Pacific. It would take approximately three
weeks to reach Ulithi. If all went well, they'd be ready to strike in
mid-August.

Meanwhile the *I-400* managed to exit the Tsugaru Strait without
being shelled. Kusaka knew the only way to avoid Halsey's Third
Fleet was to head east,[5] so he raced to put Japan behind him.

Life aboard the *I-400* was routine at first. Kondo even found
time to play a Ouija-like game called Kokkuri-san using three *hashi*
(chopsticks) tied together in a tripod. After asking a question, the
spirit of a fox assisted in moving the *hashi* until they pointed to
various *kanji* spelling out an answer. Senior officers disapproved of
the game, believing it superstitious, but the younger officers were
fascinated by it.

"Are we going to sink?" Kondo asked.

"No," the fox responded.

"Will we be attacked?"

"No, you are going home soon."

The answers were puzzling. Nevertheless, Kondo was relieved to
hear they'd survive.[6]

Once the *I-400* cleared the Japanese mainland, Kusaka had to
decide how much to travel underwater. Surface cruising was fastest but risked discovery. Traveling underwater was safer but cost
precious time. Nambu faced the same dilemma. But the question
took on even more importance after both subs encountered a typhoon.

Nambu did his best to power through the maelstrom, but the

waves rocked his boat so violently, his crew were thrown from their berths.[7] At one point, the sub's exhaust pipe was swamped, creating so much back pressure, the relief valves sounded like a cannon going off. Fearing the *Seiran* would be damaged, Nambu was forced to submerge.[8]

It's amazing how calm the ocean is 50 feet beneath the waves, and the *I-400* subs took full advantage of the peace and quiet.[9] When both subs finally surfaced, they found their *Seiran* unharmed. Unfortunately, they'd also lost valuable time.

A WEEK LATER Nambu moved through the *I-401* careful not to bump his head. It may have been the world's largest submarine, but he still had to duck when climbing through a hatch. That was the drawback of being six feet tall. Nambu spent most of his time in the control room, and since the *I-401* was Ariizumi's flagship, the commander spent his time there as well.

Command and control authority was sacrosanct aboard a submarine. The captain issued orders, and his executive officer made sure the crew carried them out. Nambu was captain of the *I-401*, so he gave the commands. But Ariizumi's presence subtly undermined Nambu's authority. The *I-401*'s officers knew that many of the orders they received from Nambu originated with their squadron commander—as far as Nambu was concerned, probably too many. It also didn't help that Nambu was the most junior of Ariizumi's four sub captains. Additionally, Nambu was the only *Sen-toku* captain who had not served in Penang with Ariizumi. Even if Nambu had served in the Indian Ocean, it's doubtful Ariizumi would have changed his command style. It wasn't his nature.

The main problem was chemistry. It wasn't just that their styles clashed; the two men's personal philosophies were fundamentally different. Ariizumi was a task-driven martinet, focused solely on the mission. Nambu, however, could see the big picture. Whereas Ariizumi wouldn't think twice about sacrificing his men in pursuit of a goal, Nambu had his crew's welfare at heart. It wasn't easy for a broad-minded man such as Nambu to serve under a narrow-minded one like Ariizumi. But Ariizumi was Nambu's commanding officer. He had to ignore the differences.

Nambu grasped the ladder in the control room and climbed into the conning tower. The *I-401*'s sonar operator was reporting numerous contacts, so Nambu raised the sub's periscope to have a look around. They were approximately two weeks out from Ominato, but as Nambu looked through the eyepiece, he was shocked by what he saw.

There were so many American warships heading west toward Japan, the sight was overwhelming. And the armada was so confident, it didn't even bother to dim its lights at night.[10] The size of the enemy's fleet gave Nambu pause. Could Japan really expect to defeat such superior numbers?[11] Given the countless U.S. warships he saw, Operation Storm threatened to become meaningless.

Normally, Nambu didn't think in defeatist terms, but what was the point of dying if it would have a negligible impact against the American Goliath? Every one of his men was prepared to lay down his life, himself included.[12] But from what Nambu saw, the U.S. fleet could easily absorb their blow and still invade Japan. Nambu was a patriot, and he had no intention of standing down. Still, a seed of doubt had been sown. He shuddered to think what awaited his countrymen.

The enemy armada forced the *I-401* to remain underwater. With a submerged speed of only two to three knots, the sub fell farther behind schedule. Nambu worried they'd miss their rendezvous if they didn't travel on the surface,[13] but the farther south they moved, the more enemy ships they encountered.

Ariizumi was concerned for a different reason. He feared the *I-401* would be discovered. Discovery would mean death, so to avoid putting the mission at risk, Ariizumi decided to make a detour. The detour he proposed involved sailing east of the Marshall Islands before rendezvousing with the *I-400* and heading to Ulithi.[14] Naturally, Nambu protested the change. The detour would significantly lengthen their journey, costing them valuable time. Importantly, the warships they saw were probably coming from Ulithi. The sooner they attacked the island's anchorage, the more ships they could sink. Finally, a detour didn't necessarily mean they'd avoid enemy contact, particularly since the Americans were everywhere. Nambu argued to maintain course.

But Ariizumi was as conservative as he was overbearing. Nambu found it maddening, though he hid his irritation. Arguing with Ariizumi never did any good. The pint-size commander just dug in his heels. After failing to change Ariizumi's mind, Nambu ordered a new course. The detour meant a new rendezvous location, which would have to be radioed to the *I-400*. It's doubtful Nambu felt comfortable with the plan. Then again, he had no choice. Those were the rules of command.

NAMBU WASN'T ALONE in his suffering. Cdr. Tsuruzo Shimizu, captain of the *I-14*, had nearly lost his sub from a grueling depth charge attack that lasted a day and a half. Shimizu's survival would add to his reputation as a lucky skipper. The *I-13*, however, had not been so fortunate. The sub had still not arrived at Truk, even though she'd left Ominato six days ahead of the *I-14*.[15] Of more concern, nothing had been heard from her since July 16, five days after she'd departed. Operation Storm depended on the *I-13* and *I-14*'s reaching Truk, getting their *Saiun* into the air, and reporting on conditions at Ulithi. It would be senseless to attack the anchorage if American carriers weren't there. Nobody wanted to repeat the mistakes of Pearl Harbor.

Nambu feared for the *I-13's* safety, and with good reason. ULTRA intelligence had not only been tracking the *I-13* and the *I-14* since their refueling stop at Chinkai, it had more than 28 mentions of Ohashi's sub in its contact logs.[16] In other words, once Nambu radioed the new rendezvous coordinates to the *I-400*, the U.S. Navy would be there to greet them. They were sailing straight into an ambush.

CHAPTER 31

CROSSED WIRES

THE *I-14* ARRIVED AT TRUK ON AUGUST 4,[1] AND FOR THE FIRST time in three weeks, her crew set foot on dry land. Shimizu was happy to have escaped the Allied dragnet and immediately sent a message to Sixth Fleet headquarters relaying his arrival.[2] Unfortunately, Truk was not what he'd expected.

What had once been the empire's premier forward naval base was now a shambles. The harbor was filled with sunken ships, and the skeletons of burned out planes littered the airfield. Those who had known Truk in its glory days could only weep at its destruction.[3] If this was what an island looked like when the enemy bypassed it, what was in store for Japan?

Under the circumstances, Shimizu's arrival was nothing short of miraculous. The *I-14* should have been lying at the bottom of the ocean, a gaping hole blown in her side, but Shimizu had run the Allied gauntlet. Ariizumi's snorkel may have had something to do with it; still, Shimizu wasn't just lucky—he was competent as well.

As soon as the *I-14* docked at Truk, her crew sprang into action. First they unloaded the two *Saiun* aircraft. Next, the planes were assembled and flown over Ulithi.[4] That same day Ariizumi received orders for another mission.[5] It seemed premature to plan a second attack before the first one had launched, but the Imperial Japanese Navy was running out of combat units. After the *I-400* and *I-401* sent their *Seiran* against U.S. carriers, the *Sen-toku* force was to travel to Hong Kong and pick up a new ten-plane squadron.[6] After refueling in Singapore, they would then return to Ulithi for a second attack.*[7] A contingent from the 631st had already been dispatched by submarine to help with preparations.[8]

Given Ulithi's heavy security, the odds the *I-401* would survive the first mission were slim at best; a second attack had only a one-in-a-million chance. It wasn't being outnumbered that put them at risk as much as a top secret U.S. intelligence operation called ULTRA, which had broken the IJN's naval codes. The IJN's high command refused to believe their codes had been compromised, but U.S. naval intelligence knew the whereabouts of virtually every remaining Japanese submarine. Fortunately, Ariizumi's sub captains had maintained radio silence since leaving Ominato.[9] There were a few exceptions, such as Shimizu's message confirming his arrival at Truk. But by and large, the *Sen-toku* subs were absent from the airwaves, which made it harder to find them.

Ariizumi was not out of touch with headquarters, though. Sixth Fleet communications were still broadcast, and the subs picked them up at night when they surfaced.[10] Receiving a radio signal was far different from sending one though—it didn't betray a sub's location. Radio silence, then, was an important reason Nambu had made it this far. It also maintained the crucial element of surprise.

WHILE THE 631ST readied ten *Seiran* for transport,[11] Asamura worried about the combat readiness of his pilots. Sub crews were kept busy with myriad tasks. Even the *Seiran* maintenance workers had plenty to do. But *Seiran* pilots and their observers had no assigned duties on board the sub.[12] As days passed, Asamura worried they were losing their edge.

In truth, *Seiran* aircrews were nothing more than high-priority passengers being transported to launch coordinates. Other than maintaining careful watch over their aircraft, they had little to oc-

---

* There is some confusion around this point. Some accounts suggest the *Sen-toku* squadron would bypass Hong Kong altogether and pick up its *Seiran* squad in Singapore when it refueled.

cupy them. Regardless, the *I-401*'s crew treated them like gods.[13] Though it was good for morale, Asamura worried that three weeks of inactivity would hurt pilot readiness.[14]

The pilots had lost their appetite, for one thing. They subsisted mainly on canned spinach, soy sauce, and ginger, hardly the breakfast of champions. Lack of exercise was another problem. The *I-401* might have been big, but it was so crammed with men and supplies that the *Seiran* pilots spent most of the day either lying in their bunks or hanging around the radio shack.[15]

Asamura passionately believed that the *Arashi* mission was their last chance for heroic achievement,[16] so he decided to do what he did best: impose a strict regimen.

One of the first things Asamura did was have his pilots assigned to lookout duty.[17] Searching for the enemy in darkness was one way to keep night flying skills sharp. Asamura didn't want to rely solely upon a special hormone designed to improve night vision that would be injected before the attack.[18] He also had his pilots rehearse takeoff procedures while sitting in the cockpit[19] and held mission briefings using photos and a scale model of Ulithi's anchorage.[20] Finally, he initiated a calisthenics program, held on deck, to keep his men in shape.[21]

It's not unusual in Japan to drill men to the point where fatigue is a greater impediment to success than lack of preparedness. This wasn't the case for Takahashi. He had it easy aboard the *I-400*. When he grew tired of lying in his bunk, he'd go to the radio room and listen to the broadcasts out of Sydney. Sometimes he'd chat with the communications officer.[22] Despite the effort to fill his days, Takahashi still had plenty of time to think. One memory he may have avoided was the atrocities he'd committed while serving aboard the *I-37*.

It was February 22, 1944, when one of the *I-37*'s lookouts spotted the *British Chivalry,* an unescorted grain carrier sailing between Melbourne and Abadan. The *I-37* sank the merchant using a combination of torpedoes and deck-gun fire. When the *Chivalry* was gone, her lifeboats were beckoned and the ship's captain ordered on board the sub. Takahashi had held a pistol while the captain was interrogated. He'd also relieved him of a briefcase full of jewels.[23]

Takahashi knew SubRon 8's policy was to execute survivors of ships they'd sunk. For justification, he was told Japanese women and children had been indiscriminately killed during the invasion of Saipan.[24] The lifeboats were too close for the sub's machine guns to be used effectively, so combat rifles were issued. Takahashi used his sidearm instead. At least 13 men were killed and five wounded.[25]

The *I-37* sank two more British merchants after that, killing their crews in a similar manner.* If Takahashi felt regret, he didn't express it. Even the "Butcher" was penitent.

As ULITHI DREW closer, the *Seiran* pilots grew increasingly sentimental. Knowing their days were numbered, they dwelled in the past even as they drilled operational details into their heads. One of the popular songs of the era, "Cherry Blossom Classmates," or *Doki no Sakura*, perfectly captures their mind-set. The song celebrates the friendship of two former classmates, now naval aviators destined to die in battle. Few things represent the Japanese view of life better than cherry blossoms, and the song expresses the wistfulness many Japanese feel about life's beautiful and transitory nature.

> *You and I, blossoms of the same cherry tree*
> *That bloomed in the Naval Academy's garden*
> *Blossoms know they must blow in the wind someday*
> *Blossoms in the wind, fallen for their country*
> *You and I, blossoms of the same cherry tree*
> *That bloomed in the flight school garden*
> *I wanted us to fall together, just as we have sworn to do*
> *Oh, why did you have to die, and fall before me?*
> *You and I, blossoms of the same cherry tree*
> *Though we fall far away from one another*
> *We will bloom together in Yasukuni Shrine*
> *Spring will find us again, blossoms of the same cherry tree* [26]

---

* The ships involved were the SS *Sutlej* and SS *Ascot*.

In addition to being sentimental, the absurdly young *Seiran* pilots weren't above wearing good luck charms. Their talisman of choice was the *senninbari,* or "stitches by a thousand people." The *senninbari* was a plain cotton wrapper worn like a cummerbund around the stomach. Designed to ward off harm, it was made by a man's mother, wife, or sister. The custom had been around since the Meiji era and was hugely popular. Even in the summer of 1945, women could be found on street corners politely asking passersby to contribute a stitch. When 1,000 stitches were collected, the *senninbari* was ready to be worn.[27]

THE DAY AFTER Ariizumi received instructions for a second assault, the *I-400* passed east of Saipan.[28] It was just before dawn the morning of August 5, and the sub had recently finished charging her batteries.[29] Shortly after Kusaka submerged, a malfunction in the maneuvering room's electrical distribution panel caused it to catch fire. Sparks shot everywhere as the board began to burn. Moments later, the power went out.[30]

Fire is the worst condition that a closed system like a sub can face underwater. It can't vent smoke, precious oxygen is consumed, and the air is soon poisoned. Kusaka ordered the maneuvering room's hatches shut and closed the *I-400*'s ventilation system, but noxious fumes had already spread.[31]

His next action was to surface. Unfortunately, the morning sun revealed a U.S. task force on the horizon, so Kusaka had no choice but to submerge again.[32] This time the *I-400* descended out of control forcing her crew to grab hold of anything they could find while the sub sank by the stern. When a gauge showed them passing their safety depth, many feared the worst.[33]

The blackout only compounded Kusaka's problems. Without bilge pumps, which require electricity to operate, water built up in the maneuvering room. The water not only risked shorting out additional equipment, it was pulling the *I-400* down at a steep angle.[34] Fortunately, Captain Kusaka regained control before his sub reached crush depth, but they were hardly out of trouble.

As the U.S. task force steamed overhead, the *I-400* slowly began to expire. It's hard to know which was worse: to die from asphyxiation or at the hands of a U.S. warship. Without ventilation, however, the temperature inside the sub soared, while the dimness of the emergency lights only added to the oppression.

The air was so noxious, the crew's eyes burned, their throats became sore, and many developed headaches.[35] Those men who weren't on duty took to their bunks to consume as little oxygen as possible.

It took more than five hours to complete the repairs.[36] Time passed so slowly, they must have felt they were already dead. By the time repairs were finished, the *I-400*'s oxygen had almost run out. Kusaka wasn't sure whether the task force was still around, but he had to surface. When the *I-400* broke through the waves, he was relieved to find the ocean clear.

Meanwhile, the *I-401* had also met the enemy. In fact, Nambu had encountered so many U.S. warships, he was forced to submerge up to ten times a day.[37] This meant the detour Ariizumi had ordered was taking longer than anticipated. Unfortunately, there was nothing Nambu could do about it. Everywhere they went, an unbroken line of U.S. warships steamed toward Japan. Though it added time to their overburdened schedule, Nambu did his best to evade them.

One morning Nambu bade Yata, his chief gunnery officer, to the conning tower to look through the periscope.

"Hey, Shooter," Nambu called, using Yata's nickname. "Look here. We could sink any of these ships with a single shot!"[38]

Nambu knew the *I-401* had to remain concealed. Mole ops had taught him restraint meant survival.[39] But it was frustrating just to watch.[40]

WHEN KUSAKA HEARD that an atomic bomb had been dropped on Japan, he was more concerned about missing his rendezvous than about the devastation. Because of the delays, his rendezvous with Nambu had been pushed back.*[41] But when Kusaka surfaced at the location after sunset August 13, the *I-401* was nowhere to be seen.[42]

Undaunted, Kusaka remained on the surface, expecting to receive the *I-401*'s identification signal at any moment.[43] When dawn approached and the *I-401* still had not appeared,[44] he began to worry. Kusaka could have radioed his commander. But to do so might have given away his position. One thing he couldn't do was remain on the surface. The area was swarming with enemy ships, and if their sharp eyes didn't spot him, their radar would. The *I-400* prepared to submerge.

Kusaka hoped the *I-401* was just delayed, but his chief navigator jumped to the more obvious conclusion.

"Either I've made a navigational error, or the *I-401* has been sunk," he told Kusaka.[45]

Unfortunately, after double-checking his calculations, the chief navigator concluded they were in the right place. That left only one explanation.

The *I-401* had been destroyed.

---

* Takahashi mentions that the rendezvous was originally scheduled for August 12. Nevertheless, Nambu says the rendezvous was to take place on August 14 and Takahashi subsequently says the same thing. It appears the rendezvous was pushed back two days from the original plan. This is not surprising given the distance involved and the number of problems both subs encountered along the way.

Chapter 32

THE EMPEROR'S VOICE

THE FIRST INDICATION THAT SOMETHING UNUSUAL WAS HAPPEN-ing came a few days before the *Segundo* left Midway on her fifth and final war patrol. A U.S. carrier strike against Japan's third-largest island was suddenly called off on August 5. Additionally, Admiral Lockwood had been told to pull back his submarines at least 100 miles from Kyushu's coast.[1] This was strange, considering U.S. forces had done nothing for the past year except press closer to Japan. If Lockwood's subs were being withdrawn, something big was up.

Five days later, on Captain Johnson's thirtieth birthday, the *Segundo* departed Midway. Several officers had been lost to crew rotation during the sub's month-and-a-half layover. New arrivals included Lt. (jg) C. A. Hennessey, Ens. R. S. Byers, and QM3c Carlo Michael Carlucci. Nevertheless, more than half the sub's original crew remained on board since her commissioning. Among them were the sub's XO, Lt. John "Silent Joe" Balson, and Lt. (jg) Lewis Rodney Johnson. Chief of the Boat Edward A. Russell had also been with the sub since the beginning, as had Chiefs Carl Stallcop and J. T. "Doggy" Downs. Together these six men had 30 war patrols under their belts. When you added seven more for Captain Johnson, the total was nearly 40. Whatever the crew might have thought of their "medal-waving" captain, the *Segundo* was a well-seasoned boat.

Lieutenant Balson wasn't bothered by the recent change in command. He knew sub captains came and went with regularity. It was always better to learn how a new skipper liked things done when he joined a boat. And if his eccentricities rubbed you the wrong way, well, a smart XO kept it to himself. Balson certainly knew how to keep things to himself; he wasn't nicknamed "Silent Joe" for nothing. Unfortunately, the other officers on board didn't always share this attitude. As the *Segundo* departed Midway, the grumbling continued.

Carlo Carlucci noticed his captain had a mouth on him right away. This was really saying something, since Carlucci was no shrinking violet when it came to colorful language. "Everything was 'fuckin' this' and 'fuckin' that,' " he recalled about his skipper.[2]

It didn't bother Carlucci. He was new to the boat and had no expectations of how his captain should behave. But a foul-mouthed sub captain suggested a degree of volatility uncommon in a line commander. It wasn't a good sign.

Carlucci was a tough guy himself. A "dese, dem, and dose" type, he could have been mistaken for a boxer or a longshoreman. Born and raised in New York City, he'd worked construction before the war and was 175 pounds of solid muscle. He was also "scared of nuthin'."[3]

When Johnson finally steamed out of Midway, the *Segundo* was in "a high state of material condition."[4] It was August 10, 1945,[5] the day after the second atomic bomb was dropped. The crew knew that two Japanese cities had been destroyed by a powerful new weapon.[6] What they didn't know was that Fat Man and Little Boy were the reason Lockwood's subs had been withdrawn from the waters around Kyushu. Though the bombing's implications were unclear, the crew realized that the war was in its final stages. Nevertheless, they still believed Japan would have to be invaded before she surrendered. Indeed, Operation Olympic, the invasion of Kyushu, was set for November, less than three months away. Based on the invasions of Iwo Jima and Okinawa, it promised to be a long, bloody fight.

In the meantime, the *Segundo* headed for the Sea of Okhotsk, steering "various courses at various speeds."[7] Russia had declared war on Japan on August 8, and though she was an American ally, the United States feared she might invade Hokkaido, Japan's northernmost island. Russia already had a foothold in the northern Kurils, and so the *Segundo* was sent to keep an eye on the Soviets.

IJN warships and enemy freighters were strangely absent as the *Segundo* neared Japan. A few fishing trawlers were spotted—none worth stopping.[8] The enemy might have been missing from the battlefield, but Johnson knew not to underestimate the Japanese. He'd experienced firsthand how brave they could be. One time, while serving aboard a different vessel, Johnson had encountered a few Japanese soldiers floating on a raft in the middle of the Pacific. When he offered to take them on board, the bedraggled group surprised him by refusing. Despite being far from land, they preferred to die rather than surrender. After giving them food and water, Johnson obeyed their wishes and left them floating in the middle of nowhere.[9] That small example of Japanese courage was enough to convince him they were a formidable foe. What American would wave off rescue in the face of certain death? You could only hope you'd never be tested.

WHILE THE *SEGUNDO* was making her way up the coast of Japan, Kusaka surfaced the *I-400*. It was the evening of August 14, and the *I-401* was still missing.[10] Time was running out as the attack date drew near, and Kusaka debated whether to wait or proceed on his own. It didn't help that the *I-400*'s radar was irreparably broken.[11] The longer he hung around, the more chances he was taking.

Kusaka was confident he had the right location (they'd been relying on astral navigation to steer their course), but Takahashi had his doubts. He knew how difficult it was to navigate by the stars. As a pilot, he had experience making the same complicated calculations. The subs had practiced astral navigation at Nanao, and not once had their calculations been correct. Takahashi suspected they hadn't found the *I-401* because somebody had made another miscalculation.[12] In other words, they were lost.

They weren't lost though. They were south of Ulithi,[13] right where they should be. The longer Kusaka waited, the more likely it seemed that the *I-401* had been sunk. The *I-14* had nearly been lost while traveling to Truk, and the *I-13* had disappeared 550 miles east of Yokosuka. Sunk by planes from the USS *Anzio* (CVE-57), as well as by the USS *Lawrence C. Taylor* (DE-415),[14] the *I-13*'s demise marked the Sixth Fleet's single largest loss of life during the war,[15] and another casualty to ULTRA intelligence. If the *I-401* was also missing, then it meant Kusaka's sub was the last one left that could launch an attack. It was prudent for him to strike now rather than wait and risk being sunk.

Takahashi thought along similar lines. If they didn't rendezvous with the *I-401* by the appointed time, they should attack on their own. Another reason to attack was the disturbing transmissions coming out of Sydney. A Japanese-language newscast aired by the Allies claimed that a special bomb had been dropped on Hiroshima, instantly reducing the city to ruins. Takahashi was amazed to hear the bomb was no bigger than a matchbox. It sounded so fantastic, he wasn't sure whether to believe it. Other broadcasts mentioned that Russia had declared war on Japan. That meant four countries (the United States, Britain, China, and Russia) were demanding Japan's immediate and unconditional surrender. Japan couldn't fight the entire world. Eventually, she'd succumb.[16]

Many of the sub's officers doubted what they heard. One of Kusaka's men even reported hearing that Japan had won the war. The crew roared their approval and discussed what they would do once they arrived in America.[17] But the more Takahashi listened, the more the newscasts rang true. One announcer claimed Japan would surrender if allowed to keep the emperor.[18] It didn't seem the kind of propaganda an enemy would spread.

Gathering the *I-400*'s pilots, Takahashi shared what he'd heard on the radio. Since no surrender had been declared, they agreed not to act rashly. If Japan did surrender, however, Takahashi wanted them to know they bore no responsibility for defeat. Whatever happened, they should remain calm. Still, the rumors were unnerving.[19]

The next day Takahashi heard an Allied broadcast discussing repatriation. It claimed that "Japanese soldiers will be . . . allowed to return to their families to lead peaceful, productive lives." But it also stated that the "crews of Japanese submarines will be punished as war criminals for the crime of massacring prisoners."[20]

Takahashi must have found the news unnerving, given his participation in the *I-37* massacres. If captured, it meant he'd be tried as a war criminal, another good reason to proceed with the attack.

Rumors of an impending surrender spread quickly throughout the *I-400*. While Kusaka remained shut in his cabin, the sub entered a kind of purgatory.[21] As time passed, the gossip increased, threatening to undermine discipline.

When dawn arrived on the morning of August 15, the *I-400* submerged once again. It had been nearly two days since her arrival, with still no word from the flagship. Kusaka debated what to do. Should he wait one more day, or should he complete the mission on his own? After thinking matters over, he decided to wait a little longer.

At dawn, Kusaka extended the *I-400*'s radio antenna above the waves to test reception. Maybe Sixth Fleet headquarters would send a message explaining the commander's whereabouts. Though radio reception was fine, there was no word from Sixth Fleet. Then, at noon Tokyo time, the *I-400* received a report from Japan.

The broadcast was so shrouded in static, it seemed someone was trying to jam the signal. This was inconceivable, because the broadcast was made by the emperor. No one on board the *I-400* had ever heard the emperor speak before. Indeed, no one in Japan, save the emperor's closest advisers, had ever been addressed by the God incarnate and certainly never by radio.

As Takahashi listened to the emperor, he found himself struggling to make sense of his words. The emperor's voice was tinny and high-pitched and his language was so vague and opaque, it was difficult to make sense of it. But when Takahashi heard the phrase "endure the unendurable," he knew what it meant. The emperor was telling them to lay down arms.[22]

WHEN PRESIDENT HARRY S. Truman announced that Japan had surrendered, Americans poured into the street to celebrate. When Emperor Hirohito announced his desire for peace, most Japanese were confused, particularly since he never used the word *surrender.* The announcement had been recorded the previous day on a phonograph record. But the emperor's language was so formal and filled with vague allusions it made comprehension difficult. Even the most educated Japanese had trouble understanding what he had said.

There was confusion aboard the *I-400* as well. Many officers couldn't believe Japan would surrender—the very concept of defeat was unimaginable—and their first reaction was to reject it. Kusaka, being a cooler character, was undecided. A transcript of the emperor's speech was radioed to all IJN vessels that evening, and though it was easier to understand than the broadcast, it was still difficult.[23] It was clear, however, that the emperor believed the only way to prevent the Japanese race from being annihilated was to surrender.[24] Peace had been declared.

The Imperial Rescript said nothing about the *I-400*'s mission though,[25] and without specific orders, Kusaka could not stand down. Though he was a loyal subject, Kusaka did not report to the emperor. He was under Sixth Fleet command. That meant until the Sixth Fleet, the Combined Fleet, or the Navy General Staff countermanded the *I-400*'s orders, Kusaka would undertake the mission. If the *I-401* didn't arrive by August 17, he would launch the attack himself.

UNKNOWN TO KUSAKA, or the Sixth Fleet for that matter, the *I-401* had not been sunk; she'd arrived at the rendezvous point as planned. Thirty minutes after sunset on the evening of August 14, Nambu surfaced, looking for Kusaka. The night was clear and the water smooth, the stars shone brightly in the sky. Conditions were perfect for two subs to meet,[26] yet the *I-400* was nowhere to be seen.

Nambu wondered whether the *I-400* had succumbed to the same fate as the *I-13*. It was possible that a navigational error had caused the two subs to miss each other. Still, they couldn't be sure. The *I-401* sent another "friendly" signal but received nothing in reply. Nambu was worried.[27]

The *I-400* was waiting of course, just not where she was supposed to be. When Ariizumi ordered a course change, the agreed-upon meeting place had also been changed. He instructed the new location be radioed to the *I-400*, but either she never received the message, or the *I-401* failed to send it. Whatever the explanation, the *I-400* was waiting in the waters off Ulithi, while the *I-401* was waiting nearly 1,000 miles due west. It was a catastrophic error, and one that remains unexplained to this day.*

What's especially surprising is that Kusaka, if he never received the change order, should have been waiting in the waters off Ponape, yet that's not where he was. For some reason he had proceeded to Ulithi, bypassing Ponape altogether. This meant he not only failed to rendezvous with the *I-401* at the new location, he went to Ulithi of his own accord. Gross failures in communication don't happen in a modern navy, at least not often and not on this scale. Additionally, there's no good reason why the two subs ended up in such different locations. Did Ariizumi assume that Nambu would send Kusaka the change in plans? It seems unlikely, given how detail oriented Ariizumi was. Did Nambu deliberately withhold the route change in order to sabotage the mission? That seems even more unlikely, given Nambu's dedication to the navy.

Nambu doesn't recall Ariizumi sending a message informing the *I-400* of the new rendezvous.[28] If this is the case, why didn't Nambu send it in his stead? Either way, Kusaka never went to the original rendezvous point. He seems to have taken a right turn north of Ponape and headed straight for Ulithi on his own. It was an astounding breakdown in communication, one that probably saved the two subs from destruction. Of such errors is fate made.

As the *I-401* waited, she picked up newscasts out of San Fran-

---

* Some accounts suggest the radio message was never sent, implying Nambu may have withheld it. Given the strict command and control structure of a submarine, it's unlikely that such an important message would have been withheld. As a result, any suggestion that Nambu was responsible is purely speculative. More likely, the message was sent and the *I-400* failed to receive it. Amazingly, ULTRA intelligence seems not to have intercepted the message either.

cisco and Melbourne suggesting that surrender was imminent. From what Nambu could tell, the broadcasts were too outrageous to believe.[29] He knew Japan was losing the war, but it never occurred to him she might actually surrender. He was truly shocked then by what the broadcasts claimed. The best explanation was that they were American propaganda devised to trick them.

Nambu wasn't sure what Ariizumi thought. The commander was keeping his mouth shut. Even if Ariizumi knew something that he wasn't telling, he agreed to keep the radio broadcasts from the crew. Neither man wanted the mission jeopardized by unsubstantiated rumors, especially when they came from the enemy.

Nambu ordered his radio officers to keep silent, but it's impossible to keep news quiet in a submarine. There are always crewmen who know how to ferret out information. Once word got out that Japan might surrender, it was all the men could talk about.

When dawn approached on the morning of August 15, Nambu wondered where his sister sub could be. Like Kusaka, he couldn't remain on the surface during daylight and had to decide whether to wait or attack Ulithi on his own. Finally, after discussion with Ariizumi, he submerged the boat and waited until evening. If the *I-400* didn't show up by then, they'd consider attacking Ulithi on their own. Time was running out.

When Nambu resurfaced that evening, the *I-400* was nowhere to be found.[30] The weather was good, the ocean remained calm.[31] The *I-401*'s communications officer busily transcribed messages, hoping for news about the *I-400*. There was none though and foreign broadcasts continued to be alarming.

It was still difficult for Nambu to take them seriously; surrender seemed impossible. But when the communications chief handed him a transcript of the emperor's broadcast his hands shook in disbelief.

"Could they possibly be this stupid?" he exclaimed. Then he barked, "Do not tell the crew!"[32]

Ariizumi was so infuriated, he didn't finish reading the Imperial Rescript. Whether he already knew what it said, or could not bear the news, Nambu wasn't sure.[33] It made no difference either way. Both men were ready to attack.

Orders from Japan followed quickly after that, though none of them made sense. One instructed the 631st air group to prepare a final defense of the Japanese homeland.[34] Another confirmed that peace had been declared but instructed all submarines to execute their predetermined missions and to attack the enemy if discovered.[35]

That was enough for Ariizumi. He was finished waiting. The *I-401* submerged and set a course for Ulithi. The empire might have surrendered, but Ariizumi had not. He was going to complete his mission.[36]

The *I-401* was going rogue.

CHAPTER 33

ANARCHY

ARIIZUMI'S DECISION TO GO ROGUE WASN'T SURPRISING. EVEN though the emperor had expressed his desire for peace, only a cease-fire had been declared; an actual surrender agreement was still three weeks away.[1] In the meantime, anything could happen, and the incoming messages weren't helping.

The orders Ariizumi received were confusing and contradictory. Importantly, no order explicitly canceled the Ulithi attack, let alone told him to stand down. In fact, one of the orders mentioned that "submarines should execute their missions as planned."[2] This meant the Ulithi attack was still on.

Besides, Ariizumi didn't take commands from the emperor, he took them from Sixth Fleet. Since the Sixth Fleet hadn't ordered him to cease combat operations, it was reasonable to assume the sub should proceed with her mission.

It's also important to remember that Ariizumi had been raised within the traditions of the IJN. Born to a navy family and educated at Etajima, he was a product of his upbringing. He'd been a line commander, attended the Naval War College, and served as an NGS staff officer. Everything he believed in, worked for, and fought for was centered on serving the IJN. If Japan's cause was just, backed by celestial will and divine guidance, then it was his job to see that they triumphed. The word *surrender* wasn't in his vocabulary.

There was also the problem of war crimes. Ariizumi had played a central role in the Indian Ocean massacres. Allied protests had already resulted in his interrogation. Still, it's doubtful that Ariizumi chose to continue the attack to avoid being tried as a war criminal. Killing prisoners might have been sickening, but he understood the reason for doing it. Besides, an officer of the Imperial Japanese Navy never disobeyed an order, and Ariizumi was dutiful if anything. Even if his decision to attack went against the emperor's wishes, going out in a blaze of glory would be Ariizumi's way of accepting responsibility for Japan's defeat. Fear of being prosecuted as a war criminal had nothing to do with it.

Ariizumi was a patriot. If the emperor in all his benevolence had decided Japan must capitulate in order to survive, so be it. But Ariizumi's honor was at stake, and honor is a powerful motivator in any culture. Yes, he'd sworn allegiance to the emperor, but if Japan had failed after many years of war, the failure was Ariizumi's. If victory was impossible, then his only recourse was death in defense of the empire. It was the honorable thing to do.

Nambu agreed with Ariizumi. He too found surrender inconceivable, though he reacted as much out of anger as conviction. And they weren't the only ones to feel this way. Acceptance of the cease-fire agreement was far from uniform in Japan. Approximately 600 military personnel, mostly officers, committed suicide over the disgrace.[3] Others resisted in different ways. Most notable was the attempted coup d'état staged by Maj. Kenji Hatanaka on the evening of August 14, designed to prevent the emperor's speech from being broadcast. Hatanaka and his men stormed the Imperial Palace searching feverishly for the phonograph record with the emperor's recording. Though Hatanaka surrendered four hours before the emperor's broadcast, the incident showed just how difficult it was for true believers to accept defeat.

And Ariizumi was a true believer. As commander of the last operational Sixth Fleet unit,[4] he wasn't willing to lay down his sword. He'd been charged with a top secret mission, the last offensive action of the war. When it came time to make his decision, Ariizumi chose to proceed as planned. In 24 hours, they'd launch against Ulithi.

MASAO OKUI, THE *I-400*'s cook, knew something was wrong when the senior officers ignored their food.[5] It was the evening of August 15, and he was serving dinner in the wardroom. Food was a high point aboard the sub, so it was unusual when somebody refused to eat. The entire senior rank was so dispirited, they hardly lifted their *hashi*.

Kusaka had chosen not to inform his enlisted men about the emperor's announcement. It was the captain's prerogative to withhold information, but Kusaka did so because he was having trouble accepting the news himself. He'd told his senior officers, of course, instructing them to keep quiet. Since orders from Japan were contradictory, he thought it best to see how things developed first.[6]

When the *I-400* surfaced after sunset the next day, Kusaka finally received a message to cease combat activities and return to Kure.[7] Instead of complying, he took the sub down to periscope depth and assembled his senior officers. Even though his orders were clear, their opinion still mattered to him. Losing the war was unprecedented. Kusaka wanted to know what his officers thought they should do.

The *I-400*'s chief navigator was first to speak. He argued they should attack Ulithi because it would be shameful to return to Japan. The *I-400* was only hours from launching her *Seiran* when the surrender announcement came, it would be easy to resume their plans. If they survived, they could launch other attacks against the enemy, commandeering food and fuel along the way. If capture appeared imminent, they could always scuttle the sub.[8]

Takahashi had the opposite reaction. The chief navigator was too quick to sacrifice the crew, he argued. Some of the officers might want to fight, but many of the enlisted men would want to go home.[9] If the chief navigator wanted to die, fine, but why should the rest of the crew be deprived of their lives?[10] Importantly, Japan had surrendered. What was the point of dying if they'd already lost? Of course, the naval command had made a grievous error. Starting a war it couldn't win had been foolish. Now that they'd admitted defeat, everyone should return home as quickly as possible.

Kusaka listened quietly with his eyes closed. When all his officers had had their say, he retired to his cabin to think things over.[11] It didn't take him long to make up his mind. He soon reassembled his officers to tell them they were returning to Kure.[12]

Though not everyone agreed with the choice (some officers even contemplated jumping into the sea wearing weights if they were captured),[13] there was palpable relief. Kusaka informed the rest of the crew by intercom. Many were surprised by Japan's defeat, but they were equally shocked to have survived the war. Takahashi was in the happy-to-return-home camp.[14] At least he wouldn't be throwing his life away to satisfy someone else's notion of honor.

The next morning Kusaka set course for Japan. It's unknown whether he feared capture because he'd massacred prisoners, but he certainly took precautions. Traveling underwater by day, Kusaka surfaced only at night, when the sub could go her fastest.[15] Obviously, no self-respecting sub captain wanted to surrender his boat to the enemy. The ignominy could only be worsened by being captured in international waters. Ideally, they'd make it back to Japan without being spotted, where they could quietly melt into the countryside. If worse came to worst and they were intercepted, it had to be in Japanese waters. Otherwise, the loss of face would be too great.

THE *I-14* WAS awaiting another recon patrol when Shimizu received a transcript of the emperor's speech.[16] He had his doubts about the message, just like the other sub captains. He even considered sailing to Singapore as originally planned.[17] But when the *I-14* was ordered to cease combat operations, Shimizu gathered his officers and read them the edict.

Lt. Michio Takamatsu, the *I-14*'s gunnery officer, was crushed by the news. This was how German naval officers must have felt at the end of World War I, he thought. Germany had paid a heavy price after the war, and Takamatsu feared the same for Japan. *Shoganai*, he said to himself—there was nothing he could do.[18]

Some of Shimizu's officers entertained wild ideas, like blowing up the sub or attacking Saipan.[19] When the Sixth Fleet ordered the

I-14 to return to Yokosuka,* Shimizu finally accepted that the war was over. The news might have depressed him, but he was ready to comply. It was time to go home.[20]

As the *I-14* departed Truk, one of its reconnaissance planes circled overhead. Though he accepted the cease-fire, Shimizu was intent on avoiding capture. Navigating underwater by day, he darkened the *I-14*'s navigation lights when traveling on the surface at night. His priority was to "bring every last crewman safely back to the mainland." The only way to do it was to avoid the enemy.[21]

Meanwhile, tempers were running hot in Fukuyama. Some of the 631st's younger officers wanted to commandeer a boat, pack it with weapons, and attack Allied ships in the Tsushima Strait. It was a joke at first. Then Lieutenant Yamamoto found a boat, loaded it with supplies, and headed for the Inland Sea with a few supporters. Things didn't end there, however. The air group's maintenance chief was so upset by the emperor's broadcast, he threatened suicide. Thinking more clearly, he packed his bags and deserted the unit instead. His colleagues took mercy on him since his Hiroshima home had recently been destroyed. Two men went to bring him back. The incident was indicative of the difficulty many had embracing defeat.[22]

THE *I-401*'s *SEIRAN* were readying for their attack on Ulithi when Nambu received orders to cease all combat activity. The blanket message was quickly followed by another specifically canceling the Ulithi mission. SubRon 1 was now ordered to Kure.[23]

It was nine o'clock the evening of August 16 when Nambu learned the attack had been canceled.[24] The order had come not a moment too soon, since the sub was close to launching her planes. Had the message arrived seven hours later, an attack so provoca-

---

* Accounts conflict, but it appears that the high command initially ordered the *Sen-toku* squadron to proceed to Kure. A subsequent order changed the destination to Ominato. See Nambu, *Beikidoukantai wo Kishuseyo,* p. 240; and Kazuo Nishijima, interview by author.

tive it could have endangered the cease-fire agreement would have commenced. As it was, the *I-401* barely avoided disaster.

There were no rules in the Japanese Navy for dealing with surrender. The samurai code taught that when given a choice between surrender and death, it is best to choose death. Imperial Naval tradition reinforced this thinking, but Nambu was too relieved to kill himself. It might have been cowardly, still he was glad to be alive.[25]

After receiving orders to stand down, Ariizumi convened a meeting in the *I-401*'s wardroom, with Nambu and his senior officers in attendance.[26] It had been nearly two days since the emperor's announcement, a seeming eternity in the minds of those who knew the truth. Now, as they squeezed around the wardroom table, their faces shiny with sweat, the officers of the *I-401* expressed their opinion about what to do next.[27]

"We can't return to Japan with our tail between our legs," one officer argued. "We should scuttle the sub instead."[28]

Ariizumi dismissed the idea. German captains who scuttled their ships at the end of World War I had demonstrated admirable fighting spirit, he explained, but their actions had resulted in higher war reparations for Germany. The commander didn't want to increase Japan's burden, especially after losing a war. Instead, he suggested they kill themselves.*[29]

"Even if we return to the mainland all soldiers will be executed as war criminals," he added.[30] Mass suicide was a better idea.

Individual accounts of the meeting vary, but Nambu's officers had little heart for such drastic action.

"Even if we commit suicide we only have six pistols," one officer pointed out. "Senior officers have a sword but their death would be messy and might discourage the [enlisted men from following their example]. It's just not practical for 200 people to kill themselves. Sinking the sub would be better, even if it burdens Japan."[31]

---

* There is some dispute over whether Ariizumi argued initially for suicide or for heading for the Sanriku coast, where the crew would disperse. Having studied Ariizumi, I find it wholly within his character for him to have first supported suicide.

Ariizumi continued to disagree. He might not have realized, however, that some of his officers preferred not to die by their own hand. Though they were ashamed to admit it, it created a dilemma. If a consensus emerged that suicide was best, the reluctant officers would be obligated to go along. In the meantime, many hoped to avoid death by coming up with an alternative solution.

One officer suggested they hide out on a Pacific island.[32] The idea was dismissed as impractical because they couldn't survive on an island without supplies.[33] Another officer, desirous of breaking the tension, suggested they become pirates.[34] With three attack planes, 20 torpedoes, and months' worth of provisions, they could sail the high seas capturing ships along the way. It was a funny idea, and no one took it seriously.[35]

If Nambu felt anything during the meeting, it was the shame of defeat.[36] It was bad enough that Japan had lost the war; the fact she had surrendered was enough to choke him. But the more Nambu thought about the situation, the more he realized what he should do. The emperor had called upon Japan's fighting men to return and rebuild their nation. Perhaps they should heed that call. Certainly, their lives would be better spent helping their country recover from a devastating war than sacrificing themselves for a cause already lost.

It was at this moment that Nambu decided what he must do. The war was over; the emperor had deemed it so. He would return his 204 crewmen safely to Japan.[37] And since the Sixth Fleet was no longer in existence, there was no one to tell him to do otherwise—no one except Ariizumi.

It was hard to know where the commander stood after the debate. After all, his first instinct had been for everyone to kill themselves. Would he back a consensus to return to Japan, or would he overrule them? There was no way to know for sure.

After the initial wardroom meeting, Muneo Bando, the *I-401*'s chief navigator, went to Ariizumi's quarters for a private audience.[38] Like many of the *I-401*'s officers, Bando was relieved the war was over.[39] Newly married, he was inclined to accept the emperor's edict.

"Commander, regarding suicide . . . ," Bando began.

"Ah, you weren't at the meeting, but I think suicide is the best choice for us."

"What do we do about the submarine, Commander, if we commit suicide?"

"We'll leave the sub afloat, so it won't cause problems for Japan in the future."

It was now or never, so Bando screwed up his courage. "There's no need to go to these lengths [i.e., kill ourselves] . . . We have fought for the emperor . . . but this time, the emperor has ordered our submission. . . . Committing suicide against his wish . . . may mean death for nothing. . . . We should follow orders and return to base."

"Do you think so?" Ariizumi asked. "No such opinion was expressed in the meeting."

"Commander, we need to think about the future of the Japanese race. It took Germany only 10 years to recover from World War I. . . . You devoted half your life to the navy, but I and the crew are young. You may have no regrets, still . . . ," Bando stopped talking to examine the commander's face.

Much to Bando's surprise, Ariizumi seemed to be taking what he said seriously. Sensing an opportunity, Bando pressed on.

"We must be the ones to rebuild Japan. Why not sail the sub to an unpopulated part of the eastern seaboard, split up, and disappear? That way we could arrive home safely and avoid surrendering to the Americans. If the enemy intercepts us, we can always submerge with the hatches open. Barring capture, we should try to get home no matter what."[40]

Yata, the *I-401*'s gunnery officer, was not senior enough to have been told of the emperor's announcement when it first happened. Now that he knew, he was glad the war was over. Nobody had thought they could win anyway, so it was a relief to hear they might be returning home. But could the *I-401* really get through such heavily guarded waters? Yata wondered. Surely the United States would catch them along the way. What would they do then?[41]

Bando's suggestion to return to Japan was the simplest, most direct response to an ambiguous situation, but the problem of how to avoid capture by the Americans remained. If they were discovered while too far south, they might be diverted to an American naval base like Saipan or Guam. Alternatively, they couldn't head for Yokosuka or Kure because both were likely to be occupied.[42] Fortunately, their classified mission gave them options. The I-401 was a top secret sub, few people knew she existed. This meant they could go anywhere they wanted and nobody would be the wiser. Being a well-kept secret had its advantage.

Alternative accounts suggest that the idea to return to Japan was not Bando's alone. Whatever the truth, the consensus was fragile. There had been so much back-and-forth, and so many conflicting opinions, that Nambu wasn't sure which agreement would stick. The commander had always been difficult, and his sense of pride naturally favored death.

Surprisingly, Ariizumi agreed to return to Japan. They would continue traveling underwater by day to escape detection, even though such an act was considered hostile. They would avoid Yokosuka, Kure, and Sasebo. Instead, they would head for the Sanriku coast, a remote area on Honshu's northeastern seaboard that the enemy was likely to overlook. Once they arrived, they would disembark and quietly scuttle the sub. Since few people knew the I-401 existed, let alone her whereabouts, they might just get away with it.[43] The two wild cards were the Americans and Ariizumi. Unfortunately, there was nothing Nambu could do about either one. If they ran into the enemy, all bets were off. He just hoped it didn't come to that.

WHEN NAMBU FINALLY informed his crew that Japan had lost the war, it was nearly 30 hours since the emperor had broadcast the same message. Many had guessed the truth. Certainly no one complained about not having been told. They were happy just to have survived.[44]

The crew might have been glad to be alive, but their mood was hardly festive. A depression descended upon the sub and deepened the farther north they got. The shock of having survived the war was replaced by the uncertainty of what awaited them at home. Were their families still alive, or had they been incinerated by B-29s? Would they be welcomed back, scorned as "ghosts" or worse, seen as responsible for the empire's defeat? After so many years of warfare, the men had difficulty grasping a future that didn't involve death. The uncertainty of postwar life weighed on them like a black cloud.[45]

Nambu received a second Imperial Rescript on August 18, this one addressed "To the officers and men of the Imperial Forces."

> Three years and eight months have elapsed since we declared war on the United States and Britain. During this time our beloved men of the army and navy, sacrificing their lives, have fought valiantly on disease-stricken and barren lands and on tempestuous waters in the blazing sun, and of this we are deeply grateful.
>
> Now that the Soviet Union has entered the war against us, to continue the war under the present internal and external conditions would be only to increase needlessly the ravages of war finally to the point of endangering the very foundation of the Empire's existence.
>
> With that in mind and although the fighting spirit of the Imperial Army and Navy is as high as ever, with a view to maintaining and protecting our noble national policy we are about to make peace with the United States, Britain, the Soviet Union and Chungking.
>
> To a large number of loyal and brave officers and men of the Imperial forces who have died in battle and from sicknesses goes our deepest grief. At the same time we believe the loyalty and achievements of you officers and men of the Imperial forces will for all time be the quintessence of our nation.
>
> We trust that you officers and men of the Imperial forces will comply with our intention and will maintain a solid unity and strict discipline in your movements and that you will bear the hardest of all difficulties, bear the unbearable and leave an everlasting foundation of the nation.[46]

Nambu had little difficulty understanding this rescript. Enough time had passed that he'd accepted Japan's defeat, and the edict, though sad, was designed to persuade the military to accept a cease-fire. Not everybody was content to surrender though. Two days later the *I-401* received a message not only diverting her from Kure to Ominato but demanding she reveal her position as well.[47]

The request put Ariizumi in a quandary. If he revealed the *I-401*'s location, the sub could be directed to an enemy port.[48]

"As a soldier of the Imperial Navy, I cannot let one of his majesty's ships fall into enemy hands," he told Nambu. "There is no need to give them our location. We'll just keep silent and return to the mainland."[49]

Clearly, Ariizumi was still in command. Deciding to attack Ulithi after the emperor's broadcast, returning to a port of his own choosing, and now refusing to reveal the sub's location were strong indications he was no longer following orders. It was remarkable in some ways that a loyal commander of the Sixth Fleet, one who had consented to massacring prisoners even though he knew the policy was despicable, behaved in this manner. Then again, they were living in remarkable times. Ariizumi was calling the shots.

A third Imperial Rescript, also addressed to the military, was received on August 25. Written to suppress the pockets of resistance that continued to plague the empire, the emperor again thanked his fighting men for their sacrifice, reminded them to cease combat activity, and made it clear that demobilization was under way. The navy minister followed up the rescript with his own message. Praising the emperor's gracious edict, it reminded IJN personnel to follow the emperor's words and focus their efforts on rebuilding the nation.

By now, the message was clear. The war was over; the Imperial Japanese Navy was no more. Nambu took the messages as evidence that he was correct in returning his crew to Japan. After posting an inspirational note to the *I-401*'s mast,[50] he retired to his cabin to pen his last poem of the war:

LET THIS DISGRACE BE HANDED DOWN AND SHARED BY
OUR CHILDREN AND GRANDCHILDREN AS IT BECOMES A
CORNERSTONE OF OUR HOMELAND.[51]

Later that night Nambu shaved off his mustache. He felt no regret doing so, though it surprised his crew. He'd been growing the mustache since before hostilities began, and its loss was his way of saying the war was over. The crew understood Nambu's action. They also grasped his intention to return them home safely. No words need be spoken. The loss of his mustache said volumes.

Traveling on the surface both day and night, Nambu raced home to Japan. On August 26, all IJN warships were instructed to dispose of their weapons and hoist the black flag of surrender.[52] Nambu had all documents collected, in keeping with the order. Everything from the important to the mundane—including the sub's logbooks, code books, personal diaries, schematics, and navigation charts—was loaded into jute sacks and weighted with ammunition.[53] Then, as the midday sun shone overhead, the crew began throwing bag after bag off the machine gun deck. Nambu watched the sacks splash into the *kuroshio* current. The water was so clear, he could trace each bag as it sank into the darkness.*[54]

Weapons disposal left Yata in a state of shock. As gunnery officer, nothing was worse than throwing munitions over the side. It made him feel numb.[55] Inouye, the *I-401*'s sonar operator, was similarly moved. Chucking weapons overboard was such a painful reminder of defeat that he found himself crying.[56]

Nambu waited until dark before disposing of their *Seiran*. The moon was playing hide-and-seek behind the clouds as the first airplane was rolled from the hangar. The aircrew left her wings folded, attached the plane to the catapult without floats, and launched her pilotless into the night sky. The first *Seiran* didn't get very far before plunging into the sea. Rather than sink right away, she settled so

---

* One reason there are so many conflicting dates in the story of the *I-400* subs is that most of the material that would allow for an accurate reconstruction of their timeline was disposed of in this manner.

slowly, it seemed as if she were putting up a fight. Nambu thought it the saddest sight he'd ever seen.

Heiji Kondo was the aircraft mechanic responsible for the second plane. He felt nothing but respect for his charge. As a result, he couldn't let her leave with a U.S. star on her wings. It would be embarrassing if someone found her. Besides, Kondo wanted everyone to know the *Seiran* had been a Japanese plane. Working quickly in the darkness, he and his maintenance crew painted over the blue and white star with a bright red Japanese sun. When they were finished, they launched their *Seiran* into the night, tears shining in their eyes.[57]

Ariizumi accompanied the launch of each *Seiran* with a lone cry of *"Banzai!"* It only added to the tragic effect.*[58] But something strange happened that night. As the third *Seiran* hurtled down the launch ramp, the plane seemed to resist leaving. A rooster tail of sparks followed in her wake, and after crashing into the ocean, she floated so close to the *I-401* that Kondo felt she was trying to return home.[59] It was a sentimental notion, but it didn't last. After struggling to remain afloat, the final *Seiran* dipped beneath the waves. The storm that had once been intended for a clear sky vanished into the night.

The *I-400* also disposed of its weapons. Surfacing shortly after sunset, Kusaka's crew began throwing sacks of documents overboard. Among them were Takahashi's personal flight records. It pained him to throw them away. But since they tied him to the *I-37*'s massacre of Allied prisoners, he had no choice.[60]

Next came the *Seiran*. A brief ceremony was held before the planes were launched. The aircrews lined up on the machine gun deck, tears running down their cheeks, before they punched holes in their planes' wings and fuselage.[61] Next the *I-400*'s crane picked up the planes, one by one, and dropped them into the ocean.†

---

* Nambu thinks it may have been Asamura who cried *"Banzai!,"* but Asamura recalls it was Ariizumi.

† Takahashi, in *Shinryu Tokubetsu Kogekitai* (p. 208), says the *Seiran* were launched into the sea by catapult rather than dumped by crane.

Even in darkness, the *Seiran*'s silver-painted body could be seen sinking slowly out of sight.

It hurt to see such good aircraft destroyed. Still, Takahashi knew that disguising the planes as American would be seen as a violation of international law. But the *I-400* was not home free yet. Amid all the hurried activity, a crewman fell overboard and drowned. It was shocking to lose someone so close to Japan, especially now that the war was over. The accident didn't stop weapons disposal though.[62] There was no time for delay.

Seiran ordnance came next. One by one the 1,760-pound bombs were plucked off the deck and dropped into the sea.[63] Okui, the cook, was sad to see the weapons go,[64] but not as sad as the sub's chief torpedo officer over what happened next. After launching the *I-400*'s bow torpedoes, Kusaka watched in dismay as one by one they leaped out of the water, turned in a half circle, and began heading back toward the boat.[65] It took only one malfunctioning torpedo to sink a submarine; several was unprecedented. Clearly, the gyros had been set incorrectly.

Incredible as it may seem, after surviving an Allied air raid, underwater mines, an electrical fire, and multiple navy task forces, the hunter was once again the hunted. Only this time, the *I-400* wasn't hunted by the enemy—she was hunting herself.

CHAPTER 34

ESCAPE

CARLO CARLUCCI WAS ASLEEP WHEN NEWS OF THE JAPANESE surrender first reached the *Segundo*. He'd finished his watch, had a bite to eat, and was sacked out in the crew's quarters when somebody turned the lights on.

"What's up?" he asked drowsily.

"War's over!" someone shouted.

Carlucci couldn't have been more surprised.

The *Segundo* was en route to the Kuril Islands when Japan accepted peace terms. It was 2:07 the afternoon of August 15 when the news came by radio. Forty-three minutes later it was followed by ComSubPac orders to cease fire.[1]

As late as July 1945, U.S. submariners were repeating the hopeful slogan "The Golden Gate in '48," so it's clear they thought fighting would last at least a little while longer.[2] But the absence of enemy ships was one indication the war was near its end.[3] The *Segundo* had seen nothing since leaving Midway. Still, as Captain Johnson approached their designated patrol area, he resolved to stay on guard. The Japanese might have accepted a cease-fire, but he knew how determined they could be. They'd have to be careful.

The Kurils are a long chain of islands extending in an arc northeast from Hokkaido to the Russian peninsula of Sredinny Khrebet. Long contested, the islands were an uneasy mix of both populations. Russia had begun invading the chain three days after the cease-fire had been declared. The Kurils may have been economically insignificant, but they had strategic value, since they could be used to launch an attack against Japan.

The *Segundo* patrolled the area for seven days. From what

Johnson could tell, the Japanese were sitting out the Russian land grab. Given the animosity between the two countries, it must have hurt. Nevertheless, Johnson's orders were to observe, not to intervene.

On August 19 the *Segundo* approached close enough to photograph one of the islands.[4] Seeing no activity, Johnson withdrew. That same day he stopped a Japanese fishing trawler. Deciding she wasn't a threat, he let her go. It was a waste to interdict fishermen,[5] and now that a cease-fire had been declared, he had no reason to sink one. In fact, Johnson became so confident, the *Segundo* remained surfaced by day, diving only when torpedo maintenance was necessary.

The *Segundo* wasn't alone on her patrol. The USS *Razorback* was also in the area. The subs exchanged recognition signals and small talk, killing time until something more interesting came their way. Then finally on August 24, Johnson was ordered south to Tokyo Bay.[6]

The *Segundo* was told to mop up any remnants of the Imperial Japanese Navy that were encountered along the way.[7] There had been enough isolated attacks since the cease-fire to warrant concern. The official surrender ceremony had even been pushed back a few days to give the Japanese military time to persuade reluctant factions to lay down arms. Any more violations and the cease-fire might be jeopardized.

Johnson knew enough to maintain a sharp lookout, but he probably didn't expect any strays.[8] Japanese warships weren't anticipated this far north, and if he did see anything, it was likely to be a small surface vessel, since most capital ships had been sunk.

But not all Japanese warships had been destroyed. The world's largest, most secret submarine was returning home, determined that nothing should get in her way. What Johnson didn't realize was that the *Segundo* stood right in her path.

THE *I-401* WAS considerably lighter after jettisoning her weapons. She now rode higher in the water than at any time since training. Her increased buoyancy also meant she traveled faster, a condition

Nambu exploited in his race to get home. For the last two days, the *I-401* had been making her way up Japan's eastern seaboard. They'd managed to avoid the enemy thus far. But one dark night, when visibility was poor, they had a bad scare.

They were still south of Tokyo when one of the lookouts spotted a shadow in the distance. There was little chance of it being a Japanese ship given all the enemy activity, so Nambu submerged, hoping to escape detection. As the *I-401*'s crew sat motionless, the sound of a U.S. Navy task force roared overhead. It would have been an excellent opportunity to attack if Nambu hadn't already disposed of their weapons. When the propellers faded, Nambu resurfaced. He could still see the huge black shadows heading toward Japan.[9] Ironically, it was the same direction he was heading in, only he wasn't a conqueror as they were—he was a fugitive. The difference was incalculable.

Avoiding capture was only one of Nambu's problems. The other was Ariizumi's increasingly erratic behavior. Just as the *Segundo*'s crew was watching Captain Johnson for signs of trigger happiness, Nambu watched Ariizumi for signs of trouble. Nambu no longer feared being killed in battle, and he was well aware that his commander had volunteered them for suicide. Since then, however, Ariizumi's strange behavior had made him feel ill at ease.

Nambu's greatest fear was that the command structure was breaking down. The *Seiran* pilots had lapsed into a kind of despondency,[10] and the rest of the crew was equally depressed. If morale collapsed, they could be in danger. It took only one mistake for a fatal accident to sink a submarine. Nambu had to find a way to keep that from happening.

Ariizumi's behavior wasn't helping matters. It was shocking to see him look so poorly. The normally stout squadron commander seemed to have shrunk to half his normal size, and his clean-shaven face only emphasized the change. Even some of the *I-401*'s officers didn't recognize him. After entering the wardroom, the *I-401*'s sonar operator thought, "Who's that sitting there?" Then he realized, "It's the boss!"[11]

It must have been devastating for Ariizumi to see his world collapse around him. He'd single-mindedly served two things in his life: the emperor and the Imperial Japanese Navy. Now both had ordered him to surrender. To make matters worse, he was returning home not only in defeat but as a war criminal. No wonder death was an appealing solution.

Ariizumi's travails were far from over. As they neared Japan, he'd felt safe enough to report the *I-401*'s location. However, the Imperial Defense Command had forwarded the information to the U.S. Navy as part of the armistice agreement.[12] It was the ultimate betrayal by the very system Ariizumi had pledged to support. Fortunately, Ariizumi had no way of knowing this—otherwise he might have taken precipitate action. In the meantime, he struggled to live within a code that fate had conspired to destroy. The truth must have been enough to drive him crazy.

BY THE EVENING of August 28, the *I-401* was less than 200 miles off the coast of Japan.[13] In ten hours they would reach the Sanriku coast, their final destination.[14] As it was, they were passing Kinkasan, a mountainous island northeast of Tokyo. Bando fantasized about evacuating the sub.[15] In the ancient past, gold had been discovered nearby, and good fortune came to those who visited the local shrine. But the *I-401* continued its journey.

In addition to raising the black surrender flag, Nambu had also angled the deck guns downward to indicate they weren't hostile. The *I-401* may have appeared chastened, but neither Nambu nor Ariizumi was willing to hand their sub to the enemy just yet.[16] It was miraculous that Nambu had gotten this far without being apprehended. In a sea brimming with enemy ships, it was virtually impossible to evade capture. Now, with his objective only ten hours away, Nambu imagined he could safely return his men to Japan. If luck would only hold.

"Something black, fifteen degrees to starboard!" a lookout shouted. "Movement unknown!"

It was near midnight when a silhouette unmistakably formed into a U.S. submarine. Radar Officer Natsume confirmed he had a ship on his screen. *We can't dive to escape,* Nambu thought, *they'll see it as an act of aggression.* The last thing he wanted, now that the war was over, was to lose his crew in a meaningless action. But he didn't want to be captured, either. And so in what amounted to an act of wishful thinking, Nambu decided upon swift withdrawal.[17]

Ordering a change in course, he felt the sub veer hard to port and accelerate to flank speed. As he watched the enemy fall away 90 degrees to starboard, he prayed they'd escaped without being discovered.[18] Unfortunately for the crew of the *I-401*, Nambu's luck had finally run out.

CHAPTER 35

INTERCEPTION

THE SUB ROCKED GENTLY ON THE SURFACE AS DAWN SPREAD across the Pacific. The sea was calm, the day gray and hazy.[1] As Nambu watched the American sub less than 500 yards off his starboard side,[2] he didn't need binoculars to see that her torpedo tubes were pointed directly at him.

The confrontation had a rallying effect on the commander. Restored to his intransigent self, Ariizumi stood beside the *I-401*'s captain staring grimly at the Americans. Nambu requested an update on port engine repairs. Informed it would take a while longer, he reviewed his options. As best as he could determine, he had three—all of them bad. They could fight, they could run, or they could surrender.

Yata, the chief gunnery officer, wanted to ram the American submarine.[3] Nambu dismissed the idea, since they'd never close the distance before being torpedoed. In fact, attacking the sub was impossible. They'd disposed of all their weapons two days earlier. The Americans didn't know this, of course, which meant Nambu could leverage their ignorance. But he wasn't ready for a banzai charge, at least not yet, which left two other options: running or surrendering. Both were unappealing.

As Nambu watched his enemy, the American sub flashed another signal. This one said "surrender." "Stop" was one thing, "surrender" quite another. The *I-401* might have been flying the black flag, but Ariizumi had no intention of honoring it.

Asamura had been sleeping when the *Segundo* first appeared. Word of the American sub quickly spread, and though there was no panic, the crew was worried. Fearful of death, a young crewman sought Asamura out for reassurance: "We'll die together, won't we?"[4]

The young man's concern was indicative of the fear some felt inside the *I-401*. Many of the enlisted men expected to die, if not at the hands of the Americans, then at the hands of their commander. After all, everyone knew Ariizumi had slaughtered Allied prisoners. Their treatment at the hands of the enemy would be no different.

Some men were convinced Ariizumi would never permit that to happen. He would kill them first, either by scuttling the sub or by ordering them to commit suicide. Either way, they were doomed.

While the crew wondered what was happening, Nambu carefully watched the *Segundo*. He had a bad feeling about the sub. Her intention to sink them seemed clear. Given his limited options, Nambu figured it was best to do nothing. A passive-aggressive approach might buy time to develop a course of action. He would wait them out.

Unfortunately for Nambu, Captain Johnson was in no mood for stalling. He'd been granted permission to torpedo the enemy if they showed resistance. The Japanese sub might have been flying the surrender flag, but nothing in her behavior indicated she would do so.

The *Segundo*'s crew knew their captain wouldn't hesitate to sink the enemy. They might have been more worried, however, had they known his real intention. For Johnson wasn't going to sink the *I-401*, at least not yet. He was going to try to board her first.[5]

THE *I-401*'S CHIEF navigator, Muneo Bando, was standing near Captain Nambu on the bridge when they received a signal from the American sub to "dispatch an officer."

"Send an officer?" Bando thought, "What do they mean send an officer? They should send someone to us!"[6] Even in the middle of a showdown, Sixth Fleet pride took precedence.

Nambu tried a different approach. Instead of refusing the request, he signaled, "We have no boat."[7]

This wasn't true, of course. Kondo, the *Seiran* mechanic, was busy preparing a rubber raft for just such a request.[8] But Nambu was reluctant to comply with the order.[9] The longer he dragged things out, the more options he might have. Though he didn't want to be torpedoed, he wasn't going to cooperate just because they'd asked.

In the meantime, Captain Johnson was losing patience. "Tell them we'll send a boat!" he snapped.

Now that the *Segundo* had called their bluff, Ariizumi needed to appoint someone to represent them. Regulations stipulated that in such situations, the chief navigator should serve as liaison. But Bando's English was poor. Nevertheless, Ariizumi wanted him to go.

"This is asking a lot, but please visit the enemy submarine," Ariizumi requested. "We have no intention of living ourselves, and I don't know what will happen to you amongst the enemy, but think of this as your final duty and go."[10]

Ariizumi had always liked Bando even though some crewmen considered him a brown-noser. Still, the navigator was able to say things to the commander that Nambu could never get away with.[11]

Bando agreed to act as liaison, but that didn't mean he had the authority to negotiate. The most he could do was communicate the commander's wishes and relay the American response. He did not have the power to accept or change terms. That was Ariizumi's call.

The biggest problem Bando faced was his weak command of the enemy's language.[12] Ariizumi knew Bando was deficient and questioned him about it.

"Can you handle them all right with your English?" he asked. "Why don't you bring along a crew member who can translate for you?"[13]

Ariizumi was probably thinking of Masao Nishimura, a Canadian-born Nisei who spoke fluent English. Nishimura had monitored the English-language broadcasts aboard the *I-401*.[14] His command of the language was excellent.

But Bando didn't want an English speaker. He was concerned that a translator might inadvertently say something he shouldn't or somehow take control of the negotiations.[15] Importantly, Bando thought it best if the Americans didn't understand everything he was saying. Obscurity could help in a situation where they had few advantages. If anything, he might be able to wear down the Americans enough that they'd grant a concession. It wouldn't be the first time the Japanese had used such a tactic.

"I can't let the enemy see our hand," Bando replied. "I will handle this myself."

Bando felt responsibility for their situation.[16] After all, he'd convinced Ariizumi not to scuttle the sub. Staying alive had made sense at the time, since they still had options. Now that they might become prisoners, he wasn't so sure. The obligation to bring matters to an honorable conclusion weighed heavily upon him. Nor did it help that he entertained thoughts of survival.[17]

If the Americans could be persuaded to allow the *I-401* to continue on her own,[18] Bando felt he could prevent Ariizumi from scuttling the sub. But if they refused, or negotiations broke down, all bets were off. In that case, Bando was prepared to die.[19]

The *Segundo* sent a small rubber raft to collect Bando. Manned by Lt. (jg) J. K. Brozo and rowed by Chief of the Boat E. A. Russell, it took the two men 15 minutes to maneuver the craft near the giant submarine. Entering a raft in a choppy sea is not an elegant process, and Bando undoubtedly got wet. Wearing shorts, a long-sleeved coat, and a short-brimmed hat, he sat in the stern practically in Lieutenant Brozo's lap. As Russell pulled away from the *I-401*, the wind picked up and the sea with it.

It took another 15 minutes to return to the *Segundo*.[20] During this time, Bando sat quietly in the raft, fearful about what might happen next. He was about to board an American submarine outmanned, outgunned, and far from help. The fate of the *I-401* rested upon his shoulders. He didn't want the crew to die in vain, but if it came to that, he wasn't going without a fight. If the enemy sank them, he resolved to give the American captain a farewell punch in the jaw.[21]

By the time the raft bumped against the *Segundo*'s hull, Bando was seriously scared. When he saw the reception party, five crewmen each with a pistol waiting to search him, he realized the

Americans considered him unpredictable. They needn't have worried. Bando had every intention of conducting himself in a manner becoming an officer of the Imperial Japanese Navy, even with a .45 stuck in his back.

Johnson was waiting on the bridge. Wearing a dark navy jacket and his lieutenant commander's hat, he maintained a casual pose as the navigator greeted him.

"I am Bando," Bando said. He followed his broken English with a Japanese-style bow.

"Hello, Mr. Bando," Johnson replied. "Nice to meet you."[22]

He then shook the navigator's hand, albeit awkwardly.[23] Formalities finished, Johnson cut to the chase.

"You surrender."[24]

"Look at my submarine," Bando responded, uncertain of his English. "We not surrender, we *hara kiri*."

Captain Johnson looked concerned. "*Hara kiri* no good," he replied.[25]

Bando was surprised that an American sub captain would know the word *hara kiri*. Johnson had even used it in his reply, leaving no doubt he understood what the ritual act of suicide meant. Bando smiled inwardly. If Captain Johnson didn't want the Japanese crew to kill themselves, it gave him negotiating leverage. He could use suicide as a threat to extract concessions from his foe.[26] That, combined with the possibility the Americans didn't know the sub had disarmed, meant they were in a stronger negotiating position than he originally realized.

As the conversation progressed, the mood remained hostile. Johnson told Bando he wanted the Japanese sub to proceed to Yokosuka accompanied by the *Segundo*. Bando refused, claiming the *I-401* had only enough fuel to reach Ominato.* Johnson didn't buy Bando's story. Yokosuka was closer than Ominato; the *I-401* should

---

* Some accounts suggest Captain Johnson initially told Bando he wanted the *I-401* to go to Guam. However, according to the *Segundo*'s Fifth War Patrol Report, August 29, 1945, 0539 and 0609, Tokyo and Yokosuka were the only destinations Johnson mentioned.

have no trouble reaching the sub base. The truth was Ariizumi didn't want to surrender at an occupied naval base. He found it too humiliating. Nevertheless, Johnson had orders to escort the *I-401* to Yokosuka whether they liked it or not.

If Johnson was surprised to be negotiating with a junior officer, he didn't show it. Bando might have had less authority than Nambu, but Johnson seemed content to deal with him. Despite a somewhat flippant manner, the *Segundo*'s captain remained calm throughout the discussion. He knew the Japanese were in no position to negotiate. The *Segundo* had them at gunpoint. But Johnson was willing to hear them out, so long as he wasn't played for a fool. At the end of the day, they would do what he said or he'd blow them out of the water. It was as simple as that.

Bando, however, proved difficult to understand. As the *Segundo*'s patrol report indicates, "A doubtful conversation [was held] in baby talk plus violent gestures."[27] It's dangerous to negotiate with a foe you don't completely comprehend. The cultural gap was wide enough, but the language barrier was almost insurmountable.

Despite the difficulty in communicating, the *Segundo*'s captain remained in control. Slouching against the bridge, his lieutenant commander's hat tipped back on his forehead, Johnson towered over the Japanese navigator. He might not have realized that Bando didn't have the authority to negotiate, especially since the chief navigator was negotiating with all his might. Nevertheless, Bando appeared almost comical. Aside from being small, he seemed exotic and out of place.

Handing him a map, Johnson pointed to where he wanted the Japanese sub to go. Yokosuka, he said. Even Bando could understand that. But the chief navigator had other ideas.

When he'd first climbed aboard the American sub, he was sure they were going to kill him. But Johnson had no more intention of killing Bando than he did of allowing the *I-401*'s crew to commit suicide. Perhaps there was an honorable alternative. If so, Bando was determined to find it.

Using pidgin English, Bando tried persuading the *Segundo*'s CO to let them go to Ominato. If he did, Bando promised, they'd turn their sub over as soon as they arrived. If Johnson insisted on the *I-401* surrendering however, they'd have no choice but to commit *hara kiri.*

Johnson shook his head.

At this point in the discussion, a *Segundo* quartermaster pulled a KA-BAR combat knife from his belt and held it in front of Bando.

"Here, take this," he said. "I've never seen someone commit *hara kiri* before." Then, to emphasize the point, he shouted down the bridge hatch, "Send up a bucket of water! We're going to have a mess up here."[28]

The story may be apocryphal, since the crewman who reported it was not on the bridge at the time, but it was indicative of the sour feelings that many of the crew felt for the Japanese. There might have been a cease-fire, but the war wasn't over, not by a long shot. And these Japanese seemed intent on restarting it.

Johnson hung tough despite his crew's doubts. Arguing that suicide would be meaningless now that the war was over, he told Bando the best thing to do was surrender and accompany him to Yokosuka.

"I'd like you to persuade your people of this," he urged Bando. "There's no point in killing yourselves."

Bando didn't understand everything the American sub captain said. Still, he sensed the man felt responsible for keeping them alive.

"They won't commit suicide before I return," Bando said, "so please don't worry. The important thing is the result of our negotiation."

But Bando was wrong. Unknown to the chief navigator, Ariizumi's patience had run out. Determined not to surrender his flagship, the commander had grown so agitated, he ordered signal flags to be used to send Bando a message.

It read: "Tell them to hurry up and sink our sub."

Bando was astonished. He'd boarded the American sub eager to save his crewmates. Now Ariizumi was telling him to facilitate their death.

"Please wait, we are negotiating," Bando signaled back.[29]

As far as Ariizumi was concerned, it was too late. The negotiations had gone on long enough. If the Americans wouldn't torpedo Ariizumi's sub, allowing him an honorable death, then he would take matters into his own hands.

"Open the Kingston valves!" he commanded.[30]

Ariizumi would sink his flagship himself.

CHAPTER 36

SPOILS OF WAR

No one was more surprised than the *I-400*'s captain to see their torpedoes jump out of the ocean, make a 180-degree turn, and head back toward the sub. Circular torpedo runs were rare in the Japanese Navy. When they did occur, they were a much-dreaded event. Kusaka immediately called for evasive action. He wasn't worried about the torpedoes exploding; they'd been disarmed before launching. But you didn't want a two-ton, steel-jacketed battering ram slamming into your hull at 50 knots, especially more than once. Even unarmed torpedoes can do damage.

Unfortunately for Kusaka, the torpedoes hadn't gone very far before circling back. He didn't have time to dive and wasn't even sure he could get out of their way, especially since their paths were officially unpredictable. His only choice would have been to make the sub's profile as small as possible. Careful not to show his starboard or port sides, he would have headed his sub straight into the oncoming weapons.

As the torpedoes began their half circle, the *I-400*'s crew would have rushed to close the watertight hatches. Next, they would have braced for impact. Fortunately, just before the first torpedo reached the sub, it headed for the bottom.[1] The others soon followed. When it was clear the sub was out of danger, Kusaka hissed a sigh of relief.

The *I-400* had avoided disaster for the time being, but the *Sen-toku* subs still had to get to Ominato without being discovered. A fleet of enemy ships awaited them, many looking for stragglers. To avoid this dragnet, they needed more than just luck—they needed the gods to help them.

Though accounts differ, the *Sen-toku* subs appear to have

received orders to return to Ominato on August 20.² If not, it's a remarkable coincidence that all three subs set sail for the same destination of their own accord (rather than Yokosuka or Kure). There's no indication that Ariizumi was in contact with his squadron, and even if he was, he seemed more interested in disembarking along the Sanriku coast than docking at Ominato. Either way, none of Ariizumi's subs were ready to surrender.

LT. ROBERT T. Mahoney was piloting a Grumman TBM Avenger when he spotted what was later described as a great whale half awash.³ It was August 27, 1945, and Mahoney was leading an air patrol off the USS *Bennington* (CV-20).⁴

"Japanese sub flying surrender colors," he reported.⁵

The first thing Kusaka did after Mahoney spotted him was put on speed. Hoping to escape before a U.S. ship intercepted him, he ordered 18 knots. Realizing that Kusaka was trying to escape, Mahoney did his best to intercede. But there's only so much an airplane can do to stop a sub. At first Mahoney used a blinker light to tell the *I-400* to reverse course. When that didn't work, he dropped a message on her deck ordering her south. Unwilling to concede, Kusaka ignored it.⁶

Takahashi watched from the *I-400*'s deck as the American pilot repeatedly signaled the sub. He could easily tell the Grumman wanted them to turn around. After circling the *I-400* several times, Mahoney grew so frustrated, he executed a reverse turn 100 feet off the sub's bow. When that didn't work, he buzzed the boat, leaned out of his cockpit, and jerked his thumb south.⁷

Kusaka eventually gave in, but not because of anything Mahoney did. When the *I-400*'s captain radioed Naval Defense Command for instructions, he was told to obey the American pilot.⁸ Even after Kusaka turned south, he still had thoughts of escaping. Slowing to six knots, he'd drag the voyage out, wait until sunset, then submerge and sneak away.⁹ In the meantime, he threw his code books overboard.¹⁰

Mahoney was not alone in pursuit of the *I-400;* the USS *Blue*

(DD-744) and USS *Mansfield* (DD-728) were also dispatched. The two Sumner-class destroyers were making 30 knots in an effort to catch the sub. At 5:30 on the evening of August 28, they sighted her 200 miles off the coast of Honshu. The *I-400* was bigger than either destroyer. That didn't prevent the *Blue* from signaling to "stop or be fired upon." Having no choice, Kusaka complied. The two destroyers began circling the sub, their deck guns at the ready.[11]

Gordon Hiatt was one of at least 37 prize crew members on board the *Blue*. A motor machinist's mate first class, he'd originally been stationed on a submarine tender in Guam. Every morning for three months, he'd mustered with the relief crew to see what needed to be done. So far there hadn't been much. Once the call for a prize crew went out,[12] Hiatt figured it was his last opportunity to see some action.[13] As luck would have it, he soon found himself on the *Blue* speeding toward a Japanese submarine the likes of which he'd never seen.

The *Blue* was first to arrive on the scene. A new 2,200-ton destroyer, she appeared too small to take on the giant enemy sub. Hiatt was in the mess hall when the *Blue* began circling what looked like a floating island. Fortunately, she soon had the *Mansfield* for company.

Nobody knew what to expect from the sub, so both destroyers kept their deck-mounted torpedo tubes armed and ready.[14] A member of the *Blue*'s gun crew asked rhetorically, "Why don't we just blow them out of the water?" He wasn't the only one who felt this way. An officer told him to keep quiet.[15]

After half an hour of circling, the *Blue*'s captain told his boarding party to capture the *I-400*.[16] Lt. John J. Rowan and 36 other men including Hiatt climbed into a 40-foot whaleboat, which was lowered into the water.[17] Hiatt had no idea what to expect as they approached the sub. Japanese submariners were thought to be part of a military elite reluctant to surrender. And since the U.S. Navy had little experience boarding enemy subs, Lieutenant Rowan wasn't sure either.

The sea was calm as the whaleboat approached. A lifeline was dropped over the *I-400*'s side, but only one man at a time could climb it. Hiatt was one of the first. Handing his rifle to a colleague, he took hold of the rope and began scaling the side. Between the bobbing launch and the slipperiness of the hull, he found it tough going. If it hadn't been for the sub's degaussing cables, he might have fallen into the sea.

Japanese sailors watched curiously as the U.S. boarding party climbed on deck. The sailors in the whaleboat kept their guns trained on the enemy crew, but the deck was so high, it was like aiming at the rooftop of a three-story building. P2/c Toshio Azuma felt sorry for the Americans. Although they were armed with Thompson submachine guns, M-1 carbines, and .45-caliber pistols, they looked nervous as they stood around on deck.[18] Hiatt now found himself surrounded by the enemy without the benefit of his rifle. No wonder Azuma thought they looked scared.

Kusaka met the boarding party on the foredeck.[19] Accompanied by an interpreter, he listened grimly as Lieutenant Rowan explained his demands. According to a pugnacious account later filed by Rowan, Kusaka "was immediately made to understand that I was in charge and that he would follow my orders." This included leaving the bridge hatch open, as well as all the interior hatches, so the sub could not submerge. Kusaka was also read the terms of surrender and asked whether he accepted them.[20]

Things did not go smoothly, according to Japanese accounts. Takahashi says Kusaka demurred when Rowan ordered the *I-400* to Guam. Arguing they only had fuel to reach Yokosuka, Kusaka refused to back down. Rowan did his best to make himself understood by drawing pictures and writing key words.[21] Kusaka remained firm.

Though ComSubPac headquarters was located at Guam, it's surprising that Rowan suggested the *I-400* should travel there. U.S. Naval Command seemed more intent on corralling Japanese subs at Yokosuka than at U.S. ports in the Pacific. Whatever the reality, it was eventually agreed that the *Blue* would escort the *I-400* to Yokosuka. Not surprisingly, Kusaka proved more cooperative than Ariizumi.[22]

Though some Japanese accounts claim the boarding party never went below deck,[23] this wasn't the case. Rowan sent two-man teams to secure the *I-400*'s radio room, torpedo compartment, conning tower, and bridge. Rowan also assigned Hiatt to find the engine room and stand guard. This wasn't as easy as one might think. Although the *I-400*'s engines were where you'd expect them, the two compartments were cavernous. It was certainly more than one man could watch on his own.[24]

But Hiatt was in for a bigger surprise. As he climbed down the engine room deck hatch M-1 in hand, a Japanese crewman reached for his gun.

"What the hell are you doing?" he yelled.

The *I-400* crewman smiled and bowed, making Hiatt realize he just wanted to help. Still, Hiatt had come so close to shooting the man, he was shaken. The Japanese crewman had only been offering to hold the rifle while Hiatt squeezed through the deck hatch. Azuma was right. The Americans were nervous.[25]

Hiatt did his best to keep watch over the engines, but he found them distracting. They were the biggest things he'd ever seen. Additionally, instead of being placed in two sequential compartments, they were located side by side with a hatch between them. Hiatt began to relax though when he realized the Japanese motor machinist's mates were more curious than hostile. In fact, they were downright friendly. Using an impromptu form of sign language, they happily answered his questions about how the engines functioned. But as Hiatt familiarized himself with their workings, he noticed a rat crawling along a bulkhead. There weren't any rats aboard a U.S. sub, and this one seemed in no hurry to escape. Hiatt had never seen anything like it.[26]

After radio communication was established with the *Blue*, Lieutenant Rowan ordered a weapons search. Swords and small arms were collected and locked inside Kusaka's cabin. Once the sub was secure, Rowan radioed the *Blue*, and the two vessels got under way for Sagami Bay, near Yokosuka.[27]

Surprisingly, the *Blue* wasn't the only one interested in capturing the *I-400*. Capt. Lew S. Parks of the 20th Submarine Squadron wanted to claim her as well. When Parks intercepted Lieutenant Mahoney's first message, he immediately contacted the USS *Proteus*

(AS-19) about assembling a prize crew to take the sub. When word came back from Admiral Halsey to "go fetch," Parks assigned Cdr. Hiram H. Cassedy to form a boarding party.[28]

"Hi" Cassedy was an experienced sub captain who'd served aboard the USS *Sailfish* (SS 192), *Searaven* (SS 196), and *Tigrone* (SS 419).[29] Overweight, overbearing, and prone to outbursts, he was every bit as gruff as Ariizumi. One thing was for certain—Cassedy had no problem taking risks. As captain of the *Searaven*, he'd distinguished himself by rescuing 31 Royal Australian Air Force personnel from enemy-held Timor.[30] More recently, he'd rescued 31 B-29 airmen downed off the coast of Japan. Since "lifeguarding" wasn't a sub captain's favorite duty, Cassedy might have been itching for glory, or he might have simply been reverting to type. Either way, he wasn't going to let anyone prevent him from "capturing" the *I-400*.

Cassedy had no trouble finding officers to join him. There was so much demand, he had to deal a poker hand to decide the winners.[31] But persuading enlisted men to volunteer was problematic. The *Proteus* was loaded with experienced submariners, many of whom just wanted to go home. There was no point risking one's life now that the war was over, especially since the navy had ceased being a long-term career.[32] Furthermore, Cassedy wanted men who not only had an intimate knowledge of how subs operated but were familiar with Japanese tactics. Forty men were eventually chosen; still, the operation was hurried and their briefing limited.[33]

Harry Arvidson was one of the men selected for Cassedy's boarding party. A baker by training, and ship's cook third class, Arvidson soon found himself along with Cassedy aboard the USS *Weaver* (DE-741). The *Weaver* had been escorting the *Proteus* from Guam to Tokyo when she was assigned to transport Cassedy's prize crew. Now the Cannon-class destroyer escort steamed at high speed to reach Mahoney's last reported coordinates.

JUST AFTER NIGHTFALL on the evening of August 27, a large black object appeared on the horizon. Cassedy's spirits must have soared when the object turned out to be a huge Jap sub. His heart sank though when he realized the sub was already being escorted by a U.S. destroyer. His prize had been claimed. The captured sub was the *I-14*, however, which Mahoney had spotted shortly before finding the *I-400*.[34] Since the USS *Murray* had the sub under control, the *Weaver* continued through the night toward Kusaka's sub.[35] When Cassedy reached the *I-400* early the next morning, he was thrilled.

The boat was at least a football field long, with a sail that rose from the port side like the leaning tower of Pisa. On deck, a humongous housing ran more than 100 feet before ending in a mysterious bulge.[36]

Cassedy knew he'd bagged "something special."[37] However, the USS *Blue* already had a prize crew on board and was escorting the sub to Tokyo Bay. But Cassedy was not about to let the *Blue* steal his thunder. Insisting that his orders took precedence, he bullied his way into the situation by claiming the *Blue*'s prize crew had no submarine experience. Though this wasn't true, the *Blue*'s captain gave way. The photographer Cassedy had brought to record the historic capture probably added some incentive.[38]

As Cassedy assembled his prize crew, the *Blue*'s boarding party assembled on the *I-400*. Lieutenant Rowan clearly had the situation in hand, but reality was not going to stand in Cassedy's way. Ordering the *Weaver* to lower two whaleboats,[39] he hurried to claim his prize.

Harry Arvidson was in one of Cassedy's boats as they made their way toward the *I-400*. The sea was choppy, and spray came off the bow. Arvidson used a tarp to keep dry, while Cassedy got wet. A less than heroic photograph shows him boarding the *I-400*, his shirt and pants completely soaked.

Arvidson wore a life belt but had no helmet or weapon, as those were reserved for officers. By the time Cassedy boarded the *I-400*, however, a weapon wasn't needed.[40] The only tension that existed was between Cassedy and Lieutenant Rowan.

As the *I-400*'s surrender flag flapped violently in the wind, Cassedy relieved Rowan of command, then went about doing everything Rowan had already done. Rowan's boarding party was not as ill prepared to manage the sub as Cassedy contended. For example,

Cassedy thought well enough of Gordon Hiatt and several of his colleagues to keep them aboard during the trip to Tokyo.

Rowan wasn't the only person perturbed by Cassedy's power play. Kusaka was irritated as well. Now the Japanese sub captain found himself having to deal with an entirely new officer. From the pained expression on Kusaka's face captured by Cassedy's photographer,[41] it's evident he didn't enjoy having yet another American tell him Japan had lost and that his sub was now a U.S. war prize.[42]

Cassedy's translator tried sweetening the pill by telling Kusaka, "We promise to treat you as gentlemen, so please cooperate and obey our commander."[43] Undoubtedly, it was politer than anything Cassedy would have said. Still, it hardly softened the blow.

Cassedy later claimed Kusaka opened up to him once he noticed the dolphins on his shirt. As Cassedy recalled, "When I told [Kusaka] that I and my . . . men were veteran submariners . . . he bowed deeply and from then on was most cooperative."[44] *Polite* would probably be a more accurate description, because Kusaka remained evasive under questioning. It would have been typical of Cassedy to assume he was smarter than the enemy. For example, he assumed the *I-400*'s size meant she was a cargo carrier.[45] He was wrong, of course, and Kusaka did nothing to disabuse him of this notion. As for his claim that Kusaka was talkative,[46] it seems self-aggrandizing given that Kusaka was not known for his eloquence either in English or Japanese. The idea that Kusaka, a battle-hardened commander, would pour his heart out just because they were fellow sub captains stretches credulity, especially when you consider that Cassedy never even bothered to learn Kusaka's name.

While Cassedy interrogated Kusaka, his prize crew checked for torpedoes. When they found they'd been disposed of, they chained the hatches open to prevent the sub from diving.[47]

Takahashi was impressed by the courtesy of the prize crew, especially Cassedy's translator.

"We're submariners too," the interpreter told him. "We know what you've been through."

"So this is democracy," Takahashi thought.[48] It was certainly better than he'd expected.

There were communication problems though. Cassedy's translator may have won the crew's sympathy, but Kusaka found his Japanese so poor as to be humorous.[49] When a prize crew member left guarding the *I-400*'s wardroom gave in to temptation and lit a cigarette, he was scolded by a Japanese officer for smoking. In other words, it wasn't always clear who was guarding whom.[50]

At noon a ceremony was staged on the *I-400*'s bridge for the benefit of the navy photographer. Cassedy looked on as Japan's battle ensign was lowered and replaced with the Stars and Stripes. Kusaka also observed the proceedings. Hoping no one would notice, he quietly wiped a tear from his eye.[51] Cassedy saw the emotion and was uncharacteristically sympathetic.[52] Even the gruff commander could feel the pain of a fellow sub captain surrendering his command.

But Cassedy's sympathy didn't extend to the crew's personal effects. Before relieving Lieutenant Rowan of command, Cassedy ordered him to leave all Japanese swords and small arms behind. Even though an officer's sword was considered part of his uniform,[53] Cassedy wanted them for war trophies.[54] In one photograph, he can even be seen with the hint of a smile as the swords are stacked like cordwood on the *I-400*'s catapult track.[55] Cassedy made sure the *Blue*'s boarding party left empty-handed, saying the swords would be turned over to the proper authorities. It was a promise unlikely to be kept.

Cassedy wasn't the only one to show interest in war booty. While walking through the *I-400*'s officers' quarters, Harry Arvidson spotted a short sword dangling from a bunk with a man lying next to it. Undeterred, Arvidson released the belt clip and calmly walked away with the prize.[56] Another enlisted man was so eager for souvenirs, he "liberated" the *I-400*'s bridge compass. Unsatisfied with his haul, he stripped insignia from a *Seiran* crewman's uniform, including the buttons, and took several sets of *hashi* from the galley. In fact, by the time the *I-400* arrived in Tokyo, the U.S. prize crew had taken pretty much anything that caught their eye, including personal letters and New Year's greeting cards. When Takahashi lost his sword, he consoled himself by saying, "It's all just worthless trash anyway."[57] Even so, it must have stung.

As the *I-400* got under way, however, Kusaka let some information slip. There was another sub at large just like the *I-400*, with the squadron commander on board. This was news to Cassedy, but what Kusaka said next was even more disconcerting. Kusaka told him he knew the commander personally and didn't believe he'd surrender without a fight.[58]

Unfortunately, Kusaka was too late. The *I-401* was already locked in a showdown with the USS *Segundo*, a showdown that Commander Ariizumi had no intention of losing. No intention, that is, unless Nambu could stop him.

CHAPTER 37

RECKONING

NAMBU KNEW ARIIZUMI MIGHT SCUTTLE THE *I-401*, BUT HE WAS still shocked when the commander ordered the Kingston valves opened. Nambu was captain; he alone had authority to issue such a command. But Ariizumi was commander, and though there was no squadron left for him to command, he naturally had a proprietary feeling toward his flagship. It was debatable whether scuttling the sub was his call to make. Unfortunately, Ariizumi decided it was, and since he was the highest-ranking officer, there was no one to stand in his way except Nambu.

Neither man had been given suicide orders.[1] This meant it was a matter of choice—killing themselves was left to their discretion. Ariizumi believed death was preferable to dishonor, while Nambu felt his responsibility was to return his crew safely to Japan. The two were so opposed that Nambu went to talk to Ariizumi in his cabin.*

Ariizumi's quarters-cum-office was small but private, with a bed, a desk, and a clock on the bulkhead. The two men could have a confidential conversation so long as they didn't raise their voices. But their relationship was beyond strained at this point. Despite both officers being products of the Imperial Japanese Navy, their personalities were so different, it only bred antagonism.

"Our duty is done," Nambu began. "I'd like to return the precious lives of my 204 crewmen to Japan."

---

* It's unclear exactly when this meeting took place. Possibly it occurred after Ariizumi ordered the *I-401* scuttled, but it seems more likely that Nambu tried to persuade Ariizumi not to scuttle the sub before the fleet commander gave the order. The following conversation is speculative, as it is Lt. Tsugio Yata's estimate of what may have been discussed.

Ariizumi was unmoved. "Please give those lives to me."

Nambu held firm. "I would like us to return to Japan and will gladly take responsibility for the decision."

But Ariizumi refused to budge.[2]

It's impossible to know exactly what Ariizumi thought, since he left no written record and never spoke of the meeting. Nevertheless, a few things can be surmised. First, Ariizumi considered Nambu impertinent if not downright mutinous for questioning his authority. Though Nambu had asked for the lives of his crew in the most formal and polite way, it didn't take much to trigger Ariizumi's temper.

Additionally, Ariizumi was under tremendous strain. Japan had lost the war, the Imperial Navy was in disgrace, and his special attack force had been scattered without firing a shot. What was supposed to be the pinnacle of his naval career had become its darkest hour.

As if that weren't enough, Ariizumi was the kind of commander to whom honor meant everything. Though he had favorites among his men, their lives were his for the taking. Nambu wanted to return to Japan, but as far as Ariizumi was concerned, it wasn't his decision to make. And though not everyone aboard the *I-401* shared Ariizumi's refined sense of honor, it was incomprehensible that the commander would surrender his flagship to an enemy he despised. These feelings contributed to Ariizumi's agitated state. He'd been wracked by depression ever since the emperor's speech, and the sweltering conditions inside the sub only exacerbated matters.

As their voices rose in heated confrontation, sweat rolled down Nambu's face. The *I-401*'s captain probably stood in the presence of his commander, making his six-foot frame intimidating. Their yelling eventually crescendoed to the point that it was heard outside the cabin. Though their words were unclear, the crew could easily tell the men were angry. Both were insistent; neither would back down. Finally Ariizumi boiled over. Refusing to accept Nambu's insubordination, he struck him in anger.[3]

It wasn't the first time Nambu had been hit. Corporal punishment was de rigueur in the Imperial Japanese Navy. But Nambu was stunned by the action. Being struck like a midshipman was the worst kind of insult. It also meant Ariizumi had lost control.

Turning on his heel, Nambu exited the cabin. His pride might have been stung, but Ariizumi's behavior had only steeled his resolve.

It's a testament to both men's stubbornness that neither could be dissuaded. Nambu planned on saving his crew, while Ariizumi intended on sinking the sub. It was a standoff comparable to the one they faced with the *Segundo*. There was a complicating factor though. A pro-Ariizumi faction existed aboard the sub. The commander embodied the Imperial Japanese Navy, and plenty of crewmen supported him. Asamura was one of them. He deeply respected Ariizumi and shared his belief in an honorable death. And Asamura wasn't the only one.

Many of the *I-401*'s officers were loyal to Nambu, however. After all, a navy's command and control structure was sacrosanct. If Ariizumi wanted the *I-401* to do something, he had to work through her commanding officer to do it. He couldn't just issue orders over his head.

There was another wild card, though. Everyone knew what Ariizumi was capable of. They'd all heard about the *I-8* massacres. One of Nambu's officers even called Ariizumi "*Gyangu*" or "gangster" behind his back.[4] When Ariizumi ordered the *I-401* scuttled, no one doubted he meant what he said.

The Kingston valves were located on the bottom of the *I-401*'s hull. When they opened, seawater flooded the boat's ballast tanks, allowing her to submerge. But for Ariizumi to scuttle the boat, the bridge hatch would also have to remain open. The moment the sub dipped below the waves, the ocean would flood in, sinking her in minutes.

It's no fun drowning this way. The force of water would hit like an explosion, knocking many of the crew unconscious. Those who survived the impact would find themselves looking for air pockets. As the sub sank deeper, the increased pressure would expel the remaining air, and the men would drown quickly. Undoubtedly, a few crew members would follow their instinct and try escaping. It would be impossible to fight the torrent of flood water though. If they succeeded in closing their compartment's watertight hatches, they might last until the boat passed her safety depth, but then the sub would implode, crushing them like paper. Trapped in the cold, dark confines of a sub plummeting out of control, you wouldn't have more than a few minutes to realize you were a goner. A bullet to the brain would have been faster and a lot less horrifying.

The commander might have been a god who rarely descended from heaven, but Nambu was the *I-401*'s captain; the crew took orders from him. Add to this the human will to live, and it was anyone's guess what would happen when Ariizumi ordered the Kingston valves opened.

When Ariizumi gave the order, most of Nambu's officers froze. The commander was a powerful personality. It was impossible to ignore him. But his order to open the sea cocks only caused confusion among the crew.[5] Enough officers sympathized with Nambu that they refused to take action. In fact, a few of them had already commandeered pistols to make sure no one complied with Ariizumi's order.[6] As the commander raged on, they pretended not to hear him.

When Ariizumi realized he was being ignored, it was as if his legs were cut out from under him. He'd played his hand and lost; Nambu retained the conn. It was a milestone of sorts. What could have been a tragic end to the world's largest submarine had become a humiliating defeat for her squadron commander. The war, and everything the Imperial Japanese Navy stood for, was over. It was a bitter defeat for Ariizumi, but Nambu finally had a chance to save his crew.

As NAMBU AND Ariizumi struggled to control the *I-401*, Johnson continued pressing Bando for concessions. He wanted his officers to board the Jap sub,[7] after which the *Segundo* would escort her to Yokosuka. Johnson was unaware of Ariizumi's resistance to his plan. Nor did he realize the commander wanted to scuttle his boat. If anything, Johnson wanted to avoid a mass suicide. It's doubtful Bando relayed Ariizumi's message asking Johnson to torpedo them. If he did, Johnson either ignored or dismissed it as too bizarre for consideration.

After 20 minutes of negotiation, Bando finally agreed to carry Johnson's terms to the *I-401*.[8]

A few minutes later, Bando was rowed to his sub.[9] As the *Segundo* shrank in the distance, he was sure he felt Captain Johnson's good wishes following him.[10] But Johnson wasn't the sentimental type. He sent Lt. (jg) J. K. Brozo to accompany Bando, giving him instructions to keep an eye on things. Johnson didn't trust Bando, at least not yet.

Ariizumi and Nambu were waiting on the bridge as Brozo and Bando climbed the ladder. Brozo had no idea about the conflict aboard the *I-401*. Bando outlined Johnson's demands, then Lieutenant Brozo pressed the point: "Sail to Yokosuka."

"We must go to Ominato in accordance with the Imperial Order," Nambu replied.

"The emperor has surrendered. You must follow General MacArthur's orders."

Nambu knew that he was quibbling and that the American officer was correct.[11] But Ariizumi, having failed to sink the *I-401*, was still against returning to Yokosuka. Nambu wasn't sure why.[12] It probably had something to do with preserving the navy's reputation.[13] Of course, the IJN's reputation was already in tatters. Still, Ariizumi's personality was such that he insisted on upholding standards to the bitter end.

Reluctantly, Ariizumi eventually agreed to go to Yokosuka. One thing he couldn't agree to though was Johnson's demand to place American officers on board his sub. That would mean the *I-401* had surrendered.[14]

And so the issue became whether the *I-401* could be boarded. Johnson had no intention of allowing the sub to go to Yokosuka on her own, especially given her past behavior. But neither

Ariizumi nor Nambu would surrender their sub before returning to Japan.

While this was going on, Vic Horgan was in the *Segundo*'s control room plotting the demise of the *I-401*. There was still a lot the Americans didn't know about the sub. They had no idea that she was the flagship of a secret armada, or even that her squadron commander was on board. Nor did they know her torpedo tubes were empty, or that her deck guns lacked ammunition. As far as Johnson was concerned, the *I-401* was armed and dangerous. And so Horgan monitored the sub's position, knowing they might have to torpedo her at any moment.[15]

As Brozo relayed an update to the *Segundo*,[16] Ariizumi and Nambu developed a plan to outwit the Americans. Neither man completely trusted the other; nor did they have reason to. Nevertheless, the two Japanese officers were not in a position to negotiate. Not only was their sub unarmed, their Naval Defense Command had ordered them to comply with the *Segundo*'s instructions. And so Ariizumi and Nambu had to find a compromise that not only met the *Segundo*'s requirements but allowed them to save face as well.

Their counteroffer was nothing short of brilliant. They would agree to be boarded based on several conditions. First, the boarding party would be composed of five petty officers; no commissioned officers would be included. Next, the boarding party would limit itself to a communications role only. This meant Nambu would continue as captain of the sub. Finally, since the boarding party was in a liaison role, they would remain on deck at all times; they would not venture inside the sub.[17]

It was a typical Japanese compromise, engineered to satisfy both parties' needs yet requiring a willing suspension of disbelief in order to work. Johnson would achieve his goal of putting men aboard the sub, while Ariizumi would retain nominal command, and the *I-401* wouldn't have to surrender until she reached Yokosuka. It was a well-crafted solution that gave both parties what they wanted.

Bando returned to the *Segundo* to sell the compromise to Johnson. Though Johnson was reluctant to send only petty officers, he eventually came round.[18] It still must have seemed farcical, since the compromise hung on a technicality. The *Segundo* got its prize crew, and the Japanese avoided surrendering outside home waters. All the prize crew had to do was not go in the sub.

The compromise was far from farcical though. It not only preserved the Japanese sense of honor—something the Americans only faintly comprehended—it gave Johnson both the boarding party and the destination he wanted. In other words, it allowed Johnson to save face as well. Johnson might not have realized this. Hardly the sympathetic type, it would have been difficult for him to appreciate the importance of saving face to the Japanese. Still, he must have sensed they were men of their word to accept such a compromise.

As Bando and Johnson continued their conversation, something curious happened.[19] The two men began warming to each other. They quickly learned that each had attended his country's naval academy. Johnson even recalled that the Japanese Navy had visited Annapolis while he was there,[20] and Bando thought he might have been on that trip.[21] But Johnson was not buying everything Bando was selling. In fact, his attitude was a bit snide, as his patrol report indicates:

THE WORD "TORPEDO" WAS AN INSURMOUNTABLE BARRIER
SO WE WERE UNABLE TO FIND OUT IF THEY HAD SUNK
ANYTHING OR HOW MANY FISH THEY CARRIED . . .
[LIEUTENANT BANDO] WAS QUITE PROUD OF THEIR DIVING
TIME (ONE MINUTE TEN SECONDS), THEIR MAXIMUM DEPTH
(ONE HUNDRED METERS) AND THEIR SPEED (17.5 KNOTS).
HE ALSO STATED THEY CARRIED TWO HUNDRED MEN. THIS
COULD QUITE POSSIBLY BE AN ERROR ON HIS PART AS I
THINK THE WAR INTERRUPTED HIS ENGLISH INSTRUCTION.[22]

Though Bando's English was poor, Johnson understood him well enough. Bando's explanation of the *I-401*'s head count, flank speed, dive time, and safety depth weren't far off the mark. Nevertheless, Johnson's sarcasm showed through when he noted, "Lt Bondo [*sic*] was one of the few persons I have ever seen who derived such obvious pleasure from saluting."[23]

Bando had his own agenda, of course. By ingratiating himself with the *Segundo*'s commanding officer, he hoped to persuade him to allow the *I-401* to fly her naval ensign rather than the Stars and Stripes until her surrender.[24] It was an important concession, one that could only have been made because of Johnson's sympathy. The allegedly impetuous sub captain was turning out to be not so impetuous after all. In fact, he'd achieved the seemingly impossible: capturing the *I-401* while honoring the Japanese refusal to surrender. It was an unconventional solution, to be sure, one that a more mature and battle-hardened sub captain might not have arrived at. Then again, the Japanese were an unconventional enemy. Johnson's out-of-the-box thinking had saved the day, plus or minus a few wisecracks.

CHAPTER 38

BOARDING PARTY

JOHNSON PICKED HIS EXECUTIVE OFFICER, LIEUTENANT BALSON, to lead the boarding party. Since Johnson had agreed that no officers would board the *I-401*, Balson stripped his shirt of rank and changed into a pair of dungarees.[1] When the boarding party was complete, five men joined Balson as the *I-401*'s prize crew: COB (chief of the boat) E. A. Russell; MM1c (motor machinist's mate first class) Ralph S. Austin; EM1c (electrician's mate first class) Kenneth H. "Skinny" Diekmann; TM2c (torpedo's mate second class) Jenison V. Halton; and QM3c (quartermaster third class) Carlo M. Carlucci. It was one more than Johnson had promised, but the enemy was in no position to object.

Balson issued each man a sidearm before boarding his raft, then at 8:45 A.M. set out for the *I-401*.[2] Balson could tell that the small group of Japanese officers who met them were tense.[3] Then again, the Japanese felt the same way about the Americans.

The first thing Balson did, once he was aboard, was chain the *I-401*'s hatches open. Next, he sent Russell to check on the torpedoes.[4] The *I-401*'s sonar operator thought the reason the rest of the Americans didn't go inside the sub was that they knew Ariizumi was on board and were afraid.[5] According to the terms Bando had negotiated, however, the *Segundo*'s boarding party was to remain topside. This meant Balson and his men camped on the aft section of the hangar roof, where they could keep an eye on the bridge.[6] Carlucci had been warned that if he heard a hissing sound, it meant the sub was submerging. In that case, he was to fire a signal flare and either run to the bridge to keep its hatch from closing or, if it was too late, inflate his "Mae West" and jump overboard.[7]

Balson and his men weren't eager to mingle with the enemy, so they were happy to remain secluded on the aft deck. They'd brought blankets for the cold as well as food, and when they needed water they hollered down the bridge hatch until someone rewarded them with a flask of sake.[8]

Finally at 9:05 A.M. the subs set course for Sagami Bay. While the *I-401* proceeded at 15 knots, the *Segundo* kept station off the sub's port quarter. It didn't take long though before Nambu tested the ropes that bound him. Less than an hour later, he reported engine trouble and slowed his sub to 11 knots.[9]

"They better get their fuckin' boat under way or I'll blow it the fuck out of the water," Johnson exclaimed.[10]

For the Japanese to be having second thoughts this early in the voyage was concerning. Fearing that their agreement was unraveling, Johnson contacted his superiors and reported the sub as hostile.[11]

The USS *Tigrone* (SS 419) was sent to assist, but three hours after the *I-401* reported engine trouble, she still lagged behind. Finally Johnson signaled the sub to fix her engine or "we'll come over and do it for you."[12]

Nambu assured them that wouldn't be necessary.[13]

Johnson was right to suspect the Japanese of second thoughts. The *I-401*'s engine had broken down,[14] but Ariizumi was also trying to find a way to avoid Yokosuka. Johnson would be damned if he'd give an inch. As far as he was concerned, he was escorting a hostile submarine barely under his control. If the *I-401* so much as looked crooked, he'd send her to the bottom.

A few minutes before six that evening, the *I-401* came to a stop and signaled she was sending an officer over. Twenty minutes later Lieutenant Bando appeared for the third time that day. Johnson was already irritated by the diversion, and hit the roof when Bando showed him dispatches ordering the *I-401* to Ominato.[15]

"I take a very dim view of your actions," Johnson told him. "We either proceed with you handling your sub, or with our Prize Crew in charge."[16]

Johnson must have thought it a childish ploy, since the only orders he obeyed came from ComSubPac. What he didn't realize was that Ariizumi had not only informed his naval command he'd been captured, he'd also requested permission to proceed to Ominato. When he was told to comply with the *Segundo*'s orders, Ariizumi had chosen to ignore the message and try to trick Johnson instead. Clearly, Ariizumi still had some fight left.

Early the next morning Johnson received orders regarding the *I-401*'s surrender. After ordering her to stop, Johnson boarded the sub to personally relay the instructions.[17]

"I's sorry you come," Nambu told him, but Johnson was in no mood for pleasantries.[18]

The meeting lasted just long enough for Johnson to tell Nambu that the Japanese naval ensign would be lowered the next morning at 5:00,[19] with a formal surrender at 11:00. Nambu would retain the conn until then. Once the *I-401* had surrendered in Sagami Bay, she would proceed to Yokosuka, where she would moor next to the *Proteus*.[20] In the meantime, the funny business was to stop.

The communication went more smoothly this time, with Nishimura serving as translator.[21] Nambu reassured Johnson he'd received the same orders, but the accommodation was not to last.

Later that night Johnson received a dispatch from Adm. William F. Halsey, commander of the Third Fleet, saying that the *I-401* was transmitting disturbing messages to Japan's Naval Defense Command.[22] Johnson suspected as much, though he thought it was Nambu (not Ariizumi) who sought to ignore his instructions. The *Segundo*'s captain certainly didn't want an enemy sub broadcasting without his permission. Disgruntled forces might home in on the signal and launch an attack.[23] Five minutes later Johnson ordered Balson to locate the radio and disable it. Once again Ariizumi's plans had been thwarted.

THAT EVENING, AS Nambu stood on the bridge, he felt a darkness inside that had nothing to do with night. He'd learned some troubling news earlier in the day. [24] The Sixth Fleet, the submarine arm of the Imperial Japanese Navy, had officially been disbanded.[25] The news infuriated him. Sixth Fleet subs were still at large, yet their command had ceased to exist.[26] These were the people who had micromanaged every operational detail since the war had begun. The same people who had ignored his advice, whether it was the difficulty in attacking a well-guarded anchorage, the need to target merchant rather than capital ships, or the foolishness of carrying out resupply operations. They'd refused to listen to the hard-won experience of their most seasoned sub captains, and he had paid the price. Now, during the sub force's darkest hour, when they should be upholding naval tradition, the Sixth Fleet had washed their hands of him. It made a travesty out of everything Nambu believed in, and left him fuming.

Nambu had every right to feel betrayed. After all, he'd been on the front lines of Japan's sub war since the attack on Pearl Harbor. He'd served on board the first sub to shell the U.S. mainland; he'd survived combat operations off Australia and mole ops in the South Pacific. Here he was, one of the war's last surviving sub captains, with a nearly insane commander, yet he was still trying to conduct himself with honor and dignity. Where was the honor in disbanding the Sixth Fleet? Abolishing it violated everything the IJN represented. What in God's name had they been fighting for?

Ariizumi was also topside that night. Standing on the deck beneath Nambu, he too stared into the darkness. Nambu was concerned with the commander's increasingly strange behavior.[27] Ever since the *I-401* had been captured, Ariizumi had wandered the sub as if he were lost. Wearing an undershirt and a white pith helmet he had worn in Penang, he haunted the compartments like a ghost.[28] Nambu had informed him their surrender would occur the next morning. He'd also told him the Sixth Fleet had been disbanded. Both pieces of news must have been a blow, which was why Ariizumi was coming apart before Nambu's eyes. Still, the question remained whether Nambu could maintain control of his sub long enough to reach home. There were only a few hours left before the surrender. If he could prevent Ariizumi from taking any action, they just might reach Yokosuka, unless the commander had other plans. Unfortunately, "other plans" was exactly what Ariizumi was thinking about as he stared out to sea.

CHAPTER 39

THE TENTH WAR GOD

THE *I-401* WAS DUE TO ARRIVE AT SAGAMI BAY EARLY THE MORN-ing of August 31. Nambu was to officially hand his sub over to Lieutenant Balson and then follow the *Segundo* into Tokyo Bay. Meanwhile, a feeling of dread pervaded the sub.

Nambu hadn't slept for days, so he retired to his cabin to get a few hours of rest. He found it difficult to sleep knowing surrender was only hours away. The oppressive heat didn't help. Suddenly, at 4:20 A.M., he was awakened by a shot.[1]

The sound came from Ariizumi's quarters. Jumping out of his bunk, Nambu ran into the passageway and pushed open the com-mander's door. What he saw was a grisly sight. The commander was seated in a chair wearing his formal naval uniform, a pistol in his right hand. The smell of gunpowder filled the cabin,[2] and the glass in the clock on the bulkhead behind him was shattered where the bullet had struck.[3]

Despite the bloodshed, Nambu thought the commander looked dignified.[4] He sat upright, his medals and merit sash[5] testimony to his many accomplishments. The gun was still in his mouth, smoke from its discharge hung in the air. Though the back of his head had been blown off, he'd been careful to aim the pistol toward the ceiling before firing. Even in death Ariizumi was meticulous.

Otherwise, the commander's cabin appeared tidy. A photo on his desk showed the nine war gods who, under his command, had bravely sailed their midget subs against Pearl Harbor. His service sword was also on the desk,[6] along with three handwritten notes.[7]

Nambu examined the letters carefully. One was addressed to the

Imperial Japanese Navy, another to Nambu, and the third to Matsu, Ariizumi's wife. Nambu fought back his emotions as he contemplated the commander's suicide. He had not gotten along with Ariizumi, but Nambu could appreciate the courage it had taken to commit such a selfless act. It was not only a magnificent accomplishment,[8] it was the honorable thing to do, and Nambu admired him for it.

Picking up the letter addressed to the Imperial Japanese Navy, Nambu read Ariizumi's final words.

> *As a professional, I have failed to fulfill my duties. This was my responsibility and I am deeply sorry. With my death, I maintain the traditions of the Imperial Japanese Navy and I take pride in having commanded a squadron that fought in the Pacific until the end of the war. I am confident my crew will serve the country as loyal subjects and I pray for the rebuilding of the Japanese Empire. Long live the Emperor.*[9]

Nambu wasn't surprised it had come to this. He'd hinted to his officers that such a thing might happen.[10] But many of his men were caught off guard. Yata had been on the bridge standing watch earlier that morning when Ariizumi had appeared wearing his pith helmet:

"Gunnery chief, anything new?" the commander asked.

It was a rule never to take one's eyes off the horizon when on watch, so Yata remained glued to his binoculars and answered, "No, sir."[11]

Yata later realized that he was probably the last person to converse with the commander, and that the crumpled paper he saw Ariizumi throw into the sea had been an early version of a suicide note. Ariizumi was a stickler for discipline; no litter was allowed inside or outside the boat. Still, his strange behavior had gone unnoticed.[12]

Ariizumi asked that his last words be shared with the naval high command.[13] Unfortunately, this request was impossible to fulfill, since the Sixth Fleet had already disbanded. But Nambu felt compelled to honor the wish even if it only meant sharing Ariizumi's words with the *I-401's* crew.[14] The second note, addressed to Nambu, was also written in Ariizumi's careful hand. In it, he made clear the reason for his death:

> *We will be forced to raise the American flag at 5:00 a.m. It is more than I can bear to see.*

Warning Nambu to "refrain from any rash or irresponsible actions until the crew had returned home," Ariizumi concluded by promising to watch over the reconstruction of Japan from his resting place in the Pacific.[15]

Ariizumi's note to his wife was written in the third person and further explained the reason for his death. "Ariizumi is sorry from the bottom of his heart for losing the war," he penned. He finished with a farewell poem outlining his hopes for their family:

> *May our children grow up to be pure of heart / And be strong and just to benefit the world.*[16]

They hardly seemed the words of a murderer.

The *I-401* was the world's largest sub, but it was a small boat when it came to gossip. Word that the commander had killed himself spread quickly.[17] Nambu was particularly concerned about the *Segundo*'s reaction. If the Americans learned that Ariizumi had killed himself, they might treat his body disrespectfully. Therefore, Nambu decided not to inform them of Ariizumi's death and to secretly bury his commander at sea.[18]

While the *I-401*'s medical officer filled out a death certificate, Nambu and Bando covered the commander's body in a blanket.[19] Next they wrapped him tightly in a Japanese naval ensign,[20] its 16 rays matching the number of petals on the emperor's chrysanthemum seal. When they were finished, they changed into formal naval dress.[21] Meanwhile, one of the *Seiran* mechanics made an ossuary box, using wood from a *shoji* game board, for presentation to Ariizumi's family.[22]

It took several men pushing and pulling to get the commander through the number-two deck hatch. Though Ariizumi had lost weight, he was still stout.[23] Keeping his voice low to avoid alerting the prize crew, Nambu presided over a brief funeral ceremony. When it was over, they saluted their commander one last time before silently committing his body to the sea. A weighted bag ensured he sank to the bottom.[24]

By the time Nambu finished his silent prayer, the sun was coming up. Though Ariizumi's burial was without benefit of sutra or song, it had been a warrior's funeral nonetheless.*[25] He had died as he had lived: fierce, unwavering, and committed to his principles. His decision to kill himself must not have been easy, but it was consistent with the values he professed and the honor he passionately embraced. Commander, mentor, loyal subject, faithful officer, father, husband, butcher, friend—Ariizumi had been all these things and more. He'd earned the respect of his men as well as their fear and had fought as valiantly as any officer in the Imperial Japanese Navy. Now he was gone to rest at the bottom of the sea. But who would forgive him his crimes?

LIEUTENANT BALSON ORDERED Carlucci to lower the *I-401*'s naval ensign and raise the American flag at 5:00 A.M. Carlucci knew it was a slap in the face to the Japanese,[26] and he performed his task with relish. Though the ceremony was largely symbolic, it meant the *I-401* was no longer a Japanese sub—she was officially an American war prize.

With Mount Fuji in the background, Nambu watched as the flags were exchanged, chafing at the sight.[27] Bando wasn't about to let the Japanese naval ensign fall into enemy hands, so when the flag came down, he secretly ordered the signal officer to burn it.[28]

The *I-401* wasn't ready to concede, even in surrender.

---

* The crew of the USS *Segundo* did in fact observe Nambu's deck gathering. When Captain Johnson demanded to know what was going on, he was told the *Sen-toku*'s squadron commander had committed suicide. Johnson doubted the truth of the statement, since he wasn't even aware Ariizumi had been on board the sub.

Chapter 40

BITTERSWEET

When the crew of the submarine tender *Proteus* saw the *I-401* approach, they began cheering with all their might.

"Wonderful! Big one!" they cried.

Yata, the *I-401*'s gunnery officer, was proud his sub caused a commotion. After all, it was the the *Sen-toku* squadron's flagship, it was only right that the Americans found her impressive.[1] But Nambu's sub almost hadn't made it to Tokyo Bay. The *Segundo* had been escorting the *I-401* when Johnson received orders to immediately reverse course and take her back to *Sagami-wan*. Adm. William "Bull" Halsey had received reports from Japanese naval officers that the *I-401* was dangerous and that U.S. ships should avoid her at all costs. Since Johnson had also reported the *I-401* as hostile and Lieutenant Balson felt the situation was not well in hand,[2] Halsey didn't want the rogue sub anywhere near his Third Fleet.

Of course, Nambu had no intention of resisting. As a sign of compliance, he'd presented Balson with his service sword at 11:00 A.M., turning over command exactly as promised. Balson informed the *Segundo* that the "formal surrender had been received."[3] By then, it was too late. The USS *Gatling* (DD-671) and USS *O'Bannon* (DD-450) had already arrived. Sent as a show of force, the Fletcher-class destroyers had orders to escort a compliant *I-401* into Tokyo Bay or blast her out of the water. With Ariizumi dead, all Nambu wanted was to return his men to Japan. Unfortunately, no one believed his good intentions after the sub's previous recalcitrance. At a time when things should have been settling down, they were heating up all over again.

Sagami Bay was crowded with Third Fleet ships, each a tempting target if Nambu had wanted to ram one. U.S. naval officials remained concerned right up to the point when the *I-401* docked near the *Proteus*. But Nambu was a man of his word. He maneuvered alongside the giant American sub tender without incident.

The biggest surprise for Nambu's crew was finding the *I-400* already there. There was sadness amid the joy, however. Both the *I-13* and the *I-14* were absent. When Takahashi tried asking the *I-401*'s crew about the missing subs, he was stopped by American MPs.[4] The *I-14* arrived shortly thereafter,[5] but the *I-13*, a casualty of war, would never return home.

The *Sen-toku* subs proved to be a popular attraction. Over the next few days, they were visited by a bevy of navy brass, including Halsey and Lockwood. Lockwood was present for the *I-400*'s arrival. When he boarded her for inspection, he immediately noticed the "lousy appearance of the enemy crew."

"Normally, a Jap is clean," Lockwood observed. "These were filthy in clothing and person."[6]

Sen-toku crews also lamented the condition of their maintenance-deferred subs. When compared to the spic-and-span standards of Allied ships, they made a poor showing.[7] Even Asamura noticed the difference. Considering the almost unlimited supply of paint they were given to refresh the *I-401*, Asamura concluded the United States must be a truly rich nation.[8]

The true purpose of the underwater aircraft carriers remained hidden, at least for a while. Lockwood was under the impression that the *I-400* had been on a supply trip to Truk. He also couldn't understand why Captain Kusaka hadn't seen any American warships en route.[9] Of course, the answer was clear—Kusaka was lying. Though Kusaka had spoken honestly when he'd said the *I-400* had never sunk an Allied ship, he'd most certainly seen them. Though it was easy to mistake the *I-400*'s airplane hangar for a warehouse, especially since the planes had been replaced with supplies, it's surprising that the commander of Pacific Fleet subs didn't learn of

Kusaka's mission until later. Unless the Japanese were launching food at captured islands, there was no reason for a catapult other than for aircraft. It's hard to imagine how anyone bought the story that the *I-400* was a cargo sub.

Not surprisingly, U.S. sailors didn't just want to see the world's largest submarines—they wanted to take a piece home with them. The *I-401*'s medical officer was so concerned that the wardroom's Japanese doll would be stolen that he burned it.*[10] Nevertheless, American sailors proved innovative scavengers. Swords and side-arms were first to go, but items necessary to the operation of the sub, including the *I-401*'s chronometer, compass, barometer, and binoculars, soon followed. It goes without saying that any sake or scotch that was discovered also disappeared.[11] Later choices were of more dubious value. When the crew's personal razors went missing, it redefined the meaning of acceptable war booty.[12]

A cease-and-desist order was issued before things got out of hand.[13] This wasn't done so much to protect the personal belongings of Japanese POWs as to ensure that the good stuff wasn't looted before higher-ups got their chance. The *I-401*'s sidearms and service swords were eventually distributed according to rank, but even Balson wasn't able to hold on to Nambu's service sword for more than a few hours. As soon as Lew Parks, commander of SubRon 20, saw it, he took it for himself.[14]

Not all the pillaging happened without consequence, as Hi Cassedy soon learned. Quick to confiscate the *I-400*'s service swords, he had planned to personally redistribute them. When Halsey got wind of it, Cassedy became the highest-ranking officer to fall afoul of souvenir fever. Though Cassedy wasn't in the dog-house long, it must have given the *Blue*'s skipper some satisfaction to know that Cassedy was the only U.S. officer ever relieved of com-

---

* According to Kazuo Nishijima, Kusaka gave a similar doll, as a token of friendship, to the U.S. officers of the *I-400*'s prize crew. When it was accidentally broken, Cassedy yelled at his officers for their rough treatment. However, one of the *I-400*'s crewmen felt sympathy for the Americans and repaired the doll for them.

mand of a Japanese sub.[15] Still, it didn't slow the stripping of the *Sen-toku* subs.

There were generous acts amid the looting. After their arrival in Yokosuka, Johnson gave Bando his Zippo lighter and invited the chief navigator to visit him in the United States after the war.[16] Bando still remembered the kindness 65 years later, suggesting that Johnson could build bridges, not just destroy them.

In fact, many of the *Segundo*'s crew had to admit they'd been wrong about Johnson. No matter what their concerns had been at the beginning of the patrol, there was no denying that he had handled himself well. He'd shown surprising restraint while chasing an unknown sub for four hours, and foresight by consulting with ComSubPac before taking action. Furthermore, he had remained calm during negotiations with a wily enemy, despite mixed signals. He'd been tough when necessary, insisting on escorting the *I-401* to Yokosuka; flexible when it came to Japanese face saving. Another skipper might have plunged them into a shooting war, but Johnson had shown grace under pressure while never letting his guard down. In other words, Stephen Lobdell Johnson had achieved something very important for a sub captain: he'd earned the respect of his crew.

LOCKWOOD MAY HAVE DESCRIBED Ariizumi's suicide as "the happy event,"[17] but it was not so for everyone. The commander's family was devastated. Matsu was every bit as much a product of the Imperial Japanese Navy as her husband. She had lived within its strictures and was proud of his success. He had not only become one of the navy's most trusted operational officers, he had done so while remaining true to his creed. Now he was gone, dead by his own hand. Yet by sacrificing himself, he'd brought honor to his family.

As much as Matsu grieved for her husband, she knew he had done the right thing. Now she resolved to join him. Just as the 47 Ronin had killed themselves after avenging their master's death, Matsu would make the ultimate sacrifice and follow in her husband's footsteps. Even though the Japan she had grown up with now lay in ruins, Matsu would uphold tradition.

For not only was Matsu going to end her own life—she was going to take the lives of her five children as well. It was a horrific decision for a mother to make, but in her mind, it was the only choice she had left.

CHAPTER 41

FREEDOM

THE *I-401*'S COMMUNICATIONS CHIEF, LT. (SG) GOICHI KATA-yama, brought Matsu her husband's suicide note.[1] He'd served aboard the *I-8* with Ariizumi and felt close to the commander. The note expressed Ariizumi's wish for a better life for his children, but Matsu could not ignore the fact that her husband had killed himself.

It was not unusual for a wife to follow her husband in suicide, especially in a feudal structure like the Imperial Japanese Navy. Wives had been following their husbands' example for centuries in Japan, and Matsu wasn't just a navy wife—her husband was an Etajima graduate, had served on the Naval General Staff, and had commanded the last submarine squadron of the Great Pacific War. Matsu was a role model for many, her actions studied and critiqued. The psychological pressure must have been enormous.

Still, she faced a dilemma. If Matsu and her children died, no one would be left to carry on the family line. Children were nec-essary to venerate the memories of their parents and ancestors, so it was crucial that the family bloodline be continued. And so Matsu chose to spare her oldest son, Nobukazu, and her younger daughter, Yasuko. Her remaining three children would follow her into death.

When the fateful day arrived, Matsu gathered her elder daugh-ter, Shizuko, and her second and third sons, Keisuke and Yosuke. Matsu had told no one about her decision save her mother, who waited quietly in the next room. The house remained dark in the shade of its garden, and the *tatami* mat floor muffled the small footsteps as the children gathered round.

Matsu used her cheeriest, high-pitched voice to address her children. Her message was honest if veiled.

"Let's go join your father."

But Keisuke, a chipper boy of four, was hungry.

"Not until we've eaten all the delicious things in our house, Mother."

"Of course, let us eat it all," she said choking back tears.

After a moment, Keisuke added, "Let's be sure to eat the persimmons too, Mother."

"Of course, the persimmons and the chestnuts," Matsu responded, for she knew the chestnut tree, which had been planted in their garden by Ariizumi's father, had borne fruit for the first time that season.

Before Matsu could make good on her promise though, Keisuke had one last question.

"Mother, the persimmons will grow again next year, won't they?"

Matsu's mother, who had been listening, was overwhelmed by the innocent question. The thought of this tiny child's death was too much to bear. Yes, their persimmon tree would bloom next year, but her grandson would not. Struggling with emotion, she interrupted the gathering.

"Death is not the only way to serve [your husband]," she said, tears in her eyes. "Please do not die."[2]

Matsu must have felt terrible as her mother's plea echoed in her ears. Sacrificing her children in the name of honor went against every maternal instinct. And yet she was the dutiful wife of a senior naval officer. She knew what she must do.

As her mother's sobbing filled the room, Matsu considered her family's fate. Her youngest son was but an infant, Keisuke no more than a toddler. Must she really sacrifice their lives to preserve the family honor? Or had Japan changed enough that her children might be spared?

Whatever else transpired in the Ariizumi house that day, Matsu decided that she and her children would survive. They would not follow her husband into death. They would live to taste persimmons another year.

SEPTEMBER 2, THE day the Japanese signed the Instrument of Surrender, was Lockwood's day in the sun. Twelve U.S. fleet subs, including the *Segundo,* were invited to participate in the ceremony and anchored in a nest alongside the *Proteus* in Tokyo Bay. Lockwood's personal three-star flag hung from the *I-400*'s bridge during the ceremony. Though he later admitted he was "gloating . . . over the enemy," Lockwood was proud of what he'd achieved.[3] One still has to wonder whether the commander of the Pacific sub force understood that he'd chosen the lesser of two submarines to gloat over. The real prize was Ariizumi's flagship, the *I-401.*

The next day the *Segundo* departed Tokyo for Pearl Harbor. It took a week to reach her destination. When the sub arrived, her crew was in for one last surprise. While the *Segundo* was in dry dock for inspection, a large dent was found in her starboard hull. A closer look revealed a yellow smear between the forward and aft engine compartments, most likely from the warhead of an enemy torpedo.[4]

Wallace Karnes remembered the bump they'd heard while approaching Sagami Bay and drew the simplest conclusion. "One of the *I-401*'s buddies must have snuck up and torpedoed us," he said. "That was funny."[5]

Funny in retrospect, maybe. But if the torpedo, depth charge, or sea mine hadn't been a dud, the *Segundo*'s last war patrol could have had a very different ending.

ONCE THE JAPANESE surrender was official, learning how to operate the *I-400* subs became the next order of business. All the subs' manuals, schematics, and diagrams had been thrown overboard, which meant U.S. submariners had to learn from scratch. Though Japanese sub design followed standard practice,[6] there was still a bewildering array of pipes, valves, dials, and switches to decipher. Turn the wrong valve, and you might flood the sub. It was time to learn how these monsters worked.

Japanese petty officers proved crucial to explaining how the subs operated.[7] They walked every inch of the surviving *Sen-toku* squadron with U.S. submariners in tow.[8] Ironically, the jailers soon learned that their prisoners were demanding taskmasters. U.S. prize crews produced drawings of every aspect of each sub's layout and systems. A Japanese-English dictionary of submarine terms also took shape. It proved helpful in understanding the strange Japanese markings that appeared everywhere. Most terms were new to the American submariners, but there was the occasional amusing display of English without *l*'s—for example, *barasuto tanku* for "ballast tank."[9]

As the prize crews grew more confident, they began entertaining visitors with demonstrations of the sub's catapult, raising and lowering her hydraulic crane, and opening her hangar door.[10] The Japanese petty officers were surprised at how fast the Americans caught on. Despite the language barrier, the learning process went quickly. After a week of training, Cdr. Joseph M. McDowell was ready to take the *I-400* out for sea trials—proof that submariners spoke the same language regardless of the country they came from.

THOUGH NAMBU RECEIVED "gentle treatment by the U.S. Navy,"[11] *Sen-toku* officers faced extensive questioning by naval intelligence. At first investigators wanted to know which ships Nambu had sunk, but they soon zeroed in on who had served in the Indian Ocean. Clearly, the Allies knew about the atrocities and wanted to find out which subs were involved.

Yata, the *I-401*'s chief gunnery officer, was taken to MacArthur's SCAP headquarters and asked whether Ariizumi had really committed suicide. Yata answered truthfully. Policemen still watched his house, however, hoping the officers they were looking for would show up.[12]

Two of Ariizumi's *Sen-toku* captains, the *I-400*'s Kusaka and the *I-14*'s Shimizu, had participated in massacres. The *Sen-toku* crews knew this, so they had something to hide. Since neither Nambu nor Yata had served in the Indian Ocean, they were eventually cleared.

Kusaka, however, didn't have it so easy. The day after the surrender ceremony, American interrogators descended upon his sub and began calling officers into the wardroom one by one.

An American translator encouraged Takahashi to tell them everything, promising, "We won't treat you badly."

Takahashi was hardly going to spill the beans, since he'd massacred prisoners himself. He chose to boast about Ulithi instead.

"It's a shame the war didn't last one more day," he told his interrogators. "If it had, I would have slammed myself into an American aircraft carrier."[13]

By the end of September, the U.S. Navy was comfortable enough operating the *I-400* subs that the *Sen-toku* crews were no longer needed. Curiously, none of the subs was ever submerged. Presumably, nobody wanted to risk operating them on anything but the surface.

Before the *Sen-toku* crews were discharged, however, American officials visited them one last time.[14] In appreciation for their cooperation, they gave the officers 20 cigarettes, a bottle of whiskey, and five ten-dollar bills. The same amount minus the whiskey was given to enlisted men. The gifts were a surprisingly Japanese thing to do—perhaps the American officers had learned something from their former enemies.

Before the translator departed though, he had important information to share.

"You will be released shortly, but the Allied War Crimes Tribunal will begin soon. The massacre of prisoners by submarines is a particular issue. If you are not careful, you may be arrested. Therefore, once you are released, it would be better to lay low."[15]

The *I-401*'s crew was mustered out of the navy on September 30, 1945.[16] By that time, the sub had been stricken from the IJN's roster of active duty ships. After a morning truck ride to a nearby demobilization center, Nambu was promoted one rank and exchanged his summer uniform for a winter one. By noon he was wandering the streets of the city, a free man.[17]

CHAPTER 42

THE LONG ROAD HOME

WHEN THE U.S. NAVAL TECHNICAL MISSION TO JAPAN LANDED in Yokosuka in September 1945, navy officials were keen to identify the latest Japanese sub technology in case it proved useful. Undersea war experts were already examining Germany's latest sub, the Type XXI, and though the state-of-the-art U-boat came too late to play a deciding role in the war, it was not too late to incorporate her design into the next generation of American fleet boats. U.S. naval officials already had a pretty good idea which Japanese subs they wanted to study, with the largest and the fastest at the top of their list.[1] Any submarine that could travel around the world without refueling to launch multiple offensive aircraft against enemy targets was undeniably unique. Not surprisingly, the *Sen-toku* squadron made the short list.

Teams of U.S. experts quickly spread out to the sub bases at Yokosuka, Kure, and Sasebo, where senior Japanese officers were interviewed about Sixth Fleet sub programs. Rear Adm. Katayama, head of submarine design and construction, and Commander Fujimori, the Naval General Staff's senior submarine officer, were extensively interviewed. Katayama had overseen construction of the *Sen-toku* force while Fujimori was familiar with her top secret operations. Both men spoke freely, helping U.S. intelligence assemble a clearer picture.[2]

Not everyone found the *I-400* subs of strategic value; some considered them nothing more than white elephants. One British Royal Navy observer dismissed them as "hopelessly under motored and . . . the very devil to stop or turn in an emergency."[3]

Though a report issued by the U.S. Navy analyzing the *I-400* subs disparaged the Japanese as pipe fitters, it also noted that this "system will hunt."[4] As a result, all three subs were sailed to Pearl Harbor for further study.

THE 4,000-MILE VOYAGE to Hawaii began in November 1945, when the subs journeyed from Yokosuka to Sasebo. Lieutenant Commander McDowell captained the *I-400*, Cdr. Edward D. Spruance captained the *I-401*, and Cdr. John S. McCain, Jr. (father of the future U.S. senator), commanded the *I-14*. The subs remained in Sasebo for several weeks loading supplies, and in a surprising twist, Hi Cassedy took command of the *I-14* from Jack McCain. Cassedy had been removed from commanding the *I-400* after his run-in with Halsey over Japanese swords. Being a Lockwood disciple, he soon found himself back in favor. And since Cassedy was the most senior officer, he was put in charge of all three subs.

The *I-400*'s prize crew developed their own logo for the voyage. Painted on a pennant, it shows an American sailor with a bulbous red nose riding the *I-400* with reins in one hand, a defeated Japanese soldier in the other. Subtle it was not.

Finally, on December 11, 1945, a minesweeper led the subs out of Sasebo harbor. The USS *Greenlet* (ASR-10) also accompanied the convoy in case one of the boats broke down. When the minesweeper reached the end of the channel, she blinked, "Bon Voyage" instead of the traditional "Good Hunting!"[5] Now that the war was over, there was no reason to hunt.

When the *Sen-toku* subs arrived at Guam eight days later, they received a tumultuous welcome. Whistles blew, a brass band played, and navy officials lined up to tour the underwater aircraft carriers. Guam was also jammed with navy surplus. In a cashless economy, it was easily exchanged for Japanese war booty. Soon the subs' aircraft hangars began filling with luxuries. Japanese rifles were exchanged for prime steaks; a coffee machine and General Electric ice cream maker joined the galley; and a porcelain toilet appeared in the *I-400*'s head. Even individual bunks were wired for music from a jukebox.[6]

Unfortunately, things didn't stop there. An irate marine lieutenant stormed aboard the *I-400* demanding that his motor scooter be returned. The chief of the boat assured the executive officer that "nobody is going to find any motor scooter in this boat."[7] The XO knew, however, that that wasn't the same as saying there was no scooter to be found. Still, the marine was told to take the matter up with his motor pool sergeant. Strangely enough, when the *I-400* sailed for Eniwetok,[8] it was the Americans, not the Japanese, that had become pirates.

A brief stop at Eniwetok enabled the *I-14* to repair her engines.[9] Unfortunately, the *I-401*'s entrepreneurial crew found themselves in hot water when they were accused of stealing the island commander's jeep. The sub was searched on the eve of her departure. The missing vehicle never turned up. When the *I-401* was finally granted permission to sail, she was told not to return, or risk being fired upon.[10]

The *Sen-toku* subs arrived at Pearl Harbor on January 6.[11] Cassedy had been informed that his subs shouldn't appear until dark, to avoid antagonizing Japanese sympathizers.[12] Since Cassedy was the highest-ranking officer, the *I-14* would be first to dock,[13] followed by the *I-401* and *I-400*. Unfortunately, as the squadron approached the submarine base, a bolt shook loose from the *I-401*'s number-one engine mount. It was no time for screw-ups, but when the *I-401* switched to battery power, her props sped up, and the sub shot past the *I-14*. Cassedy, always first, was fit to be tied.[14] It didn't help that a row of admirals and reporters were waiting at the dock.

The next day the local papers were filled with news of the *Sen-toku* squads' arrival.[15] The U.S. Navy recognized the publicity value of the subs and wanted to promote them. There was even talk of sailing them up and down the California coast, not to drop biological weapons but to raise money for war bonds. Until then, the subs were put on display at Pearl.

In February the *I-400* went into dry dock. The pungent smell of barnacles rotting in the tropical sun filled the air as sub experts crawled over Kusaka's former boat. The sub was extensively photographed both inside and out, and her systems were carefully examined for features that might be incorporated into the design of future American submarines.[16] A month later, Cdr. R. Kissinger issued a written report summarizing his findings.[17]

Though Kissinger found the sub's overall construction to be sound and cited several features of interest, he was unimpressed. Curiously, he thought the *I-400*'s hangar carried four aircraft and noted that the sub's purpose was "primarily for transportation of supplies, fuel, and planes to outlying islands."[18] Either Kissinger wasn't paying attention, or some members of the United States Navy were still in the dark as to her true mission. This discrepancy would be resolved when the U.S. Technical Mission to Japan issued its report. It's surprising though that six months after the *I-400*'s capture, the nature of her mission was still unclear.

THE FATE OF the *Sen-toku* subs was debated for several weeks.[19] The *I-400*'s XO, Lt. Thomas O. Paine, argued that the sub should be refitted for submerged operation and further evaluated. As Paine wrote, "I was convinced we should find out how such a huge submarine handled submerged . . . [and] what lessons her Japanese naval constructors [had] incorporated into her design [as well as] all the other things she could teach us."[20] Another idea was to convert her into a transport sub.[21]

Military budgets were in decline, however, and there were no funds for refitting enemy vessels. Paine was told to "stand by and await further orders."[22] Though the U.S. Navy was eager to design a new fleet of submarines, it showed little interest in underwater aircraft carriers, particularly in the midst of a demobilization. When it was discovered it would cost three quarters of a million dollars and require six months' yard work to refit the subs, decision making slowed to a crawl.[23]

On March 26, 1946, Lockwood attended the Submarine Officers' Conference in Washington, D.C. The *Sen-toku* subs were among the topics of discussion. Kissinger's report was reviewed, as were findings from the U.S. Naval Technical Mission to Japan. Several of the *I-400*'s "outstanding features" were singled out, including their sound protective coatings. Nevertheless, U.S. Navy officials found the subs too cumbersome and their number of aircraft too few to be of practical use. As the Technical Mission's report noted, the *I-400*s had many differences from U.S. submarines, but "there is little of actual technical accomplishment . . . and few items of possible value to the United States."[24]

It was agreed that no design studies should be made unless the Chief of Naval Operations believed the subs would be required in the future.[25] In other words, U.S. naval officials had no interest in using Yamamoto's underwater aircraft carriers.

The U.S. Navy might have lost interest, but the Soviets had not. When the Russians learned that the *Sen-toku* subs had been captured, they asked the United States to see them as part of an information-sharing agreement. The last thing U.S. naval officials wanted was the Russian military gaining access to a potentially disruptive technology. Given Soviet interest, U.S. officials denied the Russians access by scuttling Yamamoto's subs.

In the Japanese version of Scapa Flow, 15 Sixth Fleet subs were slated for destruction. The *I-402* was among the first to go. Early on the morning of April 1, 1946, in an operation called Road's End, a skeleton crew of Japanese sailors piloted their subs out of Sasebo harbor. One crew fastened cherry blossom sprigs to their sub's sail; another painted their sail bright green. Escorted by U.S. naval ships, the subs were led 60 miles off shore, where the water was 100 fathoms deep. Once the subs arrived, their crews were removed while demolition experts set explosive charges. Shortly after 1:00 P.M. the detonations began.[26]

The *I-402* avoided that ignominious end, but not for long. Lashed to a second sub, she was used for target practice by the USS *Everett F. Larson* (DD-830). When the two subs stubbornly refused to sink, they were scuttled. Ariizumi must have been rolling in his grave.

Four days later nine more Japanese subs were scuttled, leaving only a handful of Sixth Fleet subs at Pearl Harbor. The *I-14* was next. On May 28, 1946, she was taken eight miles off shore and used to test the newly developed Mark 10-3 exploder. The USS

Bugara (SS 331) did the honors. Three days later the *I-401* followed. At 10:51 on the morning of May 31, the USS *Cabezon* (SS 334) fired two torpedoes. Seven minutes later Nambu's sub was gone.[27]

On June 4 it was the *I-400*'s turn. The newly commissioned USS *Trumpetfish* (SS 425) hosted distinguished guests for the fireworks, including Lockwood's replacement and a medal of honor winner. As a PBY Catalina Flying Boat filmed the destruction, the *Trumpetfish* fired three Mark 18-2 torpedoes. One torpedo prematured, the other two struck in a sensational eruption of metal, foam, and fury. The *I-400*, the last of the great underwater aircraft carriers and the final Japanese submarine sunk by the United States during World War II, went down by the stern.[28]

The Russians filed a protest, but it was too late. The *Sen-toku* subs were already on the bottom. A headline in *The New York Times* read, "U.S. Said to Sink Four Japanese Subs to Balk Booty Bid." A U.S. naval official was quoted as saying, "Russia strongly disapproved the sinkings and lodged a protest."[29] The United States wasn't listening though—the cold war had begun.

CHAPTER 43

REDISCOVERY

THE OPERATIONS CENTER FOR THE HAWAII UNDERSEA RE-
search Laboratory is located on Makai Pier, on the southeast end
of Oahu. The pier is off the beaten track for most tourists. Wedged
between the Pacific Ocean, Route 72, and a steep set of cliffs, its entrance is blocked by a chain-link fence. A shed in its middle, three
stories high, is where the lab's two deep-diving submersibles, *Pisces
IV* and *V,* can be found.

Once you get past the hilarious acronym, HURL is a place where
serious science is conducted. Funded by the National Oceanic and
Atmospheric Administration's (NOAA) Underwater Research Program and overseen by the University of Hawaii, HURL has a reputation in the world of submersibles as being the scrappy underdog.
It doesn't have the budget or staff of a Woods Hole, but what it lacks
in funding, HURL makes up for in ingenuity and moxie.

The world of deep-diving submersibles is an elite and expensive
club. France has the *Nautile;* Russia has the *Mir 1* and *2;* Japan has
the *Shinkai;* China has the *Jiaolong;* and the United States has *Alvin.*
Though the *Pisces IV* and *V* are the "shallowest" members of the club,
with an operating depth of only 6,500 feet, they still accomplish a lot.

Because of budgetary constraints, HURL can't spend millions
training its submersible pilots on an expensive simulator. Instead,
they use the *Pisces* manipulator arms to practice picking up coffee
cups off the ocean bottom. The U.S. Navy dumped them there by
the thousands at the end of World War II and every desk at HURL's
operation center boasts at least one of these ceramic mugs as a pencil holder. The cup on the desk of Terry Kerby, HURL's operations
director, is stamped January 1943.

Since HURL was founded in 1981, it has made a name for itself not only by exploring the hydrothermal vents near underwater volcanoes but by finding important historical artifacts, like two of Ariizumi's previously unaccounted for midget subs. Kerby has been involved with HURL operations since their beginning. Blond, blue-eyed, and remarkably fit, he looks at least ten years younger than his age, which is what you'd expect for a man who swims two miles in the ocean every day. Wearing a dark T-shirt and khaki shorts, he is both tan and casual as he explains some of HURL's outsize discoveries.

Kerby was prompted to look for Ariizumi's midget subs by the fiftieth anniversary of the attack on Pearl Harbor. Up until 1991, only three of Ariizumi's five type-A midgets had been accounted for. One washed ashore shortly after the attack and was captured; one penetrated the harbor, was sunk, then raised weeks later, only to be used for landfill with its crew still inside; one was discovered off Oahu in the 1960s; and one was presumed sunk by the USS *Ward* (DD-139) but never found. The location of the fifth and final midget sub was a mystery.

Kerby couldn't use science assets to go "treasure hunting" though. It cost upward of $40,000 a day to operate the submersibles, so any search for Ariizumi's midget subs had to come as a by-product of a preexisting operation. Maritime artifacts were a secondary consideration.

Fortunately, HURL conducts test dives off Oahu at the beginning of each season to review safety protocols and ensure that each submersible is functioning properly. In August 2002 Kerby bested Dr. Robert Ballard, discoverer of the *Titanic,* when he found Ariizumi's fourth midget sub. Ballard had conducted his own search for the midget in 2000 but came up empty-handed. After ten years of looking, Kerby found the midget right where the *Ward* had sunk her, four miles south of Pearl Harbor, in 1,200 feet of water. The sub was remarkably well preserved despite the hole in her sail. Since her crew had the dubious distinction of becoming the Pacific War's first casualties, Kerby left the sub undisturbed.

Kerby and Ballard are more colleagues than competitors. The

two men have worked together, so it's hardly a rivalry. Still, HURL's find generated so much positive publicity that the National Park Service and NOAA's National Marine Sanctuaries encouraged them to explore further. As a result, Kerby set his sights on finding the fifth and final midget. He'd discovered her tail section in 1992. Subsequently he found two more sections, including the midget's bow.

It wasn't clear how the midget came to its final resting place or how it ended up in three neatly sundered pieces. Working with experts hired for a *NOVA* documentary, Kerby deduced that the sub had gotten lost either entering Pearl Harbor or trying to escape. When she ended up in the West Loch, her crew probably settled on the bottom, detonated the sub's self-destruct charge, and disappeared into history.

The U.S. Navy accidentally rediscovered the midget while cleaning up after an explosion in May 1944. The midget was dredged up along with other debris, cut into sections, and dumped at sea without anyone realizing what they'd found. It was only when Kerby discovered all three sections that the puzzle came together.

There's a lot of adventure in Kerby's background. He spent four and a half years in the Coast Guard, where he served on a cutter in Alaska and trained as a navigator. "It was an exciting time," Kerby says, "Alaska has the worst the sea has to offer."

After leaving the Coast Guard, he attended the Coastal School of Deep Sea Diving in Oakland, California, eventually becoming a salvage diver. After working in the San Francisco Bay Area, he journeyed to Hawaii in 1976.

"I drove by the Makai pier one day and saw them offloading a submersible," Kerby recalls. "I'd always been fascinated by ocean exploration. I had the qualifications that the company, Deep Water Exploration, were looking for, so they hired me. That's when I started working with the *Star II*."

Kerby was eager to learn about submersibles. In 1980, he was hired to pilot one for the James Bond movie *For Your Eyes Only*. The next year he was contacted by HURL.

HURL's two submersibles were built by International Hydrodynamics in Vancouver; the *Pisces IV* in 1972 and the *Pisces V* in

1973. The core of *Pisces V* is a command sphere made of high-end steel, seven feet in diameter, with room for a pilot and two observers. The pilot kneels in the middle of the floor while operating its propulsion, ballast, and other systems. The two observers lie on vinyl-covered benches on either side of the pilot. The sphere is attached to a steel frame that contains batteries, hydraulics, ballast, and propulsion systems. There are also three forward-looking viewports made of acrylic. The centermost viewport is for the pilot; each observer gets his own 14-inch-wide window as well.

Kerby describes both *Pisces,* which are nearly identical, as workhorses—utility players that can adapt to a variety of needs. It might be challenging to fly them, but Kerby appreciates their flexibility. "They can spin like a top," he says enthusiastically—something most people are happy to take his word for.

Each submersible weighs 13 tons and is 20 feet long, its most fascinating feature being its manipulator arms. Configured with parallel jaws, the manipulators collect samples off the bottom, which are then deposited in a steel basket attached to the sub's undercarriage. Both submersibles carry a battery of lights to illuminate the darkness underwater and two high-definition cameras to record what they see. Both subs are also self-propelled, meaning there is no umbilical cord tethering them to their mother ship. The *Pisces IV* was bought from the Canadian Navy in 1999 for $500,000, even though it cost $4 million to build. It's a bargain Kerby is proud of.

Except for a brief leave of absence to teach Ed Harris underwater dive technique for James Cameron's *The Abyss,* Kerby has spent 30 years at HURL. He's not only its director of operations but its chief submersible pilot as well. Part of HURL's research program is to study the susceptibility of coastal zones to pollution, but in March 2005 Kerby set their sights on another discovery: finding the *I-400* subs.

There'd been one previous attempt to find a *Sen-toku* sub. In April 2004 William Bryant, an oceanography professor at Texas A&M, launched an unsuccessful search for the *I-402* in collaboration with The Discovery Channel. Though he found 12 of the 24 submarines sunk off Japan during Operation Road's End, he did not find the *I-402*.

Once again cost was a concern. Kerby and his team hoped to find at least one of Ariizumi's subs while breaking in a new NOAA-funded navigation system. But three days of test dives is not a lot of time. A submarine can plane a good distance after being torpedoed, and U.S. Navy coordinates don't necessarily reflect where the *Sen-toku* subs came to rest. There was no guarantee Kerby would find anything.

The ocean bottom around Pearl Harbor has historically been a dumping ground for the U.S. military. Tanks, amphibious assault vehicles, trucks, ships, piers, landing craft, airplanes, and aircraft parts have been piling up for decades, making it hard for sonar to identify specific targets. The sea floor is also littered with unexploded ordnance, including Hedgehog depth charges and chemical explosives dumped by the army. You have to be careful what you approach.

The first two days of dive operations did not go well, with sonar giving many false positives.

"We used up a lot of our test dives chasing down rock formations," Kerby recalls. "A limestone reef with an outcropping on top can look a lot like a giant submarine on sonar."

On March 17, the last day of test dives, Kerby and pilot-in-training Colin Wollerman conducted emergency tracking exercises in the *Pisces IV*. Tracking exercises are a safety protocol done to test a pilot's ability to find her hypothetically stranded sister sub, in this case, the *Pisces V*. When the *Pisces V* settled on the ocean floor, pilot Max Cremer turned off her lights while pilot-in-training Steve Price activated the 27 kHz pinger that Kerby would use to locate them. The pinging sounds a lot like a cardio monitor, only faster. If the danger of dying at 6,000 feet doesn't focus your attention, the sound of a heart monitor will. At maximum dive depth, the *Pisces* experience 3,000 pounds of pressure per square inch—a fact that's enough to concentrate even the most distracted passenger.

Once tracking exercises were finished, Kerby worked his way along the ocean floor. The bottom off Barber's Point has occasional rock formations but otherwise is featureless. At 2,600 feet, the water is also silty with plankton. The submersibles' headlights make it look like you're driving through a snowstorm.

Depending on dive conditions, Kerby can see up to 20 feet underwater with the lights on. Sonar can see farther, in some cases as much as several hundred feet. Still, the *I-400* subs are such large targets, Kerby believed sonar would pick them up at 300.

Looking for wrecks is a dangerous business. Kerby knows it and is especially careful. The biggest danger is coming in too low and getting snagged on something. The current can also be a problem, especially if it changes on you. Kerby insists on approaching wrecks from downstream. That way if anything goes wrong, the current pushes you away from the wreck.

You can almost feel your brain struggling to make sense of the images on the monitor as Kerby searches for the *I-400*. The underwater hues of gray, dark blue, and green are so limited, they don't help much. It's not until Kerby says "We have it in sight!" that you even know he's found something.

Once pattern recognition kicks in, the distinctive shape of a submarine lying on its side begins to emerge. But it's not clear which sub he's found. Getting situated on a wreck in what appears to be the dead of night, especially when you don't know what shape it's in, is intimidating. Any number of objects, including floating cables, bent piping, and twisted hull plating, are waiting to grab you. Once a wreck is located, the lead submersible comes in, sits on the bottom, and conducts a sonar survey to outline the perimeter. Meanwhile the second submersible waits as backup in case anything goes wrong.

It's important to get a sense of a wreck's size and dispersement before taking a closer look. A preliminary survey helps. Though Kerby always plans for safety, accidents can happen. Backing away from the wreck, Kerby calls Cremer in *Pisces V* to announce he's found the bow section. Once he has a decent sonar signature, he'll make an initial tour to determine if there are any entanglements. The cleanest way is to fly over the wreck, but for now Kerby studies the sonar data.

As lights from the *Pisces IV* abruptly illuminate the sub's bow, Kerby spots a launch ramp. A few minutes later he's identified the hydraulic crane used to lift the sub's *Seiran*. You can also see where the plane's pontoons were stored between the catapult rails. Clearly, he's discovered one of the *Sen-toku* subs, but which one? It's hard to tell in what passes for day at 2,600 feet.

As Kerby flies farther down the sub, he soon makes a surprising discovery. The sub is broken in two just short of the sail, robbing him of a chance to identify which of the three *Sen-toku* subs he's found. The section where the bow has separated looks like the worst sort of industrial accident. Piles of tangled metal litter the bottom some 30 feet high, suggesting the destructive forces at work. The torpedoes that sunk the sub have broken her in two. It's almost painful to see.

Kerby enters the debris field to see where it leads him. A piece of deck section, with its triple-mount antiaircraft gun intact, appears in his viewport. There's some marine growth on the barrels, otherwise they're easily recognizable. As Kerby moves in for a closer look, one of his thrusters raises a cloud of sediment, obscuring his view. To the novice, it looks like *Pisces IV* is in trouble. There are lots of jagged pieces to damage a submersible, so Kerby backs away, giving the sandstorm time to disperse. As he later notes, "It's always important to know where safe water is."

The next big surprise comes when Kerby discovers the sub's aircraft hangar. Separated from the rest of the hull, it's planted in the ocean bottom like a javelin. You can barely make out its giant door buried in the sand. The rest of the hangar stands upright at a slight angle.

At some point during Kerby's inspection, Cremer reports from the *Pisces V* that he's found another sub east of his position.

"I think you've found this sub's stern," Kerby responds.

Submersible pilots don't talk much. Motivated by the spirit of exploration, they're sober minded in the driver's seat. They don't leap to conclusions, since the last thing they want is to make a scientific claim they can't support. Kerby cautions Cremer to watch out for obstructions and then continues through the debris field.

Both men sound professional, though Cremer can't quite keep the enthusiasm from infecting his voice. Aside from the clicking and whirring of machinery, the submersibles are quiet.

Once Cremer begins flying down the stern section, he can see that the hatches were left open to assist her sinking. An occasional shrimp attracted by the lights swims into view, and a ray can be seen gliding across the aft deck. The teak planks have long since rotted away, leaving only the metal cross braces, which could easily snag the skids on the *Pisces V* if Cremer gets too close.

When the boat's 5.5-inch deck gun comes into view, there is surprisingly little marine growth, save for two sea fans on its barrel. The juxtaposition is almost funny. Unfortunately, the gun can't identify the sub, since virtually all Japanese fleet boats carried the same weapon. HURL will have to proceed further if it hopes to make a positive identification.

Finally, as the *Pisces V* passes the sub's midsection, video footage shows what appears to be her sail rising from the darkness. It's speckled with yellow and red marine growth that looks surprisingly vibrant against the dark hull. The rungs of a ladder can be seen climbing up the outside just below where the sub's designation should be. The laser dot triangle of the *Pisces's* rangefinger shines against the plating like an alien targeting system.

As the high-def camera begins to pan, the characters "*I-4*" come into view. Part of the sail's plating has peeled away, however, obscuring the rest of the ID. Which sub has HURL found? Is it the *I-400* or the *I-401*? A long-legged crab clinging to the hull tries skittering out of view. When the *Pisces* maneuvers to get a better angle, the lights finally illuminate what's been hiding behind twisted steel. HURL has found Ariizumi's flagship.

Incredibly, the single white "I" character followed by three numerals can still be read 59 years later. The boat's designation was most likely painted by Americans, since the Japanese would not have drawn such a sloppy "I." Nevertheless, there is no doubt this is Nambu's sub, the same sub that he captained on the Storm mission and that the USS *Segundo* persuaded to surrender.

In subsequent video footage, one of the *Pisces* approaches the

I-401's bridge for closer inspection. The first thing you notice is that the sub's periscope, a shiny sliver of silver, is fully extended. It positively gleams in the underwater lights; not a trace of corrosion mars its shaft. You can also see that the bridge hatch is open. Part of a ladder leading into the conning tower can be seen disappearing into the darkness. The bridge compass is missing, but a set of pressure-proof binoculars remains, ready to spot enemy ships on the horizon. You can also make out the voice tubes where Nambu would have shouted his orders while navigating on the surface.

After several hours inspecting the sub, it's time for the *Pisces* to head upward. As they begin their one-hour ascent, they leave the *I-401* in darkness. It's the same darkness that envelops Ariizumi on the other side of the world. In both cases, it's a suitable resting place.

EPILOGUE

At the start of the Great Pacific War, the Imperial Japanese Navy had one of the best submarine forces in the world. The Sixth Fleet's approximately 60 submarines were on par with many of the latest U.S. fleet boats.* As the war progressed, the Japanese built an additional 126 boats, for a total of nearly 200 submarines.[1] Yet by August 1945, the Sixth Fleet had only 50 subs left, and most of them were obsolete, damaged, or inoperable.[2] The Japanese lost at least 127 submarines during the war, including the unlucky *I-33*, which, after being sunk and refloated, was sunk a second time.[†3] By comparison, the U.S. Navy lost 52 subs.[4] The casualty rate for U.S. sub crews might have been the highest of any U.S. military branch,[5] but the number of Sixth Fleet deaths was staggering by comparison.

Western historians point to these statistics when dismissing the Sixth Fleet as ineffective. And though it's true the IJN made glaring errors in administering its sub force, the courage and resolve of

---

* The actual number of Japanese submarines at the beginning of World War II varies by source. Ito says that by December 1941, Japan had 64 submarines; see *The End of the Imperial Japanese Navy*, p. 155. Bagnasco confirms this number in *Submarines of World War II*, p. 176. Other accounts cite totals ranging between 60 and 63 submarines.

† Once again it's difficult to say with absolute certainty how many Japanese subs were lost during World War II because so many files were destroyed. For example, John D. Alden says 128 Japanese subs were lost; see *The Fleet Submarine in the U.S. Navy*, p. ix. According to Boyd and Yoshida, *Japanese Submarine Force and World War II*, "127 of about 160 large submarines in service during the war were lost" (p. xiii). The actual number makes little difference. Bottom line, by August 1945 the Sixth Fleet was virtually wiped out.

Sixth Fleet crews was impressive, as were their accomplishments in the face of declining resources, poor management, and a resourceful enemy. Certainly, Japanese sub technology did not keep pace with the United States. Despite this drawback, the Sixth Fleet managed to produce the *I-201*, one of the world's fastest submarines, as well as the *I-400*s, suggesting that a touch of not-invented-here syndrome colors the historical assessment.

The Japanese sub force ultimately failed for a number of reasons. Subservience to the surface fleet, midwar deployment as cargo carriers, and the IJN High Command's almost total lack of adaptation when it came to changing circumstances all played a role. Failure to listen to the hard-won knowledge of Sixth Fleet sub captains combined with a penchant for back seat driving also didn't help. The greatest failure however, was the IJN's inability to fully utilize the submarine as a combat weapon, making Japanese sub crews (as one Sixth Fleet sub captain put it) "just so much human ammunition."[6]

SEGUNDO OFFICERS AND CREW

All five members of the *I-401*'s boarding party received the Bronze Star with combat V (for valor), including Lt. John E. Balson. After the war, Balson remained in the navy, became captain of another Balao-class sub, and retired as commander in 1961. He enjoyed a career at Electric Boat in Groton, Connecticut, as a quality control officer inspecting newly constructed submarines. As of this writing, he is retired and lives in Florida with his wife.

Capt. Stephen Lobdell Johnson received the Legion of Merit with combat V, "for exceptionally meritorious conduct in the performance of outstanding services." His citation states that "as Commanding Officer of the USS *Segundo* [he] contact[ed the] Japanese submarine *I-401* [and] accepted the hostile ship's formal surrender and brought it safe to port."[7]

Clearly, Johnson's firm hand and quick thinking saved both

the *Segundo* and the *I-401*. Lt. (jg) Victor Horgan and Lt. (jg) Rod Johnson weren't alone in sharing this conviction—the crew did as well. Though Johnson's naval career would include the occasional stumble, no one could deny he'd earned the Legion of Merit.

Stephen Johnson captained the *Segundo* until February 1946, when he was replaced by Cdr. H. M. Lytle. Two years later he was assigned command of the USS *Bergall* (SS 320), where he earned his second nickname, "Screaming" Steve Johnson, for surfacing under a tuna boat in 1949. Contrary to regulations, the tuna boat had been operating in a restricted area near Barber's Point. Ironically, it was the same area where the *I-401* had been sunk by the U.S. Navy two years earlier. The tuna boat was drifting with its engines turned off, which might have been why the *Bergall* failed to pick her up on sonar. While Johnson was surfacing his sub, he called "Up scope!" immediately followed by "Holy shit!" and an emergency dive order.[8]

The tuna boat sheared off the *Bergall*'s periscope, causing water to pour into the conning tower. Fortunately, the sub's pumps took care of the flooding and no real damage was done.[9] It was the kind of mistake that either costs a sub captain his command, leads to court martial, or both. But it didn't hurt Johnson's career any. Having an admiral in the family must have helped.

The self-admitted nonstudent later went on to earn a master's degree in international relations from American University and was awarded France's National Order of Merit for his service as naval attaché at the U.S. embassy in Paris. Johnson retired from the navy in 1969 and died in Virginia Beach, Virginia, in April 2000.

Cdr. J. D. Fulp's distinguished naval career lasted a total of 30 years. His final posting was as base commander of the U.S. naval station on Kodiak Island in the Gulf of Alaska. When a tsunami driven by a 9.2 earthquake destroyed Kodiak City in March 1964, Fulp was instrumental in aiding its recovery. After retiring from the navy, he took a job in the private sector and died of a sudden heart attack in 1979.

Lt. Victor Horgan and Lt. Rod Johnson, childhood pals from

Portland, Oregon, went their separate ways after the war but kept in touch. Horgan had a successful career as an executive in the fish canning industry. He eventually sold his company but continued traveling the world, returning to Japan, which he'd first visited aboard the *Segundo*. He died in Seattle, where he lived with his second wife, Mary Lee, shortly before this book was completed.

QM3c Carlo Carlucci returned to his former construction job after being honorably discharged. He married and raised a family and is currently living in New Jersey. Carlucci won the Bronze Star for his time aboard the *I-401*. Sixty-four years later he proudly notes, "I didn't get it for washing dishes."[10] Surprisingly, the *Segundo*'s prize crew received their Bronze Stars through the mail rather than in a formal ceremony,[11] which seems understated considering what they accomplished.

As for the *Segundo* herself, she returned to Pearl Harbor after Japan's surrender. Two of her crew managed to get arrested for taking a post office motorcycle for a joyride during their stay.[12] The sub sailed for Seattle shortly afterward and then took a victory cruise down the west coast.

The *Segundo* received four battle stars for her World War II service and was eventually assigned to SubRon 3 in San Diego. She was modernized in 1951 in the San Francisco Naval Shipyard, where she was equipped with a snorkel—which Ariizumi would have appreciated. She served numerous tours in the Far East and saw action during the Korean War. Finally, after 26 years of duty, the *Segundo* was found "unfit for naval service" and sunk during target practice on August 8, 1970.[13]

SEN-TOKU OFFICERS AND CREW

Having spent 1,380 days fighting in the Pacific,[14] the *I-401*'s captain, Lt. Cdr. Nobukiyo Nambu, struggled to make a living after the war. Trained to serve a navy that no longer existed, Nambu's life became so grim he couldn't feed his growing family. At one point, he even took in boarders to make ends meet, yet still insisted on bringing former naval officers home for dinner, much to his wife's annoyance.[15]

Nambu continued to be questioned by occupation authorities about his former squadron commander but was never charged with any crime.[16] When the predecessor to today's Japanese Maritime Self Defense Force (JMSDF) was reconstituted in 1952, Nambu joined up. He moved from Kure to Maizuru, close to where the *I-401* had undergone her final training, and eventually became superintendent of the JMSDF Submarine School; he retired as a rear admiral in 1965.[17] Like Yamamoto, Nambu enjoyed writing poetry and in 1963 was awarded a prize for his efforts by Emperor Hirohito.[18] As of this writing, he lives in an assisted living facility outside Tokyo. Even at age 97, the captain of the *Sen-toku* subs' flagship remains unstooped with a sharp mind and crisp salute, though his hearing isn't what it used to be.

Had Cdr. Tatsunosuke Ariizumi lived to see a final accounting of his *Sen-toku* squad, he would have been depressed. All five subs (*I-13*, *I-14*, *I-400*, *I-401*, *I-402*) lay at the bottom of the Pacific. Construction on the *I-403* had been canceled in October 1944,[19] while the *I-404* was almost complete when Allied bombs destroyed her while moored near Kure in July 1945.[20] The *I-405*'s keel was laid down in September 1944, but work stopped in January 1945,[21] and the sub was dismantled. Hull numbers *406* through *417* were never built, since shifting priorities led to the remaining *I-400* subs being canceled altogether.

The *I-402* was the only other *I-400* sub to become operational during the Storm mission. Commissioned on July 24, 1945,[22] just a few days after her sister subs departed for Ulithi, she was captained by Cdr. Otoji Nakamura, and immediately commenced training as part of SubRon 1. She was slightly damaged on August 11,[23] when shrapnel from a Kure bombing raid punctured one of her fuel tanks. When the cease-fire was declared, she was still undergoing her shakedown period.

As for the remaining Type A modified subs, sisters to the *I-13* and *I-14*, the *I-1* was 70 percent complete when she sank in a storm off Kobe in September 1945;[24] the *I-15* was also unfinished when the war ended and was scrapped. Three additional AM-type subs never got past the planning stage.[25]

The Allied investigation into war crimes soon uncovered Ariizumi's role in the Indian Ocean massacres. For a while, Allied authorities sought to determine whether Ariizumi might still be alive. Over time, however, they accepted that he'd killed himself just as Nambu described.

Suprisingly, some of the *Segundo*'s crew believe Ariizumi's body was cremated in a rice kettle aboard the *I-401*. Later there was speculation that Nambu killed Ariizumi after the commander threatened to scuttle the sub,[26] but the story is preposterous. Ariizumi is on record as having specifically asked the 631st chief medical officer,[27] as well as Yata, the chief gunnery officer,[28] about the best way to kill oneself with a pistol. Additionally, Ariizumi was clearly in psychological distress, not because of his role in the *I-8* massacres but because surrender was unimaginable. Given that Ariizumi probably felt as betrayed by his naval command as shaken by defeat, it's not surprising he killed himself. Everything he believed in had been destroyed.

Certainly, there was no love lost between Ariizumi and Nambu. Still, it's highly unlikely that Nambu would have turned a gun against his commanding officer given his belief in naval protocol. Even now, 66 years after the *I-401*'s surrender, Nambu refuses to speak critically of his commanding officer.

Matsu raised Ariizumi's five children in the manner he would have wished, and though the family keeps a low profile, refusing to speak to the media (including the author), relatives have occasionally appeared at *I-401* reunions.[29]

Muneo Bando, the *I-401*'s chief navigator, eventually got involved in real estate and is a rightist in his political views. He is a member of one of Tokyo's most prestigious clubs, from which the emperor's palace can be seen, and remains a somewhat controversial figure at *I-401* reunions, since his recollections don't always square with those of his former shipmates. Nevertheless, it's not hard to see what Captain Johnson found so endearing about the little navigator.

When the IJN was reconstituted as the Japanese Maritime Self Defense Force, Nambu wasn't the only *Sen-toku* officer to return to his former career. Tsugio Yata, the *I-401*'s chief gunnery officer, also signed up. In fact, Yata eventually rose to the rank of admiral, surpassing Nambu, whom he'd always admired. He served as the thirteenth chairman of the Joint Staff Council at Japan's Defense Agency, a position similar to the chairman of the Joint Chiefs of Staff in the United States. In a 1981 ceremony attended by Mrs. Douglas MacArthur, the United States awarded Yata the Legion of Merit (Degree of Commander) for exceptionally meritorious conduct in the performance of outstanding services. It was the same award Captain Johnson received for capturing the *I-401*. Yata retired from the navy in 1983 and lives with his wife in a suburb outside Tokyo.

Yata's mother also survived the war. Though she'd intended to kill herself after her son left on Operation Storm, she delayed doing so, hoping he'd return. Had she received the farewell note Yata had planned to send her, she confessed, she would have hung herself. It was Nambu's kind invitation to say goodbye to her son that saved Yata's mother from death.[30]

The *Sen-toku* squad's mission was so secret that Inouye, the *I-401*'s sonar operator, could not tell his parents where he was going, what he was doing, or whether he'd return. When months passed and Inouye's parents heard nothing from him, they assumed the worst. But when he returned home as a "ghost" in the fall of 1945, they were overjoyed. His two older brothers also survived the war, which was uncharacteristically lucky for a Japanese family. Inouye later went to work for Toyota Motors. For the past 35 years, he's run a small ramen shop with his wife in Nagoya, not far from where the *Seiran* were built.[31]

After the war, the *I-400*'s commanding officer, Cdr. Toshio Kusaka, skippered a surface ship to return demobilized soldiers to Japan.[32] He was later tried and found guilty by the Yokohama War Crimes Tribunal for massacring the survivors of the SS *Richard*

Hovey. He was sentenced to five years' hard labor in Sugamo Prison and was released after serving his sentence.[33] He later captained merchant marine ships and died in 1999 at the age of 95.[34]

On the other hand, Cdr. Tsuruzo Shimizu, captain of the *I-14*, lived up to his lucky reputation. After starting over as a farmer, he was arrested in October 1948 and confined to Sugamo Prison for atrocities committed while captaining the *I-165*. He was acquitted, however, on December 13, 1948. Though the reasons for his acquittal are unclear, it certainly wasn't because he was innocent. Most likely, evidence was lacking or a deal was struck in exchange for his cooperation. He too entered the JMSDF, eventually serving as vice-superintendent of the Yokosuka Naval Base, and retired as a rear admiral in 1963. He died in December 2001.[35]

THE PILOTS

Ens. Kazuo Takahashi, the *I-400*'s *Seiran* pilot, managed to avoid being tried as a war criminal despite his participation in the *I-37* massacres. After living a long, productive life, he died in March 2005.

Lt. Atsushi Asamura, the *Seiran* squadron leader for the *I-401*, lives in Tokyo with his wife. His apartment boasts a scale model of a *Seiran* and a photo of himself as squadron leader. He keeps in touch with his colleagues and is an unofficial spokesman for the *Sen-toku* subs, often granting television and magazine interviews. Even today he remains a stickler for protocol and has few kind words to say about his fellow *Seiran* pilot Takahashi. Not surprisingly, Asamura comes across as an unreconstructed war veteran, ready to jump into his *Seiran* and finish the job he started.

Reunions for the respective *Sen-toku* subs continued for many years after the war, though the number of attendees declined as death took its toll. Many of the *I-401* crew remain grateful to Nambu for returning them to Japan. But the *I-401*'s failure to communicate the change in rendezvous date and location to the *I-400*, as well as the conflict between Ariizumi and Nambu, splits the crew to this day.[36] When pressed for details, all Tsugio Yata will say is: "The captain is head of the sub, whereas the squadron commander is not. I suspect the opinions of Commander Ariizumi and Lt. Commander Nambu did not reach agreement."[37]

Nambu remains equally reticent. Despite having been on the receiving end of Ariizumi's psychological troubles,[38] he continues to praise his commanding officer despite their differences, saying: "I have avoided all speculation and believe the Commander was a brilliant naval officer who committed suicide in the *bushido* tradition. I have written as much and my belief will remain this way."[39]

Many *I-401* officers praise Ariizumi for his strength of character in accepting responsibility for their mission's failure. "He was a great soldier," Muneo Bando, the *I-401*'s navigator, says. "He even took his own life for his crew and country."[40]

As for Nobuo Fujita, the pilot who firebombed west coast forests from his sub-launched seaplane, he returned to Oregon in 1962 to make amends. Fujita was deeply ashamed of his attack on the U.S. mainland and traveled to Brookings, Oregon, to present his family's 400-year-old samurai sword as a symbol of his regret. Fearing the Brookings townspeople might still be angry, Fujita was prepared to disembowel himself should things turn ugly. Fortunately, it never came to that. Later he donated $1,000 to the local library to purchase children's books about Japan so there wouldn't be another war between the two countries. He died of lung cancer in 1997 at age 85.[41]

Perhaps the most unusual farewell for anyone associated with the *I-400* subs was the funeral of Hiram Cassedy. Cassedy had briefly commanded the *I-400* and later sailed the *I-14* to Pearl Harbor. In keeping with his flamboyant personality, Cassedy's ashes were placed in the forward torpedo tube of an experimental submarine and fired into the deep blue sea.[42] Presumably, he went without any Japanese naval swords.

Of course, the Tokyo War Crimes Tribunal took its toll on the IJN High Command. The *Sen-toku* crews were interrogated about Ariizumi and the *I-8* atrocities.[43] Even Carlo Carlucci was interviewed by U.S. naval intelligence when he returned to New York in

1946. "I was shown pictures of various Japanese naval officers and asked if I could identify any of them," Carlucci remembers. "They all looked alike, but I picked out one that I'd seen on the bridge staring at us with anger in his eyes."[44]

After the war, there was a trial involving participants in the Indian Ocean massacres. Vice Adm. Hisashi Ichioka, who commanded SubRon 8 when the atrocities occurred, received 20 years. Other punishments were harsher. Admiral Daigo, the sixth CINC of the Japanese sub force in five years, was executed by firing squad in 1947. Declining a blindfold, the commander in chief of the Sixth Fleet sang the "*Kimigayo,*" Japan's national anthem, before declaring *banzai* three times in honor of the emperor. When he finished, he calmly told the firing squad he was ready. Some of Daigo's officers claimed he had nothing to do with the atrocities. Six years after the Ichioka defendants were convicted for massacres committed in the Indian Ocean, their sentences were commuted.[45]

Chief of the Imperial Japanese Army General Staff Yoshijiro Umezu, who had canceled Operation PX—the plan to attack America with biological weapons—was arrested by SCAP authorities and tried as a war criminal. The International Military Tribunal for the Far East in Tokyo found him guilty of waging a war of aggression and sentenced him to life imprisonment. He converted to Christianity while in prison and died from rectal cancer in 1949.

As for the brain trust behind the *Sen-toku* subs, NGS submarine staff officer Cdr. Shojiro Iura was found guilty of failing to restrain his subordinates from killing more than 800 prisoners in the Indian Ocean and was sentenced to six years of hard labor at Sugamo Prison.[46] He was eventually released and wrote a book about his experience. Cdr. Yasuo Fujimori, who headed up the submarine section of NGS's First Division, was found guilty of similar crimes and sentenced to four years' hard labor.[47]

Kameto Kurojima, Yamamoto's favorite naval officer, was a rear admiral by the time the war ended. After Yamamoto's death, he became director of the NGS's Second Division, where he developed suicide attack plans, believing it impossible to win using conventional tactics.[48] After the war, the "weirdo officer" cooperated with

SCAP authorities. As Yamamoto's chief of planning, he provided invaluable information about the attack on Pearl Harbor and the Battle of Midway. He was not charged with any war crimes and died in 1965.

AFTERMATH

Aichi, the *Serian* manufacturer, was dissolved after the war. In its current incarnation (Aichi Machine Industry Co., Ltd.), it manufactures light trucks and automotive parts for Nissan. The private shipyards that built the *Sen-toku* subs continue to exist, including Kawasaki Heavy Industries.

At least one *Seiran* was brought to the United States after the war. Transported by a U.S. aircraft carrier along with a number of other Japanese aircraft, the last *Seiran* ever built (airframe no. 28) was studied to see if it might be of future use. When it was determined that the United States had no need for such a specialized attack plane, the *Seiran* was housed at the Alameda Naval Air Station. Ravaged by souvenir hunters and inclement weather, she was finally shipped in an advanced state of disrepair to the National Air and Space Museum in 1962, where she remained outside for another 12 years until room was found inside a storage facility.[49] Over the next ten years, she was lovingly restored at a cost of $1 million and is now on display at the Smithsonian Air and Space Museum's Udvar-Hazy Center, near Dulles International Airport in Virginia. Asamura was reunited with his beloved *Seiran* in 2003, when the Smithsonian invited him to experience it firsthand. Though beautifully refurbished, she is not capable of flight—something the residents of Washington, D.C., must feel relieved about.

A *Nanzan* was also reportedly brought to the United States. Last seen in poor condition at Seattle Naval Air Station during the 1950s, she disappeared without a trace and is presumed to have been scrapped.[50]

Despite finding Nambu's sub, the *I-401*, and Shimizu's *I-14*, the Hawaii Undersea Research Laboratory (HURL) has yet to find the

I-400. The general location of Kusaka's sub is known, and it's probably just a matter of time before HURL locates it during one of its test dives.

REAPPRAISAL

Many naval historians view the *Sen-toku* squad as a dead branch on the family tree of submarines. But the story of Yamamoto's underwater aircraft carriers is by no means over. What was once dismissed as an "undersea dinosaur"[51] takes on a more meaningful role when one realizes the *I-400*s were the strategic predecessors to today's ballistic missile submarines.

For example, Rear Adm. John D. Butler gives partial credit to the *I-400*s for the Regulus missile program,[52] lending credence to various paternity claims. Certainly the resemblance between the *I-400* subs and the Regulus missile–carrying subs is striking.

The Regulus missile program began eight years after the war ended. A primitive version of the Tomahawk cruise missile used today, Regulus missiles carried a thermonuclear warhead and were stored inside a sub's massive watertight deck hangar, similar to the *I-400*s. They also required a sizable platform for launching—another link to *I-400* paternity.

The first Regulus missile was launched from the deck of the USS *Tunny* (SSG 282) in July 1953. The *Tunny* and her sister sub, the USS *Barbero* (SSG 317), were retrofitted with a giant watertight hangar to carry the missile. They were later joined by two purpose-built Regulus submarines, the USS *Grayback* (SSG 574) and USS *Growler* (SSG 577) in 1958, and the nuclear-powered USS *Halibut* (SSGN 587) in 1960. Together these five boats formed the first U.S. nuclear deterrent patrol submarines.[53]

The ability of U.S. submarines to launch nuclear weapons undetected became the backbone of the nation's strategic deterrent force. At the very least, then, the Regulus missile program marked an important evolution of the *I-400*s as an offensive weapon. The *I-400*s helped demonstrate that a large, stable sub with a watertight deck hangar could be built to launch an offensive airborne weapon against an enemy's cities.[54] The Regulus subs even suffered the same tactical disadvantage as the *I-400*s—they had to surface before launching, making them vulnerable to attack.

The successful development of the underwater-launched Polaris missile put an end to the Regulus program. Nevertheless, Regulus missile subs were clearly a strategic descendant of the *I-400*s. Other accounts suggest *I-400* sub design was incorporated into the U.S. Navy's next generation of Tang class submarines, just as Wernher von Braun's V-2 program became the backbone for later U.S. ballistic missile and space programs. This probably gives the technology more credit than it warrants. Still, the *I-400*s proved it was possible to build a stealthy and stable underwater launch platform when it came to developing nuclear missile submarines.

LEGACY

A new Japan arose out of the ashes of World War II. Her postwar constitution mandates she remain a pacifist, nonnuclear nation, with a military deterrent focused solely on defense. Despite this fact, Japan's military budget in 2010 was the sixth largest in the world, behind the United States, China, France, the U.K., and Russia.[55] Though the U.S. security umbrella protects the Japanese from aggressors, it has made for an oddly reliant relationship. While by no means a vassal state, Japan is not wholly independent either, especially where national defense is concerned. Sixty-six years after the war ended, the United States remains "the dominant military force in the Pacific" and continues to wield a strong military, cultural, and economic influence on Japan.[56] It is precisely this fear of U.S. hegemony that drove Japan to attack Pearl Harbor in the first place. It also explains the strong nationalistic streak alive in some parts of Japan today. The United States even exercises wide influence over Japan's submarine force. For example, the JMSDF relies on diesel subs, even though it could easily afford to buy and operate nuclear ones. The U.S. military prefers it this way.

The Imperial Japanese Navy's dream of launching airplanes from a submarine was not as easily frustrated. This legacy is surprising, considering that the *Sen-toku* force saw only eight months of service between commissioning and surrender: its *Seiran* never flew in combat; its subs never fired a shot in anger; it attacked not a single enemy. But that didn't make a difference for the men who served on the subs and planes. They were prepared to die nonetheless.

It's not particularly strange, then, that the Naval General Staff's plan to bomb New York and Washington, D.C., the Panama Canal, and Ulithi is so little known. Cold war secrecy has something to do with it, as does failure. But the chief reason the *I-400s'* story is not well known is that victors rarely celebrate their enemy's courage and determination.

There are few signs today that the *I-400s* ever existed. Several items can be found in personal collections and in one or two institutions, including the USS *Bowfin* Submarine Museum at Pearl Harbor. Among the objects scattered among various prize crew members are a bridge compass, a barometer, a sword, *Seiran* aircrew insignia, uniform buttons, personal mail, chopsticks, a teacup, and the notes (written in English) that *I-401* officers used to negotiate the sub's surrender with Captain Johnson. Additional objects have been auctioned on eBay.

Among the relics thought to have been destroyed when the war ended were the *I-400s'* blueprints. The author stumbled upon the only existing set during a visit to a naval base in Japan. While discussing the *I-400s* with the base's commandant, a staff officer mentioned a box that had recently been given to them when its owner, a former IJN engineer, died. Inside the box was a complete set of the *I-400s'* plans, meticulously drawn on wax-coated silk. The engineer had taken the plans when the war ended and kept them at his house for safe keeping. Since orders had been given to destroy the blueprints at the end of the war, the staff officer had not returned them to Self Defense headquarters in Tokyo. By an accident of history, the *I-400s* continue to live.

For the most part, however, the subs are considered a historical footnote. Their story is better known in Japan (where you can build a nifty model of the *I-400* and a *Seiran*), but not by much. It mostly lives in the memories of the few surviving crew members, who are rapidly dying off. For the younger generation, World War II is about as relevant as the Hundred Years' War. Most have never heard of the *I-400*s.

The moral of the story, that courage and perseverance are not enough, is difficult to absorb. The commitment of Ariizumi, Nambu, and the *Sen-toku* crew could not overcome the poor strategic and operational planning of the IJN High Command. Both the Allies and the Japanese believed theirs was a just cause, but it takes more than sentiment to win a war. Advanced technology, adaptive ability, production efficiencies, and superior logistics are also necessary for success.

That the *I-400* subs failed in their mission is less important than the fact that they got as far as they did, given the daunting obstacles they faced. In other words, the story of the *Sen-toku* subs is about determination in the face of overwhelming odds. Yes, the storm from a clear sky never materialized as predicted, but it wasn't for want of trying.

ACKNOWLEDGMENTS

This project might never have happened if my editor at *Aviation History* magazine, Carl von Wodtke, hadn't had the courage to greenlight my story about the *I-400* subs and their *Seiran* aircraft. Still, a work of nonfiction is impossible to write without the cooperation of many people. Accordingly, I'd like to thank the following:

Martin Bennett; Dick Budzienny (in Australia); Tom and Lisa Cohen; Frits de Jong (in the Netherlands); Charles J. Doane; John W. Dower, Ford International Professor of [Japanese] History at MIT; David Dugan, Chairman of Windfall Films, Ltd.; George Gambel; Dr. Sara L. Gandy; Robert D. Hackett of Combinedfleet .com; Adam Hochschild at the Berkeley Graduate School of Journalism; Patrick Householder, national commander of United States Submarine Veterans, Inc.; Sander Kingsepp of Combinedfleet .com; Kevin Leonard of The Leonard Group; Robert C. Mikesh; Rich "Pete" Peterson, webmaster at Segundo398.org; Adm. (ret.) Maurice H. Rindskopf; Sam Saliba; Anna Saraceno and Eric Stange at Spy Pond Productions; Alan Tansman at the University of California, Berkeley; William Thibodeaux; and Norma Whitmire.

My mother, Margaret Geoghegan, offered me important moral and financial support throughout this project. Tom and Maggie Bedecarré generously provided me with a place to stay while I was completing the book; Toshiko Ozasayama believed in me despite my many failings; Hazuki Yoshino babysat and made travel arrangements; and Beth Geoghegan put me up for a month when I had no place else to go. Importantly, my brother, Michael Geoghegan, provided me with his love, support, and wisdom through every step of the process. I couldn't have done it without him.

I also owe a special debt to my interviewer/researchers, Yayoi and Takuji Ozasayama, and to my translators: Marie Abe, Laura Keehn,

Reiko Konitzer, Robin Colomb Sugiura, Yumi Kijima, and Erika Römer. Special thanks also go to my readers Kirk Citron, who suffered an early draft; Norman Polmar, columnist for the U.S. Naval Institute; Professor Emeritus Carl Boyd, Old Dominion University; Oliver Mittermaier; Jonathan Parshall; Bob McLean; Emil Petrinic; and my *sensei,* Rear Adm. (ret.) Yoichi Hirama. Illustrator and photographer Emil Petrinic rendered an exceptionally fine map and cutaway diagram of the *I-400* sub, and shot the author photograph. Thanks also to Robert Hanshew, museum curator, Photographs at the Naval History and Heritage Command in Washington, D.C., for his assistance in selecting photographs for this book.

In Japan, I'd like to thank Ken Dota, who was a tremendous help tracking down people and setting up interviews, as well as Izumi Fuji; Toshio Ichiki; Junya Katsume; Tohru Kizu, editor in chief/director at *Ships of the World;* Hiro Nagashima; Tetsukuni Watanabe; and Nobutaka Nambu, for helping me to better understand his father's long and distinguished life. I'd also like to thank Iroha-kai (Japan's Submarine Veterans Association), the *Mikasa* Preservation Society, as well as the Japanese Naval Academy (Etajima) and both Togo and Yasukuni shrines.

The Japanese Maritime Self Defense Force was also helpful in assisting my research. I'd like to extend my heartfelt appreciation to Vice Adm. (ret.) Mitsunori Akeno; Rear Adm. Izuru Fukumoto, chief of staff and commandant of Kure District, JMSDF; Rear Adm. (ret.) Masao Ikemura, secretary general of Suikou Kai (Japan Naval Association); Capt. (ret.) Greg K. Kouta; Capt. Sanji Nyui, commander of Submarine Flotilla Two, Yokosuka, JMSDF; Capt. Tahiko Tanaka, commanding officer of the Submarine Training Center, JMSDF, Kure; and his senior staff officer.

Obviously, there would have been no book without the kindness and cooperation of the *Sen-toku* squadron's officers and crew. I would like to thank the *I-401*'s captain, Nobukiyo Nambu, for his graciousness and candor. Additionally, Yoshio Andoh, Muneo Bando, Chin-Ji Inouye, and Tsugio Yata, all of the *I-401*, opened their homes and were extremely generous with their time and patience in answering my questions. Atsushi Asamura and Heiji Kondo, both of the 631st air group, also spent significant time with me, for which I am grateful.

I also want to thank the *I-400*'s officers and crew for speaking with me, including Fukumaru Koshimoto, Shoici Matsutani, Izumi Fuji (daughter of Hidetoshi Namura), Masami Nariari, Kazuo Nishijima, Masao Okui, Sutejiro Shimazu, Haruo Sugiyama, and Kazuo Takatsu, as well as Chikanori Hatanaka of the 631st air group.

An equally hearty thanks is extended to the officers and crew of the USS *Segundo* (SS 398) for speaking with me, including: John Balson, Richard Binkley, Carlo Carlucci, Leon Crouse, Vic Horgan, Rod Johnson, Wallace Karnes, Jr., Harry McCartney, Robert O'Connor, Bud Quam, and Carl Stallcop. Many of their family members also deserve thanks, including Miriam Miller Balson, Mrs. Richard Binkley, Mike Carlucci, Suze Johnson Comerford, Lynne Fulp, Mary Lee Horgan, Nadia M. Johnson, Steve Johnson, Jr., Marge McCartney, Carolie McLaughlin, and Karen Pittman.

I'm also grateful to the U.S. prize crews and their families for allowing me to interview them, including Harry Arvidson (*I-400*), Lynda Arvidson Cambron, Gordon Hiatt (*I-400*), Dave Johnson (whose father was a member of the *I-400*'s prize crew), Donald Pierson (*I-401*), Lou Reynolds (*I-14*), and Paul Wittmer (*I-401*).

Special mention should also be made of three texts that proved crucial to my understanding of the *Sen-toku* subs and their crew. The first is Lt. Cdr. Nobukiyo Nambu's memoir, *Beikidoukantai wo Kishuseyo: Sensuikuubo I-401 Kanchou No Shuki* [*Surprise Attack on the American Fleet! Memoir of the I-401 Aircraft-Carrying Submarine by Its Captain*] (Tokyo: Fuami Shobo, 1988). Next is Tsugio Sato's history of the *Sen-toku* force, *Maboroshi no Sensui Kubo* [*Phantom Submarine Carrier*] (Tokyo: Kabushiki Gaisha Kojin-sha, 1989). And finally, Ens. Kazuo Takahashi's memoir, *Shinryu Tokubetsu Kogekitai* [*Divine Dragon Special Attack Unit*] (Tokyo: Koujinsha, 2001). These three books proved immensely helpful in helping me parse fact from myth.

At the University of Hawaii's Hawaii Undersea Research Laboratory (HURL), I'd like to thank Max Cremer; operations manager

Terry Kerby, who showed me what life was like inside a deepwater submersible—I want one of those coffee cups, Terry; Rachel S. Orange; Steven L. Price; and Dr. John C. Wiltshire.

At the Smithsonian Institution's National Air and Space Museum, I'd like to thank Tom D. Crouch, senior curator of the Division of Aeronautics; and Robert M. McLean, Jr., and Matthew Nazzaro, whose loving and historically accurate restoration of the world's only *Seiran* is a feast for the eyes. Bob once told me, "Translating English and Japanese aeronautical terms is fraught with error, and requires a Zen-like comparative analysis of what is actually being said." My sentiments exactly. Frank McNally and Brian Mullen, also at the Smithsonian, graciously provided me access to the collection.

At the USS *Pampanito* (SS 383) in San Francisco, a beautifully restored Balao-class submarine, I'd like to thank Neil Chaitin, Diane Cooper, Bill Parker (who answered my numerous questions about Balao-class submarines without complaint), and Aaron Washington.

The U.S. military provided vital assistance to my research for this book. I am particularly grateful to the U.S. Department of Veterans Affairs; the U.S. National Archives and Records Administration; the National Personnel Records Center, Military Personnel Records Division, St. Louis; and the National Archives, both in Washington, D.C., and in College Park, Maryland.

I enjoyed the full cooperation and support of the U.S. Navy. The Naval History and Heritage Command; the Naval Historical Center; and the Washington Navy Yard in Washington, D.C., were also wonderful resources, but it's the people who make the difference, including Lt. Cdr. Suzanna Brugler, director at the Navy Office of Information in New York City; Navy Reserve Lt. Jonathan Groveman, public affairs specialist in Washington, D.C.; Wendy S. Gulley, archivist at the Submarine Force Museum, Naval Submarine Base, New London; Chris Zendan, public affairs officer, Naval Submarine Base, New London; William Kenny at the Submarine Learning Center Public Affairs Office; Jenny Erickson, public affairs and media relations specialist at the U.S. Naval Academy; Dorothea V. Abbott, librarian of special collections and archives at the U.S.

Naval Academy's Nimitz Library in Annapolis; James W. Cheevers, associate director and senior curator at the U.S. Naval Academy Museum in Annapolis; Skid Heyworth at the U.S. Naval Academy Alumni Association; J. Lloyd Abbot, Jr., president of the U.S. Naval Academy's Class of 1939 Alumni Association; Katie Suich, public affairs specialist at the Navy Personnel Command Communications Office; and Cdr. Patrick W. McNally, public affairs officer for the Submarine Force in Norfolk, Virginia.

Many library archives played a crucial role in helping me with my research. In particular I would like to thank Erin Kimber, information librarian, and Jill Durney, library manager, at the Macmillan Brown Library, University of Canterbury, Christchurch, New Zealand; Yvonne Hudgens at the Greenwood County Library, South Carolina; the Santa Barbara Public Library in Santa Barbara, California; and the Marin and San Mateo County public library systems in California. I'd also like to thank Janis Jorgensen, manager of the Heritage Collection, and Carol Parkinson, editorial production assistant, at the U.S. Naval Institute in Annapolis.

My agent, Jeff Kleinman at Folio Literary Management, read and responded to my book proposal within six hours of receiving it, even though he didn't know me from Adam. That's the longest Jeff's ever taken to respond to something I've sent him. Jeff, you are my hero.

I'd also like to thank my editor at Crown, Sean Desmond, whose sharp eye, discerning red pencil, and unquestionable good taste were crucial to shaping this book. I cooed like a baby in the hands of this professional.

The staff at Crown who saw my book through to completion were also terrific, including editorial assistant Annie Chagnot, designer Lauren Dong, assistant editor Stephanie Knapp, production editor Christine Tanigawa, and production manager Norman Watkins. It goes without saying that I owe a deep personal thanks to Crown's publisher, Molly Stern. God bless the lady who signs the checks.

Finally, I am deeply grateful to the SILOE Research Institute, whose mission to study and report on unusual technologies that fail to find a wider market application despite their innovative nature continues to inspire and nourish me today.

My apologies in advance to anyone I've inadvertently forgotten. As you might expect, any errors found in this book are my responsibility alone.

NOTES

It may seem odd that a topic with a paucity of sources has so many footnotes, but the contradictory nature of some personal accounts, combined with widespread document destruction at the end of the war, necessitates an understanding of where specific quotes, data, and tabular records of movements for the *Sen-toku* squadron come from. Therefore, in the interest of accurately recounting this highly unusual story, I have included as many sources I thought appropriate.

Principal Actors

1. Tsugio Sato, *Maboroshi no Sensui Kubo* [*Phantom Submarine Carrier*] (Tokyo: Kabushiki Gaisha Kojin-sha, 1989), p. 130.

Chapter 1. Face-off

1. USS *Segundo* (SS 398), Fifth War Patrol Report, August 15, 1945, 1305, http://www.segundo398.org/patrol_reports/patrol5.pdf.
2. Victor S. Horgan, interview by author.
3. Ibid.
4. John E. Balson, interview by author.
5. Ibid.
6. *Segundo*, Fifth Patrol Report, August 19, 1945, 2313–25.
7. Richard Binkley, interview by author.
8. Victor S. Horgan, interview by author.
9. Ibid.
10. Ibid.
11. Ibid
12. Ibid.
13. John E. Balson, interview by author.
14. Clay Blair, Jr., *Silent Victory: The U.S. Submarine War against Japan* (Annapolis, Md.: Naval Institute Press, 1975), p. 870.
15. L. Rodney Johnson, interview by author.
16. Victor S. Horgan, interview by author.
17. Ibid.
18. L. Rodney Johnson, interview by author.

19. *Segundo*, Fifth Patrol Report, August 28, 1945, 2353.

20. John E. Balson, interview by author; John E. Balson, interview on KXA radio, Seattle, October 27, 1945.

21. Ibid.

22. USS *Segundo* (SS 398), Fifth War Patrol Report, August 29, 1945, 0007, http://www.segundo398.org/patrol_reports/patrol5.pdf.

23. Leitch, "Chase, Capture, and Boarding."

24. L. Rodney Johnson, interview by author.

25. Victor S. Horgan, interview by author.

26. L. Rodney Johnson, interview by author.

27. Victor S. Horgan, interview by author.

28. Ibid.

29. Ibid.

30. Ibid.

31. *Segundo*, Fifth War Patrol Report, August 29, 1945, 0008.

32. John E. Balson, interview by author; John E. Balson, interview by KXA radio.

33. Ibid.

34. L. Rodney Johnson, interview by author; Victor S. Horgan, interview by author.

35. L. Rodney Johnson, interview by author.

36. John E. Balson, interview by author.

37. Carlo M. Carlucci, interview by author.

38. Ibid.

39. *Segundo*, Fifth War Patrol Report, August 29, 1945, 0417.

40. Ibid., 0419.

41. Norman Polmar and Dorr B. Carpenter, *Submarines of the Imperial Japanese Navy, 1904–1945* (London: Conway Maritime Press, 1986), p. 111.

42. Carl Boyd and Akihiko Yoshida, *The Japanese Submarine Force and World War II* (Shrewsbury, U.K.: Airlife, 1996), p. 37.

43. Ibid.

44. John E. Balson, interview by author; Victor S. Horgan, interview by author.

45. Victor S. Horgan, interview by author.

46. Atsushi Asamura, "*I-401* Sensuikan to Seiran to Watashi [The *I-401* Submarine, Seiran and Me]," *Maru* Special, *Japanese Naval Vessels*, no. 13, 1977, pp. 42–43.

Chapter 2. The *I-401*

1. Norman Polmar and Dorr B. Carpenter, *Submarines of the Imperial Japanese Navy, 1904–1945* (London: Conway Maritime Press, 1986), p. 111.

2. Zenji Orita with Joseph D. Harrington, *I-Boat Captain: How Japan's Submarines Almost Defeated the US Navy in the Pacific!* (Canoga Park, Calif.:

Major Books, 1976), p. 297. Lt. Tsugio Yata says the sub could dive in as little as 44 seconds. See Tsugio Yata, "SubRon 1 . . . Aims for U.S. Fleet at Ulithi and Panama Canal," *I-401 History, I-401* Submarine Society, Japan. Nevertheless, 56 seconds seems a more likely time.

3. Nobukiyo Nambu, *Beikidoukantai wo Kishuseyo: Sensuikuubo I-401 Kanchou No Shuki* [*Surprise Attack on the American Fleet! Memoir of the I-401 Aircraft-Carrying Submarine by Its Captain*] (Tokyo: Fuami Shobo, 1988), p. 187; Lt. Atsushi Asamura, interview, *Rekishi Gunzon,* no. 85, October 10, 2007, Gakken, pp. 154–59.

4. Nambu, *Beikidoukantai wo Kishuseyo,* pp. 226–27.

5. Atsushi Asamura, interview by author; Nambu, *Beikidoukantai wo Kishuseyo,* pp. 223–24; Tsugio Sato, *Maboroshi no Sensui Kubo* [*Phantom Submarine Carrier*] (Tokyo: Kabushiki Gaisha Kojin-sha, 1989), p. 227.

6. Nambu, *Beikidoukantai wo Kishuseyo,* p. 224.

7. Sato, *Maboroshi no Sensui Kubo,* p. 227.

8. Nambu, *Beikidoukantai wo Kishuseyo,* p. 227.

9. Ibid.

10. Ibid.; Sato, *Maboroshi no Sensui Kubo,* p. 228.

11. Nambu, *Beikidoukantai wo Kishuseyo,* p. 228; Sato, *Maboroshi no Sensui Kubo,* p. 228.

12. Nambu, *Beikidoukantai wo Kishuseyo,* p. 227.

13. Ibid.

14. Ibid., p. 231.

15. Sato, *Maboroshi no Sensui Kubo,* p. 232.

16. Orita and Harrington, *I-Boat Captain,* p. 310.

17. Ibid.

18. Ibid.

19. Nobutaka Nambu, interview by author.

20. Nambu, *Beikidoukantai wo Kishuseyo,* p. 236.

21. Sato, *Maboroshi no Sensui Kubo,* pp. 239, 241.

22. Nambu, *Beikidoukantai wo Kishuseyo,* p. 238.

Chapter 3. Birth

1. Hiroyuki Agawa, *The Reluctant Admiral: Yamamoto and the Imperial Navy* (Kodansha International, 2000), p. 233.

2. Ibid., pp. 50, 73.

3. Ibid., p. 21.

4. Ibid., pp. 32, 74.

5. Tsugio Sato, *Maboroshi no Sensui Kubo* [*Phantom Submarine Carrier*] (Tokyo: Kabushiki Gaisha Kojin-sha, 1989), pp. 39–41.

6. Agawa, *Reluctant Admiral,* p. 15.

7. Ibid., p. 36.

8. Ibid., pp. 63, 90.

9. Ibid., p. 57.
10. Ibid., pp. 8, 81.
11. Ibid., p. 217.
12. Ibid., pp. 180–81.
13. Ibid., pp. 1–2.
14. Agawa, *Reluctant Admiral*, p. 2.
15. Ibid., p. 8.
16. Ibid., p. 189.
17. Sato, *Maboroshi no Sensui Kubo*, p. 40.
18. M. G. Sheftall, *Blossoms in the Wind: Human Legacies of the Kamikaze* (New York: NAL Caliber, 2006), p. 362. Yamamoto was also concerned about Japan's unique vulnerability. See Agawa, *Reluctant Admiral*, p. 127.
19. Agawa, *Reluctant Admiral*, p. 127; Sato, *Maboroshi no Sensui Kubo*, p. 44.
20. Sato, *Maboroshi no Sensui Kubo*, p. 41.
21. Agawa, *Reluctant Admiral*, p. 91; Nobukiyo Nambu, *Beikidoukantai wo Kishuseyo: Sensuikuubo I-401 Kanchou No Shuki* [*Surprise Attack on the American Fleet! Memoir of the I-401 Aircraft-Carrying Submarine by Its Captain*] (Tokyo: Fuami Shobo, 1988), p. 58.
22. Sato, *Maboroshi no Sensui Kubo*, p. 46.
23. Ibid.
24. Agawa, *Reluctant Admiral*, p. 194, 196; Sato, *Maboroshi no Sensui Kubo*, p. 46.
25. Sato, *Maboroshi no Sensui Kubo*, pp. 48–49.
26. Ibid.
27. Nambu, *Beikidoukantai wo Kishuseyo*, p. 187.
28. Thomas S. Momiyama, "All and Nothing," *Air & Space*, Smithsonian, October–November 2001, p. 28.
29. Nambu, *Beikidoukantai wo Kishuseyo*, p. 192; U.S. Naval Technical Mission to Japan, *Reports of the U.S. Naval Technical Mission to Japan*, Series S: *Ship and Related Targets*, Index no. S-01-1: *Characteristics of Japanese Naval Vessels*, Article I: *Submarines* (Washington, D.C.: Operational Archives, U.S. Navy History Division, 1946), p. 8.
30. Robert C. Mikesh, *Aichi M6A1 Seiran: Japan's Submarine Launched Panama Canal Bomber* (Boylston, Mass.: Monogram Aviation Publications, 1975), p. 12.
31. Nambu, *Beikidoukantai wo Kishuseyo*, p. 192.
32. John D. Alden, *The Fleet Submarine in the U.S. Navy: A Design and Construction History* (Annapolis, Md.: Naval Institute Press, 1979), p. 3:101.
33. Ibid.
34. Ibid.
35. Ibid., p. 190.
36. Alden, *Fleet Submarine in the U.S. Navy*, p. 3:101.
37. Norman Polmar and Dorr B. Carpenter, *Submarines of the Imperial Japanese Navy 1904–1945* (London: Conway Maritime Press, 1986), p. 111.
38. Nambu, *Beikidoukantai wo Kishuseyo*, p. 186.

39. Carl Boyd and Akihiko Yoshida, *The Japanese Submarine Force and World War II* (Shrewsbury, U.K.: Airlife, 1996), pp. 28–29.
40. Nambu, *Beikidoukantai wo Kishuseyo*, p. 179.
41. Ibid., p. 167; Sato, *Maboroshi no Sensui Kubo*, p. 177.
42. Sato, *Maboroshi no Sensui Kubo*, p. 52.
43. Nambu, *Beikidoukantai wo Kishuseyo*, p. 179.
44. Ibid., p. 180.
45. Ibid., p. 179.

Chapter 4. Nambu

1. Carl Boyd and Akihiko Yoshida, *The Japanese Submarine Force and World War II* (Shrewsbury, U.K.: Airlife, 1996), p. 25.
2. Zenji Orita with Joseph D. Harrington, *I-Boat Captain: How Japan's Submarines Almost Defeated the U.S. Navy in the Pacific!* (Canoga Park, Calif.: Major Books, 1976), p. 40.
3. Ibid.
4. Ibid.
5. "California and the Second World War: The Attack on the SS *Larry Doheny*," California State Military History Museum, http://www .militarymuseum.org/LarryDoheny.html; Bob Hackett and Sander Kinsepp, "Sensuikan! HIJMS Submarine *I-17*, Tabular Record of Movement," CombinedFleet.com, http://www.combinedfleet.com/I-17.htm.
6. Nobukiyo Nambu, *Beikidoukantai wo Kishuseyo: Sensuikuubo I-401 Kanchou No Shuki* [*Surprise Attack on the American Fleet! Memoir of the I-401 Aircraft-Carrying Submarine by Its Captain*] (Tokyo: Fuami Shobo, 1988), p. 42.
7. Ibid.
8. According to Nambu, the shelling of Johnston and Palmyra Islands was canceled.
9. Orita and Harrington, *I-Boat Captain*, p. 41.
10. Clark G. Reynolds, "Submarine Attacks on the Pacific Coast, 1942," *Pacific Historical Review* 33 (May 1964), p. 186.
11. Nambu, *Beikidoukantai wo Kishuseyo*, p. 35.
12. Orita and Harrington, *I-Boat Captain*, p. 53.
13. Nambu, *Beikidoukantai wo Kishuseyo*, p. 42.
14. Ibid.
15. Clark G. Reynolds, "Submarine Attacks on the Pacific Coast, 1942," pp. 183–93.
16. Justin M. Ruhge, *The Western Front: The War Years in Santa Barbara County, 1937–1946* (Goleta, Calif.: Quantum Imaging Associates, 1989), p. 3–1.
17. Patrick J. O'Hara, "History: Bombs Over Ellwood," *Santa Barbara Magazine*, May–June 1991, p. 24.
18. Nambu, *Beikidoukantai wo Kishuseyo*, p. 43. It was February 23, U.S. time.

19. Orita and Harrington, *I-Boat Captain*, p. 53.

20. "California and the Second World War: The Shelling of Ellwood," California State Military Museum, http://www.militarymuseum.org/ Ellwood.html; Walker A. Tompkins, *Santa Barbara History Makers* (Santa Barbara, Calif.: McNally & Loftin, 1983), pp. 161–65, 304–306.

21. Reynolds, "Submarine Attacks on the Pacific Coast," p. 184.

22. Orita and Harrington, *I-Boat Captain*, p. 53.

23. Nambu, *Beikidoukantai wo Kishuseyo*, p. 43.

24. Ibid., p. 43; Orita and Harrington, *I-Boat Captain*, p. 53.

25. "Japanese Carry War to California Coast," *Life* 12, no. 10 (March 9, 1942), p. 20.

26. Nambu, *Beikidoukantai wo Kishuseyo*, p. 43.

27. Orita and Harrington, *I-Boat Captain*, p. 53.

28. Nambu, *Beikidoukantai wo Kishuseyo*, p. 44.

29. Ibid.

30. Reynolds, "Submarine Attacks on the Pacific Coast," p. 188.

31. Ibid.

32. Nambu, *Beikidoukantai wo Kishuseyo*, p. 44.

33. Ibid.

34. Orita and Harrington, *I-Boat Captain*, p. 54; Nambu, *Beikidoukantai wo Kishuseyo*, p. 44.

35. The gun size was 140mm.

36. Boyd and Yoshida, *Japanese Submarine Force*, p. 38.

37. "California and the Second World War: The Shelling of Ellwood," California State Military Museum, http://www.militarymuseum.org/ Ellwood.html.

38. Reynolds, "Submarine Attacks on the Pacific Coast," pp. 184–89.

39. "Japanese Carry War to California Coast," *Life* 12, no. 10 (March 9, 1942), p. 20.

40. Ibid.

41. Ibid.

42. Ibid.

43. Nambu, *Beikidoukantai wo Kishuseyo*, p. 45.

44. Ibid., p. 46.

45. James Anderson, "1942 Shelling of California Coastline Stirred Conspiracy Fears." *Los Angeles Times*, March 1, 1992.

46. "California and the Second World War: The Shelling of Ellwood," California State Military Museum, http://www.militarymuseum.org/ Ellwood.html.

47. Ibid.

48. Reynolds, "Submarine Attacks on the Pacific Coast," p. 189.

49. Justin M. Ruhge, *The Western Front: The War Years in Santa Barbara County, 1937–1946* (Santa Barbara, Calif.: Quantum Imaging Associates, 1989), pp. 3–5.

50. Ibid.

51. Ibid.

52. Nambu, *Beikidoukantai wo Kishuseyo*, p. 46.

53. George W. Edmonds, ". . . and the Shells Came," *Noticias* [Santa Barbara Historical Society], Spring 1961, pp. 3–4.

54. Reynolds, "Submarine Attacks on the Pacific Coast," p. 189.

55. Orita and Harrington, *I-Boat Captain*, p. 54.

56. Nambu, *Beikidoukantai wo Kishuseyo*, p. 46.

57. Ibid., p. 47.

58. "Japanese Carry War to California Coast," *Life* 12, no. 10 (March 9, 1942), p. 23.

59. Donald J. Young, "Phantom Japanese Raid on Los Angeles During World War II," *World War II,* September 2003; online at http://www.history net.com/phantom-japanese-raid-on-los-angeles-during-world-war-ii.htm.

60. Ibid.

61. "California and the Second World War: The Shelling of Ellwood," California State Military Museum, http://www.militarymuseum.org/ Ellwood.html.

62. Young, "Phantom Japanese Raid."

63. Ibid.

64. Ibid.

65. "Shelling of Ellwood," California State Military Museum.

66. "Japanese Carry War to California Coast."

67. "The Great Los Angeles Air Raid of 1942: An Exciting Re-creation of a Historic Controversy," http://www.theairraid.com/.

68. Young, "Phantom Japanese Raid."

69. "Japanese Carry War to California Coast."

70. "Great Los Angeles Air Raid."

71. "Shelling of Ellwood," California State Military Museum.

72. "Japanese Carry War to California Coast."

73. Young, "Phantom Japanese Raid."

74. *Los Angeles Times,* February 25, 1942, p. 1.

75. "Japanese Carry War to California Coast."

76. Young, "Phantom Japanese Raid."

77. Ibid.

78. "Great Los Angeles Air Raid."

79. Boyd and Yoshida, *Japanese Submarine Force,* p. 68.

80. Bob Hackett and Sander Kingsepp, "Sensuikan! HIJMS Submarine *I-17,* Tabular Record of Movement," CombinedFleet.com, http://www .combinedfleet.com/I-17.htm.

Chapter 5. Underwater Aircraft Carriers

1. W. J. Holmes, *Undersea Victory: The Influence of Submarine Operations on the War in the Pacific* (Garden City, N.Y.: Doubleday, 1966), p. xiii.

2. Tsugio Sato, *Maboroshi no Sensui Kubo* [*Phantom Submarine Carrier*] (Tokyo: Kabushiki Gaisha Kojin-sha, 1989), p. 135.

3. Ibid., p. 57.

4. Ibid.; Thomas S. Momiyama, "All and Nothing," *Air & Space*, Smithsonian, October–November 2001, p. 24.

5. Robert C. Mikesh, *Aichi M6A1 Seiran: Japan's Submarine-Launched Panama Canal Bomber*, Close-Up 13 (Boylston, Mass.: Monogram Aviation Publications, 1975), p. 2.

6. Ibid.

7. Ibid.

8. Ibid., p. 27.

9. Ibid., p. 2.

10. Walter J. Boyne, ed., *Air Warfare: An International Encyclopedia* (Santa Barbara, Calif.: ABC-CLIO, 2002), p. 12.

11. Mikesh, *Aichi M6A1 Seiran*, p. 2.

12. Ibid., p. 6.

13. Sato, *Maboroshi no Sensui Kubo*, p. 118.

14. Mikesh, *Aichi M6A1 Seiran*, p. 4; Momiyama, "All and Nothing," p. 24.

15. Mikesh, *Aichi M6A1 Seiran*, p. 4.

16. Ibid., p. 5.

17. Ibid.

18. Ibid., p. 6.

19. Ibid.

20. Sato, *Maboroshi no Sensui Kubo*, p. 136.

21. Momiyama, "All and Nothing," p. 25.

22. Mikesh, *Aichi M6A1 Seiran*, p. 2.

23. Henry Sakaida, Gary Nila, and Koji Takaki, *I-400: Japan's Secret Aircraft-Carrying Strike Submarine, Objective Panama Canal* (East Sussex, U.K.: Hikoki , 2006), p. 19.

24. Sato, *Maboroshi no Sensui Kubo*, p. 62.

25. Ibid., p. 70.

26. Ibid.

27. R. Kissinger, Jr., *I-400, I-401 Japanese Submarines, Description of Hull, General Arrangements, and Characteristics* (U.S. Navy, 1946), p. 4.

28. Tadeusz Januszewski, *Japanese Submarine Aircraft* (Redbourn, U.K.: Mushroom Model Publications, 2002), p. 4. The U-boat was the U-12.

29. Richard Compton-Hall, *Submarine Warfare: Monsters and Midgets* (Dorset, U.K.: Blanford Press, 1985), p. 59.

30. Ibid., p. 60.

31. Ibid.

32. Clay Blair, Jr., *Silent Victory: The U.S. Submarine War Against Japan* (Annapolis, Md.: Naval Institute Press, 1975), p. 54.

33. Norman Polmar, interview by author.

34. Compton-Hall, *Submarine Warfare*, p. 59.

35. Ibid., p. 60.

36. Ibid., pp. 63, 59.

37. Ibid., p. 63.

38. Ibid., p. 50.

39. Ibid., p. 51.

40. Ibid.

41. Zenji Orita and Joseph D. Harrington, *I-Boat Captain: How Japan's Submarines Almost Defeated the U.S. Navy in the Pacific!* (Canoga Park, Calif.: Major Books, 1976), p. 111.

42. Compton-Hall, *Submarine Warfare*, p. 65.

43. Orita and Harrington, *I-Boat Captain*, p. 111; Januszewski, *Japanese Submarine Aircraft*, pp. 15–16.

44. Carl Boyd and Akihiko Yoshida, *The Japanese Submarine Force and World War II* (Shrewsbury, U.K.: Airlife, 1996), p. 21.

45. Compton-Hall, *Submarine Warfare*, p. 65.

46. Boyd and Yoshida, *Japanese Submarine Force*, p. 22.

47. Compton-Hall, *Submarine Warfare*, p. 65.

48. Ibid.

49. Boyd and Yoshida, *Japanese Submarine Force*, pp. 24–25. These subs were the *I-15*, *I-17*, *I-19*, *I-21*, *I-23*, and *I-25* through *I-39*.

50. Ibid., p. 23. These subs were the *I-9* through *I-11*.

51. Ibid.

52. Mochitsura Hashimoto, *Sunk!* (New York: Avon, 1954), p. 36.

53. Holmes, *Undersea Victory*, p. 43; Hashimoto, *Sunk!*, p. 36.

54. Forest Garner, "Submarines of the Imperial Japanese Navy," CombinedFleet.com, http://www.combinedfleet.com/ss.htm.

Chapter 6. Proof of Concept

1. Zenji Orita and Joseph D. Harrington, *I-Boat Captain: How Japan's Submarines Almost Defeated the U.S. Navy in the Pacific!* (Canoga Park, Calif.: Major Books, 1976), p. 113.

2. Tsugio Sato, *Maboroshi no Sensui Kubo* [*Phantom Submarine Carrier*] (Tokyo: Kabushiki Gaisha Kojin-sha, 1989), p. 38.

3. Tadeusz Januszewski, *Japanese Submarine Aircraft* (Redbourn, U.K.: Mushroom Model Publications, 2002), p. 44.

4. Orita and Harrington, *I-Boat Captain*, pp. 110–11.

5. Ibid., p. 110; Nobuo Fujita and Joseph D. Harrington, "I Bombed the USA," *U.S. Naval Institute Proceedings*, June 1961, p. 65.

6. Fujita and Harrington, "I Bombed the USA," p. 64.

7. Orita and Harrington, *I-Boat Captain*, pp. 111–12.

8. Fujita and Harrington, "I Bombed the USA," p. 66.

9. Ibid.

10. "Prince Takamatsu," Wikipedia, http://en.wikipedia.org/wiki/Prince _Takamatsu.
11. Fujita and Harrington, "I Bombed the USA," pp. 66–67.
12. Ibid., p. 67.
13. Sato, *Maboroshi no Sensui Kubo*, p. 36.
14. Fujita and Harrington, "I Bombed the USA," p. 65; Sato, *Maboroshi no Sensui Kubo*, p. 36.
15. Orita and Harrington, *I-Boat Captain*, p. 112.
16. Fujita and Harrington, "I Bombed the USA," p. 65.
17. Ibid.
18. Ibid.
19. Ibid.
20. Ibid., p. 67.
21. Orita and Harrington, *I-Boat Captain*, p. 116.
22. Fujita remembers it as the *Ryuho*. Orita, however, says it was the *Chitose*. Since Fujita was there, his recollection seems most reliable.
23. Fujita and Harrington, "I Bombed the USA," p. 67.
24. Robert C. Mikesh, *Aichi M6A1 Seiran: Japan's Submarine Launched Panama Canal Bomber*, Close-Up 13 (Boylston, Mass.: Monogram Aviation Publications, 1975), p. 2.
25. Orita and Harrington, *I-Boat Captain*, p. 115.
26. Fujita and Harrington, "I Bombed the USA," p. 67.
27. Ibid., p. 64.
28. Ibid.
29. Ibid.
30. Ibid.
31. Orita and Harrington, *I-Boat Captain*, p. 114.
32. Fujita and Harrington, "I Bombed the USA," p. 64.
33. Ibid.
34. Tadeusz Januszewski, *Japanese Submarine Aircraft* (Redbourn, U.K.: Mushroom Model Publications, 2002), p. 35.
35. Orita and Harrington, *I-Boat Captain*, p. 115.
36. Fujita and Harrington, "I Bombed the USA," p. 64.
37. "Japanese Submarine Attacks on Curry County in World War II," Port Orford Heritage Society, 2000, http://www.portorfordlifeboatstation.org/article1.html.
38. Ibid.
39. Fujita and Harrington, "I Bombed the USA," p. 67; Orita and Harrington, *I-Boat Captain*, p. 115.
40. Orita and Harrington, *I-Boat Captain*, p. 115.
41. Fujita and Harrington, "I Bombed the USA," p. 67.
42. Ibid.
43. Orita and Harrington, *I-Boat Captain*, p. 116.
44. Fujita and Harrington, "I Bombed the USA," p. 67.
45. Ibid., p. 68.

46. Ibid.
47. Orita and Harrington, *I-Boat Captain,* p. 116.
48. Fujita and Harrington, "I Bombed the USA," p. 68.
49. Ibid.
50. Fujita and Harrington, "I Bombed the USA," p. 68.
51. Ibid.
52. Ibid.
53. Nicholas D. Kristof, "Nobuo Fujita, 85, Is Dead; Only Foe to Bomb America," *New York Times,* October 3, 1977.

Chapter 7. Challenges

1. Tsugio Sato, *Maboroshi no Sensui Kubo* [*Phantom Submarine Carrier*] (Tokyo: Kabushiki Gaisha Kojin-sha, 1989), pp. 72, 100.
2. Shizuo Fukui, *Japanese Naval Vessels at the End of the War,* Administrative Division, Second Demobilization Bureau, April 25, 1947, p. 36.
3. Sato, *Maboroshi no Sensui Kubo,* p. 135.
4. Fukui, *Japanese Naval Vessels at the End of the War,* p. 36.
5. Norman Polmar and Dorr B. Carpenter, *Submarines of the Imperial Japanese Navy 1904–1945* (London: Conway Maritime Press, 1986), p. 110.
6. Sato, *Maboroshi no Sensui Kubo,* p. 62.
7. Robert C. Mikesh, *Aichi M6A1 Seiran: Japan's Submarine Launched Panama Canal Bomber,* Close-Up 13 (Boylston, Mass.: Monogram Aviation Publications, 1975), p. 3.
8. Ibid.
9. Ibid., p. 2.
10. Ibid., p. 3.
11. Ibid., p. 4.
12. Sato, *Maboroshi no Sensui Kubo,* p. 62; Mikesh, *Aichi M6A1 Seiran,* p. 5.
13. Nambu, *Beikidoukantai wo Kishuseyo,* p. 183.
14. Sato, *Maboroshi no Sensui Kubo,* p. 71, quoting Shojiro Iura.
15. Ibid.
16. Ibid., p. 70.
17. Ibid., p. 71.
18. W. J. Holmes, *Undersea Victory: The Influence of Submarine Operations on the War in the Pacific* (Garden City, N.Y.: Doubleday, 1966), p. 221.

Chapter 8. Reduction and Revival

1. W. J. Holmes, *Undersea Victory: The Influence of Submarine Operations on the War in the Pacific* (Garden City, N.Y.: Doubleday, 1966), p. 221.
2. Tsugio Sato, *Maboroshi no Sensui Kubo* [*Phantom Submarine Carrier*] (Tokyo: Kabushiki Gaisha Kojin-sha, 1989), p. 74.

3. U.S. Strategic Bombing Survey (Pacific), Naval Analysis Division, *Interrogations of Japanese Officials: Submarine Warfare*, p. 294.
4. Sato, *Maboroshi no Sensui Kubo*, p. 73.
5. Ibid., p. 74.
6. Ibid., p. 73.
7. Ibid., p. 82.
8. Ibid., p. 79.
9. Ibid., pp. 80, 134.
10. Ibid., p. 74.
11. Ibid., p. 80.
12. Ibid., p. 75.
13. Ibid., p. 88.
14. Ibid., p. 89.
15. Ibid.
16. Ibid.

Chapter 9. Nambu Under Fire

1. Nobukiyo Nambu, *Beikidoukantai wo Kishuseyo: Sensuikuubo I-401 Kanchou No Shuki* [*Surprise Attack on the American Fleet! Memoir of the I-401 Aircraft-Carrying Submarine by Its Captain*] (Tokyo: Fuami Shobo, 1988), p. 59.
2. Ibid., p. 63. Boys Day is known in Japanese as *Tango No Sekku*.
3. Nambu, *Beikidoukantai wo Kishuseyo*, p. 64.
4. Muneo Bando, interview by author.
5. Nambu, *Beikidoukantai wo Kishuseyo*, p. 25.
6. Ibid.
7. David Stevens, *A Critical Vulnerability: The Impact of the Submarine Threat on Australia's Maritime Defense 1915–1954* (Canberra, Australia: Department of Defence, Sea Power Centre, 2005, 1943), pp. 233–35, http://www.navy.gov.au/w/images/PIAMA15_ch8.pdf.
8. Nambu, *Beikidoukantai wo Kishuseyo*, pp. 68–69.
9. Nambu, *Beikidoukantai wo Kishuseyo*, pp. 74–75.
10. Bob Hackett and Sander Kingsepp, "Sensuikan! IJN Submarine I-174, Tabular Record of Movement," June 4, 1943, CombinedFleet.com, http://www.combinedfleet.com/I-174.htm.
11. Nambu, *Beikidoukantai wo Kishuseyo*, pp. 74–75.
12. Ibid., pp. 76–77.
13. Stevens, *Critical Vulnerability*, p. 233.
14. Hackett and Kingsepp, "IJN Submarine I-174," June 4, 1943.
15. Robert Wallace, *The Secret Battle 1942–1944: The Convoy Battle off the East Coast of Australia During World War II* (Ringwood, Australia: Lamont, 1995), p. 85.
16. Nambu, *Beikidoukantai wo Kishuseyo*, pp. 78–80.

17. Wallace, *Secret Battle 1942–1944*, p. 85.

18. Nambu, *Beikidoukantai wo Kishuseyo*, p. 78.

19. Stevens, *Critical Vulnerability*, p. 233.

20. Nambu, *Beikidoukantai wo Kishuseyo*, p. 80.

21. Stevens, *Critical Vulnerability*, pp. 233–35.

22. Ibid.

23. Wallace, *Secret Battle*, p. 87.

Chapter 10. Nambu Becomes a Mole

1. Zenji Orita and Joseph D. Harrington, *I-Boat Captain: How Japan's Submarines Almost Defeated the U.S. Navy in the Pacific!* (Canoga Park, Calif.: Major Books, 1976), p. 167.

2. Nobukiyo Nambu, interview by author.

3. Richard N. Billings, *Battleground Atlantic* (New York: NAL Caliber, 2006), p. 19.

4. Nobukiyo Nambu, *Beikidoukantai wo Kishuseyo: Sensuikuubo I-401 Kanchou No Shuki* [*Surprise Attack on the American Fleet! Memoir of the I-401 Aircraft-Carrying Submarine by Its Captain*] (Tokyo: Fuami Shobo, 1988), p. 83.

5. Carl Boyd and Akihiko Yoshida, *The Japanese Submarine Force and World War II* (Shrewsbury, U.K.: Airlife, 1996), p. 105.

6. Orita and Harrington, *I-Boat Captain*, p. 176.

7. Mochitsura Hashimoto, *Sunk!* (New York: Avon, 1954), p. 70.

8. Masanori Ito, *The End of the Imperial Japanese Navy: A Japanese Account of the Rise and Fall of Japan's Seapower* (New York: Macfadden Books, 1965), p. 67.

9. Hashimoto, *Sunk!*, p. 70.

10. Orita and Harrington, *I-Boat Captain*, p. 171.

11. Hashimoto, *Sunk!*, p. 71.

12. Orita and Harrington, *I-Boat Captain*, p. 170.

13. Ibid., p. 176.

14. Ibid., p. 170.

15. Ibid.; Hashimoto, *Sunk!*, p. 71.

16. Orita and Harrington, *I-Boat Captain*, p. 176.

17. Hashimoto, *Sunk!*, p. 71.

18. Nambu, *Beikidoukantai wo Kishuseyo*, p. 82.

19. Hashimoto, *Sunk!*, p. 94.

20. Ibid., p. 70.

21. Nambu, *Beikidoukantai wo Kishuseyo*, p. 85.

22. Ibid., p. 87.

23. Ibid., p. 88.

24. Ibid., pp. 99–100.

25. Ibid., p. 96.

Chapter 11. *Seiran* Takes Flight

1. Tsugio Sato, *Maboroshi no Sensui Kubo* [*Phantom Submarine Carrier*] (Tokyo: Kabushiki Gaisha Kojin-sha, 1989), p. 72.

2. Ibid. The date was October 2.

3. Ibid. Sato says the *I-404* was to be constructed at the Go Shipyards in Kure; Nambu says Sasebo. Nevertheless, it appears Kure is correct.

4. At least one Japanese and one Western source report that the *I-405* began construction at Kawasaki Heavy Industries. See Seiji Azuma, "Sekai Ni Hirui Naki '*I-400* Gata, *I-13* Gata' No Kouzou to Seinou [The Construction and Efficiency of the Unparalleled *I-400* and *I-13*]," *Maru* Special, *Japanese Naval Vessels*, no. 13 (Tokyo: Kojinsha, 1977), p. 28; Norman Polmar and Dorr B. Carpenter, *Submarines of the Imperial Japanese Navy, 1904–1945* (London: Conway Maritime Press, 1986), p. 111.

5. Nobukiyo Nambu, *Beikidoukantai wo Kishuseyo: Sensuikuubo I-401 Kanchou No Shuki* [*Surprise Attack on the American Fleet! Memoir of the I-401 Aircraft-Carrying Submarine by Its Captain*] (Tokyo: Fuami Shobo, 1988), p. 199, quoting Funada.

6. Thomas S. Momiyama, "All and Nothing," *Air & Space*, Smithsonian, October–November 2001, p. 25,

7. Robert C. Mikesh, *Aichi M6A1 Seiran: Japan's Submarine Launched Panama Canal Bomber*, Close-Up 13 (Boylston, Mass.: Monogram Aviation Publications, 1975), p. 7.

8. Momiyama, "All and Nothing," p. 29.

9. Nambu, *Beikidoukantai wo Kishuseyo*, p. 199.

10. Ibid.; Ikuhiko Hata, *Dainiji Taisen Koukuju Shiwa* [*Historical Aviation Stories of World War II*], trans. Shojo Jonda and Sandy Kita (Japan: Chuukou Bunko, n.d.), chap. 10.

11. Hata, *Dainiji Taisen Koukuju Shiwa*, chap. 10.

12. Nambu, *Beikidoukantai wo Kishuseyo*, p. 200; Hata, *Dainiji Taisen Koukuju Shiwa*, chap. 10.

13. Henry Sakaida, Gary Nila, and Koji Takaki, *I-400: Japan's Secret Aircraft-Carrying Strike Submarine, Objective Panama Canal* (East Sussex, U.K.: Hikoki, 2006), p. 20.

14. Mikesh, *Aichi M6A1 Seiran*, p. 6.

15. Nambu, *Beikidoukantai wo Kishuseyo*, p. 200; Sakaida, Nila, and Takaki, *I-400*, p. 20.

16. Nambu, *Beikidoukantai wo Kishuseyo*, p. 200.

17. Mikesh, *Aichi M6A1 Seiran*, p. 23.

18. Atsushi Asamura, interview by author.

19. Mikesh, *Aichi M6A1 Seiran*, pp. 9, 32. Funada remembers it as 1,300 shp.

20. Ibid., pp. 31, 6.

21. Nambu, *Beikidoukantai wo Kishuseyo*, p. 200; Sato, *Maboroshi no Sensui Kubo*, p. 136; Hata, *Dainiji Taisen Koukuju Shiwa*, chap. 10.

22. Momiyama, "All and Nothing," p. 24.

23. Nambu, *Beikidoukantai wo Kishuseyo,* p. 186.
24. Momiyama, "All and Nothing," p. 24.
25. Kazuo Takahashi, *Shinryu Tokubetsu Kogekitai [Divine Dragon Special Attack Unit]* (Tokyo: Koujinsha Corporation, 2001), p. 158; Mikesh, *Aichi M6A1 Seiran,* p. 9.
26. Mikesh, *Aichi M6A1 Seiran,* inside front cover.
27. Sakaida, Nila, and Takaki, *I-400,* p. 25, quoting Lt. Cmdr. Tadashi Funada's *Development and Records of Famous Aircraft.*

Chapter 12. The Panama Canal

1. Tsugio Sato, *Maboroshi no Sensui Kubo [Phantom Submarine Carrier]* (Tokyo: Kabushiki Gaisha Kojin-sha, 1989), p. 97.
2. Ibid., p. 99.
3. Ibid., p. 97.
4. David McCullough, *The Path Between the Seas* (New York: Simon & Schuster, 1977), p. 606.
5. Sato, *Maboroshi no Sensui Kubo,* pp. 98, 99.
6. Panama Canal Authority, www.pancanal.com.
7. Ibid.
8. McCullough, *Path Between the Seas,* p. 596.
9. Ibid., p. 598.
10. Ibid., p. 596.
11. Ibid.
12. Panama Canal Authority, www.pancanal.com.
13. Ibid.
14. Mark Skinner Watson, *The War Department, Chief of Staff: Prewar Plans & Preparations* (Washington, D.C.: U.S. Army Center of Military History, 1991), p. 459, http://www.history.army.mil/books/wwii/csppp/ch14.htm.
15. McCullough, *Path Between the Seas,* p. 589.
16. "Panama Canal—Defending the Canal," GlobalSecurity.org, 2009, http://www.globalsecurity.org/military/facility/panama-canal-defense.htm.
17. Sato, *Maboroshi no Sensui Kubo,* pp. 98, 99.
18. Ibid., p. 100.
19. Ibid., p. 98.
20. Ibid., p. 75.

Chapter 13. Ariizumi

1. F. de Jong, statement, Document no. 8388, Exhibit no. 2099, p. 1, Macmillan Brown Library, University of Canterbury, Christchurch, New Zealand (hereafter MBL), Archives Reference: MB 1549, Tokyo War Crimes Tribunal, Item 2099, Box 266, Exhibits 1944.

2. Carl Boyd and Akihiko Yoshida, *The Japanese Submarine Force and World War II* (Shrewsbury, U.K.: Airlife, 1996), p. 174.

3. Ibid., p. 128.

4. Tsugio Sato, *Maboroshi no Sensui Kubo* [*Phantom Submarine Carrier*] (Tokyo: Kabushiki Gaisha Kojin-sha, 1989), p. 104.

5. Ulrich Straus, *The Anguish of Surrender: Japanese POWs of World War II* (Seattle: University of Washington Press, 2005), p. 8.

6. Sato, *Maboroshi no Sensui Kubo*, p. 104.

7. Ibid.

8. Masataka Chihaya, "Organization of the Naval General Staff Headquarters in Tokyo," in Donald M. Goldstein and Katherine V. Dillon, eds., *The Pacific War Papers: Japanese Documents of World War II* (Dulles, Va.: Potomac Books, 2005), p. 41.

9. Yamamoto did not approve their inclusion until October 1941.

10. Hiroyuki Agawa, *The Reluctant Admiral: Yamamoto and the Imperial Navy* (Tokyo: Kodansha International, 2000), p. 266.

11. *Hunt for the Samurai Subs*, Wild Life Productions for National Geographic Channel, broadcast in Japan on NHK, 2009.

12. Michael Wilson, *A Submariner's War: The Indian Ocean 1939–1945* (Gloucestershire, U.K.: Spellmount, 2008), p. 100.

13. Jan Dekker, statement, March 15, 1946, Pro Justitia, War Crimes Investigation Unit, Amsterdam, no. 47, p. 2, MBL.

14. Motohide Yanabe, statement, Sugamo Prison, August 30, 1948, p. 3, MBL.

15. Ibid.

16. Motohide Yanabe, letter, Sugamo Prison, August 23, 1948, p. 3, MBL

17. Ibid.

18. Sadao Motonaka to chairman of the Parole Board, Legal Section, GHQ, SCAP, APO 500, September 28, 1950, pp. 1–2, MBL.

19. Dekker statement, MBL; Jiro Nakahara, statement, October 13, 1948, p. 2, MBL.

20. De Jong statement, pp. 3–4, MBL; Nakahara statement, MBL.

21. De Jong statement, pp. 3–4; Nakahara statement, p. 2; Nakahara affidavit, p. 2; Dekker statement, p. 3; all MBL.

22. Dekker statement, p. 2.

23. Frits de Jong and Henk Slettenaar, *De Chinalijn in Oorlogstijd* [*The China Line in Wartime*] (Doetinchem, Netherlands: Association of Former Employees of the Koninklijke Java-China-Parketvaart Lijnen N.V. [Royal Interocean Lines], 2004), pp. 44–57.

24. Motonaka to chairman of Parole Board, pp. 1–2, MBL.

25. Dekker statement, p. 2, MBL; *United States of America vs. Hisashi Ichioka*, Case File no. 339, March 30, 1949, p. 40, MBL.

26. Nakahara statement, p. 2, MBL.

27. Yanabe statement, p. 4 (also marked as p. 8 of 30), MBL.

28. Nakahara statement, p. 3, MBL.
29. Motonaka to chairman of Parole Board, p. 1, MBL.
30. Ibid., p. 3.
31. Yanabe statement, p. 4, MBL.
32. De Jong statement, p. 4, MBL.
33. Ibid.
34. Jiro Nakahara, testimony to Tokyo War Crimes Tribunal, pp. 38, 139, and 38, 140, MBL.
35. Ibid., pp. 38, 140; Nakahara statement, p. 2, MBL.
36. Ibid.
37. Mark Felton, *Slaughter at Sea: The Story of Japan's Naval War Crimes* (Annapolis, Md.: Naval Institute Press, 2007), p. 134.
38. Nakahara statement, p. 2, MBL.
39. Nakahara affidavit, pp. 1–2, MBL.
40. Nakahara statement, p. 5, MBL.
41. Yanabe statement, p. 4, MBL.
42. Nakahara statement, p. 5, MBL.
43. Yanabe statement, p. 3 (also marked as p. 7 of 30), MBL.
44. Ibid.
45. Nakahara statement, p. 4, MBL.
46. Ibid.
47. Motonaka to chairman of Parole Board, p. 2, MBL.
48. Yanabe statement, p. 4, MBL.
49. Nakahara affidavit, p. 3, MBL.

Chapter 14. Ariizumi Under Fire

1. Francisco Fereza, statement, June 11, 1944, Macmillan Brown Library, University of Canterbury, Christchurch, New Zealand (hereafter MBL).
2. Bob Hackett and Sander Kingsepp, "Sensuikan! HIJMS Submarine I-8, Tabular Record of Movement," June 29, 1944, CombinedFleet.com, http://www.combinedfleet.com/I-8.htm.
3. *United States vs. Hisashi Ichioka et al.,* Case no. 339, March 30, 1949, p. 46, MBL.
4. John Alexander McDougall, testimony, Tokyo War Crimes Tribunal, pp. 15, 123, MBL.
5. Hackett and Kingsepp, "HIJMS Submarine I-8," July 2, 1944.
6. Mark Felton, *Slaughter at Sea: The Story of Japan's Naval War Crimes* (Annapolis, Md.: Naval Institute Press, 2007), p. 153.
7. Motohide Yanabe, statement, Sugamo Prison, August 30, 1948, p. 4 (also marked as p. 8 of 30), MBL.
8. Ibid., p. 5, MBL.
9. Ibid.

10. Ibid., pp. 5–6.

11. Ibid., p. 6.

12. Clay Blair, Jr., *Silent Victory: The U.S. Submarine War Against Japan* (Annapolis, Md.: Naval Institute Press, 1975), p. 49.

13. Ibid., pp. 49–51.

14. W. J. Holmes, *Undersea Victory: The Influence of Submarine Operations on the War in the Pacific* (Garden City, N.Y.: Doubleday, 1966), pp. 19, 46–47.

15. Blair, *Silent Victory*, p. 18.

16. Holmes, *Undersea Victory*, p. 47.

17. Mochitsura Hashimoto, *Sunk!* (New York: Avon , 1954), pp. 156–57.

18. *United States vs. Hisashi Ichioka et al.*, pp. 36–39, 54, MBL.

19. Yanabe statement, p. 3, MBL.

20. *United States of America vs. Hisashi Ichioka et al.*, Case no. 339, March 30, 1949, pp. 36, 54, MBL.

21. Ibid., p. 38.

22. Ibid.

23. Hisashi Ichioka, statement, July 6, 1948, Document no. 927, Tokyo War Crimes Tribunal, Prosecution Exhibit no. 98, p. 2, MBL.

24. Tsugio Sato, *Maboroshi no Sensui Kubo* [*Phantom Submarine Carrier*] (Tokyo: Kabushiki Gaisha Kojin-sha, 1989), p. 272.

25. Motohide Yanabe, letter, Sugamo Prison, August 23, 1948, p. 2, MBL; *United States vs. Hisashi Ichioka et al.*, p. 38, MBL.

26. Lord Russell of Liverpool, *Knights of Bushido: A History of Japanese War Crimes During World War II* (New York: Skyhorse, 2008), pp. 213–27.

27. Ibid.

28. Swedish Minister in Tokyo to the Imperial Japanese Minister for Foreign Affairs, June 5, 1944, Document no. 23221-a, pp. 2, 3, MBL.

29. Russell of Liverpool, *Knights of Bushido*, pp. 213–27.

30. Ibid.

31. Henry Sakaida, Gary Nila, and Koji Takaki, *I-400: Japan's Secret Aircraft-Carrying Strike Submarine, Objective Panama Canal* (East Sussex, U.K.: Hikoki, 2006), p. 37.

Chapter 15. The *Segundo* (SS 398)

1. Richard Binkley, interview by author.

2. John D. Alden, *The Fleet Submarine in the U.S. Navy: A Design and Construction History* (Annapolis, Md.: Naval Institute Press, 1979), p. 3:79.

3. Ibid., p. 3:80.

4. Edward L. Beach, *Run Silent, Run Deep* (New York: Henry Holt, 1955), p. 116.

5. Alden, *Fleet Submarine in U.S. Navy*, p. 3:79.

6. Ibid., p. 3:78.

7. Clay Blair, Jr., *Silent Victory: The U.S. Submarine War Against Japan* (Annapolis, Md.: Naval Institute Press, 1975), p. 198.

8. Alden, *Fleet Submarine in U.S. Navy*, p. 3:84.

9. Ibid.

10. Ibid., p. 3:105.

11. Department of the Navy, *Dictionary of American Naval Fighting Ships* (1976), pp. 6:429–30, entry for USS *Segundo* (SS-398), http://www.hazegray.org/danfs/submar/ss398.txt.

12. Beach, *Run Silent, Run Deep*, p. 90.

13. James D. Fulp, U.S. Navy, Officer Biography Sheet, August 10, 1949, at National Personnel Records Center, Military Personnel Records, St. Louis.

14. James D. Fulp, U.S. Naval Academy, Certificate from Secondary School, June 12, 1928, at National Personnel Records Center, Military Personnel Records, St. Louis.

15. Lt. Cmdr. D. E. Barbey to Col. J. D. Fulp, December 11, 1929, at National Personnel Records Center, Military Personnel Records, St. Louis.

16. Rear Adm. S. S. Robison, Superintendent of U.S. Naval Academy, Special Order no. 2-30, January 3, 1930, at National Personnel Records Center, Military Personnel Records, St. Louis.

17. James D. Fulp, U.S. Naval Academy, Report of Delinquency, December 24, 1929, at National Personnel Records Center, Military Personnel Records, St. Louis.

18. U.S. Naval Academy, *Lucky Bag* Yearbook, Class of 1934, p. 222, at National Personnel Records Center, Military Personnel Records, St. Louis.

19. Michael S. Sanders, *The Yard: Building a Destroyer at the Bath Iron Works* (New York: Perennial, 2001), p. 174.

20. Beach, *Run Silent, Run Deep*, p. 94.

21. L. Rodney Johnson, interview by author.

22. Ibid.

23. Ibid.

24. USS *Segundo* (SS 398) Deck Log, July 5, 1944.

25. Johnson interview.

26. Blair, *Silent Victory*, pp. 724–27.

Chapter 16. Decline

1. W. J. Holmes, *Undersea Victory: The Influence of Submarine Operations on the War in the Pacific* (Garden City, N.Y.: Doubleday, 1966), pp. 349–50.

2. Ibid., p. 350.

3. Carl Boyd and Akihiko Yoshida, *The Japanese Submarine Force and World War II* (Shrewsbury, U.K.: Airlife, 1996), p. 143; Zenji Orita with Jo-

seph D. Harrington, *I-Boat Captain* (Canoga Park, Calif.: Major Books, 1976), pp. 214–15.

4. Boyd and Yoshida, *Japanese Submarine Force,* p. 143.

5. Orita and Harrington, *I-Boat Captain,* pp. 214–15.

6. W. J. Holmes, *Double-Edged Secrets* (US Naval Institute Press, 1998), p. 172.

7. Ibid., p. 141.

8. Ibid., p. 147.

9. M. G. Sheftall, *Blossoms in the Wind: Human Legacies of the Kamikaze* (New York: NAL Caliber, 2006), p. 265.

10. Nobukiyo Nambu, *Beikidoukantai wo Kishuseyo: Sensuikuubo I-401 Kanchou No Shuki* [*Surprise Attack on the American Fleet! Memoir of the I-401 Aircraft-Carrying Submarine by Its Captain*] (Tokyo: Fuami Shobo, 1988), p. 144.

11. Ibid., p. 148.

12. Nobukiyo Nambu, interview by author; Nambu, *Beikidoukantai wo Kishuseyo,* p. 156.

13. Nambu, *Beikidoukantai wo Kishuseyo,* p. 158.

14. Ibid., p. 165.

Chapter 17. Nambu and the *I-401*

1. Bob Hackett and Sander Kingsepp, "Sensuikan! HIJMS Submarine *I-8,* Tabular Record of Movement," October 9, 1944, CombinedFleet.com, http://www.combinedfleet.com/I-8.htm.

2. Tsugio Sato, *Maboroshi no Sensui Kubo* [*Phantom Submarine Carrier*] (Tokyo: Kabushiki Gaisha Kojin-sha, 1989), p. 106.

3. Ibid., p. 68.

4. Ibid., p. 107.

5. Ibid.

6. Ibid., p. 268.

7. Nobukiyo Nambu, *Beikidoukantai wo Kishuseyo: Sensuikuubo I-401 Kanchou No Shuki* [*Surprise Attack on the American Fleet! Memoir of the I-401 Aircraft-Carrying Submarine by Its Captain*] (Tokyo: Fuami Shobo, 1988), p. 165.

8. Ibid., p. 167.

9. Ibid., p. 168.

10. Kazuo Takatsuka, *Memories of the I-400,* 3 parts (Japan: privately published, 1996).

11. R. Kissinger, Jr., *I-400, I-401 Japanese Submarines, Description of Hull, General Arrangements, and Characteristics* (U.S. Navy, 1946), p. 4.

12. Seiji Azuma, "Sekai Ni Hirui Naki '*I-400* Gata, *I-13* Gata' No Kouzou to Seinou [The Construction and Efficiency of the Unparalleled *I-400*

and *I-13*]," *Maru* Special, *Japanese Naval Vessels*, no. 13 (Tokyo: Kojinsha, 1977), p. 30.

13. Kissinger, *I-400, I-401 Japanese Submarines*, p. 4.
14. Henry Sakaida, Gary Nila, and Koji Takaki, *I-400: Japan's Secret Aircraft-Carrying Strike Submarine, Objective Panama Canal* (East Sussex, U.K.: Hikoki, 2006), p. 102.
15. Kissinger, *I-400, I-401 Japanese Submarines*, p. 7.
16. Thomas O. Paine, "The Transpacific Voyage of HIJMS *I-400*: Tom Paine's Journal: July 1945–January 1946," February 1991, http://www .pacerfarm.org/i-400/. Other sources claim the drop may have been as much as thirty feet.
17. Heiji Kondo, interview by author.
18. Paine, "Transpacific Voyage of HIJMS *I-400*."
19. Takatsuka, *Memories of I-400*, pt. 2, March 1, 1974.
20. Sakaida, Nila, and Takaki, *I-400*, p. 109.
21. Paine, "Transpacific Voyage of HIJMS *I-400*."
22. Sakaida, Nila, and Takaki, *I-400*, p. 103.
23. Ibid., p. 101.
24. Kissinger, *I-400, I-401 Japanese Submarines*, p. 4. The actual length was 102 feet, 3 inches.
25. Ibid. The actual diameter was 11 feet and 9½ inches. The hangar itself sat 15 inches to starboard of centerline.
26. Nambu, *Beikidoukantai wo Kishuseyo*, p. 202.
27. Azuma, "Sekai Ni Hirui Naki," p. 30.
28. Kissinger, *I-400, I-401 Japanese Submarines*, p. 6.
29. Robert C. Mikesh, *Aichi M6A1 Seiran: Japan's Submarine Launched Panama Canal Bomber*, Close-Up 13 (Boylston, Mass.: Monogram Aviation Publications, 1975), p. 12.
30. Nambu, *Beikidoukantai wo Kishuseyo*, pp. 203, 192.
31. Sakaida, Nila, and Takaki, *I-400*, pp. 100, 101.
32. Kissinger, *I-400, I-401 Japanese Submarines*, p. 5.
33. Ibid.
34. U.S. Naval Technical Mission to Japan, *Reports of the U.S. Naval Technical Mission to Japan*, Series S: *Ship and Related Target*, Index no. S-01-1: *Characteristics of Japanese Naval Vessels*, Article I: *Submarines* (Washington, D.C.: Operational Archives, U.S. Navy History Division, 1946), p.10.
35. Ibid.
36. Kissinger, *I-400, I-401 Japanese Submarines*, p. 14.
37. U.S. Naval Technical Mission to Japan, *Reports of the U.S. Naval Technical Mission to Japan, Submarines*, p. 10.
38. The *I-401*'s layout is primarily based on the description provided in the Kissinger Report. See Kissinger, *I-400, I-401 Japanese Submarines*, pp. 1–20. Additionally, a rough layout of the sub based on U.S. Navy sources was also referred to. It appears in Norman Polmar and Dorr B.

Carpenter, *Submarines of the Imperial Japanese Navy, 1904–1945* (London: Conway Maritime Press, 1986), p. 115. Finally, Shizuo Fukui's *Japanese Naval Vessels at the End of the War*, Administrative Division, Second Demobilization Bureau, April 25, 1947, was also used.

39. Paine, "Transpacific Voyage of HIJMS *I-400*."

40. W. J. Holmes, *Undersea Victory: The Influence of Submarine Operations on the War in the Pacific* (Garden City, N.Y. Doubleday, 1966), pp. 11–14.

41. "Japanese Torpedoes," Type 95, CombinedFleet.com, http://www.combinedfleet.com/torps.htm.

42. Mochitsura Hashimoto, *Sunk!* (New York: Avon, 1954), p. 143.

43. Sakaida, Nila, and Takaki, *I-400*, p. 17.

44. Paine, "Transpacific Voyage of HIJMS *I-400*"; Lloyd R. Vasey, "The *I-400* Class of Japanese Submarines," *Mustang News* [National Order of Battlefield Commissions] 29, no. 3 (Fall 2008).

45. Vasey, "*I-400* Class of Japanese Submarines."

46. Sakaida, Nila, and Takaki, *I-400*, photo on p. 114.

47. Chin-Ji Inouye, interview by author; Takatsuka, *Memories of the I-400*, pt. 2.

48. Paine, "Transpacific Voyage of HIJMS *I-400*."

49. Zenji Orita with Joseph D. Harrington, *I-Boat Captain: How Japan's Submarine Force Almost Defeated the U.S. Navy in the Pacific!* (Canoga Park, Calif.: Major Books, 1976), p. 46.

50. Atsushi Asamura, "*I-401* Sensuikan to Seiran to Watashi to [The *I-401* Submarine, Seiran and Me]," *Maru* Special, *Japanese Naval Vessels*, no. 13 (1977), pp. 42–43.

51. Kazuo Takatsu, interview by author.

52. Tsugio Yata, interview by author.

53. Nambu, *Beikidoukantai wo Kishuseyo*, p. 66.

54. Sakaida, Nila, and Takaki, *I-400*, photo on p. 115.

55. Victor S. Horgan, interview by author; Paul Wittmer, interview by author.

56. Nambu, *Beikidoukantai wo Kishuseyo*, p. 245. The *I-400* also had a doll in her wardroom. See Kazuo Takahashi, *Shinryu Tokubetsu Kogekitai* [*Divine Dragon Special Attack Unit*] (Tokyo: Koujinsha, 2001), photo on p. 202.

57. Heiji Kondo, interview by author.

58. Hashimoto, *Sunk!*, p. 143.

59. Nambu, *Beikidoukantai wo Kishuseyo*, p. 217.

60. Masanori Ito, *The End of the Imperial Japanese Navy: A Japanese Account of the Rise and Fall of Japan's Seapower* (New York: Macfadden Books, 1965), p. 19.

61. Dr. Ellen Schattschneider, "The Mystery of Mascot Dolls," Pacific Wrecks.com: http://www.pacificwrecks.com/history/doll/.

62. Sutejiro Shimazu, interview by author.

63. Kazuo Takatsuka, *Memories of the I-400* (Japan: privately published, 1996), pt. 3, September 20, 1974.

64. Muneo Bando, interview by author.

65. Ibid.

66. M. G. Sheftall, *Blossoms in the Wind: Human Legacies of the Kamikaze* (New York: NAL Caliber, 2006), p. 368.

67. Hashimoto, *Sunk!*, p. 143.

68. Henry Sakaida, Gary Nila, and Koji Takaki, *I-400: Japan's Secret Aircraft-Carrying Strike Submarine, Objective Panama Canal* (East Sussex, U.K.: Hikoki, 2006), p. 56.

69. Chin-Ji Inouye, interview by author.

70. Kissinger, *I-400, I-401 Japanese Submarines*, p. 6.

71. Nobukiyo Nambu, interview by author.

72. *Japanese Navy Submarine 1–400 Assembly Instruction Booklet*, Tamiya, p. 19.

73. Sakaida, Nila, and Takaki, *I-400*, p. 117.

74. Kissinger, *I-400, I-401 Japanese Submarines*, p. 5.

75. Ibid.

76. Kazuo Takatsuka, *Memories of the I-400*, pt. 1, September 1, 1973.

77. Ibid.

78. Harry Arvidson, interview by author.

79. Paine, "Transpacific Voyage of HIJMS *I-400*."

80. Takatsuka, *Memories of the I-400*, pt. 3, September 20, 1974; Orita and Harrington, *I-Boat Captain*, p. 210.

81. Orita and Harrington, *I-Boat Captain*, p. 210.

82. Ibid., p. 250.

83. Masao Okui, interview by author.

84. Ibid.

85. Hashimoto, *Sunk!*, p. 142.

86. Ibid.

87. Ibid., p. 47.

88. Kissinger, *I-400, I-401 Japanese Submarines*, p. 4.

89. Paine, "Transpacific Voyage of HIJMS *I-400*."

90. U.S. Naval Technical Mission to Japan, *Ship and Related Targets: Characteristics of Japanese Naval Vessels: Submarines*, p. 10.

91. Erminio Bagnasco, *Submarines of World War II* (London: Cassell, 2000), p. 194.

92. Kissinger, *I-400, I-401 Japanese Submarines*, pp. 1, 10.

93. U.S. Naval Technical Mission to Japan, *Ship and Related Targets: Characteristics of Japanese Naval Vessels: Submarines*, p. 14.

94. John E. Long, "Japan's Undersea Carriers," *U.S. Naval Institute Proceedings*, June 1950, p. 612.

95. Sato, *Maboroshi no Sensui Kubo*, p. 206.

96. Charles A. Lockwood and Hans Christian Adamson, *Hellcats of the Sea* (New York: Bantam Books, 1988), p. 67.

97. Vasey, *I-400 Class of Japanese Submarines*. One source claims there was at least one shower on each of the *I-400* subs.

98. Shoici Matsutani, interview by author.

99. Kissinger, *I-400, I-401 Japanese Submarines*, pp. 3, 11.
100. Paine, "Transpacific Voyage of HIJMS *I-400*."
101. Ibid.
102. Ibid.
103. Nambu, *Beikidoukantai wo Kishuseyo*, p. 167.

Chapter 18. The 631st

1. Nobukiyo Nambu, *Beikidoukantai wo Kishuseyo: Sensuikuubo I-401 Kan-chou No Shuki* [*Surprise Attack on the American Fleet! Memoir of the I-401 Aircraft-Carrying Submarine by Its Captain*] (Tokyo: Fuami Shobo, 1988), p. 194.
2. Ibid., pp. 195–96.
3. Ibid., pp. 196–97.
4. U.S. Naval Technical Mission to Japan, *Reports of the U.S. Naval Technical Mission to Japan*, Series S: *Ship and Related Targets*, Index no. S-17, *Japanese Submarine Operations* (Washington, D.C.: Operational Archives, U.S. Navy History Division, 1946), chap. 2. December 30, 1944, has also been given as a squadron formation date.
5. Tsugio Sato, *Maboroshi no Sensui Kubo* [*Phantom Submarine Carrier*] (Tokyo: Kabushiki Gaisha Kojin-sha, 1989), p. 123; Tsugio Yata, "Sub-Ron 1 . . . aims for U.S. fleet at Ulithi and Panama Canal," *I-401 History*, *I-401* Submarine Society, Japan; Norman Polmar and Dorr B. Carpenter, *Submarines of the Imperial Japanese Navy, 1904–1945* (London: Conway Maritime Press, 1986), p. 110; Sato, *Maboroshi no Sensui Kubo*, p. 36.
6. Sato, *Maboroshi no Sensui Kubo*, p. 123.
7. Ibid.; Jim Main and David Allen, *Fallen: The Ultimate Heroes, Footballers Who Never Returned from the War* (Victoria, Australia: BAS, 2002); Main and Allen, "The Ultimate Tiger Heroes" (2002), http://www.afl.com .au/news/newsarticle/tabid/208/newsid/2941/default.aspx.
8. Sato, *Maboroshi no Sensui Kubo*, p. 124; Fukui, *Japanese Naval Vessels at the End of the War*, p. 36.
9. Nambu, *Beikidoukantai wo Kishuseyo*, p. 165.
10. Robert C. Mikesh, *Aichi M6A1 Seiran: Japan's Submarine Launched Pan-ama Canal Bomber*, Close-Up 13 (Boylston, Mass.: Monogram Aviation Publications, 1975), p. 7.
11. Ibid.
12. Sato, *Maboroshi no Sensui Kubo*, p. 138.
13. Mikesh, *Aichi M6A1 Seiran*, pp. 9–10.
14. Kazuo Takahashi, *Shinryu Tokubetsu Kogekitai* [*Divine Dragon Special Attack Unit*] (Tokyo: Koujinsha 2001), p. 161.
15. Nambu, *Beikidoukantai wo Kishuseyo*, p. 175.
16. Takahashi, *Shinryu Tokubetsu Kogekitai*, p. 191.
17. Ibid., p. 104.

18. Henry Sakaida, Gary Nila, and Koji Takaki, *I-400: Japan's Secret Aircraft-Carrying Strike Submarine, Objective Panama Canal* (East Sussex, U.K.: Hikoki, 2006), p. 23.
19. Takahashi, *Shinryu Tokubetsu Kogekitai*, pp. 156, 157.
20. Ibid., pp. 158, 157.
21. Ibid., pp. 158, 159.
22. Sakaida, Nila, and Takaki, *I-400*, p. 25.
23. Satoru Fukuoka, oral interview transcript, Smithsonian Air & Space Museum, March 12, 1998.
24. Takahashi, *Shinryu Tokubetsu Kogekitai*, p. 160.
25. Ibid.
26. Ibid., p. 164.
27. Thomas S. Momiyama, "All and Nothing," *Air & Space*, Smithsonian, October–November 2001, p. 25.
28. Mikesh, *Aichi M6A1 Seiran*, p. 5.
29. M. G. Sheftall, *Blossoms in the Wind: Human Legacies of the Kamikaze* (New York: NAL Caliber, 2006), pp. 267–68.
30. Ibid.
31. Atsushi Asamura, interview, *Rekishi Gunzou*, Gakken, Issue no. 85, October 10, 2007, pp. 154–59.
32. Seventieth class.
33. Asamura interview, *Rekishi Gunzou*, pp. 154–59.
34. Takahashi, *Shinryu Tokubetsu Kogekitai*, p. 164.
35. Ikuhiko Hata, *Dainiji Taisen Koukuju Shiwa* [*Historical Aviation Stories of World War II*], trans. Shojo Jonda and Sandy Kita (Japan: Chuukou Bunko, n.d.), chap. 10.
36. Takahashi, *Shinryu Tokubetsu Kogekitai*, p. 164.
37. Mikesh, *Aichi M6A1 Seiran*, p. 7.
38. Ibid., p. 11.
39. Sato, *Maboroshi no Sensui Kubo*, p. 138.
40. Takahashi, *Shinryu Tokubetsu Kogekitai*, pp. 191, 166.
41. Nambu, *Beikidoukantai wo Kishuseyo*, p. 198.
42. Sakaida, Nila, and Takaki, *I-400*, p. 42.
43. Nambu, *Beikidoukantai wo Kishuseyo*, p. 199.
44. Ibid., p. 198.
45. Carl Boyd and Akihiko Yoshida, *The Japanese Submarine Force and World War II* (Shrewsbury, U.K.: Airlife, 1996), p. 183.
46. Nambu, *Beikidoukantai wo Kishuseyo*, p. 198.
47. Ibid.
48. Mochitsura Hashimoto, *Sunk!* (New York: Avon, 1954), p. 138.
49. Sato, *Maboroshi no Sensui Kubo*, p. 138.
50. Mikesh, *Aichi M6A1 Seiran*, p. 12.
51. Takahashi, *Shinryu Tokubetsu Kogekitai*, pp. 168–69.
52. Ibid., p. 126.
53. Ibid., pp. 139, 169.

54. Sato, *Maboroshi no Sensui Kubo*, pp. 144, 169, 170.
55. Nambu, *Beikidoukantai wo Kishuseyo*, p. 201.
56. Takahashi, *Shinryu Tokubetsu Kogekitai*, pp. 170–71, 173–75.

Chapter 19. Fulp on Patrol

1. James L. Mooney, "History of USS *Segundo* (SS-398)," *Dictionary of American Naval Fighting Ships* (Washington, D.C.: Navy Department, Naval Historical Center, Ships' History Branch, 1959–81); USS *Segundo* (SS 398), First War Patrol Report, September 13, 1944, 0802, at http://www.segundo398.org/patrol_reports/patrol1.pdf.
2. USS *Segundo* (SS 398), Deck Logs, October 6, 1944.
3. Harry W. McCartney, interview by author.
4. Wallace C. Karnes, Jr., interview by author.
5. L. Rodney Johnson, interview by author.
6. Clay Blair, Jr., *Silent Victory: The U.S. Submarine War Against Japan* (Annapolis, Md.: Naval Institute Press, 1975), pp. 725, 202, 715.
7. Ibid., p. 715.
8. Ibid., p. 844.
9. *Segundo* Deck Logs, October 29, 1944.
10. Wallace C. Karnes, Jr., interview by author.
11. Ibid.
12. Victor S. Horgan, interview by author.
13. USS *Segundo* (SS 398), Second War Patrol Report, November 16, 1944, 1435, at http://www.segundo398.org/patrol_reports/patrol2.pdf.
14. Mooney, "History of USS *Segundo*."
15. *Segundo*, Second War Patrol Report, December 6, 1944, 1804, 1953; *Segundo* Deck Logs, December 6, 1944.
16. *Segundo*, Second War Patrol Report, December 6, 1944, 2046.
17. Ibid.
18. L. Rodney Johnson, interview by author.
19. Bob Hackett, Sander Kingsepp, and Peter Cundall, "Kuchikukan! IJN Second Class Destroyer, *Kuretake*: Tabular Record of Movement," CombinedFleet.com, http://www.combinedfleet.com/Kuretake_t.htm.
20. Bob Hackett, Sander Kingsepp, and Peter Cundall, "Kusentei! IJN Subchaser, CH-33: Tabular Record of Movement," CombinedFleet.com, http://www.combinedfleet.com/CH-33_t.htm.
21. L. Rodney Johnson, interview by author.
22. Ibid.
23. Ibid.; *Segundo*, Second Patrol Report, December 6, 1944, 2258, 2210–2300. The *Segundo*'s patrol report indicates that the torpedoes were fired from 2,300 yards, possibly to appear more prudent. See *Segundo*, Second Patrol Report, December 6, 1944, 1953–0500. *Segundo* Deck Logs, December 6, 1944; Mooney, "History of USS *Segundo*."

24. L. Rodney Johnson, interview by author.

25. Richard Binkley, interview by author.

26. *Segundo,* Second Patrol Report, December 6, 1944, 2300.

27. Victor S. Horgan, interview by author.

28. John E. Balson, interview by author.

29. *Segundo,* Second Patrol Report, December 6, 1944, 2300.

30. Richard Binkley, interview by author.

31. Mooney, "History of USS *Segundo.*"

32. USS *Segundo* (SS 398) Second War Patrol Report, December 6, 1944; 2300; *Segundo* Deck Logs, December 6, 1944.

33. Mooney, "History of USS *Segundo.*"

34. *Segundo,* Second Patrol Report, December 6, 1944, 2347.

35. Ibid., 2326–47.

36. Victor S. Horgan, interview by author.

37. Blair, *Silent Victory,* p. 803.

38. Wallace C. Karnes, Jr., interview by author.

39. *Segundo* Deck Logs, December 9, 1944.

40. Ellsworth R. Quam quoted in "Over the Sea, and Under the Sea," *Minnesota Legionnaire,* http://www.mnlegion.org/paper/html/quam.html.

41. Wallace C. Karnes, Jr., interview by author.

42. *Segundo,* Second Patrol Report, December 9, 1944, 2153–2330.

43. Ibid., 2330; Robert O'Connor, interview by author.

44. L. Rodney Johnson, interview by author.

45. Richard Binkley, interview by author.

46. *Segundo,* Second Patrol Report, December 9, 1944, 2153–2330.

47. "World War II Pacific Typhoons Battered U.S. Navy," *USA Today,* 2008, http://www.usatoday.com/weather/hurricane/history/typhoons-ww2 -navy.htm.

48. *Segundo* Deck Logs, December 19, 1944.

49. *Segundo,* Second Patrol Report, December 26, 1944, 2030.

50. Victor S. Horgan, interview by author.

51. *Segundo,* Second Patrol Report, December 26, 1944, 2030–2146.

52. Ibid.

53. Ibid.

54. Ibid.

55. Victor S. Horgan, interview by author.

56. *Segundo,* Second Patrol Report, December 27, 1944, 1100.

57. Ibid., December 31, 1944, 2354.

58. Recommendation for Award to Cmdr. James D. Fulp, Jr., February 3, 1945, at National Personnel Records Center, Military Personnel Records, St. Louis.

59. Recommendation for Award to Cmdr. James D. Fulp, Jr., February 11, 1945, at National Personnel Records Center, Military Personnel Records, St. Louis. (Two copies of the citation exist, dated separately and with slightly different wording.)

Chapter 20. Kure

1. Tsugio Sato, *Maboroshi no Sensui Kubo* [*Phantom Submarine Carrier*] (Tokyo: Kabushiki Gaisha Kojin-sha, 1989), p. 146.

2. Henry Sakaida, Gary Nila, and Koji Takaki, *I-400: Japan's Secret Aircraft-Carrying Strike Submarine, Objective Panama Canal* (East Sussex, U.K.: Hikoki, 2006), pp. 40–41.

3. Ibid.

4. Sato, *Maboroshi no Sensui Kubo*, p. 105.

5. Bob Hackett and Sander Kingsepp, "Sensuikan! HIJMS Submarine *I-165*, Tabular Record of Movement," December 16, 1943, Combined-Fleet.com, http://www.combinedfleet.com/I-165.htm.

6. Ibid., January 16, 1944.

7. Ibid., March 18, 1944.

8. *United States of America vs. Hisashi Ichioka*, Case File no. 339, March 30, 1949, p. 44, Macmillan Brown Library, University of Canterbury, Christchurch, New Zealand (hereafter MBL).

9. Hackett and Kingsepp, "I-165, Tabular Record of Movement," March 18, 1944.

10. Sakaida, Nila, and Takaki, *I-400*, pp. 40–41.

11. Yukio Matsuyama, "The Need to Wait for a Generation Change," in Ronald Dore, ed., *Japan, Internationalism and the UN* (London: Routledge, 1997), p. 167.

12. Sato, *Maboroshi no Sensui Kubo*, p. 147.

13. Norman Polmar and Dorr B. Carpenter, *Submarines of the Imperial Japanese Navy, 1904–1945* (London: Conway Maritime Press, 1986), p. 111.

14. Sato, *Maboroshi no Sensui Kubo*, p. 147.

15. Ibid., p. 139.

16. Ibid.

17. Ibid., p. 140.

18. Ibid., pp. 139–140.

19. Ibid., p. 144.

20. Kazuo Takahashi, *Shinryu Tokubetsu Kogekitai* [*Divine Dragon Special Attack Unit*] (Tokyo: Koujinsha, 2001), p. 179.

21. Ibid., pp. 188, 178, 176.

22. Ibid., p. 178.

23. "Jisaburo Ozawa," CombinedFleet.com, http://www.combinedfleet.com/officers/Jisaburo_Ozawa.

24. Yoshio Enoh quoted in "Navy Planned Bacteriological Warfare, U.S. Attack Operation Revealed," *Sankei* [newspaper], August 14, 1977.

25. Denis Warner, Peggy Warner, and Sadao Seno, *The Sacred Warriors* (New York: Van Nostrand Reinhold, 1982), pp. 282–83.

26. Mark Felton, *The Fujita Plan: Japanese Attacks on the United States and Australia during the Second World War* (South Yorkshire, U.K.: Pen & Sword Military, 2006), pp. 182–83.

27. "Navy Planned Bacteriological Warfare," *Sankei.*
28. Ibid.
29. Ibid., p. 16; Warner, Warner, and Seno, *Sacred Warriors,* pp. 282–83.
30. "Navy Planned Bacteriological Warfare," *Sankei.*
31. Polmar and Carpenter, *Submarines of the Imperial Japanese Navy,* p. 54.
32. Nobukiyo Nambu, *Beikidoukantai wo Kishuseyo: Sensuikuubo I-401 Kanchou No Shuki* [*Surprise Attack on the American Fleet! Memoir of the I-401 Aircraft-Carrying Submarine by Its Captain*] (Tokyo: Fuami Shobo, 1988), p. 161.
33. Carl Boyd and Akihiko Yoshida, *The Japanese Submarine Force and World War II* (Shrewsbury, U.K.: Airlife, 1996), p. 174.
34. Bob Hackett and Sander Kingsepp, "Sensuikan! HIJMS Submarine I-8, Tabular Record of Movement," March 30, 1945, CombinedFleet.com, http://www.combinedfleet.com/I-8.htm.
35. Zenji Orita with Joseph D. Harrington, *I-Boat Captain: How Japan's Submarine Force Almost Defeated the U.S. Navy in the Pacific!* (Canoga Park, Calif.: Major Books, 1976), p. 274.
36. Mochitsura Hashimoto, *Sunk!* (New York: Avon, 1954), p. 136.
37. Ibid.
38. Ibid.
39. Hackett and Kingsepp, "*I-8*, Tabular Record of Movement," March 31, 1945.
40. Hashimoto, *Sunk!*, p. 136.
41. Orita and Harrington, *I-Boat Captain*, pp. 274–75; Hashimoto, *Sunk!*, p. 136.
42. Hackett and Kingsepp, "*I-8*, Tabular Record of Movement," March 31, 1945.
43. Orita and Harrington, *I-Boat Captain*, pp. 274–75. In Hashimoto's *Sunk!* (p. 136), Petty Officer Takamasa Mukai, the sole survivor of the *I-8*, contradicts his own account in Orita's *I-Boat Captain*, by saying he was wounded before his 25mm gun crew was able to fire.
44. Orita and Harrington, *I-Boat Captain*, pp. 274–75.
45. Hashimoto, *Sunk!*, p. 136.
46. Boyd and Yoshida, *Japanese Submarine Force*, p. 174.
47. Ibid.
48. Hashimoto, *Sunk!*, p. 136.
49. Orita and Harrington, *I-Boat Captain*, p. 275.
50. Fukumoto Izuru, interview by author.
51. Chin-Ji Inouye, interview by author.
52. Satoru Fukuoka, oral interview transcript, Smithsonian Air & Space Museum, March 12, 1998.
53. Tsugio Yata, "SubRon 1 . . . Aims for U.S. Fleet at Ulithi and Panama Canal," *I-401 History, I-401* Submarine Society, Japan.
54. Tsugio Yata, interview by author.

55. Yata, "SubRon1."
56. Sakaida, Nila, and Takaki, *I-400,* p. 43.
57. Kazuo Takatsuka, *Memories of the I-400* (Japan: privately published, 1996).
58. Yata, "SubRon1."
59. Fukumaru Koshimoto, interview by author.
60. Chin-Ji Inouye, interview by author.
61. Takahashi, *Shinryu Tokubetsu Kogekitai,* p. 179.
62. Arizuka, *Memories of the I-400.*
63. Chin-Ji Inouye, interview by author.
64. Takahashi, *Shinryu Tokubetsu Kogekitai,* p. 179; Sato, *Maboroshi no Sensui Kubo,* p. 144.
65. Takahashi, *Shinryu Tokubetsu Kogekitai,* p. 180.
66. Ibid., p. 179.
67. Ibid., p. 180.
68. Ibid., pp. 179–80.
69. Ibid.
70. Tsugio Yata, interview by author.
71. Ibid.
72. Nambu quoted in Sato, *Maboroshi no Sensui Kubo,* p. 145.
73. Chin-Ji Inouye, interview by author.
74. Arizuka, *Memories of the I-400.*
75. Yata, "SubRon1."
76. Chin-Ji Inouye, interview by author.
77. Arizuka, *Memories of the I-400.*
78. Sato, *Maboroshi no Sensui Kubo,* p. 145.
79. Ibid.; Nambu, *Beikidoukantai wo Kishuseyo,* p. 206.

Chapter 21. Adversity

1. Tsugio Sato, *Maboroshi no Sensui Kubo* [Phantom Submarine Carrier] (Tokyo: Kabushiki Gaisha Kojin-sha, 1989), p. 145.
2. Fukumaru Koshimoto, interview by author. Sato, in *Maboroshi no Sensui Kubo,* says only one man, the *I-400*'s machine gunner, was killed (p. 145).
3. Sato, *Maboroshi no Sensui Kubo,* says the *I-14* departed Kure on March 19 (p. 147). However, since this is the day the Allies attacked Kure, it probably left on March 18. The difference in dates might also be ascribed to U.S. versus Japan time.
4. Kazuo Takahashi, *Shinryu Tokubetsu Kogekitai* [Divine Dragon Special Attack Unit] (Tokyo: Koujinsha, 2001), p.180.
5. Max Hastings, *Retribution: The Battle for Japan, 1944–1945* (New York: Alfred A. Knopf, 2007), p. 305.

6. Robert C. Mikesh, *Aichi M6A1 Seiran: Japan's Submarine Launched Panama Canal Bomber,* Close-Up 13 (Boylston, Mass.: Monogram Aviation Publications, 1975), p. 7.

7. Hastings, *Retribution,* p. 310.

8. Sato, *Maboroshi no Sensui Kubo,* chap. 5

9. Hastings, *Retribution,* p. 310.

10. Sato, *Maboroshi no Sensui Kubo,* p. 146, 168.

11. U.S. Naval Technical Mission to Japan, *Reports of the U.S. Naval Technical Mission to Japan,* Series S: *Ship and Related Targets,* Index no. S-17, *Japanese Submarine Operations* (Washington, D.C.: Operational Archives, U.S. Navy History Division, 1946), chap. 2.

12. Zenji Orita with Joseph D. Harrington, *I-Boat Captain: How Japan's Submarine Force Almost Defeated the U.S. Navy in the Pacific!* (Canoga Park, Calif.: Major Books, 1976), p. 298.

13. Nobukiyo Nambu, *Beikidoukantai wo Kishuseyo: Sensuikuubo I-401 Kanchou No Shuki* [*Surprise Attack on the American Fleet! Memoir of the I-401 Aircraft-Carrying Submarine by Its Captain*] (Tokyo: Fuami Shobo, 1988), p. 201.

14. Ibid.

15. Ibid., p. 202; Sato, *Maboroshi no Sensui Kubo,* p. 142.

16. Nambu, *Beikidoukantai wo Kishuseyo,* p. 202; Henry Sakaida, Gary Nila, and Koji Takaki, *I-400: Japan's Secret Aircraft-Carrying Strike Submarine, Objective Panama Canal* (East Sussex, U.K.: Hikoki, 2006), p. 28.

17. Nambu, *Beikidoukantai wo Kishuseyo,* p. 202.

18. Ibid.

19. Atsushi Asamura, "*I-401* Sensuikan to Seiran to Watashi to [The *I-401* Submarine, *Seiran* and Me]," *Maru* Special, *Japanese Naval Vessels,* no. 13, 1977, pp. 42–43.

20. Ikuhiko Hata, *Dainiji Taisen Koukuju Shiwa* [*Historical Aviation Stories of World War II*], trans. Shojo Jonda and Sandy Kita (Japan: Chuukou Bunko, n.d.), chap. 10.

21. Satoru Fukuoka, oral interview transcript, Smithsonian Air & Space Museum, March 12, 1998.

22. Sakaida, Nila, and Takaki, *I-400,* p. 45.

23. Takahashi, *Shinryu Tokubetsu Kogekitai,* pp. 182–83.

24. Charles A. Lockwood and Hans Christian Adamson, *Hellcats of the Sea* (New York: Bantam Books, 1988), p. 67.

25. Dan Kurzman, *Fatal Voyage: The Sinking of the USS Indianapolis* (New York: Broadway Books, 2001), pp. 45–46.

26. Hata, *Dainiji Taisen Koukuju Shiwa,* chap. 10.

27. Nambu, *Beikidoukantai wo Kishuseyo,* p. 206.

28. Philip Henshall, *Vengeance: Hitler's Nuclear Weapon—Fact or Fiction?* (Gloucestershire, U.K.: Sutton, 1998), p. 154.

29. Sato, *Maboroshi no Sensui Kubo,* p. 167.

30. Richard Compton-Hall, *Submarine Warfare: Monsters and Midgets* (Dorset, U.K.: Blanford Press, 1985), p. 71.

31. U.S. Naval Technical Mission, *Japanese Submarine Operations*, chap. 2; W. J. Holmes, *Undersea Victory: The Influence of Submarine Operations on the War in the Pacific* (Garden City, N.Y.: Doubleday, 1966), pp. 472, 478, 485.

32. Nambu, *Beikidoukantai wo Kishuseyo*, p. 189.

33. M. G. Sheftall, *Blossoms in the Wind: Human Legacies of the Kamikaze* (New York: NAL Caliber, 2006), p. 34.

34. Holmes, *Undersea Victory*, p. 478.

35. Sato, *Maboroshi no Sensui Kubo*, p. 167.

36. Nambu, *Beikidoukantai wo Kishuseyo*, p. 203; Tsugio Yata, "SubRon 1 . . . Aims for U.S. Fleet at Ulithi and Panama Canal," *I-401 History*, *I-401* Submarine Society, Japan.

37. Nambu, *Beikidoukantai wo Kishuseyo*, p. 207; Yata, "SubRon1."

38. Nambu, *Beikidoukantai wo Kishuseyo*, p. 207.

39. Chin-Ji Inouye, interview by author.

40. Yata, "SubRon1."

41. Ibid.; Muneo Bando, interview by author.

42. Chin-Ji Inouye, interview by author.

Chapter 22. Attacking the Canal

1. Nobukiyo Nambu, *Beikidoukantai wo Kishuseyo: Sensuikuubo I-401 Kanchou No Shuki* [*Surprise Attack on the American Fleet! Memoir of the I-401 Aircraft-Carrying Submarine by Its Captain*] (Tokyo: Fuami Shobo, 1988), p. 207; Tsugio Sato, *Maboroshi no Sensui Kubo* [*Phantom Submarine Carrier*] (Tokyo: Kabushiki Gaisha Kojin-sha, 1989), p. 168.

2. Nambu, *Beikidoukantai wo Kishuseyo*, p. 207.

3. Chin-Ji Inouye, interview by author.

4. Nambu, *Beikidoukantai wo Kishuseyo*, p. 207.

5. Chin-Ji Inouye, interview by author.

6. Muneo Bando, interview by author.

7. Henry Sakaida, Gary Nila, and Koji Takaki, *I-400: Japan's Secret Aircraft-Carrying Strike Submarine, Objective Panama Canal* (East Sussex, U.K.: Hikoki, 2006), pp. 37–38.

8. Ibid., p. 38.

9. *United States of America v. Hisashi Ichioka et al.*, Case no. 339, March 30, 1949, p. 45. Kusaka sank the *Richard Hovey* on March 29, 1944.

10. Kazuo Nishijima, interview by author.

11. Haruo Sugiyama, interview by author.

12. Kazuo Nishijima, interview by author.

13. Nambu, *Beikidoukantai wo Kishuseyo*, p. 207; Robert C. Mikesh, *Aichi*

M6A1 Seiran: Japan's Submarine Launched Panama Canal Bomber, Close-Up 13 (Boylston, Mass.: Monogram Aviation Publications, 1975), p. 12.

14. Kazuo Takatsuka, *Memories of the I-400* (Japan: privately published, 1996), pt. 1, September 1, 1973.

15. Sato, *Maboroshi no Sensui Kubo,* p. 168.

16. Nambu, *Beikidoukantai wo Kishuseyo,* p. 207.

17. Takatsuka, *Memories of the I-400,* pt. 1, September 1, 1973.

18. The *I-400*'s original fuel requirements may have been reduced with their redesign, from 1,750 tons to 1,660 tons. See Sato, *Maboroshi no Sensui Kubo,* p. 101, and Nambu, *Beikidoukantai wo Kishuseyo,* p. 189.

19. Nambu, *Beikidoukantai wo Kishuseyo,* p. 208; Takatsuka, *Memories of the I-400,* pt. 1, September 1, 1973.

20. Nambu, *Beikidoukantai wo Kishuseyo,* p. 208.

21. Takatsuka, *Memories of the I-400,* pt. 1, September 1, 1973.

22. Mikesh, *Aichi M6A1 Seiran,* p. 12.

23. Nambu, *Beikidoukantai wo Kishuseyo,* says that the *I-400* returned to Kure on April 27. However, other sources indicate that the *I-400* was back in port as early as April 25, just another example of how difficult it is to pin down exact dates given conflicting memories and the destruction of records.

24. Nambu, *Beikidoukantai wo Kishuseyo,* p. 208.

25. Sato, *Maboroshi no Sensui Kubo,* p. 169.

26. John D. Alden, *The Fleet Submarine in the U.S. Navy: A Design and Construction History* (Annapolis, Md.: Naval Institute Press, 1979), p. 3:91.

27. "History: 20th Century," Portsmouth Naval Shipyard, http://www.navsea .navy.mil/shipyards/portsmouth/Pages/20th%20Century.aspx.

28. Nambu, *Beikidoukantai wo Kishuseyo,* p. 209; Sato, *Maboroshi no Sensui Kubo,* p. 169; Tsugio Yata, "SubRon 1 . . . Aims for U.S. Fleet at Ulithi and Panama Canal," *I-401 History,* I-401 Submarine Society, Japan.

29. Ikuhiko Hata, *Dainiji Taisen Koukuju Shiwa* [*Historical Aviation Stories of World War II*], trans. Shojo Jonda and Sandy Kita (Japan: Chuukou Bunko, n.d.), chap. 10.

30. Kazuo Takahashi, *Shinryu Tokubetsu Kogekitai* [*Divine Dragon Special Attack Unit*] (Tokyo: Koujinsha, 2001), p. 185. The meeting date varies by source.

31. Nambu, *Beikidoukantai wo Kishuseyo,* p. 205.

32. Takahashi, *Shinryu Tokubetsu Kogekitai,* p. 185.

33. Sakaida, Nila, and Takaki, *I-400,* p. 45.

34. Takahashi, *Shinryu Tokubetsu Kogekitai* p. 185.

35. Nambu, *Beikidoukantai wo Kishuseyo,* p. 205.

36. Sakaida, Nila, and Takaki, *I-400,* p. 46.

37. Sato, *Maboroshi no Sensui Kubo,* p. 158.

38. Takahashi, *Shinryu Tokubetsu Kogekitai,* p. 186.

39. Nambu, *Beikidoukantai wo Kishuseyo,* p. 205.
40. Takahashi, *Shinryu Tokubetsu Kogekitai,* p. 186.
41. Sato, *Maboroshi no Sensui Kubo,* pp. 159–62.
42. Ibid., pp. 164–66.
43. Atsushi Asamura, "*I-401* Sensuikan to Seiran to Watashi to [The *I-401* Submarine, *Seiran* and Me]," *Maru* Special, *Japanese Naval Vessels,* no. 13, 1977, pp. 42–43.
44. Takahashi, *Shinryu Tokubetsu Kogekitai,* pp. 187, 188.
45. Sakaida, Nila, and Takaki, *I-400,* p. 49.
46. Takahashi, *Shinryu Tokubetsu Kogekitai,* p. 188.
47. Sato, *Maboroshi no Sensui Kubo,* p. 162.
48. Takahashi, *Shinryu Tokubetsu Kogekitai,* p. 188.
49. Ibid.
50. Ibid.

Chapter 23. Green Light

1. Tsugio Sato, *Maboroshi no Sensui Kubo* [*Phantom Submarine Carrier*] (Tokyo: Kabushiki Gaisha Kojin-sha, 1989), pp. 151, 160.
2. Henry Sakaida, Gary Nila, and Koji Takaki, *I-400: Japan's Secret Aircraft-Carrying Strike Submarine, Objective Panama Canal* (East Sussex, U.K.: Hikoki, 2006), p. 45.
3. Sato, *Maboroshi no Sensui Kubo,* p. 160.
4. Kazuo Takahashi, *Shinryu Tokubetsu Kogekitai* [*Divine Dragon Special Attack Unit*] (Tokyo: Koujinsha, 2001), p. 189.
5. Sato, *Maboroshi no Sensui Kubo,* p. 173.
6. Takahashi, *Shinryu Tokubetsu Kogekitai,* p. 189.
7. Nobukiyo Nambu, *Beikidoukantai wo Kishuseyo: Sensuikuubo I-401 Kanchou No Shuki* [*Surprise Attack on the American Fleet! Memoir of the I-401 Aircraft-Carrying Submarine by Its Captain*] (Tokyo: Fuami Shobo, 1988), p. 209.
8. Takahashi, *Shinryu Tokubetsu Kogekitai,* p. 190.
9. Sato, *Maboroshi no Sensui Kubo,* p. 175.
10. Nambu, *Beikidoukantai wo Kishuseyo,* p. 174.
11. Chin-Ji Inouye, interview by author.
12. Ibid.
13. Ibid.
14. R. Kissinger, Jr., *I-400, I-401 Japanese Submarines, Description of Hull, General Arrangement and Characteristics* (U.S. Navy, 1946), p. 1.
15. Chin-Ji Inouye, interview by author.
16. Ibid.
17. Nambu, *Beikidoukantai wo Kishuseyo,* p. 209; Zenji Orita with Joseph D. Harrington, *I-Boat Captain: How Japan's Submarine Force Almost Defeated*

the U.S. Navy in the Pacific! (Canoga Park, Calif.: Major Books, 1976), p. 276.

18. Ikuhiko Hata, *Dainiji Taisen Koukuju Shiwa* [*Historical Aviation Stories of World War II*], trans. Shojo Jonda and Sandy Kita (Japan: Chuukou Bunko, n.d.), chap. 10.
19. Nambu, *Beikidoukantai wo Kishuseyo*, p. 209.
20. Ibid.
21. Hata, *Dainiji Taisen Koukuju Shiwa*, chap. 10.
22. Nambu, *Beikidoukantai wo Kishuseyo*, p. 210.

Chapter 24. Fulp's Last Patrol

1. USS *Segundo* (SS 398) Deck Logs, January 5, 1945.
2. USS *Segundo*, Third War Patrol Report, Prologue, http://www.segundo398.org/patrol_reports/patrol3.pdf.
3. Victor S. Horgan, interview by author.
4. Charles A. Lockwood and Hans Christian Adamson, *Hellcats of the Sea* (New York: Bantam Books, 1988), p. 43.
5. L. Rodney Johnson, interview by author.
6. Wallace C. Karnes, Jr., interview by author.
7. *Segundo*, Third Patrol Report, February 1, 1945, 1630.
8. Clay Blair, Jr., *Silent Victory: The U.S. Submarine War Against Japan* (Annapolis, Md.: Naval Institute Press, 1975), p. 225.
9. Ibid., p. 844.
10. *Segundo*, Third Patrol Report, February 9, 1945, 1438.
11. L. Rodney Johnson, interview by author.
12. *Segundo*, Third Patrol Report, February 19, 1945, 1913–2130.
13. Ibid., March 6, 1945, 2355.
14. Ibid., March 11, 1945, 0413.
15. USS *Segundo* (SS 398) Fourth War Patrol Report, April 26, 1945, 1330, http://www.segundo398.org/patrol_reports/patrol4.pdf.
16. *Segundo* Deck Logs, May 17, 1945, 1328.
17. *Segundo*, Fourth Patrol Report, May 18, 1945, 1730.
18. Ibid., May 29, 1945, 1318.
19. Ibid., May 29, 1945, 1318–1720.
20. *Segundo*, Fourth Patrol Report, May 29, 1945, 1343–1429.
21. Victor S. Horgan, interview by author.
22. *Segundo*, Fourth Patrol Report, May 29, 1945, 1500.
23. Ibid., May 31, 1945, 2150.
24. Ibid., May 31, 1945, 2253.
25. Ibid., June 8, 1945, 2209.
26. *Segundo*, Fourth Patrol Report, June 9, 1945, 0022.
27. Ibid.

28. Ellsworth Russel "Bud" Quam, interview by author.
29. *Segundo* Deck Logs, June 8, 1945.
30. *Segundo*, Fourth Patrol Report, June 9, 1945, 0022; Quam, interview by author.
31. L. Rodney Johnson, interview by author.
32. Carl Stallcop, interview by author. Stallcop had been promoted to chief after the *Segundo*'s second war patrol, due to his quick work in the pump room.
33. Carl Stallcop, interview by author.
34. Victor S. Horgan, interview by author.
35. Ibid.; Wallace C. Karnes, Jr., interview by author; Richard Binkley, interview by author.
36. Richard Binkley, interview by author.
37. Cmdr. James Douglas Fulp, Jr., Gold Star citation, at National Personnel Records Center, Military Personnel Records, St. Louis.
38. Carl Stallcop, interview by author.

Chapter 25. Nanao Bay

1. Nobukiyo Nambu, *Beikidoukantai wo Kishuseyo: Sensuikuubo I-401 Kanchou No Shuki* [*Surprise Attack on the American Fleet! Memoir of the I-401 Aircraft-Carrying Submarine by Its Captain*] (Tokyo: Fuami Shobo, 1988), p. 209.
2. Tsugio Sato, *Maboroshi no Sensui Kubo* [*Phantom Submarine Carrier*] (Tokyo: Kabushiki Gaisha Kojin-sha, 1989), p. 174.
3. Nambu, *Beikidoukantai wo Kishuseyo*, p. 210; Sato, *Maboroshi no Sensui Kubo*, p. 175.
4. Sato, *Maboroshi no Sensui Kubo*, p. 175.
5. Ibid., p. 142; Robert C. Mikesh, *Aichi M6A1 Seiran: Japan's Submarine Launched Panama Canal Bomber*, Close-Up 13 (Boylston, Mass.: Monogram Aviation Publications, 1975), p. 13.
6. Chin-Ji Inouye, interview by author.
7. Nambu, *Beikidoukantai wo Kishuseyo*, p. 212.
8. Mikesh, *Aichi M6A1 Seiran*, p. 13.
9. Thomas S. Momiyama, "All and Nothing," *Air & Space*, Smithsonian, October–November 2001, p. 28.
10. Nambu, *Beikidoukantai wo Kishuseyo*, p. 203.
11. Ibid., p. 201.
12. Ibid.
13. Sato, *Maboroshi no Sensui Kubo*, p. 176; Mikesh, *Aichi M6A1 Seiran*, p. 12.
14. Sato, *Maboroshi no Sensui Kubo*, p. 176.
15. Atsushi Asamura, interview by author.
16. Atsushi Asamura, interview, *Rekishi Gunzou*, Gakken, Issue no. 85, October 10, 2007, pp. 154–59; Tsugio Yata, "SubRon 1 . . . Aims for U.S.

Fleet at Ulithi and Panama Canal," *I-401 History, I-401* Submarine Society, Japan.

17. Atsushi Asamura, "*I-401* Sensuikan to Seiran to Watashi to [The *I-401* Submarine, *Seiran* and Me]," *Maru* Special, *Japanese Naval Vessels,* no. 13, 1977, pp. 42–43.

18. Thomas O. Paine, "The Transpacific Voyage of HIJMS *I-400*: Tom Paine's Journal: July 1945–January 1946," February 1991, http://www.pacerfarm.org/i-400/.

19. Atsushi Asamura, interview by author.

20. Nambu, *Beikidoukantai wo Kishuseyo,* p. 201.

21. Sato, *Maboroshi no Sensui Kubo,* p. 176; Ikuhiko Hata, *Dainiji Taisen Koukuju Shiwa [Historical Aviation Stories of World War II]*, trans. Shojo Jonda and Sandy Kita (Japan: Chuukou Bunko, n.d.), chap. 10.

22. Sato, *Maboroshi no Sensui Kubo,* p. 176.

23. Kazuo Takahashi, *Shinryu Tokubetsu Kogekitai [Divine Dragon Special Attack Unit]* (Tokyo: Koujinsha, 2001), p. 191.

24. Sato, *Maboroshi no Sensui Kubo,* p. 176.

25. Ibid.

26. Mikesh, *Aichi M6A1 Seiran,* p. 13.

27. Sato, *Maboroshi no Sensui Kubo,* pp. 176–77; Nambu, *Beikidoukantai wo Kishuseyo,* p. 211.

28. Sato, *Maboroshi no Sensui Kubo,* p. 181.

29. Takahashi, *Shinryu Tokubetsu Kogekitai,* p. 192.

30. Nambu, *Beikidoukantai wo Kishuseyo,* p. 211.

31. Takahashi, *Shinryu Tokubetsu Kogekitai,* p. 192.

32. Nambu, *Beikidoukantai wo Kishuseyo,* p. 211.

33. Heiji Kondo, interview by author.

34. Chin-Ji Inouye, interview by author.

35. Kazuo Takatsuka, *Memories of the I-400* (Japan: privately published, 1996).

36. *CINCPAC-CINCPOA Bulletin,* no. 108-45, *Japanese Naval Vessels,* Special Translation no. 64, May 18, 1945, pp. 8, 66, 83.

37. Division of Naval Intelligence, ONI 222-J, *The Japanese Navy,* Official U.S. Navy Reference Manual, June 1945, p. 85.

38. Momiyama, "All and Nothing," p. 25.

Chapter 26. The Taste of Persimmon

1. Chin-Ji Inouye, interview by author.

2. Nobukiyo Nambu, *Beikidoukantai wo Kishuseyo: Sensuikuubo I-401 Kanchou No Shuki [Surprise Attack on the American Fleet! Memoir of the I-401 Aircraft-Carrying Submarine by Its Captain]* (Tokyo: Fuami Shobo, 1988), p. 212.

3. Bob Hackett and Sander Kingsepp, "Sensuikan! IJN Submarine *I-222*, Tabular Record of Movement," June 10, 1945, CombinedFleet. com,http://www.combinedfleet.com/I-122.htm.

4. Nambu, *Beikidoukantai wo Kishuseyo*, p. 212.

5. Zenji Orita with Joseph D. Harrington, *I-Boat Captain: How Japan's Submarine Force Almost Defeated the U.S. Navy in the Pacific!* (Canoga Park, Calif.: Major Books, 1976), pp. 275–76.

6. Tsugio Sato, *Maboroshi no Sensui Kubo* [*Phantom Submarine Carrier*] (Tokyo: Kabushiki Gaisha Kojin-sha, 1989), pp. 133, 143.

7. Ibid., p. 179.

8. Orita and Harrington, *I-Boat Captain*, p. 299.

9. Sato, *Maboroshi no Sensui Kubo*, pp. 178–80.

10. Ibid., p. 180.

11. Ibid.

12. Kazuo Takahashi, *Shinryu Tokubetsu Kogekitai* [*Divine Dragon Special Attack Unit*] (Tokyo: Koujinsha, 2001), p. 193.

13. Ibid.

14. Nambu, *Beikidoukantai wo Kishuseyo*, p. 214.

15. Ibid.

16. John E. Long, "Japan's Undersea Carriers," *U.S. Naval Institute Proceedings*, June 1950, p. 613.

17. Richard N. Billings, *Battleground Atlantic* (New York: NAL Caliber, 2006), p. 170. It's possible her destination could have been Penang.

18. Ibid., pp. 168–69.

19. Philip Henshall, *Vengeance: Hitler's Nuclear Weapon—Fact or Fiction?* (Gloucestershire, U.K.: Sutton 1998), p. 157; Billings, *Battleground Atlantic*, pp. 256–59.

20. Billings, *Battleground Atlantic*, pp. 173–76.

21. Sato, *Maboroshi no Sensui Kubo*, p. 214.

22. Nambu, *Beikidoukantai wo Kishuseyo*, p. 214.

23. Tsugio Yata, "SubRon 1 . . . Aims for U.S. Fleet at Ulithi and Panama Canal," *I-401 History*, I-401 Submarine Society, Japan.

24. Nambu, *Beikidoukantai wo Kishuseyo*, p. 214.

25. Sato, *Maboroshi no Sensui Kubo*, p. 182.

26. Ibid.

27. Nambu, *Beikidoukantai wo Kishuseyo*, p. 214.

28. Orita and Harrington, *I-Boat Captain*, p. 299.

29. M. G. Sheftall, *Blossoms in the Wind: Human Legacies of the Kamikaze* (New York: NAL Caliber, 2006), p. 38.

30. Quoted in Sato, *Maboroshi no Sensui Kubo*, p. 180; Takahashi, *Shinryu Tokubetsu Kogekitai*, p. 193.

31. Quoted in Orita and Harrington, *I-Boat Captain*, p. 300.

32. Nambu, *Beikidoukantai wo Kishuseyo*, p. 214.

Chapter 27. Johnson Takes Command

1. Richard Binkley, interview by author.
2. Suze Johnson Comerford, interview by author.
3. U.S. Naval Academy, Executive Department, Abstract of Conduct, Midshipman S. L. Johnson, Class of 1939, January 5, 1939.
4. Ibid.
5. Medical Officer of the Watch to Commandant of Midshipmen, Report of sobriety examination, Stephen Lobdell JOHNSON, Mid. 1c 4th Batt., January 2, 1939, Medical Department, U.S. Naval Academy, Annapolis, Md., at National Personnel Records Center, Military Personnel Records, St. Louis.
6. U.S. Naval Academy, Executive Department, Abstract of Conduct, Midshipman S. L. Johnson, Class of 1939, January 5, 1939, at National Personnel Records Center, Military Personnel Records, St. Louis.
7. Corrine Callahan (Mrs. David Callahan) to Superintendent, U.S. Naval Academy, Annapolis, Maryland, January 9, 1939, at National Personnel Records Center, Military Personnel Records, St. Louis.
8. Stephen Lobdell Johnson, Class of 1939 Alumni Notes, *Nine Years Later*, p. 94.
9. Ibid., p. 91.
10. Navy Secretary James Forrestal to Stephen Lobdell Johnson, Silver Star Medal citation, September 17, 1944, rewritten February 28, 1947, at National Personnel Records Center, Military Personnel Records, St. Louis.
11. C. A. Lockwood, Jr., to Stephen Lobdell Johnson, Gold Star in lieu of second Silver Star citation, July 7, 1947, rewritten February 18, 1949, at National Personnel Records Center, Military Personnel Records, St. Louis.
12. George Gambel, interview by author.

Chapter 28. Operation Storm

1. Bob Hackett and Sander Kingsepp, "Operation Tan No. 2: The Japanese Attack on Task Force 58's Anchorage at Ulithi," CombinedFleet .com, http://www.combinedfleet.com/Tan%20No.%202.htm.
2. Tsugio Sato, *Maboroshi no Sensui Kubo* [*Phantom Submarine Carrier*] (Tokyo: Kabushiki Gaisha Kojin-sha, 1989), p. 151.
3. Ibid., p. 183.
4. Thomas O. Paine, "The Transpacific Voyage of HIJMS *I-400*, Tom Paine's Journal: July 1945–January 1946," February 1991, http://www .pacerfarm.org/i-400/.

5. Zenji Orita with Joseph D. Harrington, *I-Boat Captain: How Japan's Submarine Force Almost Defeated the U.S. Navy in the Pacific!* (Canoga Park, Calif.: Major Books, 1976), p. 293.

6. Max Hastings, *Retribution: The Battle for Japan, 1944–1945* (New York: Alfred A. Knopf, 2007), p. 315.

7. Ibid., p. 182.

8. Sato, *Maboroshi no Sensui Kubo*, pp. 183, 184.

9. Kazuo Takahashi, *Shinryu Tokubetsu Kogekitai* [*Divine Dragon Special Attack Unit*] (Tokyo: Koujinsha, 2001), p. 192.

10. Hackett and Kingsepp, "Operation Tan no. 2."

11. Sato, *Maboroshi no Sensui Kubo*, p. 181.

12. Ibid., pp. 187–88.

13. Orita and Harrington, *I-Boat Captain*, p. 299.

14. Sato, *Maboroshi no Sensui Kubo*, p. 188.

15. Orita and Harrington, *I-Boat Captain*, p. 299; Paine, "Transpacific Voyage of HIJMS *I-400*."

16. Sato, *Maboroshi no Sensui Kubo*, p. 189.

17. Ibid., p. 191.

18. Takahashi, *Shinryu Tokubetsu Kogekitai*, p. 195.

19. Ibid., pp. 194–95.

20. Ibid., p. 195.

21. Ibid.

22. Sato, *Maboroshi no Sensui Kubo*, pp. 181, 193; Takahashi, *Shinryu Tokubetsu Kogekitai*, p. 195.

23. Takahashi, *Shinryu Tokubetsu Kogekitai*, p. 196.

24. Ibid.

25. Ibid.

26. Sato, *Maboroshi no Sensui Kubo*, pp. 197–98.

27. Ibid., p. 193.

28. Nobukiyo Nambu, *Beikidoukantai wo Kishuseyo: Sensuikuubo I-401 Kanchou No Shuki* [*Surprise Attack on the American Fleet! Memoir of the I-401 Aircraft-Carrying Submarine by Its Captain*] (Tokyo: Fuami Shobo, 1988), pp. 215–18, 227.

29. Charles A. Lockwood, *Sink 'Em All* (New York: Bantam, 1984), p. 339.

30. Sato, *Maboroshi no Sensui Kubo*, p. 194.

31. Nambu, *Beikidoukantai wo Kishuseyo*, p. 217.

32. Sato, *Maboroshi no Sensui Kubo*, p. 194; Tsugio Yata, "SubRon 1 . . . Aims for U.S. Fleet at Ulithi and Panama Canal," *I-401 History*, I-401 Submarine Society, Japan.

33. Nambu, *Beikidoukantai wo Kishuseyo*, p. 218.

34. Yata, "SubRon1."

35. Nambu, *Beikidoukantai wo Kishuseyo*, p. 218; Sato, *Maboroshi no Sensui Kubo*, p. 194.

36. Takahashi, *Shinryu Tokubetsu Kogekitai*, p. 196; Sato, *Maboroshi no Sensui Kubo*, p. 194.

37. Sato, *Maboroshi no Sensui Kubo*, p. 195.

38. Ibid.

39. Ibid.

40. Nambu, *Beikidoukantai wo Kishuseyo*, p. 218.

41. Henry Sakaida, Gary Nila, and Koji Takaki, *I-400: Japan's Secret Aircraft-Carrying Strike Submarine, Objective Panama Canal* (East Sussex, U.K.: Hikoki, 2006), p. 53.

42. Nambu, *Beikidoukantai wo Kishuseyo*, p. 218.

43. Ibid.

44. Ibid., p. 219.

45. Takahashi, *Shinryu Tokubetsu Kogekitai*, p. 197.

Chapter 29. Departure

1. Nobukiyo Nambu, *Beikidoukantai wo Kishuseyo: Sensuikuubo I-401 Kanchou No Shuki* [*Surprise Attack on the American Fleet! Memoir of the I-401 Aircraft-Carrying Submarine by Its Captain*] (Tokyo: Fuami Shobo, 1988), p. 219.

2. Kazuo Takahashi, *Shinryu Tokubetsu Kogekitai* [*Divine Dragon Special Attack Unit*] (Tokyo: Koujinsha, 2001), p. 197.

3. Ibid.

4. Tsugio Sato, *Maboroshi no Sensui Kubo* [*Phantom Submarine Carrier*] (Tokyo: Kabushiki Gaisha Kojin-sha, 1989), p. 196.

5. Nambu, *Beikidoukantai wo Kishuseyo*, p. 219.

6. Sato, *Maboroshi no Sensui Kubo*, p. 195.

7. Thomas O. Paine, "The Transpacific Voyage of HIJMS *I-400*, Tom Paine's Journal: July 1945–January 1946," February 1991, http://www.pacerfarm.org/i-400/.

8. Max Hastings, *Retribution: The Battle for Japan, 1944–1945* (New York: Alfred A. Knopf, 2007), p. 313.

9. Ibid., p. 300; Sato, *Maboroshi no Sensui Kubo*, p. 206.

10. Nambu, *Beikidoukantai wo Kishuseyo*, p. 246. Nambu contradicts himself here, since he notes on p. 186 that the *I-404* was built in Sasebo. Nevertheless, the *I-404* appears to have been laid down in Kure on July 7, 1944.

11. Zenji Orita with Joseph D. Harrington, *I-Boat Captain: How Japan's Submarine Force Almost Defeated the U.S. Navy in the Pacific!* (Canoga Park, Calif.: Major Books, 1976), p. 303; Norman Polmar and Dorr B. Carpenter, *Submarines of the Imperial Japanese Navy, 1904–1945* (London: Conway Maritime Press, 1986), p. 111. Nambu, in *Beikidoukantai wo Kishuseyo*, does not mention the *I-404* being sunk by U.S. planes, but he does say it was dismantled after the war (p. 246).

12. Sato, *Maboroshi no Sensui Kubo*, p. 134; Nambu, *Beikidoukantai wo Kishuseyo*, p. 246; Seiji Azuma, "Sekai Ni Hirui Naki '*I-400* Gata, *I-13*

Gata' No Kouzou to Seinou [The Construction and Efficiency of the Unparalleled *I-400* and *I-13*]," *Maru* Special, *Japanese Naval Vessels*, no. 13 (Tokyo: Kojinsha, 1977), p. 28.

13. Erminio Bagnasco, *Submarines of World War II* (London: Cassell, 2000), p. 194.

14. Nambu, *Beikidoukantai wo Kishuseyo*, p. 216.

15. Sato, *Maboroshi no Sensui Kubo*, p. 196.

16. João Paulo Julião Matsuura, "Nakajima C6N *Saiun* (Painted Cloud)," CombinedFleet.com, http://www.combinedfleet.com/ijna/c6n.htm.

17. Sato, *Maboroshi no Sensui Kubo*, p. 196.

18. Nambu, *Beikidoukantai wo Kishuseyo*, p. 216.

19. Takahashi, *Shinryu Tokubetsu Kogekitai*, p. 195.

20. Nambu, *Beikidoukantai wo Kishuseyo*, p. 216.

21. Takahashi, *Shinryu Tokubetsu Kogekitai*, pp. 194, 212; Nambu, *Beikidoukantai wo Kishuseyo*, p. 216.

22. Sato, *Maboroshi no Sensui Kubo*, pp. 191–92.

23. Clay Blair, Jr., *Silent Victory: The U.S. Submarine War Against Japan* (Annapolis, Md.: Naval Institute Press, 1975), p. 868.

24. James D. Hornfischer, *Ship of Ghosts* (New York: Bantam Books, 2007), p. 393.

25. Ibid., pp. 392–93.

26. Nambu, *Beikidoukantai wo Kishuseyo*, p. 217.

27. Ibid.; Takahashi, *Shinryu Tokubetsu Kogekitai*, p. 194.

28. Nambu, *Beikidoukantai wo Kishuseyo*, p. 161.

29. Ibid., p. 219. Sato, in *Maboroshi no Sensui Kubo* (p. 196), recalls the date as July 22, while Takahashi, in *Shinryu Tokubetsu Kogekitai* (p. 198), says the subs arrived on July 21. Asamura recalls the date even earlier, saying it was July 13; see Atsushi Asamura, interview, *Rekishi Gunzou*, Issue no. 85, October 10, 2007, Gakken, pp. 154–59. As a result, it's difficult to know with confidence which date is correct, but July 22 seems most likely.

30. Takahashi, *Shinryu Tokubetsu Kogekitai*, p. 198.

31. Sato, *Maboroshi no Sensui Kubo*, p. 198.

32. Takahashi, *Shinryu Tokubetsu Kogekitai*, p. 198.

33. Sato, *Maboroshi no Sensui Kubo*, p. 198.

34. Ibid., pp. 196–97. Eyewitness accounts suggest the *I-400 Seiran* may have been painted at Maizuru, while the *I-401* planes were painted later at Ominato.

35. Heiji Kondo, interview by author; Sato, *Maboroshi no Sensui Kubo*, p. 198.

36. Sato, *Maboroshi no Sensui Kubo*, p. 198.

37. Takahashi, *Shinryu Tokubetsu Kogekitai*, p. 199.

38. Nambu, *Beikidoukantai wo Kishuseyo*, p. 219.

39. Chin-Ji Inouye, interview by author.

40. Nambu, *Beikidoukantai wo Kishuseyo*, p. 219.

41. Sato, *Maboroshi no Sensui Kubo*, p. 202.
42. Chin-Ji Inouye, interview by author.
43. Nambu, *Beikidoukantai wo Kishuseyo*, p. 220.

Chapter 30. Under Way

1. Tsugio Sato, *Maboroshi no Sensui Kubo* [*Phantom Submarine Carrier*] (Tokyo: Kabushiki Gaisha Kojin-sha, 1989), p. 202.
2. Nobukiyo Nambu, *Beikidoukantai wo Kishuseyo: Sensuikuubo I-401 Kanchou No Shuki* [*Surprise Attack on the American Fleet! Memoir of the I-401 Aircraft-Carrying Submarine by Its Captain*] (Tokyo: Fuami Shobo, 1988), p. 220.
3. Zenji Orita with Joseph D. Harrington, *I-Boat Captain: How Japan's Submarine Force Almost Defeated the U.S. Navy in the Pacific!* (Canoga Park, Calif.: Major Books, 1976), p. 300; Kazuo Takahashi, *Shinryu Tokubetsu Kogekitai* [*Divine Dragon Special Attack Unit*] (Tokyo: Koujinsha, 2001), p. 199.
4. Sato, *Maboroshi no Sensui Kubo*, p. 203; Nambu, *Beikidoukantai wo Kishuseyo*, p. 220.
5. Ibid., p. 199.
6. Kazuo Takatsuka, *Memories of the I-400* (Japan: privately published, 1996).
7. Takahashi, *Shinryu Tokubetsu Kogekitai*, p. 199.
8. Sato, *Maboroshi no Sensui Kubo*, p. 200.
9. Ibid, p. 202.
10. Hidetoshi Namura, "Watashi wa *I-400* Sen Yojo Kofuku no tachianinin datta (I was a witness to the *I-400* surrender]," *Maru* [magazine], September 1976, p. 82.
11. Sato, *Maboroshi no Sensui Kubo*, pp. 202, 204.
12. Ibid.
13. Ibid.
14. Ibid., p. 203.
15. Takahashi, *Shinryu Tokubetsu Kogekitai*, pp. 194, 212.
16. Correspondence with Carl Boyd.

Chapter 31. Crossed Wires

1. Nobukiyo Nambu, *Beikidoukantai wo Kishuseyo: Sensuikuubo I-401 Kanchou No Shuki* [*Surprise Attack on the American Fleet! Memoir of the I-401 Aircraft-Carrying Submarine by Its Captain*] (Tokyo: Fuami Shobo, 1988), p. 217.
2. Tsugio Sato, *Maboroshi no Sensui Kubo* [*Phantom Submarine Carrier*] (Tokyo: Kabushiki Gaisha Kojin-sha, 1989), p. 193.

3. Ibid.
4. Ibid.
5. Ibid., p. 190.
6. Hidetoshi Namura, "Watashi wa *I-400* Sen Yojo Kofuku no tachianinin datta [I was a witness to the *I-400* surrender]," *Maru* [magazine], September 1976, p. 81.
7. Sato, *Maboroshi no Sensui Kubo,* pp. 188, 189, 215.
8. Ibid., p. 190.
9. Ibid., p. 216.
10. Ibid.
11. Ibid., p. 215.
12. Atsushi Asamura, interview by author.
13. Ibid.
14. Ikuhiko Hata, *Dainiji Taisen Koukuju Shiwa* [*Historical Aviation Stories of World War II*], trans. Shojo Jonda and Sandy Kita (Japan: Chuukou Bunko, n.d.), chap. 10; Nambu, *Beikidoukantai wo Kishuseyo,* p. 222.
15. Hata, *Dainiji Taisen Koukuju Shiwa,* chap. 10.
16. Nambu, *Beikidoukantai wo Kishuseyo,* p. 222.
17. Ibid., p. 221.
18. Atsushi Asamura, "*I-401* Sensuikan to *Seiran* to Watashi to [The *I-401* Submarine, *Seiran* and Me]," *Maru* Special, *Japanese Naval Vessels,* no. 13, 1977, pp. 42–43.
19. Nambu, *Beikidoukantai wo Kishuseyo,* p. 222 quoting Atsushi Asamura; Sato, *Maboroshi no Sensui Kubo,* p. 221.
20. Sato, *Maboroshi no Sensui Kubo,* p. 221.
21. Asamura, "*I-401* Sensuikan to *Seiran* to Watashi," pp. 42–43; Sato, *Maboroshi no Sensui Kubo,* p. 221.
22. Kazuo Takahashi, *Shinryu Tokubetsu Kogekitai* [*Divine Dragon Special Attack Unit*] (Tokyo: Koujinsha, 2001), pp. 200, 201.
23. Ibid., p. 116.
24. Ibid., p. 118.
25. Michael Wilson, *A Submariner's War: The Indian Ocean 1939–1945* (Gloucestershire, U.K.: Spellmount, 2008), p. 103.
26. M. G. Sheftall, *Blossoms in the Wind: Human Legacies of the Kamikaze* (New York: NAL Caliber, 2006), pp. 333–34.
27. Ibid., pp. 237–38.
28. Sato, *Maboroshi no Sensui Kubo,* p. 200.
29. Shoichi Matsutani, interview by author; Kazuo Takatsuka, *Memories of the I-400,* pt. 2, March 1, 1974.
30. Takatsuka, *Memories of the I-400,* pt. 2, March 1, 1974.
31. Ibid.
32. Namura, "Watashi wa *I-400* Sen Yojo Kofuku no tachianinin datta," p. 82.
33. Takatsuka, *Memories of the I-400,* pt. 2, March 1, 1974.
34. Ibid.

35. Ibid.
36. Ibid.
37. Sato, *Maboroshi no Sensui Kubo,* p. 203.
38. Tsugio Yata, interview by author.
39. Nambu, *Beikidoukantai wo Kishuseyo,* p. 220.
40. Nobukiyo Nambu, interview by author.
41. Takahashi, *Shinryu Tokubetsu Kogekitai,* p. 202.
42. Ibid. Some accounts suggest this date was August 14.
43. Sato, *Maboroshi no Sensui Kubo,* p. 223.
44. Takahashi, *Shinryu Tokubetsu Kogekitai,* p. 202.
45. Ibid.

Chapter 32. The Emperor's Voice

1. W. J. Holmes, *Undersea Victory: The Influence of Submarine Operations on the War in the Pacific* (Garden City, N.Y.: Doubleday, 1966), p. 481.
2. Carlo M. Carlucci, interview by author.
3. Ibid.
4. USS *Segundo* (SS 398), Fifth War Patrol Report, Prologue, http://www .segundo398.org/patrol_reports/patrol5.pdf.
5. Ibid.
6. Victor S. Horgan, interview by author.
7. USS *Segundo* (SS 398) Deck Log, August 10, 1945.
8. Victor S. Horgan, interview by author.
9. Steve L. Johnson, Jr., interview by author.
10. Nobukiyo Nambu, *Beikidoukantai wo Kishuseyo: Sensuikuubo I-401 Kanchou No Shuki* [*Surprise Attack on the American Fleet! Memoir of the I-401 Aircraft-Carrying Submarine by Its Captain*] (Tokyo: Fuami Shobo, 1988), p. 226.
11. Hidetoshi Namura, "Watashi wa *I-400* Sen Yojo Kofuku no tachianinin datta [I was a witness to the *I-400* surrender]," *Maru* [magazine], September 1976, p. 82.
12. Kazuo Takahashi, *Shinryu Tokubetsu Kogekitai* [*Divine Dragon Special Attack Unit*] (Tokyo: Koujinsha, 2001), p. 202.
13. Nambu, *Beikidoukantai wo Kishuseyo,* p. 226.
14. Tsugio Sato, *Maboroshi no Sensui Kubo* [*Phantom Submarine Carrier*] (Tokyo: Kabushiki Gaisha Kojin-sha, 1989), p. 192.
15. Bob Hackett and Sander Kingsepp, "Sensuikan! IJN Submarine *I-13,* Tabular Record of Movement," August 1, 1945, CombinedFleet.com, http://www.combinedfleet.com/I-13.htm.
16. Takahashi, *Shinryu Tokubetsu Kogekitai,* pp. 203, 200.
17. Kazuo Takatsuka, *Memories of the I-400* (Japan: privately published, 1996), pt. 3, September 20, 1974.
18. Takahashi, *Shinryu Tokubetsu Kogekitai,* p. 201.

19. Ibid., p. 202.
20. Ibid.
21. Ibid, p. 203.
22. Ibid.
23. Sato, *Maboroshi no Sensui Kubo*, p. 231.
24. Takahashi, *Shinryu Tokubetsu Kogekitai*, p. 203.
25. Sato, *Maboroshi no Sensui Kubo*, p. 231.
26. Nambu, *Beikidoukantai wo Kishuseyo*, p. 223; Sato, *Maboroshi no Sensui Kubo*, pp. 229, 223.
27. Nambu, *Beikidoukantai wo Kishuseyo*, pp. 220, 225.
28. Nambu, *Beikidoukantai wo Kishuseyo*, p. 226.
29. Ibid., p. 223.
30. Sato, *Maboroshi no Sensui Kubo*, p. 223.
31. Nambu, *Beikidoukantai wo Kishuseyo*, p. 226.
32. Ibid., p. 227.
33. Ibid.
34. Takahashi, *Shinryu Tokubetsu Kogekitai* p. 204; Sato, *Maboroshi no Sensui Kubo*, p. 228.
35. Ibid., p. 204; Sato, *Maboroshi no Sensui Kubo*, p. 228; Nambu, *Beikidoukantai wo Kishuseyo*, p. 227.
36. Nambu, *Beikidoukantai wo Kishuseyo*, p. 228; Sato, *Maboroshi no Sensui Kubo*, p. 223.

Chapter 33. Anarchy

1. Kazuo Takahashi, *Shinryu Tokubetsu Kogekitai* [*Divine Dragon Special Attack Unit*] (Tokyo: Koujinsha, 2001), p. 204
2. Nobukiyo Nambu, *Beikidoukantai wo Kishuseyo: Sensuikuubo I-401 Kanchou No Shuki* [*Surprise Attack on the American Fleet! Memoir of the I-401 Aircraft-Carrying Submarine by Its Captain*] (Tokyo: Fuami Shobo, 1988), pp. 227–28; Tsugio Sato, *Maboroshi no Sensui Kubo* [*Phantom Submarine Carrier*] (Tokyo: Kabushiki Gaisha Kojin-sha, 1989), pp. 228, 230.
3. Takahashi, *Shinryu Tokubetsu Kogekitai*, p. 207.
4. Tsugio Yata, "SubRon 1 . . . Aims for U.S. Fleet at Ulithi and Panama Canal," *I-401 History*, I-401 Submarine Society, Japan; Sato, *Maboroshi no Sensui Kubo*, p. 271.
5. Masao Okui, interview by author.
6. Takahashi, *Shinryu Tokubetsu Kogekitai*, p. 204.
7. Ibid.; Hidetoshi Namura, "Watashi wa *I-400* Sen Yojo Kofuku no tachianinin datta [I was a witness to the *I-400* surrender]," *Maru* [magazine], September 1976, p. 83.
8. Takahashi, *Shinryu Tokubetsu Kogekitai*, pp. 204–205.
9. Henry Sakaida, Gary Nila, and Koji Takaki, *I-400: Japan's Secret*

Aircraft-Carrying Strike Submarine, Objective Panama Canal (East Sussex, U.K.: Hikoki, 2006), p. 59

10. Takahashi, *Shinryu Tokubetsu Kogekitai*, p. 206.
11. Ibid., p. 205.
12. Ibid., p. 206.
13. Kazuo Takatsuka, *Memories of the I-400* (Japan: privately published, 1996), pt. 3, September 20, 1974.
14. Takahashi, *Shinryu Tokubetsu Kogekitai*, p. 206.
15. Ibid., pp. 206–207.
16. Sato, *Maboroshi no Sensui Kubo*, p. 231.
17. Bob Hackett and Sander Kingsepp, "Sensuikan! IJN Submarine *I-14*, Tabular Record of Movement," August 15, 1945, CombinedFleet.com, http://www.combinedfleet.com/I-14.htm.
18. Sato, *Maboroshi no Sensui Kubo*, pp. 228–32.
19. Ibid., p. 249.
20. Sato, *Maboroshi no Sensui Kubo*, pp. 228, 231.
21. Ibid., p. 250.
22. Ibid., pp. 234, 250.
23. Ibid., p. 229.
24. Ibid., p. 230.
25. Ibid.
26. Nambu, *Beikidoukantai wo Kishuseyo*, p. 229; Sato, *Maboroshi no Sensui Kubo*, pp. 234–35.
27. Nambu, *Beikidoukantai wo Kishuseyo*, p. 229; Sato, *Maboroshi no Sensui Kubo*, pp. 234–35.
28. Sato, *Maboroshi no Sensui Kubo*, p. 235.
29. Ibid., p. 236.
30. Ibid., pp. 238, 273.
31. Ibid., p. 238.
32. Tsugio Yata, interview by author.
33. Ibid.
34. Nambu, *Beikidoukantai wo Kishuseyo*, p. 229.
35. Ibid., p. 230.
36. Sato, *Maboroshi no Sensui Kubo*, p. 236.
37. Ibid., p. 229.
38. Muneo Bando, "Go Dai-yonhyakuichi (401) Sensuikan Kitou No Omoide [Memories of the I-401's Return]," *I-401 History, I-401* Submarine Society, Japan, p. 136.
39. Muneo Bando, interview by author.
40. Bando, "Memories of the I-401's Return," pp. 136–40; Sato, *Maboroshi no Sensui Kubo*, pp. 235, 237.
41. Tsugio Yata, interview by author.
42. Nambu, *Beikidoukantai wo Kishuseyo*, p. 231.
43. Sato, *Maboroshi no Sensui Kubo*, p. 239.

44. Ibid., pp. 230–31.
45. Tsugio Yata, interview by author.
46. Imperial Rescript Granted the Ministers of War and Navy, August 17, 1945, reproduced in *Psychological Warfare*, pt. 2, supp. 2, *CINCPAC-CINCPOA Bulletin*, no. 164-45.
47. Namura, "Watashi wa I-400 Sen Yojo Kofuku no tachianinin data," p. 83.
48. Nambu, *Beikidoukantai wo Kishuseyo*, p. 235; Sato, *Maboroshi no Sensui Kubo*, p. 241.
49. Sato, *Maboroshi no Sensui Kubo*, pp. 238–39.
50. Ibid., p. 242.
51. Nambu, *Beikidoukantai wo Kishuseyo*, p. 236.
52. Ibid., pp. 234, 236.
53. Sato, *Maboroshi no Sensui Kubo*, p. 199; Haruo Sugiyama, interview by author.
54. Nambu, *Beikidoukantai wo Kishuseyo*, p. 236.
55. Tsugio Yata, interview by author.
56. Chin-Ji Inouye, interview by author.
57. Heiji Kondo, interview by author.
58. Sato, *Maboroshi no Sensui Kubo*, p. 243; Nambu, *Beikidoukantai wo Kishuseyo*, p. 237.
59. Heiji Kondo, interview by author.
60. Takahashi, *Shinryu Tokubetsu Kogekitai*, p. 206.
61. Takatsuka, *Memories of the I-400*, pt. 3, September 20, 1974.
62. Takatsuka, *Memories of the I-400*, pt. 3, September 20, 1974.
63. Henry Sakaida, Gary Nila, and Koji Takaki, *I-400: Japan's Secret Aircraft-Carrying Strike Submarine, Objective Panama Canal* (East Sussex, U.K.: Hikoki, 2006), p. 60.
64. Masao Okui, interview by author.
65. Kazuo Nishijima, interview by author.

Chapter 34. Escape

1. USS *Segundo* (SS 398) Deck Logs, August 15, 1945.
2. Thomas O. Paine, "The Transpacific Voyage of HIJMS *I-400*, Tom Paine's Journal: July 1945–January 1946," February 1991, http://www.pacerfarm.org/i-400/.
3. John E. Balson, interview by author.
4. USS *Segundo* (SS 398), Fifth War Patrol Report, August 19, 1945, 0725, http://www.segundo398.org/patrol_reports/patrol5.pdf.
5. USS *Segundo* (SS 398) Deck Logs, August 18–24, 1945.
6. *Segundo*, Fifth Patrol Report, August 24, 1945, 1504.
7. Tsugio Sato, *Maboroshi no Sensui Kubo* [*Phantom Submarine Carrier*] (Tokyo: Kabushiki Gaisha Kojin-sha, 1989), p. 245.

8. John E. Balson, interview by author.

9. Nobukiyo Nambu, *Beikidoukantai wo Kishuseyo: Sensuikuubo I-401 Kanchou No Shuki* [*Surprise Attack on the American Fleet! Memoir of the I-401 Aircraft-Carrying Submarine by Its Captain*] (Tokyo: Fuami Shobo, 1988), p. 233.

10. Ibid.

11. Chin-Ji Inouye, interview by author.

12. Ikuhiko Hata, *Dainiji Taisen Koukuju Shiwa* [*Historical Aviation Stories of World War II*], trans. Shojo Jonda and Sandy Kita (Japan: Chuukou Bunko, n.d.), chap. 10.

13. Sato, *Maboroshi no Sensui Kubo*, p. 256.

14. Nambu, *Beikidoukantai wo Kishuseyo*, p. 238.

15. Muneo Bando, interview by author.

16. Sato, *Maboroshi no Sensui Kubo*, p. 257.

17. Nambu, *Beikidoukantai wo Kishuseyo*, p. 238.

18. Ibid.

Chapter 35. Interception

1. Victor S. Horgan, interview by author.

2. USS *Segundo* (SS 398), Fifth War Patrol Report, August 29, 1945, 0425, http://www.segundo398.org/patrol_reports/patrol5.pdf.

3. Tsugio Yata, interview by author.

4. Atsushi Asamura, interview by author.

5. Alex Leitch, "The Chase, Capture and Boarding of a Japanese Submarine," *Polaris,* December 1985.

6. Muneo Bando, interview by author.

7. Nobukiyo Nambu, *Beikidoukantai wo Kishuseyo: Sensuikuubo I-401 Kanchou No Shuki* [*Surprise Attack on the American Fleet! Memoir of the I-401 Aircraft-Carrying Submarine by Its Captain*] (Tokyo: Fuami Shobo, 1988), p. 239.

8. Heiji Kondo, interview by author.

9. Nambu, *Beikidoukantai wo Kishuseyo*, p. 239.

10. Tsugio Sato, *Maboroshi no Sensui Kubo* [*Phantom Submarine Carrier*] (Tokyo: Kabushiki Gaisha Kojin-sha, 1989), p. 258; Muneo Bando, "Memories of the I-401's Return," p. 141.

11. Muneo Bando, interview by author.

12. Heiji Kondo, interview by author.

13. Muneo Bando, interview by author.

14. Chin-Ji Inouye, interview by author; Nambu, *Beikidoukantai wo Kishuseyo*, p. 223.

15. Mueno Bando, "Memories of the I-401's Return," p. 141.

16. Ibid., p. 142.

17. Muneo Bando, interview by author.

18. Sato, *Maboroshi no Sensui Kubo,* p. 258.
19. Muneo Bando, interview by author.
20. *Segundo,* Fifth Patrol Report, August 29, 1945, 0505–0539.
21. Sato, *Maboroshi no Sensui Kubo,* p. 258.
22. Muneo Bando, interview by author.
23. Sato, *Maboroshi no Sensui Kubo,* p. 259.
24. Muneo Bando, interview by author.
25. Ibid.; Sato, *Maboroshi no Sensui Kubo,* p. 259.
26. Muneo Bando, interview by author.
27. *Segundo,* Fifth Patrol Report, August 29, 1945, 0539.
28. Wallace C. Karnes, Jr., interview by author.
29. Sato, *Maboroshi no Sensui Kubo,* p. 259.
30. Nambu, *Beikidoukantai wo Kishuseyo,* p. 241.

Chapter 36. Spoils of War

1. Kazuo Nishijima, interview by author.
2. Nobukiyo Nambu, *Beikidoukantai wo Kishuseyo: Sensuikuubo I-401 Kanchou No Shuki* [*Surprise Attack on the American Fleet! Memoir of the I-401 Aircraft-Carrying Submarine by Its Captain*] (Tokyo: Fuami Shobo, 1988), p. 240; Kazuo Nishijima, interview by author; Hidetoshi Namura, "Watashi wa *I-400* Sen Yojo Kofuku no tachianinin datta [I was a witness to the *I-400* surrender]," *Maru* [magazine], September 1976, p. 83.
3. John E. Long, "Japan's Undersea Carriers," *U.S. Naval Institute Proceedings,* June 1950, p. 607.
4. Henry Sakaida, Gary Nila, and Koji Takaki, *I-400: Japan's Secret Aircraft-Carrying Strike Submarine, Objective Panama Canal* (East Sussex, U.K.: Hikoki, 2006), p. 61.
5. Long, "Japan's Undersea Carriers," p. 607.
6. Sakaida, Nila, and Takaki, *I-400,* p. 60.
7. Ibid., p. 61.
8. Ibid.
9. Kazuo Takahashi, *Shinryu Tokubetsu Kogekitai* [*Divine Dragon Special Attack Unit*] (Tokyo: Koujinsha, 2001), p. 208.
10. Namura, "Watashi wa *I-400* Sen Yojo Kofuku no tachianinin data," p. 84.
11. Sakaida, Nila, and Takaki, *I-400,* pp. 60, 62.
12. Gordon Hiatt, interview by author.
13. Sakaida, Nila, and Takaki, *I-400,* p. 65.
14. Takahashi, *Shinryu Tokubetsu Kogekitai,* p. 209.
15. Sakaida, Nila, and Takaki, *I-400,* p. 63.
16. Ibid.
17. Gordon Hiatt, interview by author.
18. Sakaida, Nila, and Takaki, *I-400,* p. 63.

19. Takahashi, *Shinryu Tokubetsu Kogekitai*, p. 209.
20. Sakaida, Nila, and Takaki, *I-400*, pp. 63–64.
21. Ibid., p. 63.
22. Takahashi, *Shinryu Tokubetsu Kogekitai*, p. 209.
23. Ibid.
24. Sakaida, Nila, and Takaki, *I-400*, p. 63.
25. Ibid.
26. Gordon Hiatt, interview by author.
27. Sakaida, Nila, and Takaki, *I-400*, p. 63.
28. Ibid.
29. Long, "Japan's Undersea Carriers," p. 607.
30. Clay Blair, Jr., *Silent Victory: The U.S. Submarine War Against Japan* (Annapolis, Md.: Naval Institute Press, 1975), p. 196.
31. Long, "Japan's Undersea Carriers," p. 607.
32. Sakaida, Nila, and Takaki, *I-400*, p. 63.
33. Long, "Japan's Undersea Carriers," p. 607.
34. Tsugio Sato, *Maboroshi no Sensui Kubo* [*Phantom Submarine Carrier*] (Tokyo: Kabushiki Gaisha Kojin-sha, 1989), pp. 246–47.
35. Long, "Japan's Undersea Carriers," p. 608.
36. Ibid.
37. Ibid.
38. Sakaida, Nila, and Takaki, *I-400*, p. 64.
39. Harry Arvidson, interview by author.
40. Ibid.
41. Sakaida, Nila, and Takaki, *I-400*, p. 64.
42. Long, "Japan's Undersea Carriers," p. 608.
43. Takahashi, *Shinryu Tokubetsu Kogekitai*, p. 210.
44. Long, "Japan's Undersea Carriers," p. 608.
45. Charles A. Lockwood, *Sink 'Em All* (New York: Bantam Books, 1984), p. 339.
46. Long, "Japan's Undersea Carriers," p. 608.
47. Ibid.
48. Takahashi, *Shinryu Tokubetsu Kogekitai*, p. 210.
49. Robert C. Mikesh, *Aichi M6A1 Seiran: Japan's Submarine Launched Panama Canal Bomber*, Close-Up 13 (Boylston, Mass.: Monogram Aviation Publications, 1975), p. 22.
50. Takahashi, *Shinryu Tokubetsu Kogekitai*, p. 210.
51. Ibid.; Sato, *Maboroshi no Sensui Kubo*, p. 248.
52. Long, "Japan's Undersea Carriers," p. 608.
53. Mikesh, *Aichi M6A1 Seiran*, p. 21.
54. Takahashi, *Shinryu Tokubetsu Kogekitai*, p. 209.
55. Mikesh, *Aichi M6A1 Seiran*, p. 21.
56. Harry Arvidson, interview by author.
57. Takahashi, *Shinryu Tokubetsu Kogekitai*, p. 210.
58. Long, "Japan's Undersea Carriers," p. 609.

Chapter 37. Reckoning

1. Nobukiyo Nambu, *Beikidoukantai wo Kishuseyo: Sensuikuubo I-401 Kanchou No Shuki* [*Surprise Attack on the American Fleet! Memoir of the I-401 Aircraft-Carrying Submarine by Its Captain*] (Tokyo: Fuami Shobo, 1988), p. 218.
2. Tsugio Yata, interview by author.
3. Muneo Bando, interview by author.
4. Jiro Nakahara, testimony, Tokyo War Crimes Tribunal, pp. 38, 140, Macmillan Brown Library, University of Canterbury, Christchurch, New Zealand (hereafter MBL).
5. Nambu, *Beikidoukantai wo Kishuseyo,* p. 241.
6. Tsugio Sato, *Maboroshi no Sensui Kubo* [*Phantom Submarine Carrier*] (Tokyo: Kabushiki Gaisha Kojin-sha, 1989), p. 260.
7. Ibid., p. 261.
8. Ibid.
9. USS *Segundo* (SS 398), Fifth War Patrol Report, August 29, 1945, 0539, http://www.segundo398.org/patrol_reports/patrol5.pdf.
10. Muneo Bando, interview by author.
11. Nambu, *Beikidoukantai wo Kishuseyo,* p. 240.
12. Ibid.
13. Sato, *Maboroshi no Sensui Kubo,* p. 262.
14. Ibid.
15. Victor S. Horgan, interview by author.
16. *Segundo,* Fifth Patrol Report, August 29, 1945, 0609.
17. Ibid.
18. Sato, *Maboroshi no Sensui Kubo,* p. 262.
19. Ibid.
20. Henry Sakaida, Gary Nila, and Koji Takaki, *I-400: Japan's Secret Aircraft-Carrying Strike Submarine, Objective Panama Canal* (East Sussex, U.K.: Hikoki, 2006), p. 68.
21. Muneo Bando, interview by author.
22. *Segundo,* Fifth Patrol Report, August 29, 1945, 0905.
23. Ibid.
24. Muneo Bando, interview by author.

Chapter 38. Boarding Party

1. John E. Long, "Japan's Undersea Carriers," *U.S. Naval Institute Proceedings,* June 1950, p. 609; John E. Balson, interview by KXA radio, Seattle, October 27, 1945.
2. USS *Segundo* (SS 398), Fifth War Patrol Report, August 29, 1945, 0845, http://www.segundo398.org/patrol_reports/patrol5.pdf.
3. John E. Balson, interview by author.

4. L Rodney Johnson, interview by author.
5. Chin-Ji Inouye, interview by author.
6. John E. Balson, interview by author.
7. Carlo M. Carlucci, interview by author.
8. Ibid.; John E. Balson, interview by author; Alex Leitch, "The Chase, Capture, and Boarding of a Japanese Submarine," *Polaris*, December 1985, http://home.earthlink.net/~richandannie/id71.html.
9. *Segundo*, Fifth Patrol Report, August 29, 1945, 0905, 0845, 0945; USS *Segundo* (SS 398), Deck Logs, August 29, 1945.
10. Carlo M. Carlucci, interview by author.
11. Tsugio Sato, *Maboroshi no Sensui Kubo* [*Phantom Submarine Carrier*] (Tokyo: Kabushiki Gaisha Kojin-sha, 1989), p. 266.
12. *Segundo*, Fifth Patrol Report, August 29, 1945, 1125. 1325.
13. Ibid., August 29, 1945, 1340.
14. Muneo Bando, interview by author.
15. *Segundo*, Fifth Patrol Report, August 29, 1945, 1755, 1815.
16. Ibid.
17. Ibid., August 30, 1945, 0220, 0945.
18. Ibid., August 30, 1945, 0955.
19. Sato, *Maboroshi no Sensui Kubo,* p. 265.
20. *Segundo*, Fifth Patrol Report, August 30, 1945, 0955.
21. Heiji Kondo, interview by author.
22. *Segundo*, Fifth Patrol Report, August 30, 1945, 2120.
23. Long, "Japan's Undersea Carriers," pp. 609–10.
24. Nobukiyo Nambu, *Beikidoukantai wo Kishuseyo: Sensuikuubo I-401 Kanchou No Shuki* [*Surprise Attack on the American Fleet! Memoir of the I-401 Aircraft-Carrying Submarine by Its Captain*] (Tokyo: Fuami Shobo, 1988), pp. 242–43; Sato, *Maboroshi no Sensui Kubo,* pp. 266, 242.
25. Sato, *Maboroshi no Sensui Kubo,* p. 264.
26. Nambu, *Beikidoukantai wo Kishuseyo,* p. 242.
27. Sato, *Maboroshi no Sensui Kubo,* p. 273.
28. Chin-Ji Inouye, interview by author; Tsugio Yata, interview by author.

Chapter 39. The Tenth War God

1. Nobukiyo Nambu, *Beikidoukantai wo Kishuseyo: Sensuikuubo I-401 Kanchou No Shuki* [*Surprise Attack on the American Fleet! Memoir of the I-401 Aircraft-Carrying Submarine by Its Captain*] (Tokyo: Fuami Shobo, 1988), pp. 243–44.
2. Ibid., p. 243.
3. Heiji Kondo, interview by author.
4. Tsugio Sato, *Maboroshi no Sensui Kubo* [*Phantom Submarine Carrier*] (Tokyo: Kabushiki Gaisha Kojin-sha, 1989), p. 267.
5. Ibid.

6. Ibid.
7. Nambu, *Beikidoukantai wo Kishuseyo,* p. 244.
8. Ibid.
9. Ibid.; Sato, *Maboroshi no Sensui Kubo,* p. 268.
10. Tsugio Yata, "SubRon 1 . . . Aims for U.S. Fleet at Ulithi and Panama Canal," *I-401 History, I-401* Submarine Society, Japan.
11. Ibid.; Tsugio Yata, interview by author.
12. Yata, "SubRon 1"; Tsugio Yata, interview by author.
13. Nambu, *Beikidoukantai wo Kishuseyo,* p. 244.
14. Yata, "SubRon 1," p. 271.
15. Sato, *Maboroshi no Sensui Kubo,* pp. 267, 271.
16. Ibid., pp. 271, 268.
17. Atsushi Asamura, interview by author.
18. Nambu, *Beikidoukantai wo Kishuseyo,* p. 244; Kazuo Takahashi, *Shinryu Tokubetsu Kogekitai* [*Divine Dragon Special Attack Unit*] (Tokyo: Koujinsha, 2001), p. 212.
19. Nambu, *Beikidoukantai wo Kishuseyo,* p. 244.
20. Sato, *Maboroshi no Sensui Kubo,* p. 270.
21. Chin-Ji Inouye, interview by author.
22. Heiji Kondo, interview by author.
23. Chin-Ji Inouye, interview by author.
24. Henry Sakaida, Gary Nila, and Koji Takaki, *I-400: Japan's Secret Aircraft-Carrying Strike Submarine, Objective Panama Canal* (East Sussex, U.K.: Hikoki, 2006), p. 68.
25. Yata, "SubRon 1."
26. Carlo M. Carlucci, interview by author.
27. Sato, *Maboroshi no Sensui Kubo,* p. 266.
28. Nambu, *Beikidoukantai wo Kishuseyo,* p. 245.

Chapter 40. Bittersweet

1. Tsugio Yata, interview by author.
2. Charles A. Lockwood, *Sink 'Em All* (New York: Bantam Books, 1984), p. 340.
3. USS *Segundo* (SS 398), Fifth War Patrol Report, August 31, 1945, 1127, http://www.segundo398.org/patrol_reports/patrol5.pdf.
4. Kazuo Takahashi, *Shinryu Tokubetsu Kogekitai* [*Divine Dragon Special Attack Unit*] (Tokyo: Koujinsha, 2001), p. 211.
5. Ibid. Others recall the *I-14* arriving before the *I-401.* See Hidetoshi Namura, "Watashi wa *I-400* Sen Yojo Kofuku no tachianinin datta [I was a witness to the *I-400* surrender]," *Maru* [magazine], September 1976, p. 85.
6. Lockwood, *Sink 'Em All,* pp. 338–39.
7. Henry Sakaida, Gary Nila, and Koji Takaki, *I-400: Japan's Secret*

Aircraft-Carrying Strike Submarine, Objective Panama Canal (East Sussex, U.K.: Hikoki, 2006), p. 69.

8. Atsushi Asamura, interview by author.
9. Lockwood, *Sink 'Em All*, p. 339.
10. Nobukiyo Nambu, *Beikidoukantai wo Kishuseyo: Sensuikuubo I-401 Kanchou No Shuki* [*Surprise Attack on the American Fleet! Memoir of the I-401 Aircraft-Carrying Submarine by Its Captain*] (Tokyo: Fuami Shobo, 1988), p. 245.
11. Carl Stallcop, interview by author.
12. Chin-Ji Inouye, interview by author.
13. Carl Stallcop, interview by author.
14. John E. Balson, interview by author.
15. Clay Blair, Jr., *Silent Victory: The U.S. Submarine War Against Japan* (Annapolis, Md.: Naval Institute Press, 1975), p. 872; Lloyd R. Vasey, "The *I-400* Class of Japanese Submarines," *Mustang News* 29, no. 3 (Fall 2008).
16. Muneo Bando, interview by author; Tsugio Sato, *Maboroshi no Sensui Kubo* [*Phantom Submarine Carrier*] (Tokyo: Kabushiki Gaisha Kojin-sha, 1989), p. 262.
17. Lockwood, *Sink 'Em All*, p. 341.

Chapter 41. Freedom

1. Tsugio Sato, *Maboroshi no Sensui Kubo* [*Phantom Submarine Carrier*] (Tokyo: Kabushiki Gaisha Kojin-sha, 1989), p. 270.
2. Ibid., p. 268.
3. Charles A. Lockwood, *Sink 'Em All* (New York: Bantam Books, 1984), p. 343.
4. Wallace C. Karnes, Jr., interview by author.
5. Ibid.
6. Thomas O. Paine, "The Transpacific Voyage of HIJMS *I-400*, Tom Paine's Journal: July 1945–January 1946," February 1991, http://www.pacerfarm.org/i-400/.
7. Ibid.
8. Don Pierson, interview by author.
9. Paine, "Transpacific Voyage of HIJMS *I-400*."
10. Ibid.
11. Nobukiyo Nambu, interview by author.
12. Tsugio Yata, "SubRon 1 . . . Aims for U.S. Fleet at Ulithi and Panama Canal," *I-401 History*, I-401 Submarine Society, Japan.
13. Kazuo Takahashi, *Shinryu Tokubetsu Kogekitai* [*Divine Dragon Special Attack Unit*] (Tokyo: Koujinsha, 2001), p. 213.
14. Ibid., p. 215.
15. Ibid., p. 216.
16. Ibid. Others recall the date as September 29, 1945. See Hidetoshi

Namura, "Watashi wa *I-400* Sen Yojo Kofuku no tachianinin datta [I was a witness to the *I-400* surrender]," *Maru* [magazine], September 1976, p. 85.

17. Takahashi, *Shinryu Tokubetsu Kogekitai*, p. 216.

Chapter 42. The Long Road Home

1. Carl Boyd and Akihiko Yoshida, *The Japanese Submarine Force and World War II* (Shrewsbury, U.K.: Airlife, 1996), p. 185.
2. U.S. Naval Technical Mission to Japan, *Reports of the U.S. Naval Technical Mission to Japan*, Series S: *Ship and Related Targets*, Index no. S-01-1: *Characteristics of Japanese Naval Vessels*, Article I: *Submarines* (Washington, D.C.: Operational Archives, U.S. Navy History Division, 1946), p. 3.
3. Henry Sakaida, Gary Nila, and Koji Takaki, *I-400: Japan's Secret Aircraft-Carrying Strike Submarine, Objective Panama Canal* (East Sussex, U.K.: Hikoki, 2006), p. 84, quoting R. B. Larkin.
4. R. Kissinger, Jr., *I-400, I-401 Japanese Submarines, Description of Hull, General Arrangement and Characteristics* (U.S. Navy, 1946), pp. 3, 16, 19.
5. Thomas O. Paine, "The Transpacific Voyage of HIJMS *I-400*, Tom Paine's Journal: July 1945–January 1946," February 1991, http://www.pacerfarm.org/i-400/.
6. Ibid.
7. Ibid.
8. Ibid.
9. Paul Wittmer, interview by author.
10. Paine, "Transpacific Voyage of HIJMS *I-400*."
11. Paul Wittmer, interview by author.
12. Henry Sakaida, Gary Nila, and Koji Takaki, *I-400: Japan's Secret Aircraft-Carrying Strike Submarine, Objective Panama Canal* (East Sussex, U.K.: Hikoki, 2006), p. 85.
13. Don Pierson, interview by author.
14. Paul Wittmer, interview by author.
15. Ibid.
16. *New York Times*, June 3, 1946, p. 2.
17. Kissinger, *I-400, I-401 Japanese Submarines*.
18. Ibid., p. 1.
19. John E. Long, "Japan's Undersea Carriers," *U.S. Naval Institute Proceedings*, June 1950, p. 613.
20. Paine, "Transpacific Voyage of HIJMS *I-400*."
21. Norman Polmar and Kenneth J. Moore, "Flights from the Deep," *Air Force Magazine* 87, no. 3 (March 2004).
22. Paine, "Transpacific Voyage of HIJMS *I-400*."
23. Polmar and Moore, "Flights from the Deep."

24. U.S. Naval Technical Mission, *Characteristics of Japanese Naval Vessels*, Article I: *Submarines*, p. 10.

25. Polmar and Moore, "Flights from the Deep."

26. Norman Polmar and Dorr B. Carpenter, *Submarines of the Imperial Japanese Navy, 1904–1945* (London: Conway Maritime Press, 1986), p. 60.

27. Henry Sakaida, Gary Nila, and Koji Takaki, *I-400: Japan's Secret Aircraft-Carrying Strike Submarine, Objective Panama Canal* (East Sussex, U.K.: Hikoki, 2006), p. 86.

28. Ibid.

29. *New York Times*, June 3, 1946, p. 2.

Epilogue

1. Ermino Bagnasco, *Submarines of World War II* (London: Cassell, 2000), pp. 175–76.

2. Masanori Ito, *The End of the Imperial Japanese Navy: A Japanese Account of the Rise and Fall of Japan's Seapower* (New York: Macfadden Books, 1965), p. 18; Bagnasco, *Submarines of World War II*, p. 176.

3. Norman Polmar and Dorr B. Carpenter, *Submarines of the Imperial Japanese Navy, 1904–1945* (London: Conway Maritime Press, 1986), p. 65.

4. Clay Blair, Jr., *Silent Victory: The U.S. Submarine War Against Japan* (Annapolis, Md.: Naval Institute Press, 1975), p. 877.

5. Ibid. It was 22 percent.

6. Mochitsura Hashimoto, *Sunk!* (New York: Avon, 1954), p. vii.

7. Stephen Lobdell Johnson, Legion of Merit citation, March 17, 1947, at National Personnel Records Center, Military Personnel Records, St. Louis.

8. George Gamble, interview by author.

9. Ibid.

10. Carlo M. Carlucci, interview by author.

11. Alex Leitch, "The Chase, Capture and Boarding of a Japanese Submarine," *Polaris,* December 1985, http://home.earthlink.net/~richandannie/id71.html.

12. Robert O'Connor, interview by author.

13. USS *Segundo* (SS 398), in *Dictionary of American Naval Fighting Ships* (1976), pp. 6:429–30, http://www.hazegray.org/danfs/submar/ss398.txt.

14. Nobukiyo Nambu, *Beikidoukantai wo Kishuseyo: Sensuikuubo I-401 Kanchou No Shuki* [*Surprise Attack on the American Fleet! Memoir of the I-401 Aircraft-Carrying Submarine by Its Captain*] (Tokyo: Fuami Shobo, 1988), p. 247.

15. Nobutaka Nambu, interview by author.

16. Tsugio Sato, *Maboroshi no Sensui Kubo* [*Phantom Submarine Carrier*] (Tokyo: Kabushiki Gaisha Kojin-sha, 1989), p. 275.

17. Henry Sakaida, Gary Nila, and Koji Takaki, *I-400: Japan's Secret Aircraft-Carrying Strike Submarine, Objective Panama Canal* (East Sussex, U.K.: Hikoki, 2006), p. 87.

18. Nobutaka Nambu, interview by author.

19. Sato, *Maboroshi no Sensui Kubo*, p. 134.

20. Fukui, *Japanese Naval Vessels at the End of the War*, p. 35.

21. Nambu, *Beikidoukantai wo Kishuseyo*, p. 246; Fukui, *Japanese Naval Vessels at the End of the War*, p. 35. A different Japanese source says work on the *I-405* was canceled (not begun) in September 1944 and the sub dismantled. See Seiji Azuma, "Sekai Ni Hirui Naki '*I-400* Gata, *I-13* Gata' No Kouzou to Seinou [The Construction and Efficiency of the Unparalleled *I-400* and *I-13*]," *Maru* Special, *Japanese Naval Vessels*, no. 13, 1977, p. 28.

22. Nambu, *Beikidoukantai wo Kishuseyo*, p. 246; Sato, *Maboroshi no Sensui Kubo*, p. 279.

23. Fukui, *Japanese Naval Vessels at the End of the War*, p. 36.

24. Azuma, "Sekai Ni Hirui Naki," p. 33.

25. Polmar and Carpenter, *Submarines of the Imperial Japanese Navy*, p. 110.

26. John E. Long, "Japan's Undersea Carriers," *U.S. Naval Institute Proceedings*, June 1950, p. 610.

27. Sato, *Maboroshi no Sensui Kubo*, p. 276.

28. Tsugio Yata, interview by author.

29. Heiji Kondo, interview by author.

30. Tsugio Yata, "SubRon 1 . . . Aims for U.S. Fleet at Ulithi and Panama Canal," *I-401 History, I-401* Submarine Society, Japan.

31. Chin-Ji Inouye, interview by author.

32. Henry Sakaida, Gary Nila, and Koji Takaki, *I-400: Japan's Secret Aircraft-Carrying Strike Submarine, Objective Panama Canal* (East Sussex, U.K.: Hikoki, 2006), p. 87.

33. *United States of America vs. Hisashi Ichioka et al.*, Case no. 339, April 14, 1949, p. 20, MBL.

34. Sakaida, Nila, and Takaki, *I-400*, p. 87.

35. Ibid.

36. Kazuo Nishijima, interview by author; Tsugio Yata, interview by author.

37. Tsugio Yata, interview by author.

38. Sato, *Maboroshi no Sensui Kubo*, p. 274.

39. Ibid., p. 275.

40. Muneo Bando, interview by author.

41. Nicholas D. Kristof, "Nobuo Fujita, 85, Is Dead; Only Foe to Bomb America," *New York Times*, October 3, 1977.

42. Blair, *Silent Victory*, p. 885.

43. Chin-Ji Inouye, interview by author.

44. Carlo M. Carlucci, interview by author.

45. Zenji Orita with Joseph D. Harrington, *I-Boat Captain: How Japan's Sub-*

marine Force Almost Defeated the U.S. Navy in the Pacific! (Canoga Park, Calif.: Major Books, 1976), p. 315.

46. *United States vs. Hisashi Ichioka et al.,* Case no. 339, March 30, 1949, p. 3; April 14, 1949, pp. 5, 19, Macmillan Brown Library, University of Canterbury, Christchurch, New Zealand.

47. Ibid., pp. 6, 20.

48. "War Responsibility: Delving into the Past (15); Lower-Ranked Officers Also to Blame," *Daily Yomiuri,* August 15, 2006, http://www.yomiuri.co .jp/dy/features/0007/15.htm.

49. Robert C. Mikesh, *Aichi M6A1 Seiran: Japan's Submarine Launched Panama Canal Bomber,* Close-Up 13 (Boylston, Mass.: Monogram Aviation Publications, 1975), p. 27.

50. Ibid., pp. 9, 27.

51. Thomas O. Paine, "The Transpacific Voyage of HIJMS *I-400,* Tom Paine's Journal: July 1945–January 1946," February 1991, http://www .pacerfarm.org/i-400/.

52. John D. Butler, *Coming of Age: The SSGN Concept,* pt. 1, "Undersea Warfare Professional Development," August 2002, http://www.globalsecurity .org/military/library/report/2002/ssgn-001.pdf.

53. Ibid.

54. Norman Polmar, interview by author.

55. Stockholm International Peace Research Institute (SIPRI).

56. Edward Wong, "China Navy Reaches Far, Unsettling Region," *New York Times,* June 15, 2011, p. A11.

Sources

Books

Agawa, Hiroyuki. *The Reluctant Admiral: Yamamoto and the Imperial Navy.* Kodansha International, 2000.

Alden, John D. *The Fleet Submarine in the U.S. Navy: A Design and Construction History.* Annapolis, Md.: Naval Institute Press, 1979.

Arizuka, Yoshihisa, Lt. *Memories of the I-400.* Japan: Privately published, 1996.

Bagnasco, Erminio. *Submarines of World War II.* London: Cassell, 2000.

Beach, Edward, L. *Run Silent, Run Deep.* New York: Henry Holt, 1955.

Billings, Richard N. *Battleground Atlantic.* New York: NAL Caliber, 2006.

Blair, Clay, Jr. *Silent Victory: The U.S. Submarine War Against Japan.* Annapolis, Md.: Naval Institute Press, 1975.

Boyd, Carl, and Akihiko Yoshida. *The Japanese Submarine Force and World War II.* Shrewsbury, U.K.: Airlife, 1996.

Boyne, Walter J., ed. *Air Warfare: An International Encyclopedia.* Santa Barbara, Calif.: ABC-CLIO, 2002.

Compton-Hall, Richard. *Submarine Warfare: Monsters and Midgets.* Dorset, U.K.: Blanford Press, 1985.

Cook, Haruko, and Theodore F. Taya. *Japan at War: An Oral History.* New York: New Press, 1992.

Curtis, Tony. *Tony Curtis: The Autobiography.* New York: William Morrow, 1993.

Cussler, Clive, and Dirk Cussler. *Black Wind.* New York: Berkley Books, 2006.

Daso, Drik, ed. *America's Hangar: Steven F. Udvar-Hazy Center.* Washington, D.C.: Smithsonian National Air and Space Museum, 2004.

De Jong, Frits, and Henk Slettenaar. *De Chinalijn in Oorlogstijd* [*The China Line in Wartime*]. Doetinchem, Netherlands: Association of Former Employees of the Koninklijke Java-China-Parketvaart Lijnen N.V. (Royal Interocean Lines), 2004.

Dictionary of American Naval Fighting Ships. Washington, D.C.: Naval History and Heritage Command, Department of the Navy, Navy Historical Center, 1959–81, http://www.history.navy.mil/danfs/.

Dower, John W. *War Without Mercy: Race and Power in the Pacific War.* New York: Pantheon, 1986.

———. *Embracing Defeat: Japan in the Wake of World War II.* New York: W. W. Norton, 2000.

Dull, Paul S. *Battle History of the Imperial Japanese Navy, 1941–1945*. Annapolis, Md.: Naval Institute Press, 1978.

Edwards, Bernard. *Blood and Bushido: Japanese Atrocities at Sea, 1941–1945*. New York: Brick Tower Press, 1997.

Evans, David C., and Mark R. Peattie. *Kaigun: Strategy, Tactics, and Technology in the Imperial Japanese Navy*. Annapolis, Md.: Naval Institute Press, 1997.

Felton, Mark. *The Fujita Plan: Japanese Attacks on the United States and Australia During the Second World War*. South Yorkshire, U.K.: Pen and Sword Military, 2006.

———. *Slaughter at Sea: The Story of Japan's Naval War Crimes*. Annapolis, Md.: Naval Institute Press, 2007.

Ferguson, Niall. *Colossus: The Price of America's Empire*. New York: Penguin Press, 2004.

Gibney, Frank, ed. *Senso: The Japanese Remember the Pacific War*. Translated by Beth Cary. Armonk, N.Y.: M. E. Sharpe, 1995.

Gold, Hal. *Unit 731 Testimony*. Tokyo; Rutland, Vt.; and Singapore: Tuttle, 1996.

Goldstein, Donald M., and Katherine V. Dillon, eds. *The Pacific War Papers: Japanese Documents of World War II*. Dulles, Va.: Potomac Books, 2005.

Grew, Joseph C. *Report from Tokyo: A Message to the American People*. New York: Simon & Schuster, 1942.

Gunton, Dennis. *The Penang Submarines: Penang and Submarine Operations, 1942–1945*. Penang, Malaysia: City Council of George Town, 1970.

Harris, Sheldon H. *Factories of Death: Japanese Biological Warfare, 1932–45, and the American Cover-Up*. London and New York: Routledge, 2004.

Hashimoto, Mochitsura, *Sunk!* New York: Avon, 1954.

Hastings, Max. *Retribution: The Battle for Japan, 1944–1945*. New York: Alfred A. Knopf, 2007.

Hata, Ikuhiko. *Dainiji Taisen Koukuju Shiwa* [*Historical Aviation Stories of World War II*], trans. Shojo Jonda and Sandy Kita. Japan: Chuukou Bunko, n.d.

Henshall, Philip. *Vengeance: Hitler's Nuclear Weapon—Fact or Fiction?* Gloucestershire, U.K.: Sutton, 1998.

Holmes, W. J. *Undersea Victory: The Influence of Submarine Operations on the War in the Pacific*. Garden City, N.Y.: Doubleday, 1966.

———. *Double-Edged Secrets: U.S. Naval Intelligence Operations in the Pacific During World War II*. Annapolis, Md.: Naval Institute Press, 1998.

Hornfischer, James D. *Ship of Ghosts*. New York: Bantam Books, 2007.

Ito, Masanori. *The End of the Imperial Japanese Navy: A Japanese Account of the Rise and Fall of Japan's Seapower*. New York: Macfadden Books, 1965.

Januszewski, Tadeusz. *Japanese Submarine Aircraft*. Redbourn, U.K.: Mushroom Model, 2002.

Lamont-Brown, Raymond. *Ships from Hell: Japanese War Crimes on the High Seas*. Charleston, S.C.: History Press, 2002.

Lenton, H. T. *Navies of the Second World War: American Submarines*. London: Macdonald, 1973.

Lockwood, Charles A. *Sink 'Em All*. New York: Bantam Books, 1984.

Lockwood, Charles A., and Hans Christian Adamson. *Hellcats of the Sea.* New York: Bantam Books, 1988.

Main, Jim, and David Allen. *The Ultimate Heroes: Footballers Who Never Returned from War.* Victoria, Australia: Crown Content, 2002.

McCullough, David. *The Path Between the Seas.* New York: Simon & Schuster, 1977.

Mikesh, Robert C. *Aichi M6A1 Seiran: Japan's Submarine Launched Panama Canal Bomber.* Boylston, Mass.: Monogram Aviation Publications, 1975.

Miller, Edward S. *War Plan Orange: The U.S. Strategy to Defeat Japan 1897–1945.* Annapolis, Md.: U.S. Naval Institute Press, 1991.

Morison, Samuel Eliot. *History of the U.S. Naval Operations in World War II.* Vols. 1 and 14. Boston: Little, Brown, 1957.

Nambu, Nobukiyo. *Beikidoukantai wo Kishuseyo: Sensuikuubo I-401 Kanchou No Shuki [Surprise Attack on the American Fleet! Memoir of the I-401 Aircraft Carrying Submarine by Its Captain].* Tokyo: Fuami Shobo, 1988.

Nihon Kaigun Sensuikan Shi Kankôkai [Association for the Publishing of Japanese Navy Submarine History]. *Nihon Kaigun Sensuikan shi [A History of Japanese Navy Submarines].* Shinkosha, 1979.

Nolte, Carl. *USS Pampanito: A Submarine and Her Crew.* San Francisco: San Francisco Maritime National Park Association, 2001.

Offley, Ed. *Scorpion Down.* New York: Basic Books, 2007.

O'Kane, Richard H. *Wahoo: The Patrols of America's Most Famous World War II Submarine.* New York: Presidio Press, 1987.

Orita, Zenji, with Joseph D. Harrington. *I-Boat Captain: How Japan's Submarines Almost Defeated the US Navy in the Pacific!* Canoga Park, Calif.: Major Books, 1976.

Parkinson, Roger. *The Origins of World War II.* New York: G. P. Putnam's Sons, 1970.

Polmar, Norman, and Dorr B. Carpenter. *Submarines of the Imperial Japanese Navy, 1904–1945.* London: Conway Maritime Press, 1986.

Prados, John. *Combined Fleet Decoded: The Secret History of American Intelligence and the Japanese Navy in World War II.* Annapolis, Md.: Naval Institute Press, 1995.

Prange, Gordon W., with Donald M. Goldstein and Katherine V. Dillon. *God's Samurai: Lead Pilot at Pearl Harbor.* Dulles, Va.: Brassey's, 1990.

Price, Alfred. *Aircraft versus Submarine in Two World Wars.* South Yorkshire, U.K.: Pen and Sword Aviation, 2004.

Ruhge, Justin M. *The Western Front: The War Years in Santa Barbara County, 1937–1946.* Goleta, Calif.: Quantum Imaging Associates, 1989.

Russell of Liverpool, Lord. *Knights of Bushido: A History of Japanese War Crimes During World War II.* New York: Skyhorse, 2008.

Sadler, A. L. *The Code of the Samurai.* Rutland, Vt., and Tokyo: Tuttle, 1998.

Sakaida, Henry, Gary Nila, and Koji Takaki. *I-400: Japan's Secret Aircraft-Carrying Strike Submarine, Objective Panama Canal.* East Sussex, U.K.: Hikoki, 2006.

Sanders, Michael S. *The Yard: Building a Destroyer at the Bath Iron Works.* New York: Perennial, 2001.

Sato, Tsugio. *Maboroshi no Sensui Kubo* [*Phantom Submarine Carrier*]. Tokyo: Kabushiki Gaisha Kojin-sha, 1989.

Sheftall, M. G. *Blossoms in the Wind: Human Legacies of the Kamikaze.* New York: NAL Caliber, 2006.

Sterling, Forest J. *Wake of the Wahoo: The Heroic Story of America's Most Daring World War II Submarine.* Riverside, Calif.: R.A. Cline, 1999.

Stern, Robert C. *U.S. Subs in Action.* Carrollton, Tex.: Squadron/Signal Publications, 1983.

———. *USS Pampanito.* Carrollton, Tex.: Squadron/Signal Publications, 2008.

Stille, Mark. *Imperial Japanese Navy Submarines, 1941–1945.* Oxford, U.K.: Osprey, 2007.

Straus, Ulrich. *The Anguish of Surrender: Japanese POWs of World War II.* Seattle: University of Washington Press, 2004.

Takahashi, Kazuo. *Shinryu Tokubetsu Kogekitai* [*Divine Dragon Special Attack Unit*]. Tokyo: Koujinsha, 2001.

Takatsuka, Kazuo. *Memories of the I-400.* Part 1, September 1, 1973; Part 2, March 1, 1974; Part 3, September 20, 1974. Japan: privately published, 1996.

Thompson, Paul W., Harold Doud, John Scofield, and Milton A. Hill. *How the Jap Army Fights.* New York: Penguin, 1942.

Tompkins, Walker A. *Santa Barbara Past and Present: An Illustrated History.* Santa Barbara, Calif.: Schauer, 1975.

Tompkins, Walker A. *It Happened in Old Santa Barbara.* Santa Barbara, Calif.: Sand Dollar Press for the Santa Barbara National Bank, 1976.

———. *Santa Barbara History Makers.* Santa Barbara, Calif.: McNally and Loftin, 1983.

Treadwell, Terry C. *Strike from Beneath the Sea: A History of Aircraft-carrying Submarines.* Gloucestershire, U.K.: Tempus, 1999.

Ugaki, Matome. *Fading Victory: The Diary of Admiral Matome Ugaki, 1941–1945*, translated by Masataka Chihaya, Donald M. Goldstein, and Katherine V. Dillon, eds. Annapolis, Md.: Naval Institute Press, 1991.

U.S. Naval Intelligence. *Japanese Naval Vessels of World War II: As Seen by U.S. Naval Intelligence.* Annapolis, Md.: Naval Institute Press, 1987.

Wallace, Robert. *The Secret Battle 1942–1944: The Convoy Battle off the East Coast of Australia during World War II.* Ringwood, Australia: Lamont, 1995.

Warner, Denis, Peggy Warner, and Sahao Seno. *Sacred Warriors.* New York: Van Nostrand Reinhold, 1982.

Wilson, Michael. *A Submariner's War: The Indian Ocean 1939–1945.* Gloucestershire, U.K.: Spellmount, 2008.

U.S. MILITARY SOURCES

Brown, C. Donald. USS *Razorback* (SS 394). *War Patrol no. 3*, February 1, 1945–March 26, 1945.

Fukui, Shizuo. *Japanese Naval Vessels at the End of the War.* Administrative Division, Second Demobilization Bureau, April 25, 1947.

General Headquarters, Far East Command, Military History, Japanese Research Division. *Outline of Operations Prior to Termination of War and Activities Connected with Cessation of Hostilities.* Japanese Monograph No. 119.

Intelligence Division, Office of Chief of Naval Operations, Navy Department. *Intelligence Report: Japan Navy Aircraft in Submarines,* January 22, 1942.

Kissinger, R., Jr. *I-400, I-401 Japanese Submarines, Description of Hull, General Arrangements, and Characteristics.* U.S. Navy, 1946.

Medical Research Laboratory Report no. 34. *Outline and Discussion of Methods Used in Selecting Enlisted Candidates for Submarine Training,* 1943.

Morton, D. W. USS *Wahoo* (SS-238). *Third War Patrol Report.* January 16, 1943–February 7, 1943.

Submarine School, U.S. Submarine Base, New London, Conn. *The Periscope, For the 75th Officer's Class of the School, Graduated April 1944.* Philadelphia: Hollander and Feldman Studios.

———. *Command Class Curriculum,* revised, November 1, 1945.

U.S. Army Forces, Far East Command, Headquarters, Military History Section. *Japanese Monograph Series, No. 163, Submarine Operations in Third Phase (Parts 1–5).*

U.S. Chief of Naval Operations, "Submarine Warfare Division." http://www.navy.mil/navydata/cno/n87/n77.html.

U.S. Civilian Production Administration. *Submarine Operations in Third Phase Operations.* Part 5, *From March 1945 to the Termination of War.* Second Historical Records Section, Repatriation Relief Bureau, Ministry of Welfare, September 1945.

U.S. Government. *Imperial Rescript Granted the Ministers of War and Navy,* August 17, 1945. Reproduced in facsimile as Serial 2118, in "Psychological Warfare," Part Two, Supplement 2 CINCPAC-CINCPOA *Bulletin* no. 164–45.

U.S. Naval Technical Mission to Japan. Index No. S-01-1, *Ship and Related Targets, Characteristics of Japanese Naval Vessels, Article 1—Submarines,* 1946.

———. Index Nos. S-01-6 and S-01-7, *Ship and Related Targets of Japanese Naval Vessels, Submarines, Supplement 2,* January 1946 and February 1946.

———. *Japanese Submarine Operations: Late March 1945–Late May 1945.*

———. *The Fleet Type Submarine,* Navpers 16160. Produced by ComSubLant by Standards and Curriculum Division, Training, Bureau of Naval Personnel, June 1946.

U.S. Navy. CINCPAC-CINCPOA, Bulletin No. 108–45, *Japanese Naval Vessels,* Special Translation Number 64, May 18, 1945.

U.S. Navy. *Japanese Ship List, Know Your Enemy!* Submarines, December 18, 1944, p. 11.

U.S. Office of Naval Intelligence. ONI 222-J, *The Japanese Navy: Official United States Navy Reference Manual,* June 1945.

"USS *Segundo* (SS-398)," http://www.hazegray.org /danfs/submar/ss398.txt.

USS *Segundo* (SS-398). Deck Logs. May 9, 1944, to October 30, 1946, National Archives, Washington, D.C.

"USS *Segundo* (SS-398)." Navsource Online, http://www.navsource.org/archives/08/08398.htm.

"USS *Segundo* (SS-398)," http://www.segundo398.org/.

USS *Segundo* (SS-398). War Patrol Reports #1–5: October 21, 1944–September 12, 1945, National Archives, Washington, D.C.

U.S. Strategic Bombing Survey. *Summary Report (Pacific War)*. Washington, D.C., July 1, 1946.

———. Pacific Theater. Naval Analysis Division. *073: Campaigns of the Pacific War*. Washington, D.C., July 1, 1946.

———. Pacific Theater. Naval Analysis Division. *Interrogations of Japanese Officials*, OPNAV-P-03–100. "Submarine Warfare," Nav. No. 72, USSBS No. 366.

Watson, Mark Skinner. *Chief of Staff: Prewar Plans and Preparations*. United States Army in World War II. Washington, D.C.: Center of Military History, 1950.

ARTICLES AND ONLINE SOURCES

Ahoy—Mac's Web Log: http://ahoy.tk-jk.net/.

"Aichi Seiran." Smithsonian National Air and Space Museum, http://www.nasm.si.edu/museum/garber/aichi/aichi.htm

"Aichi B7A2 Ryusei (Shooting Star)," Smithsonian National Air and Space Museum, http://www.nasm.si.edu/collections/artifact.cfm?id=A19630360000.

"Aichi M6A1 Seiran (Clear Sky Storm)," Smithsonian National Air and Space Museum, http://www.nasm.si.edu/collections/artifact.cfm?id=A19630308000.

Anderson, James. "1942 Shelling of California Coastline Stirred Conspiracy Fears." *Los Angeles Times*, March 1, 1992.

Asamura, Atsushi. "I-401 Sensuikan to Seiran to Watashi to [The I-401 Submarine, Seiran and Me]." *Maru* Special, *Japanese Naval Vessels*, no. 13. Tokyo: Kojinsha, 1977.

Azuma, Seiji. "Sekai Ni Hirui Naki '*I-400* Gata, *I-13* Gata' No Kouzou to Seinou [The Construction and Efficiency of the Unparalleled *I-400* and *I-13*]." *Maru* Special, *Japanese Naval Vessels*, no. 13. Tokyo: Kojinsha, 1977.

Bando, Muneo. "Go Dai-yonhyakuichi (401) Sensuikan Kitou No Omoide [Memories of the I-401's Return]." *I-401 History*, *I-401* Submarine Society, Japan.

Berger, John. "Can of Fruit Symbolizes Survival." *Honolulu Star-Bulletin*, March 29, 2001.

Burlingame, Burl. "U Team Locates Huge Japanese Sub." *Honolulu Star-Bulletin*, March 20, 2005.

Butler, John D. *Coming of Age: The SSGN Concept,* pt. 1, "Undersea Warfare Professional Development," August 2002, GlobalSecurity.org, http://www.globalsecurity.org/military/library/report/2002/ssgn-001 .pdf.

"California and the Second World War: The Shelling of Ellwood." California Military Museum, http://www.militarymuseum.org/Ellwood.html.

"California and the Second World War: The Battle of Los Angeles." California Military Museum, http://www.militarymuseum.org/BattleofLA. html.

"California and the Second World War: The Attack on the SS *Emidio.*" California Military Museum, http://www.militarymuseum.org/BattleofLA .html.

"California and the Second World War: The Attack on the SS *Somoa.*" California Military Museum, http://www.militarymuseum.org/Samoa.html.

"California and the Second World War: The Attack on the SS *Larry Doheny.*" California Military Museum, http://www.militarymuseum.org/Larry Doheny.html.

Deck Log, http://www.decklog.com/homeport.asp.

Edmonds, George W. ". . . and the Shells Came." *Noticias* [Santa Barbara Historical Society] 7, no. 1 (Spring 1961).

"First Root Resolution Will Force Submarines to Take All the Risks in Trying to Halt Ships." *New York Times,* January 1, 1922.

"Fleet of Sunken Japanese Subs Found." *Los Angeles Times,* June 14, 2004.

Fountain, Henry. "2 Sunken Japanese Subs Are Found Off Hawaii." *New York Times,* November 13, 2009.

Fujita, Nobuo, and Joseph D. Harrington. "I Bombed the USA." *Proceedings,* June 1961.

Gakken Pacific War Series, vol. 17, *I-Go Sensuikan* [*Type I Submarines*]. Tokyo: Gakken, 2000.

Geoghegan, John J. "Japan's Panama Canal Buster." *Aviation History* 18, no. 5 (May 2008), http://www.historynet.com/japans-panama-canal-buster.htm.

Goat Locker, http://www.goatlocker.org/.

"The Great Los Angeles Air Raid of 1942: An Exciting Re-creation of a Historic Controversy." Associated Press, http://www.theairraid.com/.

Hackett, Bob, and Sander Kingsepp. "OPERATION TAN NO. 2: The Japanese Attack on Task Force 58's Anchorage at Ulithi." CombinedFleet .com, http://www.combinedfleet.com/Tan%20No.%202.htm.

———. "Sensuikan! HIJMS Submarine I-8, Tabular Record of Movement." CombinedFleet.com, http://www.combinedfleet.com/I-8.htm.

———. "Sensuikan! IJN Submarine I-13, Tabular Record of Movement." CombinedFleet.com, http://www.combinedfleet.com/I-13.htm.

———. "Sensuikan! IJN Submarine I-14, Tabular Record of Movement." CombinedFleet.com, http://www.combinedfleet.com/I-14.htm.

———. "Sensuikan! HIJMS Submarine I-17, Tabular Record of Movement." CombinedFleet.com, http://www.combinedfleet.com/I-17.htm.

————. "Sensuikan! HIJMS Submarine I-165, Tabular Record of Movement." CombinedFleet.com, http://www.combinedfleet.com/I-165.htm

————. "Sensuikan! IJN Submarine I-174, Tabular Record of Movement." CombinedFleet.com, http://www.combinedfleet.com/I-174.htm.

————. "Sensuikan! IJN Submarine I-222, Tabular Record of Movement." CombinedFleet.com, http://www.combinedfleet.com/I-122.htm.

————. "Sensuikan! HIJMS Submarine I-362, Tabular Record of Movement." CombinedFleet.com, http://www.combinedfleet.com/I-362.htm.

————. "Sensuikan! IJN Submarine I-400, Tabular Record of Movement." CombinedFleet.com, http://www.combinedfleet.com/I-400.htm.

————. "Sensuikan! IJN Submarine I-401, Tabular Record of Movement." CombinedFleet.com, http://www.combinedfleet.com/I-401.htm.

————. "Sensuikan! IJN Submarine I-402, Tabular Record of Movement." CombinedFleet.com, http://www.combinedfleet.com/I-402.htm.

Hackett, Bob, Sander Kingsepp, and Peter Cundall. "Kuchikukan! IJN Second Class Destroyer *Kuretake*: Tabular Record of Movement." CombinedFleet.com, http://www.combinedfleet.com/Kuretake_t.htm.

————. "Kusentei! IJN Subchaser CH-33: Tabular Record of Movement." CombinedFleet.com, http://www.combinedfleet.com/CH-33_t.htm.

Historic Naval Ships Association, http://www.hnsa.org/index.htm.

"I-400-Class Submarine 'Sen Toku Type,'" CombinedFleet.com, http://www.combinedfleet.com/ships/i-400.

I-Go Sensui Kan [I-Type Submarines] 15 (2003).

"Imperial Japanese Navy," http://candamo.eu/Japon/ibarcos.htm.

"Japanese Carry War to California Coast." *Life* 12, no. 10 (March 9, 1942).

"Japanese Submarine Attacks on Curry County in World War II." Port Orford Lifeboat Station, http://www.portorfordlifeboatstation.org/article1.html.

"Japanese Submarine Sunk at Pearl Harbor Is Found." *New York Times*, August 30, 2002.

"Japanese Torpedoes." CombinedFleet.com, http://www.combinedfleet.com/torps.htm.

"Jisaburo Ozawa." CombinedFleet.com, http://www.combinedfleet.com/officers/Jisaburo_Ozawa.

Kennosuke, Torisu, and Masataka Chihaya. "Japanese Submarine Tactics." *Proceedings*, U.S. Naval Institute, Annapolis, Md., June 1961.

"Killer Sub Fleet Located." *Daily Telegraph*, June 15, 2004.

Kristof, Nicholas D. "Nobuo Fujita, 85, Is Dead; Only Foe to Bomb America." *New York Times*, October 3, 1977.

"L.A. Area Raided." *Los Angeles Times*, February 25, 1942, p. 1.

Langenberg, William. "Japanese Bomb the Continental U.S. West Coast." *Aviation History* 18, no. 11 (November 1988), http://www.historynet.com/japanese-bomb-the-continental-u-s-west-coast.htm.

————. "Weapons: The Giant French Submarine Surcouf's Mysterious Fate

Made Her the True Flying Dutchman of World War II." *Military Heritage*, June 2007.

Leitch, Alex. "The Chase, Capture and Boarding of a Japanese Submarine." *Polaris*. United States Submarine Veterans of World War II, December 1985.

Long, John E. "Japan's Undersea Carriers." *U.S. Naval Institute Proceedings*, June 1950.

"Los Angeles Air Raid." Associated Press, http://www.theairraid.com.

Main, Jim, and David Allen. "The Ultimate Tiger Heroes, The Bill Cosgrove Story." August 27, 2002. AFL.com, http://www.afl.com.au/news/newsarticle/tabid/208/newsid/2941/default.aspx.

Maloney, Bill. "Surrender of I-14 Submarine to DE USS Bangust, August 28, 1945," http://www.williammaloney.com/Dad/WWII/DadWWII/Surrendering-Japanese/index.htm.

Matsuura, Joao Paolo Juliao. "Aichi M6A *Seiran* (Mountain Haze)." CombinedFleet.com, http://www.combinedfleet.com/ijna/m6a.htm.

Matsuyama, Yukio. "Japan, Internationalism and the UN." Part 2, *Other Points of View*, 1997.

"Military Expenditure." Stockholm International Peace Research Institute, http://www.sipri.org/research/armaments/milex.

Momiyama, Thomas S. "All and Nothing." *Air and Space*, Smithsonian, October/November 2001.

"Nakajima C6N Saiun (Painted Cloud)." CombinedFleet.com, http://www.combinedfleet.com/ijna/c6n.htm.

Nambu, Nobukiyo. "Ninon Niha Sekaiichi No Himitsu Sensuikan Kuubo Ga Atta [Japan's Greatest Secret Submarine Aircraft Carrier in the World]." *I-401 History*, I-401 Submarine Society, Japan.

Namura, Hidetoshi. "Watashi wa I-400 Sen Yojo Kofuku no tachianin datta [I Observed the Surrender of the I-400]." *Maru*. Tokyo: Kojinsha, September 1976.

Naval History and Heritage Command, http://www.history.navy.mil/.

"Navy Planned Bacteriological Warfare, U.S. Attack Operation Revealed." *Sankei Shimbun* [newspaper], August 14, 1977.

"Nihon Kaigun Kantei Shashin Shu [Warships of the Imperial Japanese Navy]." *Maru*, no. 20. Tokyo: Kojinsha, 1998.

"Nippon Sensuikan shi [History of Japanese Submarines]." *Sekai no Kansen* [*Ships of the World*], Special Issue no. 137, no. 469. Tokyo: Kojinsha, 1993.

O'Hara, Patrick J. "History: Bombs over Ellwood." *Santa Barbara Magazine*, May–June 1991.

Pacific Wrecks.com, http://www.pacificwrecks.com/

Paine, Thomas O. "I Was a Yank on a Japanese Sub." *U.S. Naval Institute Proceedings*, September 1986.

———. "The Transpacific Voyage of HIJMS *I-400*: Tom Paine's Journal: July 1945–January 1946." February 1991, http://www.pacerfarm.org/i-400/.

"Panama Canal—Defending the Canal, 2009." GlobalSecurity.org, http:// www.globalsecurity.org/military/facility/panama-canal-defense.htm.

Panama Canal Authority, www.pancanal.com.

Panama Canal Museum, http://panamacanalmuseum.org/index.php.

Polmar, Norman, and Kenneth J. Moore. "Flights from the Deep." *Airforce Magazine* 87, no. 3 (March 2004).

Portsmouth Naval Shipyard, http://www.navsea.navy.mil/shipyards /portsmouth/Pages/20th%20Century.aspx.

Quam, Ellsworth R. "Over the Sea, and Under the Sea." *Minnesota Legionnaire*, http://www.mnlegion.org/paper/html/quam.html.

Rekishi Gunzou, no. 85 (October 10, 2007). Tokyo: Gakken.

Reynolds, Clark G. "Submarine Attacks on the Pacific Coast, 1942." *Pacific Historical Review* 33 (May 1964).

Ships Histories: Dictionary of American Naval Fighting Ships, http://www.history .navy.mil/danfs/index.html.

Stevens, David. "The Naval Campaigns for New Guinea." *Journal of the Australian War Memorial*, n.d., http://www.awm.gov.au/journal/j34/stevens.asp.

———. "The ASW Crisis—1943," chap. 8 of *A Critical Vulnerability: The Impact of the Submarine Threat on Australia's Maritime Defense, 1915–1954*. Canberra, Australia: Department of Defence, Sea Power Centre, 2005, http://www.navy.gov.au/w/images/PIAMA15_ch8.pdf.

"The Submarine Weapon of Rengo Katai," http://candamo.eu/Japon/isub mari.htm.

"Submarines." DANFS Online, http://www.hazegray.org/danfs/submar/.

"Submarines of the Imperial Japanese Navy." *B-29s Over Korea,* http://b-29s -over-korea.com/Submarines-of-the-IMPERIAL-JAPANESE-NAVY/ Submarines-of-the-Imperial-Japanese-Navy.html.

"Submarines of the Imperial Japanese Navy." CombinedFleet.com, http:// www.combinedfleet.com/ss.htm.

Submarinesailor.com, http://www.submarinesailor.com/.

TenderTale.com. http://www.tendertale.com/.

Tulleys Port, http://www.propnturret.com/tully/.

"Type AM." CombinedFleet.com, http://www.combinedfleet.com/type_am .htm.

Uboat.net, http://www.uboat.net/.

"U.S. Said to Sink Four Japanese Submarines to Balk Booty Bid; Soviet Protest Reported." *New York Times,* June 3, 1946.

Users.bigpond.net.

"USS *Bangust* (DE-739)." Navsource Online, http://www.navsource.org/ archives/06/739.htm.

"USS *Euryale* (AS-22)." Navsource Online, http://www.navsource.org/ archives/09/36/3622.htm.

USS *Euryale* (AS-22), http://www.katiebuglove.com/euryaleindex.html.

"USS *Greenlet* (ASR-10)." Navsource Online, http://www.navsource.org/ archives/09/32/3210.htm.

USS *Pampanito* (SS-383), http://www.maritime.org/pamphome.htm.

"USS *Tuscaloosa* (CA-37)." Navsource Online, http://www.navsource.org/archives/04/037/04037.htm.

"USS *Winslow* (DD-359)." Destroyer History Foundation, http://destroyer history.org/goldplater/usswinslow/.

Valoratsea.com, http://www.valoratsea.com/wolfpacks.htm.

Vasey, Lloyd R. "The I-400 Class of Japanese Submarines." *Mustang News* [National Order of Battlefield Commission] 29, no. 3 (Fall 2008).

Wittmer, Paul, homepage, http://www.subvetpaul.com/.

Wong, Edward. "China Navy Reaches Far, Unsettling Region." *New York Times,* June 15, 2011.

World War II Database, http://ww2db.com/.

"World War II Pacific Typhoons Battered U.S. Navy." *USA Today*, http://www.usatoday.com/weather/hurricane/history/typhoons-ww2-navy.htm.

Yata, Tsugio, Lt. "SubRon 1 . . . Aims for U.S. Fleet at Ulithi and Panama Canal." *I-401 History, I-401* Submarine Society, Japan.

Young, Donald J. "Phantom Japanese Raid on Los Angeles During World War II." Historynet.com, June 12, 2006, http://www.historynet.com/phantom-japanese-raid-on-los-angeles-during-world-war-ii.htm.

ALLIED WAR CRIMES TRIBUNAL, JAPAN, MACMILLAN BROWN LIBRARY, UNIVERSITY OF CANTERBURY, CHRISTCHURCH, NEW ZEALAND

Bagge, W. *Copy of Note of 28 July 44 from the Swedish Minister in Tokyo to the Imperial Japanese Minister for Foreign Affairs.* Document No. 23221-A.

Cross-examination of Vice Admiral Ichioka. *Re: Miltary Tribunal in Connection with Vice Admiral Ichioka and Others Connected with the Submarine Operations in the Indian Ocean.* Prosecution Exhibit no. 98.

De Jong, Frits. Statement by Chief Officer, SS *Tjisalak*, sunk 26 March 1944. Document no. 8388, Exhibit no. 2099, p. 1, Macmillan Brown Library. Archives Reference: MB 1549, Tokyo War Crimes Tribunal, Item 2099, Box 266, Exhibits 1944.

Dekker, Jan. Statement by Second Mate and Armaments Officer, SS *Tjisalak*, March 15, 1946, Pro Justitia, War Crimes Investigation Unit, Amsterdam, no. 47.

Fereza, Francisco. Statement by a Survivor of the SS *Nellore,* June 11, 1944.

Ichioka, Hisashi. Statement, 6 July 1948, Doc. no. 927, Tokyo War Crimes Tribunal, Prosecution Exhibit no. 98.

McDougall, John Alexander. Testimony by Able Bodied Seaman, SS *Jean Nicolet*, Tokyo War Crimes Tribunal.

Miwa, Shigeyoshi. Transcript of Interrogation. United States Strategic Bombing Survey (Pacific), Interrogations of Japanese Officials,

OPNAV-P-03–100, Naval Analysis Division, Interrogation Nav no. 72, USSBS no. 366, October 10, 1945.

Motonaka, Sadao. Letter to Chairman of the Parole Board, Legal Section, GHQ, SCAP, APO 500, September 28, 1950.

Nakahara, Jiro. Affidavit, IPS Document no. 3347; Exhibit no. 3842, January 6, 1948.

———. Statement, October 13, 1948.

———. Testimony to Tokyo War Crimes Tribunal.

Simpson, H. C. Report of the Senior Survivor of SS *Nellore.* July 12, 1944.

Swiss Minister to Mamoru Shigemitsu, Foreign Minister, Tokyo, Doc. no. 8401, June 19, 1944.

United States of America vs. Hisashi Ichioka et al., Case no. 339, March 30, 1949.

United States of America vs. Hisashi Ichioka et al., Case no. 339, April 14, 1949.

Yanabe, Motohide, Letter, Sugamo Prison, August 23, 1948, and August 30, 1948.

Multimedia Sources

"Doctor of Death." *Dateline NBC,* August 15, 1995.

Hunt for the Samurai Subs. Wild Life Productions, National Geographic Channel, 2009.

"Interview with Lieutenant John E. Balson," KXA radio, October 27, 1945, Seattle.

Japanese SuperSub. Windfall Films and Spy Pond Productions for Thirteen in Association with National Geographic Channel and WNET.org, 2010.

"Killer Subs in Pearl Harbor." A *NOVA* Production by Lone Wolf Documentary Group for WGBH/Boston in association with NHK and Channel 4, January 5, 2010.

Manatsu no Orion [*Last Operations under the Orion/Battle under the Orion*], Toho, TV Asahi, 2009.

Samurai and the Swastika. A&E Television Networks, History Channel, 2000.

Sen Toku: Search for Japan's Ghost Fleet. Parallax Film Productions for the Discovery Channel, April 2005.

The Silent Service: Japanese Submarines. A&E Television Networks, The History Channel, 2003.

Submarine I-52: Search for WWII Gold. A National Geographic Special Presentation, 2000.

INDEX

Printed in the United States
by Baker & Taylor Publisher Services